I0477175

Painting Explained

Painting Explained

A Professional Artist Reveals the
Secrets of the Masters

Thomas Gullick

Assisted by John Timbs

Edited by Paul Dennis Sporer

Valerius Press

ANZA PUBLISHING, Chester, NY 10918
Valerius Press is an imprint of Anza Publishing

This work is a new, unabridged edition of *Painting Popularly Explained,* by Thomas John Gullick, originally published in 1864.

Library of Congress Cataloguing-in-Publication Data
Gullick, Thomas John.
Painting explained / Thomas Gullick ;
edited by Paul Dennis Sporer.
p. cm.
Originally published under title:
Painting Popularly Explained. London : Lockwood & Co., 1864.
Includes index.
ISBN 1-932490-30-2 (hardcover : alk. paper)
1. Painting.
2. Painting—Technique.
I. Sporer, Paul D. II. Title.
ND1135.G9 2005
751—dc22 2005021080

ISBN 1-932490-30-2 (hardcover)

∞ This book is printed on acid-free paper.

CONTENTS

Editor's Preface

A common lament among artists is that there are no books available that give specific, practical information about the procedures used by those creative geniuses collectively known as the Old Masters. The reason for this dearth is that such a work's author would have to possess extraordinarily wide-ranging expert knowledge and skills. Thomas Gullick's credentials indicate a great capability in taking up this challenge, and his book is truly a worthy contribution to the field. As a well-informed professional artist living in the mid-19th century, he was in an exemplary position to discuss the intricacies of traditional techniques, and to compare modern systems to the styles and methods of previous eras. As a scholar, he expounds on art history and aesthetic theory, and skilfully appraises different genres of painting across a wide expanse of time. And as someone with keen insight into human nature, he relates pertinent details and witty anecdotes from the life stories of many well-known, and not so well-known, artists.

This present work is based upon the 1864 Lockwood & Co. edition originally entitled *Painting Popularly Explained.* It has not been republished since that time, and an original copy, which in its day was given to students and teachers as a prize for outstanding achievement, is quite rare. A further indication of the high level of respect that Gullick commanded, was that on the rich, dark brown cover of this exquisitely printed book was embossed the insignia V R, an official sign of acceptance by the Queen.

Gullick's spelling for names, locations, types of materials, etc. have been kept intact. However, we have made changes to the text in various places in order to extend the readability of the work, and to correct the relatively few errors. We have given numbers to the originally unnumbered chapters, and the book's footnotes were converted into endnotes for the purpose of clarity and flow. We have also included a comprehensive new index.

PAUL DENNIS SPORER

Author's Preface

Numerous eloquent and also some 'dry-as-dust' books have been written on the theory of painting. Modern German writers, more especially, have speculated very ingeniously, as well as very vaguely, upon the nature of those high faculties in man through which he derives pleasurable perceptions and refining emotions from the beautiful in the material world; and these speculations have been, under the name of aesthetics, elevated to the dignity of a science. The history of Art has afforded more tangible subjects for a large class of authors; while practical treatises for the exclusive guidance of art-students already exist of, perhaps, adequate authority and in sufficient number. We are, however, acquainted with very few books containing precisely those explanations of the processes and materials employed in painting which we believe can be given, and would greatly assist, not only the student, but the general public to understand and appreciate pictures, and to estimate how far material and technical relations have had historical influence on painting-books which, in fact, contain the particular information which an artist might be presumed best capable of communicating.

To supply (from practical acquaintance with painting) such information is the chief aim of the present volume. In working out such a design, the opportunity will not always be afforded for even attempting to increase the attractiveness of the subject by literary embellishment: but our desire is to be useful, and we are content to rough-hew the cornerstone, if we may not foliate the capital. Nevertheless, as the better part, beyond all comparison, of painting consists of those mental and imaginative elements which entitle it to rank with the sister-art of poetry, we shall take all occasions which may appear fitting to press the superior importance of these higher qualities upon the reader's consideration. We would not, from professional prejudice, and still less disingenuously, seek to obtain the reception of an overestimate of the value of technical and professional knowledge. Without such, knowledge, truth, beauty, and sentiment in pictures may undoubtedly be enjoyed. But we submit that even this enjoyment may sometimes be heightened in degree, other gratification assuredly derived, and the power of appreciating the relative merits and comparative value of paintings certainly gained, through the knowledge to which we have alluded. All who have practised painting will likewise, we think, allow, that experience gained with the pencil has removed many misconceptions respecting at least surface appearances in pictures. Artists will, we feel assured, candidly admit that some portion of the art consists of definite operations and definable modes of manipulation, and may therefore be compared to a delicate description of workmanship, requiring a regular apprenticeship and long practice. To carry out the comparison, then, to its legitimate issue, we beg the good-natured reader who would listen to the man who could make only an indifferent watch, if he had anything to say about its mechanism, to kindly lend his attention to what we have to say about the mechanism of a picture.

As all men cannot be painters or watchmakers—cannot all learn 'how to do it,' or even see it done—surely the next best thing must be to get a trustworthy description of *how* it is done. This will at all events save them from making some awkward mistakes. If Pliny, for example, could have anticipated the numerous sneers with which his shade has been insulted, he would not have attempted to write about painting while ignorant of some of its simplest operations. This consideration may touch self-respect, but another must reach self-interest. We allude to the fact that a knowledge of the nature of the materials employed for painting will also almost necessarily include acquaintance with the precautions indispensable for the possessor of pictures to take in order to secure the preservation of his art-treasures, and to display them to the best advantage.

But—and this is of great general importance—the reader who accompanies us through this volume will hardly deny the important influence of materials and processes upon the painter's fidelity of imitation; and even upon his modes of conception, and the higher manifestations of painting as a form of poetical utterance. The reader will, in succession, see what gave value to the encaustic picture, in the eyes of rich Roman collectors, and that the too exclusive employment of the more mechanical process of mosaic hastened the decline and degradation of art. He will see how the separate introduction of gold into the mediaeval tempera picture led to hard outlines, a patchwork character, absence of 'tone,' and an unnatural scale of colour; while the material limitations of fresco seem, on the contrary, only to have compelled greater attention to the higher and more essential qualities of art. He will see how 'depth,' the greatest recommendation of oil painting, is simply a property of the 'vehicle' employed; and how chiaroscuro,[1] or light and shade of pictures, has been influenced by the painter's habitual use of a light or dark ground, or his custom of painting in full daylight or a darkened studio. Lastly, the reader will see that the early Flemish painters followed a definite series of processes, which would alone secure the purity of colour, the transparency and accuracy of detail so noticeable in their works: a system which presents a marked contrast to what has been the too prevalent practice in modern painting, both in oil and watercolours —in which, from the facility of making alterations, meaningless licence has been allowed to the play of the brush, and effects have been repeated in proportion as they are easily gained.

The chronological arrangement adopted in this work is explained in the Introduction. Early Christian and Mediaeval Art having rapidly grown in public estimation, and possessing besides a kind of geological, novel interest, we have, we trust, worked out this rich vein with satisfactory industry. Great importance has also been attached to historical inquiries into the origin of methods and materials; because we believe such inquiries are in the highest degree instructive; but where individual painters have rendered eminent service to art, they are noticed in a more biographic spirit. At the same time we have endeavoured to render the book in every respect as complete as possible: it has, in fact, been attempted not only to give a description of every kind of painting, but also some account of the art in every age, together with sketches of the principal painters of the different schools.

We repeat, that our great ambition has been to be useful; and no inconsiderable result will have been achieved if we only succeed in directing attention to the best source of information on every subject, and especially to the stores of material accumulated in such works as those by Sir Charles Eastlake and Mrs. Merrifield. To the former as an author, and the latter as an editor of valuable ancient MSS., we shall have frequently to acknowledge our obligations; but, in the words of Quintilian, 'if we can say what is right we shall be delighted, though it may not be of our own invention.'

The explanation of every kind of technicality has been one of the objects of this work; in every instance, therefore, where a technical term first occurs, it is explained either in the text itself or in a note; so that the reader who follows the order of the book need anticipate no difficulty in this particular. Should, however, the clue to the exact meaning of any artistic word or phrase be lost, a copious index has been added, the references of which, instead of affording the dry definitions a mere glossary would supply, will, it is hoped, be found at once to define the word and illustrate its application.

In conclusion, we would still further conciliate the reader's confidence by assuring him that—as we have already intimated—nearly all the technical explanations in this book are derived from a more than usually varied practical acquaintance with painting. The writer whose name occurs on the title-page has not merely contributed largely to the press for some years past on the subject of Art, but he is (though the reader may be unaware of the fact) also a painter by profession. It may perhaps be asked, with a smile, how it happens that he did not prefer—like, and in the words of, Annibale Carracci—'only to speak by works,' meaning, of course, pictures. The answer to this is that his natural tendencies have inclined equally to literary and to artistic pursuits; and the observation may be ventured, though at the risk of provoking unfavourable comparisons, that—whatever may be his own fate—many painters have been better known by the productions of their pen than by those of their pencil.

Chapter 1

Introduction

Coleridge says 'Painting is something between a thought and a thing.' With a little more circumlocution, painting is the art of conveying thoughts by the imitation of things. The principle of imitation in painting as regards form is, however, abstractly unreal; for imitation, to be complete, must include the relief or roundness of objects, as in sculpture, while painting is restricted to a flat surface. But no art pretends in the fullest sense to imitate Nature, that is to say, to realize all her infinity. Imitation carried as far as possible would only end with reproduction. Each art has characteristic qualities, which its rivals do not possess in equal degree; and upon these stress is laid, in order to compensate for the deficiencies. Thus, although painting does not have the power of giving actual relief like sculpture, it yet can, by means of imitating the effects of form, light, and shadow on the eye, sufficiently secure the impression of relief, so that no want is suggested; and, in the addition of colour, it has the means of imitating a very beautiful class of facts in nature, beyond the scope of sculpture. So, on comparing representation with description: language, as a vehicle for conveying ideas of natural objects, is far less definite than painting; but it can narrate the succession of events, which painting cannot do. On the other hand, painting can embody impressions of simultaneous action and effect, and thus obtain innumerable harmonious combinations, which it would be impossible for mere words, even if the highest poetry, to do more than indefinitely suggest.

Although a degree of imitation is necessary in a work of art for the conveyance of thought, the quantity or exactitude of imitation in a picture forms by no means a measure of the amount of thought or emotion which it may awaken, apart from the simple ideas which the mind receives through the painted resemblance of natural objects. Indeed, literal imitation is sometimes so much dissociated from imagination, that Haydon went so far as to say, that 'the power of representing things as they are, constituted merely the painter of domestic art;' adding, with characteristic boldness and enthusiasm, 'while that of restoring them to what they were at creation constitutes the great painter in High Art.' When we reflect, however, upon the inexhaustible richness of nature, a more humble spirit of imitation appears not only excusable, but laudable. Modern pre-Raphaelitism is on this ground—viz., that of protest—chiefly serviceable to art. For it is a mistake to suppose that artistic imitation can ever be entirely mechanical, that it is only a means to an end, or that it is but as language is to thought. The eye has its own poetry, and the faithful rendering of the simplest object in nature has a special value and beauty that touches some of the pleasantest chords of our being. Still we must unhesitatingly give the preference to those works in which we have not only the inherent and intrinsic poetry of art, but also subject and incident conveying thought, expression, and sentiment. Moreover, though art is finite, yet nearly every branch is too comprehensive in its means for one man to do justice to all its capabilities; hence a larger measure than usual of the judgment and taste necessarily shown in *selection* and *adaptation* is justly allowed to distinguish and elevate the artist. 'Style' in the highest sense arises from the peculiar bias the artist takes in this selection and adaptation. But 'style' is also applied to the several methods of painting materially considered; for the painter is a curious combination of poet and mechanic, as his picture is a curious compromise 'between a thought and a thing.'

There have been, in the history of art, four grand styles, taking the word in the last or material sense, of imitating nature—Tempera, Encaustic, Fresco, and Oil. These, together with the minor modes of painting, we propose to arrange as nearly as possible in chronological sequence; but our design being to offer an explanation of the art derived from practical acquaintance, rather than attempt to give its history, we shall confine ourselves principally to that portion of the history of painting necessary to elucidate the origin of the different practices which have obtained at different periods.

We shall therefore give, in the first place, a full description of each method of painting as historically introduced, together with explanations of its technicalities, and then add connecting notices, following always the order of time. In this way we shall trace tempera from remote antiquity to the works of the later Roman painters. After long neglect, it will reappear in the thirteenth century, and prevail till supplanted by the introduction of Oil painting. Encaustic will furnish an episode at the period of the greatest refinement in Greece. The Byzantine school of Christian art must be estimated from Mosaics, which for some four centuries were almost the only form of art; and for the Romanesque style and period we must dip into Missals. The fourteenth century gave us (genuine) Fresco, in which, in the sixteenth century, the noblest monuments of the art of painting were executed. The improvement effected at the commencement of the fifteenth century in oil painting by the Van Eycks having led to such remarkable results, the subject will engross a large share of our attention, more especially as recent research has thrown considerable light on questions connected therewith. The recently introduced Stereochrome or Water-glass is in reality the simplest and purest form of Watercolour painting, and, together with what we understand as Watercolour, and also distemper, is but a variety of tempera, taking the last word in its broadest signification. Our modern 'Watercolour' painting has, however, received such distinct and extraordinary development during the last fifty years, that it is entitled to the separate consideration we have given it.

Chapter 2

Painting in Tempera

We place tempera first, because it is unquestionably the most ancient method of painting; but we shall confine our attention in the first instance more particularly to the process employed by the painters of Christian art in Italy, and termed generally by the Italians painting *à guazzo,* both because their works are preserved and may be examined, and because they have of late risen so rapidly in public estimation. Merely from any dissimilarity in the appearance of the painting, it would occur to few ordinary visitors to a collection of pictures which included works by the earliest Italian painters, that these are not oil paintings at all. Indeed, it has been found impossible to distinguish between a painting executed with oil colours and a tempera picture which has imbibed the oil varnish. Yet, though sometimes not betraying the fact by any great peculiarity of outward appearance, before the introduction of the so-called invention of oil painting by the Van Eycks, all paintings were executed in tempera, or by some other method very dissimilar to that of oil. There have been many statements of impossibilities made, and contradictory opinions given, in reference to 'tempera'; these we shall endeavour to qualify or reconcile.

Painting in tempera is so named because the colours are 'tempered,' or mixed with and diluted by a 'medium,'[2] to a proper consistence, to be conveniently taken by and applied with the brush, and to adhere to the surface —this medium with the mediaeval painters being neither oil nor simply water. The Italian noun *tempera* admits, nevertheless, of the widest application, and would include any medium, even oil; but in its most restricted and proper acceptation it means a vehicle in which yolk of the egg (beaten sometimes with the white) is the chief ingredient, diluted as required with the milky juice expressed from the shoots of the fig-tree. This is the painting strictly termed *à uovo* by the Italians. Vinegar probably replaced the fig-tree juice among the northern artists, from the difficulty of obtaining the latter, and in modern use vinegar is substituted. Hayden says vinegar should be used, to prevent the putrefaction of the yolk of the egg; but the early Italian painters preferred the egg vehicle when it had been suffered to stand until it had become decomposed—hence the phrase, painting *'à putrido.'* The artist is often compelled to have recourse to very offensive media to make known his most refined revelations. On walls, and for coarser work, such as painting on linen, warm size was occasionally used; but the egg vehicle undiluted was generally preferred for altar-pieces on wood. For various purposes and at different periods, however, milk, beer, wine, and media composed of water and more or less glutinous ingredients, soluble at first in water, such as gums, &c., have also been used. Such are the media, or vehicles, described by the chief Italian writers as used in the days of Cimabue, Giotto, and Fra Angelico, and by the early painters before the invention and improvement of oil painting. Pliny also mentions milk and the egg vehicle as employed for ancient wall paintings. The finer egg tempera, in dry climates, has been found to attain so firm a consistence as to withstand ordinary solvents. The use of wine in diluting these glutinous vehicles was common for a long period. Buffalmacco, of whom so many humorous stories are told by Boccaccio and Vasari, is related to have persuaded some nuns for whom he painted to supply him with their choicest wines, ostensibly for the purpose of diluting the colours, but really to be slily imbibed by the thirsty painter himself. The northern artists were sometimes obliged to content themselves with beer. In the works of the northern tempera painters there are, however, very marked differences observable in their *impasto* or body of colour; it is certain, therefore, that these painters employed media of different degrees of consistency.

In the 'distemper' of scene painting (see note C in Appendix) the medium is weak size of glue (glue dissolved), but plaster of Paris, sufficiently diluted, is worked into the colours. This carbonate of lime, or whitening, is less active as a basis for colours than the pure lime of fresco; but it is entirely destructive of transparency. When the more viscid media were employed by the tempera painters, the effect must, with their purer use of the colours (some of which, moreover, were transparent), have been very lustrous and powerful in comparison with the 'distemper' of modern scene painters, and these qualities were heightened by the addition of a strong varnish; still, however, tempera fell far short of oil painting in richness and transparency.

GROUNDS, ETC.

The ancients, it appears, were unacquainted with oil painting: they painted in tempera (or part fresco and part tempera) and encaustic, on wood, clay, plaster, stone, parchment, and canvas. Few, however, of the great painters of Greece painted upon walls. Apelles never did; and even the works of Polygnotus at Delphi are supposed to have been painted on panels inserted into the wall. As they were subsequently removed, the same may be inferred of the pictures of the Poecile at Athens. According to one account, canvas was not used until the time of Nero; and though this statement appears to be doubtful, yet, as there is no mention of its having been employed by the Greek painters of the best ages, its use was most probably of late introduction. Pliny notices, as one of the extravagances of the time, that Nero had his portrait painted on canvas 120 feet high.

Tempera pictures for the altar-pieces, triptychs, &c. (see note D in Appendix), of the Middle Ages, were generally executed on panels of wood. The painters of that period always used a 'ground' (or substratum on which the picture was executed) of pure white plaster of Paris (in Italian *gesso)* or washed chalk (whitening) with size: a preparation which has been employed without change from remote antiquity, the ground of the paintings on Egyptian mummy cases being of this description. Such a ground, unless exceedingly thin, becoming brittle with age, is evidently unsafe on canvas, especially if the picture should ever be exposed to be rolled for convenience of removal. The Venetians, therefore, who from the first preferred cloth or canvas[3] of fine texture, took the precaution of spreading the composition of size and *gesso* as thinly as possible. The fine picture by Mantegna, in the National Gallery, and 'The Triumph of Julius Caesar,' at Hampton Court, are in tempera on cloth. Wood, however, was frequently covered (particularly in the earliest or Byzantine pictures) with parchment, leather, or linen.

Walls which were to receive paintings of a finer description appear also to have been prepared with cloth glued over the surface.

Upon the gesso ground the old tempera painters were accustomed to apply a coat of Armenian bole mixed with glue, on which they spread leaf-gold; and though the practice was gradually discontinued, it was occasionally adopted in oil painting in Italy; and in Flanders was continued even to a comparatively late period, it being considered that the gold ground gave great brilliancy to the colours.

When the white ground was used, it was very carefully prepared; and the tempera picture was frequently commenced by tracing the design from a drawing or cartoon[4] on which it had been accurately studied, in a similar manner to that (which we shall fully describe) practised in fresco painting. Cennini,[5] however, does not speak of a cartoon, but recommends that the drawing should be first sketched on the white ground in charcoal (which admits of being readily obliterated), and then outlined in ink with a minever pencil; the shadows to be afterwards washed in. The effect of this insisting, as it were, upon the outline with ink, will partly account for the hard outlines and sharp edginess so conspicuous in these ancient[6] works. The mode of commencing a picture by tracing the outline was followed by the early oil painters without change, and even greater care. An example of this is presented in the original pen-and-ink drawing from which was traced the small picture by Raphael, 'The Vision of the Knight.' The drawing is placed under the picture in the National Gallery, and the holes pricked in the outline by the tracing point are very plainly to be seen.

From the thickness of the vehicle generally employed, and its unmanageable nature, the tints, as in fresco, were mixed to the required local hues,[7] or the colour proper to each particular portion of the object represented, as seen modified by light and shade (not the *local colour,* which is the 'self-colour' of an object, and what we mean when we talk of a 'red coat' or a 'green field'). The practice of using these compound or mixed tints was commonly adopted by the early oil painters, and continued when the movements of the pencil became far more free, the blending being continued more or less on the picture when applied.

Portions of the tempera picture were finished while the ground was left untouched elsewhere. Cennini directs that the head should be finished last. This practice of finishing parts separately was likewise adopted by the first oil painters, excepting that they did not reserve the flesh for the last. A picture by Leonardo da Vinci, in the Milan Gallery, has some parts nearly finished, with others merely outlined; and the remarkable Holy Family, in the possession of the Right Hon. H. Labouchere, attributed to Michael Angelo by Dr. Waagen (as the second existing easel picture he executed), is in a similar condition.

A mode of painting, 'transparencies' as they would now be called, on linen, appears to have been practised during the fourteenth century in Germany; but more extensively, if not originally, in England. At all events, if the English method was not peculiar to the country, it was distinguished for its greater transparency when held before the light. The artists worked with watercolours on closely woven linen. The linen was saturated with gum-water; when dry it was stretched on the floor over coarse woollen and frieze cloths, and the artist drew and coloured his subjects walking over the linen with clean feet, the superabundant moisture being absorbed by the woollen cloths underneath. When finished, the semi-transparency of the linen was not lessened, as the colours had no body. It was common in the fifteenth century to hang rooms, instead of tapestry, with large works on linen executed in the ordinary tempera; but as late as the beginning of the sixteenth century, a German mode of painting on cloth was distinguished for its transparency from the Italian tempera. For Vasari mentions, in his Life of Raphael, that a drawing sent by Albert Dürer to the great Italian, was painted in watercolours on a fine linen cloth, which showed the transparent lights on both sides without white, watercolours only being added, while the cloth was left for the lights; 'which thing appeared wonderful to Raphael.' Sir Charles Eastlake, in his invaluable work with the modest title, *Materials for a History of Oil Painting,* seems to be of opinion that the introduction of this German method of painting into Venice, influenced the schools of the north of Italy, and may explain the preference always given to canvas by the Venetians, that the linen was chosen fine in texture, and that their works were executed in a comparatively thin though not transparent tempera. Sir Charles instances, also, the studies of Squarcione, Leonardo da Vinci, Luini, and other of the pupils of Leonardo, as executed in this manner; and says that the cloth of fine texture was frequently employed by them, even for their finished pictures in oil. The great recommendation of this mode of tinting linens opposed to the solid tempera, no doubt was, that in the amid climate of England and the Netherlands it was less able to be affected by damp than colouring with more 'body' or substance.

Mrs. Merrifield, in her *Ancient Practice of Painting,* thinks it not at all improbable that some of the early transparent paintings executed in Germany, France, and England may have been intended and used occasionally in stead of glass or windows, when glass was extremely rare and costly. A practice prevailed also in England, previous to the introduction of printing with blocks, of painting linen cloth intended for wearing apparel, as well as probably altar-cloths and hangings of apartments, with figures, flowers, and various devices, in imitation of embroidery.

Gilding, Etc.

The splendour of gold and gilded embellishment has been largely introduced into the arts of all nations. Mr. Layard tells us that the Assyrians were prodigal of its employment. The Egyptians used it, and we read of it frequently in the Bible. The solid precious metal was lavished by the Greeks on their chryselephantine (or gold and ivory) sculpture. Every school-boy can talk of 'the golden house of Nero;' and one of the principal features of the art and decorative work of the Middle Ages was the profuse employment of gold. The era from the earliest Christian period to the beginning of the fifteenth century may be termed literally (if not symbolically) the *golden age* in art. In the ancient mosaics gold behind glass was used for the ground; or, perhaps more properly speaking, background—the open-air being intended—and the dresses. The Byzantine and early Italian pictures, missals, and wall paintings were similarly adorned, though the gold is so thickly covered with dark varnish on some Byzantine pictures as to be scarcely recognisable. This decoration was retained, although kept more subordinate, long after the introduction of oil painting. Domenico Ghirlandajo was the first, according to Vasari, who discovered the method of imitating gold with colours. This is somewhat singular, seeing that this great master was originally a goldsmith.[8] One of the disadvantages of gold applied to pictures is, that it gives, especially when seen in situations where it reflects the light, a peculiar heavy leaden effect to the subjects or portions painted, and diminishes the beauty of the colours and destroys the harmony of the picture by its superior brilliancy.

In the early pictures, the proportion of the surface covered with the precious metal far exceeded that over which the colours were spread. Even in the Augustan age, the indulgence in the tempting richness of gold could scarcely have been carried so far as in the works of Christian art of the fourteenth century. The painters of this period used gold so generally, that figures in gold dresses with shining glories (see note E in Appendix) round their heads were placed upon gold backgrounds without any shadow 'cast' from the figures. A most imposing example of the application of gold may he seen in the large altar-piece by Andrea Orcagna in the National Gallery. In the early Frankish or Carlovingian MSS. silver is frequently blended with gold. The backgrounds in the oldest Italian pictures (Sienese school) is pure smooth gold; a characteristic borrowed from the most richly-illuminated MSS. of the same period: but subsequently the gold had patterns or diapers stained, embossed (as in bookbinding), or painted on it. When the background was not gold, it was still diapered, as in the extraordinary painting preserved at Wilton House, believed, we know not upon what sufficient grounds, to be the work of a foreign artist, and which contains the most authentic portrait of our Richard II. The gold and diapered backgrounds have been revived by Hess and other modern painters of the German school; and in Mr. Holman Hunt's picture, 'The Light of the World,' the head of our Saviour encircled with a golden nimbus. In Greek (Byzantine) works and the earliest Italian paintings, even the lights on the dresses of the figures are heightened with gold applied in lines. After the year 1400 all painters seem to have discarded the flat gold background, with the exception of Fra Angelico da Fiesole. In the north, open backgrounds tempera pictures, before the time of Van Eyck, are extremely rare. In German art the nimbus is comparatively seldom seen; where gold objects are represented in the picture itself, they are laid in with the flat leaf, then outlined, and the shadows, as it were, etched with pure black lines, such as we find in large early woodcuts. Sometimes the lines are crossed and sometimes dotted, as in the woodcuts of Albert Dürer.

The gilding on many old wall paintings is in such a remarkable state of preservation, that it is desirable to ascertain how the gold was applied. The gold-leaf itself was thicker, the number of leaves obtained from an equal quantity of metal having been gradually increased since the time of the Romans. The mordants[9] were of two kinds, one of which served for miniatures and places not exposed to damp; the other and more durable being, according to some documentary evidence, an oil mordant; but the most ancient was probably glutinous. Prof. Branchi, from a chemical analysis of some portions of the gold ground of the mural paintings by Benozzo Gozzoli and Buffalmacco, in the Campo Santo at Pisa, concludes that wax was the principal ingredient of the mordant there used.

The gold was always supplied by the persons who ordered the picture; and when these were either unable or unwilling pay for the precious metal, it was usual to substitute for on wall paintings leaves of tin-foil covered with a yellow varnish (auripetrum). In order to economise gold, the old rasters had another invention called 'porporino,' a composition of quicksilver, tin, and sulphur, that produced a yellow metallic powder, and which they employed instead of gold.

A substance of a similar nature is used to this day in England as a substitute for gold on coloured woodcuts and chromolithographs. Silver likewise served as a foil over which yellow and other colours ground with oil were glazed; it was also used in representations of armour, as may be seen in the remarkable picture of 'The Battle of Sant' Egidio,' by Paolo Ucello, in the National Gallery.

Besides these, other decorations were introduced into the Italian pictures of the fourteenth century, such as stucco ornaments in relief; and actual gems (or imitations of them), termed 'nouches,' which were inserted where jewellery was to be represented, more especially in the raised diadems of saints. Such decorations, together with the draperies which we shall see later were already executed in oil,[10] and the carved framework, tabernacle, or surrounding *ornamento* itself of the picture were completed first. The face and hands, which at this period were always in tempera, were added afterwards—at least after the draperies and background were finished. In early times the artist executed all the various operations connected with his picture himself. Hence the number of arts practised in the cloisters, and included in the practical directions given by the monks in mediaeval MSS. In later times the work was divided; and Sir Charles Eastlake tells us that 'the decorator or gilder was sometimes a more important person than the painter. Thus some works of an inferior Florentine artist were ornamented with stuccos, carving, and gilding by the celebrated Donatello, who in his youth practised this art in connection with sculpture. Vasari observed the following inscription under a picture: "Simone Cini, a Florentine, wrought the carved work, Gabriello Saracini executed the gilding, and Spinello di Lucca, of Arezzo, painted the picture, in the year 1385."'

'We may pause to consider for a moment,' says a writer in the *Quarterly Review* (1847), in whom the reader will hardly fail to recognise the author of *Modern Painters,* 'what effect upon the mental habits of these earlier schools might result from the separate and previous completion of minor details. It is to be remembered that the painter's abject in the backgrounds of works of this period (universally, or nearly so, of religious subjects) was not the deceptive representation of a natural scene, but the adornment and setting forth of the central figures with precious work; the conversion of the picture, as far as might be, into a gem, flushed with colour and alive with light. The processes necessary for this purpose were altogether mechanical; and those of stamping and burnishing the gold, and of enamelling, were necessarily performed before any delicate tempera work could be executed. Absolute decision of design was therefore necessary throughout; and hard linear separations were unavoidable between the oil colour and the tempera, or between each and the gold or enamel. General harmony of affect, aerial perspective [the effect of distance given by imitating the influence of atmosphere], or deceptive chiaroscuro became totally impossible; and the dignity of the picture depended exclusively on the lines of its design, the purity of its ornaments, and the beauty of expression which could be obtained in those portions (the faces and hands) which, set off and framed by this splendour of decoration, became the cynosure of eyes. The painter's entire energy vas given to these portions, and we can hardly imagine any discipline more calculated to ensure a grand and thoughtful school of art than the necessity of discriminating character and varied expression imposed by this peculiarly separate and prominent treatment of the features. The exquisite drawing of the hand also, at least in outline, remained for his reason even to late periods one of the crowning excellences of the religious schools. It might be worthy the consideration of our present painters whether some disadvantage may not result from the exactly opposite treatment now frequently adopted, the finishing the head before the addition of its accessories. A flimsy and indolent background is almost a necessary consequence, and probably also a false flesh-colour, irrecoverable by any after apposition.'

The technical operations so characteristic of the Italian art of this period correspond greatly with what was the practice in England; as, for instance, in the splendid decoration of St. Stephen's Chapel, after it was rebuilt by Edward III in the middle of the fourteenth century; for the habits of the painters in England closely resembled those of the followers of Giotto. Nevertheless the practice of gilding, stamping ornaments, and the employment of mosaic, is thought not to have been indigenous to this country.

The rarity of examples in which such decorations occur, where the rest of the work seems English, points to the conclusion that they never formed so essential an element in English art as they did in Italian (see latter half of note D in Appendix).

The latest modifications of gold and silver, glazed or lacquered foil-grounds, appear in the works of Holbein and his contemporaries. The Italians did not paint on gold grounds after the time of Titian, though large yellow-coloured radiating glories are common in his works, as well as in those of Tintoretto and Guido, Murillo and other Spanish masters.

HATCHING AND STIPPLING; FUSION OF TINTS, ETC.

In the finishing of their pictures the tempera painters met with a difficulty that is, however, common to various branches of art. It was, we need not say, impossible to prepare as many tints as there are gradations, or as they are popularly termed, shades, in nature. The tints when laid, covered flatly certain definable patches and breadths. The vehicle dried too quickly to allow much blending or fusion of the colours on the surface of the picture, and for the same reason they could not be readily lightened or darkened in tone.[11] Therefore, for portions requiring very delicate gradations—such, for instance, as the features, in order to convey the impression of relief, or that parts are raised or project beyond others, to do, in fact, on a flat surface what the sculptor does with his modelling—it was necessary to adopt the expedients of 'hatching' and 'stippling.' *Hatching* consists of lines —*stippling* of dots. By patiently placing these, one by one, more or less closely together, or of more or less thickness, and with mechanical regularity, it is found that the most insensible or the most abrupt gradations can be obtained. Stipple gives its name to that species of engraving brought to perfection by Bartolozzi, and employed in imitations of chalk drawings. 'Hatching' is a variation of the word 'etching,' through which it is derived from the German *Etzen.* The methods are frequently mixed, stippling being used to soften and fill up spaces left by the crossed hatchings; and both are of very general application, not only in tempera, but in engraving, drawing, oil, missal, miniature, watercolour, and fresco painting. One explanation will, however, serve for all.

Hatching is the only method which can imply any knowledge of forms beyond that distinctly developed by the appearances produced by the tinting. Several refinements, by which lines were rendered more descriptive, were introduced by the great masters in their drawings, and by the early Italian engravers, that were apparently unknown to the more ancient tempera painters. Such was the principle, derived probably from observation of striped draperies, that objects which are rounded have their rotundity best expressed by curved lines; and that those portions which recede above the level of the eye, or what is the same thing, the horizontal line, should have the lines arched like a bridge; while to represent the portions which recede below that line, the curves should be inverted, like the reflection of the bridge in the water. If we were to suppose a number of threads arranged like a stave in music or the strings of a harp, and held between the light and some irregular and rounded object, the shadows of the threads would follow the depressions and elevations of the surface on which they fell, and illustrate the practice to which we allude, and which is carried to perfection in line-engraving. Other conventional principles which have been established are, that lines, while assisting the 'modelling,' should be crossed, in order, by forming reticulations, to prevent the eye following their direction; to remove the impression of the surface they are intended to describe being polished; and also to indicate the degree of roughness or smoothness intended, by drawing the lines to intersect at a more or less acute or obtuse angle. The tempera painters, on the contrary, seldom curved the stroke of their brush when at any distance from the outline, or allowed the lines to intersect, and probably never upon a scientific principle. The process of hatching may still be seen, after the lapse of front four to six hundred years, very distinctly in several of the tempera paintings, so many of which have lately been added to the National Gallery. Where the touch is large, as in a small 'Holy Family' by Pietro Perugino, the straight (vertical) strokes are very conspicuous; but in others, as, for instance, the presumed portrait of Isotta da Rimini by Piero della Francesca, the lines (in this case oblique) are so fine as to be scarcely perceptible.

Tempera, as we shall see, was adopted as complementary to fresco, and when so used (to add at leisure force and gradation to the necessarily hastily executed groundwork of true fresco) hatching was indispensable; but hatching was also employed most extensively in the actual process of fresco painting. Here, however, as indeed in many other cases, it was serviceable not only for purposes of modelling and gradation, but to procure a flat tint (which is not easy to obtain in fresco), and likewise to conceal the joinings in the mortar. The great works of Michael Angelo in the Sistine Chapel are all executed by hatchings (with lines which do not cross); an elaborate mechanical process, scarcely to be expected from the painter's impatient temperament. The simple straight lines of the tempera painters were derived from the practice of the Byzantine missal painters; but even in etchings by Rembrandt and other masters we frequently see a rounded surface represented by the same means. In the frescoes of Raphael in the Vatican there was, however, no hatching before they were 'restored' by Carlo Maratta; nor is there in those of Correggio. But in the earlier oil pictures by Raphael the hatching is often very evident—witness the St. Catherine in the National Gallery. Leonardo da Vinci, in the minute stipple of his works, furnishes an example of an analogous method, and a method which was adopted by many other of the first Italian painters in oil, and has been continued to our day, as may be seen in the more recent works of the learned President of the Royal Academy; and also, though very dissimilar, in the pictures of our contemporary pre-Raphaelites.

These modes of finishing were, however, never in favour with the northern painters, either in tempera or oil, at least it is not perceptible in their smallest and highly-finished pictures. In these the touch is either free from mechanical regularity, as, for a late example, in Teniers, or the tints are laid to appear as nearly as practicable like an even wash, as in the partially tempera pictures of Meister Stephen, in the National Gallery; in the oil paintings of Van Eyck, and later of Mieris, and many other Dutch painters of cabinet[12] pictures. This is surprising when we remember the engraving and pen-drawing they often practised; and that some of them, including Van Eyck, were also illuminators, in which stippling is inevitable. For in missal painting, from the impossibility of spreading a flat tint on the vellum of which the ancient books were composed, the illuminators were compelled to have recourse to what Fuseli calls the 'elaborate anguish' of the system. The modern miniature painter is also placed under similar conditions, the hard smooth surface of ivory obliging him to finish, as it is pleasantly termed, with line, 'dot and go one.' Finally, many painters in water-colours choose these methods, because by them greater richness and finish can be obtained.

We have said that the fig-tree juice was replaced among the German and

English tempera painters by vinegar; but this would not retard the rapidly drying vehicle sufficiently to explain the careful rounding of forms by fusion of tints observable in many of their works. This was effected, it appears, by the addition of honey. The more obviously laborious process with lines and dots was alone that which was, with few exceptions, known or practised by the earlier artists of Italy. After the middle of the fifteenth century the exceptions are less rare, but wax and other ingredients besides honey were probably employed at this period.

The lines and dots of the tempera painters are generally of the same hue, though lighter or darker than the colour which they cover. Occasionally, however, as in one of the examples of Botticelli in the National Gallery, we see some indication of a principle, invaluable for the attainment of purity and richness of effect, carried to perfection by Mr. W. Hunt and other water-colour artists; viz., the placing side by side separate touches of unbroken, but diverse colour, and leaving them for the ere to blend and unite. The system of shading with a 'self-colour,' as pink with crimson, and light blue or yellow with deeper tints of the same colour, was afterwards shown in the Roman schools to be compatible with the most elevated style of painting, though not of actual imitation. In the very early works of the Sienese this system we find did not obtain: salmon coloured lights are placed in the flesh over very dissimilar hues, not to speak of the ghastly contrast they present with the green shadows and pink cheeks of the faces.

The Varnish

A short inquiry into the nature of the varnish used by the tempera painters at the end of the fourteenth century, acquires considerable interest for the general reader from the circumstance that, as we shall see in treating of Oil Painting, it was, there is little doubt, in the search for a more eligible varnish, that Van Eyck effected the great improvement in the vehicle of oil painting, by which tempera was finally everywhere superseded.

It is probable that varnishes composed of resins dissolved in oil have been used in the most ancient times. It is believed that the composition of varnish was known in Persia, India, and China before the best period of painting in Greece; and it is, then, not to be supposed that the Greeks were unacquainted with the means of preparing it. Yet such would have been the case, if we give credit to what may be inferred from a paragraph in Pliny, in which he tells us that the great painter Apelles was indebted for his unequalled colouring to the employment of a liquid which he call, 'atramentum,' with which he covered his pictures when they were finished, and with which no other painter was acquainted. Pliny observes, 'There is in the pictures of Apelles a certain effect that cannot be equalled,' and that 'tone was obtained by means of *atramentum,* which fluid he passed over his pictures when the painting was completely finished.' 'This liquid,' we are further told, 'brought out all the brightness and fulness of the colours, and also prevented the dust or similar substances from impairing their lustre. It was so transparent that it was not perceptible until you were very near to it.' One of its greatest advantages was, that the brightest colours under its influence, so far from dazzling the sight, seemed as if viewed from a distance, or through a glassy medium, which imperceptibly lowered the tone of the most brilliant tints, rendering them more chaste and agreeable to the eye. Sir J. Reynolds thought he saw in this passage an authority for glazing.[13] At all events, the word *atramentum* would seem to imply that the transparent varnish was of a brownish tint; and Sir Charles Eastlake has even suggested that, as the varnishes of the mediaeval painters were all of a red or brown tinge, their dusky hue was possibly traditionally derived from the best ages of Greece. We have a distinct mention of a varnish by Aetius, a medical writer of as early as the end of the fifth century. From the eighth century till the time of Van Eyck the mention of oil varnishes (linseed-oil from its more readily drying being generally preferred to nut-oil) occurs occasionally in MSS.; sandarac and mastic resin being the ingredients commonly boiled in the oil, although oil alone, thickened to the consistence of a varnish, was used in the twelfth century. Such varnishes continued in use in Italy till the Raphael era, when the Italians began to employ varnishes prepared with the far more rapidly drying essential oils. Varnish, in addition to its other use, was employed by the early Venetian and other decorators in gilding the back of glass, and likewise for painting on glass, as distinguished from glass enamelling, in which the colours are fired in.

But the question remains to be determined—What was the nature of the varnish ordinarily employed by the tempera painters about the time of Van Eyck, and spoken of by Cennini and others under the familiar title of 'Vernice liquida?' The derivation of the word *vernix* bears materially on the question. This word, variously modified, is proved by Sir Charles Eastlake, with much philological research, to have been, in its primitive form, 'Berenice,' the original Greek name for amber. The possibility is even intimated that the name Berenice, or Pherenice, borne by more than one daughter of the Ptolemies, was the original word. Further—'The literal coincidence of this name and its modifications with the vernice of the Middle Ages, might almost warrant the supposition that amber, which by the best ancient authorities was considered a mineral, may at an early period have been distinguished by the name of a constellation, the constellation of Berenice's (golden) hair.'—*Materials*, &c., p. 230.

If amber was the original material it was, however, confounded with other materials, which gradually served either as substitutes or entirely superseded it. Among these were copal and sandarac resin. The latter resembles amber less than copal; but it is proved, from abundant and conclusive evidence, that, on account of its greater cheapness and easier solubility in oil, it was the usual substitute for amber; and that, when dissolved by beat in linseed oil, it was the 'Vernice liquida,' the customary varnish for tempera pictures. Concrete turpentine (or the resin in its dry state), previously prepared over a slow fire until it ceased to swell, was sometimes added to assist the liquefaction, first in Venice, where the material was easily procured (hence the name 'Venice turpentine'), and afterwards in Florence. All varnishes are affected by air sooner or later, and this is less durable than amber or copal. In some old tempera pictures, the whole surface, or large spaces, may be observed freed from the original varnish, while it remains in detached dark-brown spots on others. This cracking of the varnish seldom affects the painting underneath, a proof that it was applied when the tempera was quite dry. The 'Vernice liquida' was subjected to long boiling, to render it to more drying; but the disadvantages of this mode of preparation were not only that the varnish became so thick as actually to require to be spread with the hand, but also that by this long boiling it became at the same time so dark as to materially affect the tints over which it was passed.

'It is not impossible,' says Sir Charles Eastlake, 'that the lighter style of colouring introduced by Giotto may have been intended by him to counteract the effects of this varnish, the appearance of which in the Greek pictures he could not fail to observe. Another peculiarity in the works of the painters of the time referred to, particularly those of the Florentine and Sienese schools, is the greenish tone of their colouring in the flesh; produced by the mode in which they often prepared their works, viz., by a green underpainting. The appearance was neutralized by the red sandarac varnish, and pictures executed in the manner described must have looked better before it was removed.' The mediaeval painters were so accustomed to this red appearance in varnishes, that they even supplied the tint when it did not exist.

THE COLOURS

Our knowledge respecting the colours used by the painters in classical times is derived chiefly from a few passages in ancient authors; but some information has been drawn from experiments on the colours in the remains of ancient paintings, and on pigments[14] that were found at Pompeii, and in vases beneath the ruins of the palace of Titus at Rome. On the authority of a passage in Pliny, it has been frequently stated that Apelles and other celebrated Greek painters used only four colours, viz., white, yellow, red, and *atramentum;* but it must be a mistake to suppose that they were acquainted only with these colours, or that they never used any others. Indeed, unless Pliny be supposed to point out a distinction in this respect between the practice of the earlier and later painters, the gossiping amateur contradicts himself; for in all he enumerates no less than five different whites, three yellows, nine reds or purples, two blues, two greens, and one black (atramentum), which, moreover, appears to be a generic expression that includes bitumen, charcoal, ivory or lamp-black, and probably a blue-black, which thinned would supply a blue tint; and a longer list might be made out from other authors. Most certainly, however, from the four colours named, innumerable hues and tints might be composed; and Sir Humphry Davy says, very justly, in the account of his experiments on the ancient colours: 'If red and yellow ochres, blacks and whites, were the colours most employed by Protogenes and Apelles, so they were likewise the colours most employed by Raphael and Titian in their best style.' And it must be remembered that from the superior importance attached to design, great soberness in the use of colours prevailed for a long time in antiquity. 'Even the Ionic school,' according to Müller, 'which loved florid colouring, adhered to the so-called *four* colours even down to the time of Apelles ; that is, four principal colouring materials, which, however, had not only natural varieties themselves, but also produced such by mixing; for the pure application of a few colours only belonged to the imperfect painting of the architectural works of Egypt, the Etruscan hypogea, and the Grecian earthenware. Along with these leading colours, which appeared stern and harsh to a later age, brighter and dearer colouring materials were gradually introduced.'—*Ancient Art and its Remains.*

The light tone of colouring so characteristic of most of the works of the later Christian painters in tempera, has, it has been observed, been referred to the allowance made for the darkening effect of the varnish. But there is another reason for the pale colouring of the period. The pigments in use had little intensity of tone; the browns, for instance, were by no means dark. Hence, with the imperfect monotonous system of shading already described, those painters had no means of producing depth of effect. And it would appear that they sought to compensate for this by preserving the local colours in their full strength and purity. The delicacy which they seem in most instances to have aimed at in their flesh tints, may, however, have induced a similar treatment of the rest of the work.

The tempera painters kept their pigments when ready for use in small earthenware saucers.

Chapter 3

Wax Painting or Encaustic

Encaustic having been a favourite method of painting in classical times, it is desirable to attempt to ascertain its nature before proceeding to offer an historical sketch of ancient art.

The explanations given of the ancient wax painting are, however, almost inextricably confused and contradictory. There appears to have been three distinct methods, so entirely dissimilar that we shall best avoid confusion by describing them, according to the best authorities, separately.

Of the art of using colours prepared with wax, and of fixing pictures so executed by the aid of fire, the application of the term 'encaustic,' which strictly means 'burning in,' is scarcely sufficiently descriptive. Yet, in whatever operations wax was subjected to the action of beat, the process appears to have been considered by the ancients a species of encaustic. Polishing walls, for example, was denominated *kausis,* and the varnishers of statues were called *encaustai.* After the later pagan painters, the prevalence of encaustic painting among the Christian artists led to the gradual application of the term to all kinds of painting; and even when it was superseded by mosaic, and the process itself scarcely survived, the term was still applied to other modes of painting. In illuminating, for example, the purple and vermilion used for the imperial signatures, and in caligraphy, received the name of 'encaustic.' Later, the more ordinary materials of writing were called by the mediaeval writers 'incaustum;' and this has finally degenerated into the 'inchiostro' of the Italians, and the English 'ink.'

According to Pliny,[15] 'there were originally two modes of painting in encaustic, the one with wax, the other on ivory, by means of the *cestrum,* or graver, till ships began to be painted. This was the third mode introduced, and in this the brush was used, the wax being dissolved by fire.' As the brush is only mentioned in the last, it is evident that in the two former modes a metal instrument alone was employed.

In the first mode, then, we find that a heated metal instrument called the *rhabdion* (which might have varied in shape, as brushes do now) or *cestrum*[16] (for the terms are employed sometimes indiscriminately), was used to blend the tints. The variously coloured wax pigments were prepared in cakes or sticks, like coloured crayons in the present day. The rhabdion was used much in the same way as Turner and other painters have dexterously handled the palette-knife, drawing with the point and regulating the impasto, or body of colour, with the side of the instrument. The process was elaborate: hence it was only suited for works of limited dimensions, and its difficulty probably contributed to give the small encaustic pictures of Pausias, executed in this style, their proverbial value in the eyes of rich Roman collectors.

In the second method, the metal point, *cestrum,* or *viriculum,* as it was otherwise called, was used; but for the purpose of actually engraving, by means of encaustic outlines on ivory and other substances. Sir Charles Eastlake, however,—whose descriptions of the different styles of encaustic painting are the best with which we are acquainted,—thinks that even in this instance the word encaustic need not be taken literally, since forms burnt on ivory could not have been very delicate works of art. It may rather be supposed that the outlines were first drawn on waxed ivory, for the facility of correcting then when necessary; that they were afterwards engraved like a seal, in a sort of intaglio in the substance; and that the finished and shadowed design was filled in with one or more colours; being ultimately covered with a wax varnish by the aid of heat.

The third style was termed *pencillum* encaustic, because brushes were substituted for the metal point. The colours were kept in pots mixed with wax, and the wax was dissolved previous to painting, sufficiently to render the pigments fit to be applied with the brush. The wax crayons or cakes may also possibly have been used. But the chief characteristic of this third method was the use of the *cauterium.* This instrument was a pan of live coals or some kind of charcoal heater. When the picture was in other respects finished, the cauterium was held before it till 'the colours frothed,' and this regulated fusion united the whole surface.[17]

This was the generally practised wax painting of the late pagans and early Christians, and is the chief authorization of the term encaustic. This style somewhat resembled the first. The artists painted on wood (larch being preferred for all pictures); but ultimately sometimes on walls. Pausias, Nicias, and other painters who practised the first process, generally adopted this likewise. It is clear that, as the brush was used in this method, the wax must have been softened and dissolved in some other way than by heat, in order to fit it as a vehicle; for, merely melted by heat, although with friction serviceable as a varnish, it would cool much too rapidly for the application of the colours with the brush. But it is remarkable that, although the ancient mode of bleaching wax has been fully described by classic authors, no passage has been found which clearly describes the process of converting it into a vehicle for painting. From this uncertainty, innumerable controversies, theories, and experiments have arisen.

Pliny, we have seen, states that the third style of wax painting was first adopted for ships, and he adds that it was 'proof against the sun's heat, the salt of the sea, and the winds.' The common varnish for ships was, there is reason to believe, not pitch, but wax and resin, dissolved probably by an essential oil,[18] although the word 'zopissa' is used indifferently for pitch and comparatively light-coloured resin. This varnish, more carefully prepared in order to render it as pale as possible, was, in all probability, the vehicle used, as it has the qualities enumerated by Pliny.

Experienced chemical analysis has proved that the colours of a mummy cloth had been mixed with pure wax, and it is concluded that the wax was held in solution by a volatile oil, such as naphtha. We have seen, from the experiments of Prof. Branchi, that in the Middle Ages the mordant for gilding was wax; and the chemist inclines to think it was dissolved in an essential oil, rather than a fixed drying oil. The same Professor ascertained that wax had been also used either with or over the colours as a varnish in the early Pisan and Florentine pictures before the middle of the fourteenth century, and that from a resinous residuum it was probably dissolved by spirits of turpentine wax was likewise used at this period in colouring statues, and as a cement for mosaics. From a few passages in mediaeval MSS., it appears that wax was also sometimes employed as a vehicle, and that its solution was effected by a *lixivium,* that is to say, by some agency which will allow the wax when ground, or in some other way united with the pigment, to be mixed with water. Potass and lime are mentioned as thus used, and a similar mode is still practised by the monks of Mount Athos, who retain many other Byzantine traditions. Alkaline reagents, which convert the pigments into a kind of soap, have had many modern advocates. No direct evidence in support of the employment of a lixivium, or the solution of wax by maceration, instead of its liquefaction by fire, can, however, be adduced from ancient authors. All that is distinctly mentioned is the solution of wax by means of heat in a fixed oil: walls and statues at least were certainly sometimes varnished with wax dissolved in olive oil, and afterwards polished by means of heat and friction, as already alluded to the cloths removing the superfluous oil, as in the polishing of furniture at the present day. Of the more artistic kind of wax painting applied to statues we shall speak later.

The wax painting of antiquity was valued for its durability, resistance to moisture, and ordinary heat, and the gloss of which it was susceptible. The last was a great recommendation to the ancients, especially when encaustic was employed not only for painting on panels, but for mural decoration; for the walls of their sumptuous apartments were very carefully stuccoed, and polished like mirrors. When painted and varnished, no lodgment was afforded for dust, and there was the utmost facility for cleaning the surface. Hence, upon the introduction of the larger style, wax painting was applied to ceilings, and, at a later period, even to the walls of baths. It is true that tempera pictures were varnished and had consequently a shining surface, but not, perhaps, when tempera was employed for wall painting; and certainly we should venture to say the lime painting, either when fresco was employed alone — if ever it was so employed — or when it was combined with tempera, was not rendered superficially glossy. A higher quality, artistically speaking, was that the *pencillum encaustic* was susceptible of more depth and richness, and therefore of more force, brilliancy of colour, and gradation. And of this we are assured, that the later encaustic pictures of the Romans were esteemed as much as the works of the great artists executed in the older method, notwithstanding that art was then declining. Encaustic certainly never had entirely favourable conditions for the development and appreciation of its resources.

Chapter 4

Tempera and Encaustic in Antiquity and the Middle Ages

Having explained the principal processes of painting employed by the ancients and in the Middle Ages, a few connecting notices of the practice at different periods, together with a glance at inferior branches of the art—such for instance as vase painting—are necessary to complete a general view of the subject. Of the origin of painting various theories have been entertained. Prof. Gottfried Semper and others seem to think it originated in the ornamentation of woven fabrics; while Müller believes it arose from the colouring of statues and reliefs; and writers on ceramics follow the opinion of Pasiteles (quoted by Pliny), that pottery was the parent of the arts. Haydon says in one of his *Lectures,* and we would use the same words, 'I shall not plague you or myself with a useless discussion as to where the arts first had origin, whether in India or Egypt, Italy or Greece, before the Flood, or after the building of Babel. According to my principle, the very first man born after the Creation, with such a peculiar and intense sensibility to receive impressions through the eye, on the brain, of the beauty of colour, light and shadow, and form, so as to be irresistibly impelled in his earliest childhood to attempt the imitation of what he saw and felt by lines and colours to convey his innocent thought, and combinations, in him originated PAINTING.'

1. The Egyptians

Undoubtedly the oldest remains of painting are Egyptian; and the earliest, namely, those executed in the Pharaonic period, are by far the best, the arts having been constantly in a state of decline, from the earliest known examples, through the Ptolemaic period to the Roman. Three classes of paintings have been discovered in Egypt: those on the walls, those on the cases and cloths of mummies, and those on papyrus rolls. Of these, the paintings in the tombs and temples are first in merit and interest. The Egyptians were remarkably fond of variety of patterns on the walls and ceilings of their houses and tombs, and on their hangings, dresses, furniture, and vases. Sir J. Gardner Wilkinson says, 'some of the oldest ceilings show that the chevron (so common in Egyptian baskets and vases), together with the chequer, as well as the scroll and guilloche, ascribed too hastily to the comparatively modern Greeks, were adopted in Egypt more than 2000 years before our era. An infinite variety of purely *conventional* devices had been invented and were in common use during the eighteenth and nineteenth dynasties, long before the Trojan war, as well as the lotus and other ornaments, directly imitated from natural objects.'

Painting in Egypt was practised under peculiar conditions. Painters and sculptors were forbidden by a jealous priesthood to introduce any change or innovation whatever into the practice of their respective arts, or in any way to add to them. Thus art remained stationary from generation to generation. It was indeed considered a necessary part of the system that painting and sculpture should not be practised by illiterate people, lest they should attempt anything contrary to the established order of things. The consequences were that art preserved many, so to speak, infantine characteristics.[19] Even the imitation of nature was not carried in painting beyond an outlined diagram, arbitrarily coloured; a generalization of human form was adopted by the Egyptian sculptors and painters, but they did not attain to that ideal beauty which the Greeks were the first to comprehend and embody. Nor did the Egyptians understand the beauty and true province of bas-relief like the Greeks: in their battle scenes they attempted to make a picture; and in order to obviate the confusion resulting from a number of sculptured figures one behind the other, they placed them in all parts of the same field, regardless of the sky or of perspective, providing only against everything which might interfere with the hero of the subject—the king—who depended on colossal size, instead of art, for his importance.

Everything being prescribed and predetermined in Egyptian art, we shall not be surprised to learn that there was a regular system of conventional proportions, and that previous to commencing a painting the walls were squared out with lines. Accordingly, we find that the divisions prescribed by the canons or rules then in use are very commonly found on unfinished works, and are sometimes to be detected under the paint in finished paintings and statues. We likewise possess in the British Museum an ancient tablet, on which is preserved an outline, exhibiting the canon of the proportions of the human frame, in use among the painters and sculptors of that country in the age of Amunopth III, about 1250 years before our era.

The method of executing a wall painting has been thus described by Mr. Owen Jones: 'The wall was first chiselled as smooth as possible, the imperfections of the stone were filled up with cement or plaster, and the whole was rubbed smooth and covered with a coloured wash; lines were then ruled perpendicularly and horizontally with red colour, forming squares all over the wall, corresponding with the proportions of the figures to be drawn upon it. The subjects of the painting and of the hieroglyphics were then drawn on the wall with a *red line,* most probably by the priest or chief scribe, or by some inferior artist, from a document divided into similar squares; then came the chief artist, who went over every figure and hieroglyphic with a *black line,* and a firm and steady hand, giving expression to each curve—deviating here and confirming there the former red line. The line thus traced was then followed by the sculptor. In this stage there are instances of a foot or head having been completely sculptured, whilst the rest of the figure remains in outline. The next process was to paint the figure in the prescribed colours; and in some cases the painted line deviates from the sculptured line, showing that the painter was the more important workman, and that even in this last process no possible improvement was omitted. There are other instances where a considerable deviation from the position of a leg or arm has been made after the sculpture was finished and painted: the part was recarved, and the defective portion filled in with plaster; which, having since fallen out, furnishes us with this curious evidence of their practice.' Exactly corresponding with this is the description given by Belzoni of the executing and painting of the Egyptian bassi-relievi which he found in the Biban el Molouk, or Tombs of the Kings, at Thebes.

The colours were mixed with dissolved glue, and apparently, sometimes, even with wax: there is an example in the British Museum of the colours being mixed with wax (mistaken sometimes for an oil painting), in a small funeral group of two figures. The ordinary colours seen upon the sculptures and paintings are red, yellow, green, and blue, of which there are two tints; black also was used; but for white, the white ground, which was prepared as fine as letter paper, was of course sufficient. These colours are sometimes modified by admixture with chalk, but they are always applied singly and unmixed together. Different colours were reserved for different objects. Men and women were painted red—the men of a darker tint than the women. Black men also frequently occur, and some captives of, probably, a race with lighter complexions, are painted yellow, with black beards. According to the best chemical analyses of Egyptian colours, the *blues* appear to be oxides of copper with a small intermixture of iron: none of them contain cobalt. Belzoni, therefore, who supposed the Egyptian blues to be indigo, appears to be in error. The *reds* are red oxide of iron mixed with lime. The *yellows,* which are sometimes of a pure bright sulphur colour, appear to be generally vegetable colours; the greens are a mixture of this vegetable yellow with copper blue; the vegetable, it has been suggested, might be the *henné* plant, which is still used in the East for such purposes. The bluish-green which sometimes appears on Egyptian antiquities is a faded blue. The *blacks* might be from wine-lees, burnt pitch, charcoal, or soot. Painters and sculptors held in Egypt a rank similar to that of architects and professional scribes—indeed, painting, sculpture, and architecture were so intimately united that it is almost impossible to separate them. 'The same kind of wooden palette, or inkstand, was used by the limner in drawing outlines, as by the scribe in writing upon a papyrus; and the same kind of reed pen was employed for both purposes. The inkstand contained two colours, black and red, the latter being used at the beginning of a subject, and for the division of certain sentences—showing this custom to have been as old as that of holding the pen behind the ear, often portrayed in the paintings of the tombs. Some palettes contained more than two colours black, red, blue, green, and white. They were of the same long shape as the ordinary inkstand, with the usual case in the centre for holding the pens, and some were of square or oblong form, made of wood or stone, with a larger cavity for each colour. Slabs and pestles [mullers] for grinding colours are also commonly found in the tombs of Thebes, as well as lumps of ochre, green, blue, and other colours. The sacred scribes were of the priestly order, but the royal scribes might be either priests or military men, and they were generally sons of the king, or of the chief men of the court. The public scribes were also men of great trust and consequence, to whom the settlement of public and private accounts was committed, and they assisted or performed the office of magistrates, in condemning defaulters to punishment.'—*Sir J. Gardner Wilkinson.* For further information on this interesting subject, see this author's work on *The Private Life, Manners, and Customs of the Ancient Egyptians.*

The Egyptians, besides painting the bas-reliefs, painted also detached statues: the group of the man, woman, and child, of sandstone, in the British Museum (No. 31), has been painted. They also painted obelisks, sarcophagi, and other similar objects. There is a painted sarcophagus in the Museum (No. 39), which has been varnished. Some of the Egyptian varnishes were made of glue, others appear to be resinous.

A few words may be considered not out of place on the hieroglyphs (literally 'sacred sculptures'), the 'picture-writing' of the Egyptians. The hieroglyphs were generally coloured on the great monuments when complete; and three principal kinds have been remarked by M. Champollion: 1. Sculptured, but not painted. 2. Sculptured and painted. 3. Drawn in outline with a pencil and then painted. Besides which, they may be classed as: 4. *Polychrome,* or painted with various colours. 5. *Monochrome,* or having only one tint throughout the inscription. As it is probable that all were painted, the first class can only apply to certain inscriptions of which the colours have disappeared. The second was that in use for monuments of the highest importance. On these, by means of simple primitive colours and flat tints, the Egyptians endeavoured to imitate conventionally the objects which the hieroglyphs represented: thus the heaven was coloured blue, the hills red, the moon yellow; men with red flesh and white garments, the folds of which are sometimes traced in red, &c. Some idea may be formed in the Egyptian Court of the Crystal Palace of the beautiful appearance which the tombs presented, and the gay and artistic effect produced by lines of these pure hieroglyphs, appropriately coloured with simple colour to imitate the objects they represent. Alphabetic writing compared to it is as mean and tasteless as the 'Frank' dress compared with the Oriental costume. It is evident, however, that so elaborate a system of writing was not calculated for monuments, unless they were of the greatest importance. Consequently, for the books or rolls of papyri and other objects, such as sarcophagi and tablets, another kind of hieroglyphs, to which the term *linear* has been applied, were used. These were engraved with a pointed tool when cut, and traced with the reed when written in black or red ink; and either by tracing the outline of the object, or by giving the principal characteristics in one thick line. The linear hieroglyphs are indeed capable of many minute divisions and subdivisions of style, according as they approach to, or recede from, in their finish, the pure hieroglyphs. They are generally black, but the leading words of the chapters and direction pages are written in red like the rubrics of prayer-books; and sometimes the work is accompanied throughout by vignettes, one to each chapter, elaborately painted like those of missals.[20]

Yet, with undeniable mechanical merit, scarcely a single principle of art is illustrated in any kind of Egyptian painting—yet discovered, if we except perhaps one or two of the small cedar portraits which have been found in mummy cases, and in which we see, in addition to the outline, the relief distinctly expressed by light and shade. In no Egyptian painting is there the slightest indication of a knowledge of perspective.

2. THE ASSYRIANS

Mr. Layard tells us that traces of colour and gilding were found upon nearly all the bas-reliefs discovered at Nineveh; thus showing that the Assyrians, like other nations, painted their sculptures and the architectural ornaments of their buildings. The art displayed in the sculptures, although rude and primitive, was distinguished by considerable truth of outline and elegance of detail, and was in some respects superior to the Egyptian. It has now taken its place amongst other styles of ancient art, and is easily recognised by its peculiar characteristics, especially in the treatment of the human form, marked by the strong development of the limbs and muscles; in the nature of its ornamentation frequently distinguished by considerable grace and beauty; and in the conventional mode of portraying natural objects, such as mountains, trees, rivers, &c. The colours employed, as far as they have yet been analysed, were mineral pigments. There are, however, grounds for believing that vegetable colours were not unknown to the Assyrians, but were extensively used in decorating the walls of their palaces being, however, subject to more rapid decay than the mineral pigments, they have disappeared. The colours discovered in the ruins were a blue of great brilliancy, derived from copper; red, yellow, white, black, and green. These colours, with several hues and tints, may be seen on bricks brought from the ruins, and preserved in the British Museum. The dark black outline is a distinguishing feature of Assyrian art. As on Egyptian monuments, colours were probably used conventionally—that is to say, the same colours were always employed for a certain class of objects. From the drawings made from painted walls at Khorsabad, recently sent to Paris, it would appear, however, that human flesh was closely imitated in colour. The Assyrians seem also to have been fond of using only two colours, such, for instance, as yellow and blue, in very elaborate decorations, combining them so as skilfully to produce a very pleasing effect.

3. The Greeks

Painting is said to have passed through several stages in Greece, commencing with simple *skiagraphy,* or shadow-painting; by which is meant giving the exterior outline, or shape of an object, without any intermediate lines. According to the well-known pretty fable, the origin of painting is attributed to an effort in skiagraphy—viz., that of the Greek maiden to trace the outline of the shadow of her departing lover on the wall. The *monographic* style consisted also of lines, but the inner lines or markings were given as well as the exterior outline. In the ancient monochromatic compositions, as is intimated by the derivation of the word, one colour only was used (the black designs on the vases were probably considered monochrome paintings);

while in *polychromy* several colours are, of course, employed. Finally, *zoography* appears to have been the full art of painting to the life, and applying colours duly subordinated to the laws of light and shade.

Painting was later than sculpture in becoming an independent art in Greece, partly because the Grecian worship stood in little need of it. For a long time all paintings consisted in colouring statues and reliefs of wood and clay. Homer speaks only of red-prowed and purple-prowed ships; he alludes, however, to elegant and elaborate embroidery as , something not uncommon, and this is painting in principle, though not actually in practice: it is textile painting, or painting with the needle, and this is what it is termed by the Romans; such expressions are used by Cicero, by Virgil, and by Horace. But of painting itself there is little to be said before about 500 B.C. Aristotle mentions a very remarkable piece of embroidery, which was made for Alcisthenes, one of the luxurious natives of Sybaris. A description of this shawl, which was the wonder of the Heliots, will be found in Grote's *History of Greece.* By the Greek artistic traditions, the first advances in painting are ascribed to the Corinthians and Sicyonians, who are mentioned without much credibility, however, as the inventors of outline drawing and monochrome painting. At Corinth, 'the city of potters,' painting was certainly very early united with the fabrication of vases; and the connection of this city with Tarquinii might have been the means of conveying the antique style of vase painting to Etruria, for the Etruscans probably borrowed their art from the Greeks. The manufacture of vases was from an early period divided into two main branches: the light yellow vases without gloss, of broader and more depressed forms, with red, brown, and violet figures, which, for the most part, represent animal shapes of an arabesque character; and the dark yellow vases, which were better varnished and of a more tasteful form, with black figures, chiefly of a mythological nature. Both were fabricated in Greece and Italy. The archaic, or oldest painted vases, furnish, by the rudeness and clumsiness of their figures, the most distinct idea of the stages through which the art of design must have passed before it could arrive at an established and regular national style. See Birch's *Ancient Pottery,* 1858.

From about 600 B.C. to 400 B.C. may be dated the period of development in painting. The *essential* qualities of form and expression were exhibited in historical painting, constituting what has since been called High Art. Cimon of Cleone, who by some is believed to have lived nearly a century before Polygnotus, is the first Greek artist of importance. He made great progress in the perspective treatment of subjects. He is recorded as the inventor of *foreshortening,*[21] or the first to make oblique or inclined views of the figure *obliquæ imagines,* which the Greeks, according to Pliny, termed *Catagrapha.* He is said also to have been the first to mark the articulations, indicate the muscles and veins, and give natural folds to drapery. Vase painting remained more restricted in its resources. The art had been at this period introduced from its two metropolises Corinth and Athens into Italy and Sicily, but was still less advanced in these countries. The Chalcidian Greeks in Lower Italy (Magna Grecia), took Attic models as their ground-work, both in subjects and forms. Black figures on reddish-yellow clay were now the prevailing characteristics; but the earlier peculiarities were broadly retained. Thus we find the chief muscles and joints excessively prominent, the drapery stiffly adhering or regularly folded, the postures constrained and abrupt. Owing, however, to the facility of exercising this art, there was a great variety of styles or manners, peculiar to particular places of manufacture, often with an intentional striving at the bizarre, or caricature. The origin of *Scenography* or perspective scene painting, is ascribed by Aristotle to a painter of this period named Sophocles, after whom it figured as a separate art.

From 460 B.C. to 366 B.C., that is to say, from Pericles down to Alexander, painting reached in three great stages a degree of perfection which made it, at least in the opinion of the ancients—and surely they were qualified judges—a worthy rival of the plastic art (sculpture); even in the age when Phidias produced those marvellous works, the very dilapidated fragments of which, the Elgin marbles of the British Museum, so much excite our astonishment and admiration. Ancient painting appears, however, to have long remained more closely allied to sculpture than the modern. Forms predominated over the effects of light; the design was sharp and distinct;

different figures were separated in order not to confuse their outlines; the light was uniformly distributed, clear illumination being preserved throughout; and violent foreshortenings were avoided, notwithstanding considerable knowledge of linear perspective.

Polygnotus was the first painter of great renown. Accurate drawing and a noble and distinct manner of characterizing the different mythological forms was his great merit; his females were graceful and attractive, and he was an excellent colourist. His works were arranged according to symmetrical and architectural principles. He decorated some of the principal temples of Delphi and the Athenian Acropolis. His most important performances were those in the *Lesche,* a public ball or portico (such as are called *loggie* by the Italians) near the temple of Apollo at Delphi. '"As Homer," says De Pauw, "was the founder of epic poetry, so was Polygnotus the founder of historic painting." From Polygnotus may be dated the commencement of subjective style in painting; that is, its subjective treatment. *Subjective* is here used in contradistinction to *Objective:* a work of Art may be said to be subjectively treated when it is characterized more by the peculiar aesthetic[22] or idiosyncratic development of the artist himself, than by the ordinary condition of the object or objects treated.'[23] Dionysias, Micon, Panænus, and others are mentioned, together with Polygnotus, as distinguished painters of the temples and porticoes. Prize contests in painting were now instituted in Greece.

Apollodorus of Athens was the first great master of light and shade, and of their effects on colour, and Plutarch attributes to him the invention of tone. He received the surname of the *Shadower,* from the force and effectiveness of his chiaroscuro. He has been termed the Greek Rembrandt. As art now became established, it gradually assumed a more dramatic and less sculpturesque character.

With Zeuxis (born not later than 450 B.C.) began the second phase of Greek painting. For though the peculiar excellence of Zeuxis was a grand style of form, he united with it a higher execution, and arrived at illusion of the senses and external charm. He was also equally distinguished for the representation of female beauty; his most celebrated work being his

'Helena' at Crotona, said, like the Venus of Milo the sculptor, but upon questionable authority in both cases, to have been painted from the selected charms of five beautiful girls of that place. But he is allowed to have been surpassed by Parrhasius of Ephesus.

Parrhasius gave great beauty to his contours (outlines), and excelled in the drawing of extremities — a severe test of draughtsmanship. He is said also to have combined in some of his works the effect of Apollodorus, the design of Zeuxis, and the invention and expression of Polygnotus. There are several hardly intelligible stories of illusive pictures by the last two painters — as that of the 'Grapes,' which deceived birds, by Zeuxis; the picture representing a *linen curtain,* which Parrhasius brought forward in his contest with Zeuxis, and which Zeuxis himself mistook for a real curtain; and the tradition bearing on this, that Zeuxis laughed himself to death over the portrait of an old woman painted by himself. These stories, taken alone, might convey the impression that mere illusion in painting was estimated by the Greeks beyond its true value. But so far from this being the case, in the highly-extolled grand style of Polygnotus it could not possibly exist; and there is scarcely a passage out of Pliny — and he was certainly one of the least critical of ancient writers — in which the qualities which produce illusion are eulogised. That illusive effects were produced proves, however, that the execution of this period, and all the technical parts of the art, were brought to great perfection. The story told by Seneca of Parrhasius crucifying an old Olynthian captive, in order to paint more truly the agony of Prometheus chained, in a picture of that subject, is highly improbable, and is in all likelihood as utterly without foundation as are the similar stories told of Giotto and Michael Angelo. The numerous pictures by Parrhasius of gods and heroes (as his Theseus) attained a canonic consideration in art. He was, however, defeated in a prize competition at Samos by Timanthes of Cythnos.

This ingenious painter Timanthes, at another victorious competition (with Colotes of Teos), produced a picture containing a device which was greatly admired by the ancients, but has been the occasion of perhaps more criticism than any other pictorial incident. The subject of the picture was the 'Sacrifice of Iphigenia,' and the painter represented her father Agamemnon concealing his face in his mantle, in order, it has been assumed, to convey the expression of an intensity of grief at which art only dared to hint. Fuseli remarked, however, that the picture no doubt grave the moment that preceded the sacrifice, and that therefore Agamemnon could scarcely be represented in any ether way; for, although many considerations why he should sanction the deed might render his presence at the sacrifice absolutely necessary, still be could not be expected to have the fortitude to look upon his daughter's immolation—it would be unnatural.

The Asiatic school, as it was called, formed by Zeuxis, Parrhasius, and his followers, we have seen, was distinguished from the older Grecian school, the chief seat of which was at Athens; and now an essentially different school, that of Sicyon, was established by Eupompus, his pupil Pamphilus, and others in the Peloponnesus. Scientific cultivation, artistic knowledge, and the greatest accuracy and ease in drawing, were its distinguishing characteristics.

This school brings us to the time of Alexander, which has been termed the period of refinement. Varieties of effect and execution now distinguished the various masters, and ultimately were permitted to supersede the more essential qualities of art: conventional and artificial grace indicated the tendency to decline; sentiment was merged in the sensuous, and the spirit or essence was lost in the form. The whole course of Grecian art so much resembles the history of modern art in Italy, that any attentive observer might draw a very exact parallel between them. At this period encaustic painting was cultivated; but, according to Pliny, it had been already exercised by Polygnotus. The school of Pamphilus, already mentioned, acquired great celebrity: among his pupils were Apelles, Pausias, and Melanthius. The course of study, which occupied ten years—nor would Pamphilus take a pupil for a shorter period—comprehended instruction in drawing, arithmetic, geometry, anatomy, and painting in all its branches.

The school of Thebes produced two very celebrated painters—Nichomachus, whose execution was remarkably bold and vigorous, and who, according to Pliny, was the most rapid painter of his time; and his younger brother, Aristides, who was considered to be the greatest master of expression among the Greek painters.[24]

But before all was ranked Apelles (from about 350 to 310 B.C.); though his real superiority is not very clearly apparent. Hayden attributes it to the circumstance of his having been a 'fashionable' portrait-painter. Certainly he painted very 'flattering' portraits of his master Alexander; as, for example, that famous one in the temple of Diana at Ephesus, in which Alexander is represented wielding the lightnings of Jupiter, 'his hand,' says Pliny, 'standing quite out of the picture;' and he was paid accordingly, receiving no less than fifty talents of gold (upwards of 50,000*l.*) from the royal treasury. But the fact of his having been a portrait-painter does not lessen his claim to be considered a great artist. On the contrary, the greatest masters have been distinguished as portrait-painters; and Apelles' style was evidently that of the highest 'historical' portraiture. A still more celebrated work was his picture of Venus Anadyomene, or Venus rising out of the Waters, taken from the people of Cos by Augustus in lieu of one hundred talents tribute. His works were principally distinguished for a certain *charis* or *grace;* but he allowed that Protogenes equalled him in all respects save knowing when to leave off.[25]

Protogenes, whose too careful finish is here alluded to, was a comparatively self-taught artist; yet who, by faithful study of nature, rendered his works invaluable. The anecdote told of Apelles, that finding Protogenes was not appreciated by the Rhodians, he offered to purchase the unsold pictures of his brother-artist at his own price—that when Protogenes named a sum far below their value, Apelles fixed fifty talents, allowing it to be reported at Rhodes that be intended to dispose of them as his own, and thus opened the eyes of the Rhodians to the merit of their painter, and induced them to secure the pictures for themselves at the price named—is highly honourable to the generous Grecian. But much more within the scope of this book is the story of the celebrated contest of lines between these painters, which has given rise to much discussion. The anecdote is given to the following effect by Pliny: Apelles, upon his arrival at Rhodes, immediately sought out the studio of Protogenes, who happened to be from home; but an old woman was in attendance, and a large panel was standing ready prepared on the easel. When the old woman inquired what name she should give to her master upon his return, Apelles answered by taking a pencil wet with colour, and drawing a line *(linea)* on the panel, saying, simply, *'His.'* When Protogenes returned, the old woman mentioned what had happened; and when Protogenes saw the panel, he instantly exclaimed, 'Apelles has been here, for that is the work of no other hand.' Whereupon he took a pencil, and drew upon the same line or panel a still finer line, and going away, gave orders to the old woman, that when Apelles returned, she was to show him 'that,' and tell him it was whom he sought. Apelles returned, and blushing to see himself surpassed, drew a third *line* between or upon these two *(secuit lineas),* in a third colour, and attained the ultimatum of subtlety, leaving no possibility of being surpassed. When Protogenes returned a second time, he confessed himself vanquished, and immediately sought out Apelles. This panel, continues Pliny, was handed down a wonder for posterity, and particularly to artists; for, notwithstanding it contained only those three scarcely visible lines, still it was the most noble work in the gallery of the Imperial Palace on the Palatine, although surrounded by the finest paintings of the most renowned masters. Now this gallery was destroyed by the first fire which consumed that palace in the time of Augustus; the picture was, therefore, not seen by Pliny, and he must consequently have described it, either from a written account or front some other indirect source; and to this circumstance, perhaps, is owing much of the obscurity of this subject.

It is just possible to conceive, as many antiquaries have believed, that the word *linea* may be interpreted quite literally, as a simple line: supposing the three lines to have been one within the other. The feat then would have been, in the first instance, the drawing a line with mathematical nicety. But this performance was surpassed by drawing another line so subtle as to be contained within the former: and still more surprising would be a third and final contained line, because of its transcendent delicacy. The three colours would be absolutely necessary to distinguish each separate effort, and the third line may be strictly said to have cut the other two *(secuit lineas).* The command of hand necessary to trace with a brush three lines (the last, at least, of which must have been nearly invisible) one within the other, would be most extraordinary. It is true that this implies mere manual dexterity, which is not especially calculated to excite the admiration of painters now; but the difficulty was in this case certainly enormous, and a panel with such a singular history of two of the greatest masters of their art attached to it, might have been an especial object of wonder to painters, and by a kind of esoteric process it might even come to be considered the most noble work *(omnique opere nobiliorem) of* the Palatine collection.

However, if the text of Pliny will not allow us to interpret the lines, as three distinct rival sketches, it is far more probable to suppose that Apelles made outlines of some part of the human figure according to the ideal standard of antiquity, which was improved upon by Protogenes, whose line was in its turn surpassed by the second effort of Apelles, the final faultless line passing both *upon* and *between* the original line of Apelles and the correcting line of Protogenes: thus the two former lines were intersected, but all three were easily distinguishable because executed in distinct colours. It is greatly in support of this view that we know the ancients paid extreme attention to delicate and finely undulating outline drawing; in which long preparatory exercises, both with the style or stylus *(graphis),* and brush *(pencillias),* sometimes with black on a white ground, and sometimes with white on a black, were considered necessary before the scholar was permitted to use colours. Fuseli remarks, also, that, instead of imagining superhuman facility of execution in sweeping in the figures on vases without any guiding design beneath, we need only admire the care and dexterity with which the preparatory outlines must have been executed. The fact that in this contest the painters used different colours, favours, likewise, this explanation; for, had not the lines been intermingled, there would have been no occasion for different colours.

Of this Protogenes, who was a famous animal painter, is told the somewhat apocryphal story, that, having tried unsuccessfully over and over again to represent foam on the mouth of a dog, he threw a sponge at the dog's head in a fit of impatience, which, to his astonishment, obtained the desired effect. Another story is more probable, viz., that, having introduced a bird into a picture, and finding, from the excellent manner in which it was painted, that it attracted attention from more important parts of his work, the artist for this reason effaced it. Pliny states that a picture of Jalysus, by Protogenes, was painted over four times, in order that, should the uppermost picture be destroyed, another might be found underneath uninjured. The reason assigned by Pliny seems too absurd to require comment; in the 'four times' we may perhaps see, however, a resemblance to the modern method of dead colouring, first and second painting, glazing, &c.

Another famous painter of this period was Euphranor. He painted in encaustic, and was equally celebrated both as sculptor and painter. Pausias and Nicias were, however, the two greatest encaustic painters. Pausias distinguished himself by his figures of children, his animal and flower pieces, and (which began with him) the painting of lacunaria—that is, the decorative ceiling pictures, afterwards common, consisting of single figures, flowers, and arabesques. The ornamenting of lacunaria with painted stars and the like, had previously been practised in temples. Nicias declined to sell his masterpiece to Ptolemy I of Egypt, for a sum offered of about 14,000*l.*: he presented it to the city of Athens. The subject of this picture was the 'Region of Hades,' from the Odyssey. Athenion (another encaustic painter), Echion, Theon, and Asclepiodorus were also celebrated.

The glorious art of this period is lost to us: yet even the pictures on vases (with thinly scattered bright figures) give us an exalted idea of the progress of art, if from the productions of generally little more than common handicraftsmen we draw conclusions as to the works of the first artists. Among the excavations at Volci were found numerous specimens of vases, illustrating different styles; but, of those discovered at Nola, the mass are of this later date, and some exhibit exquisite ease, delicacy, and grace.

From the time of Alexander (or, at least, from about 300 B.C.) art rapidly deteriorated, scarcely another name of note occurring. The subjects chosen prove the decay of the higher branches. Caricatures are common, and rhyparography, *still-life* or *genre,*[26] makes its appearance, Pyreicus being its most famous master. Scenography was applied to the decoration of the palaces of the great. The love of magnificence even demanded the decoration of painting for floors; whence mosaic art arose, and soon became so developed that great combats of heroes and battle-scenes were represented. Vase painting died out during this period, and soonest in the mother country. Pillage and devastation now commenced with the victories of the Roman generals, till the porticoes and temples at Rome were filled with stolen works of art.

Two questions are often asked in reference to both the painting and sculpture of ancient Greece: Did the artists work from any prescribed system or established canon of the relative proportions of the human figure? and, Were they acquainted with anatomy?

In regard to the first question, it may be affirmed that the ancients certainly did consider a standard of human form desirable; and they recognised at least one statue, viz., the Lance-bearer of Polycletus, as canonical. Vitruvius, also, takes human proportion as a measure of perfection, applying its rules to architecture, and indeed to every object of taste. The text of the canon preserved in the third book of the *Treatise on Architecture* by Vitruvius, is, however, obscure and unimportant. But Mr. Bonomi, in a little pamphlet on the *Proportions of the Human Figure,* states that there exists in the library of the Academy of Venice a drawing by Leonardo da Vinci, and a translation into Italian by that celebrated artist, of that part of the treatise of the ancient architect which clears up the obscurity in all the existing editions, in a way that makes it probable Leonardo must have had access to some copy of Vitruvius which has not come down to us. The drawing of a man inscribed in a circle and a square, together with the translation of Leonardo, are given by Mr. Bonomi, but perspective would certainly render these and similar rules in many cases of limited application in painting. Flaxman remarks, however, that 'It is impossible to see the numerous figures springing, jumping, dancing, and falling in the Herculaneum paintings, on the painted vases, and the antique bassi-relievi, without being assured that the painters and sculptors must have employed geometrical figures to determine the degrees of curvature in the body, and angular and rectilinear extent of the limbs, and to fix the centre of gravity.' Nevertheless, in the face even of this authority, we believe that the general experience of those who have drawn the human figure will be found to be, that a few simple measures of various parts of the human figure are all that are really available in practice, and that the advantages of such geometrical figures would necessarily be limited, if, indeed, not altogether problematical.

In answer to the second question — Were the ancient Greek masters acquainted with anatomy?—we may reply, not necessarily, if, by anatomy, is merely meant dissection. In the dead subject all that can be learnt is the origin and insertion of the muscles—knowledge to be obtained sufficiently without dissection. The muscles themselves become too flaccid, and too much unlike the living fibre, to render the study of them indispensable to the artist. But anatomy, we have seen, was in some way taught in the school of Pamphilus, and Haydon believed that the Greeks dissected. Sir Charles Bell—the best authority we can adduce—says, however, that 'Although in Greece the dead were burned, and no artists dissected the human body, yet they certainly had the means of learning the nature of a bone, muscle, and tendon. No more was necessary; the rest was before them. Fine as their athlete were in youth, they were subject to the decay of age. Now, in comparing the frame of a man advanced in years, especially if in earlier life he had been remarkable for "thews and sinews," with the young and active, everything essential to the painter and sculptor may be observed. If the Greeks had before them the most admired forms of youth and manhood, they had also the "time-honoured wrestler," who in old age exhibited, almost as in the dead anatomy, every muscle, origin, and insertion, every tendon and every vein. I know how far this manner of demonstrating the anatomy may be carried. Having in my lectures on surgery taken the living man, the academy model, to illustrate the practice in fractures and dislocations, I was accustomed to introduce a powerful muscular fellow to my class, with this appeal "In the exercise of your profession you have to judge of the displacement of the limbs, and the joints disfigured by dislocations, fractures, or tumour; but not one of you, perhaps, has ever looked on the natural body itself." In giving these lessons, I became aware how much of the structure of the muscles and articulations might be demonstrated without actual dissection.'—*Anatomy of Expression,* p.205. This passage seems to us to dispose of this second query.

It may be mentioned here, that it is no longer a question whether the Greeks did or did not apply polychromy to architecture and sculpture. From existing traces and remains, it is certain that such decoration was added to many parts of their architectural details; at all events, to the intaglio parts of reliefs, the concave parts of capitals, flutings, &c. Some English and modern German and French writers on the subject are of opinion that the raw colour of the new marble was not merely tinted and toned, but that the entire surface was covered with a thin coating of stucco, and coloured.

With regard to the colouring of statues, it is established upon indisputable historical evidence, that the Greeks did paint their statues, although the practice may have been not universal. There is, in particular, one passage in Pliny which appears of itself decisive. Speaking of Nicias (lib. xxxv. cap. 11), Pliny says, that Praxiteles, when asked which of his marble works best satisfied him, replied, 'those which Nicias [the encaustic painter] has had under his hands.' 'So much,' adds Pliny, 'did he prize his *circumlitio'* —*tantum circumlitioni ejus tribuebat.* It has been supposed by some that the word *circumlitio* meant simply a finish to the marble, or a coating of some kind. It is, however, incredible that any services of a painter of eminence should be called in requisition except those of his particular art. Nor does the word seem to have been applied only to a coating of coloured wax rubbed in by the aid of heat, as others have suggested. When Vitruvius mentions this latter process—the καυσις of the Greeks—he does not apply to it any term similar to *circumlitio;* and that the word signified 'painting' is proved by the 'pictura in quâ nihil circumlitum est' of Quintilian (viii. 5, 26); by Seneca's saying (Ep. lxxxvi. 5), 'illis (marmoribus) undique operosa et in *picturæ* modum *variata circumlitio* prætexitur', as well as by the frequent use, in later times, with reference to *painting,* of derivatives from the verb *lino.* The difficulty we have in believing that the ancients coloured their statues—many of them at least, but not all, as we might quote authorities to prove—has arisen from seeing antique statues invariably deprived of whatever colouring they may originally have had, though agreeably toned by the cunning hand of time. Throughout the Middle Ages polychromy was applied to the painting of the statues and reliefs in marble, stone, and wood, of our Saviour, the Madonna, saints,&c., used so extensively in the Roman Catholic church.

4. The Etruscans

Etruscan painting generally is only a branch of the Greek, though the particular form of mural painting seems to have been practised in Etruria sooner than we hear of it in Greece. Numerous sepulchral chambers, especially at Tarquinii, are painted with figures, the colours of which are laid almost pure and unmixed on the stucco with which the walls are coated, and although not true to nature, are harmonious. The style of drawing passes from a severity and care, which show an affinity with early Greek works, into the hasty and caricature-like manner which prevailed in the later works of the Etruscans. Greek vase painting, we have said, was earlier known to the Etruscans; but it is probable that the Greek pottery was either introduced by commerce, or that Greek artists visited the country. The comparatively few vases, inferior in artistic value, which are inscribed with Etruscan characters, can alone afford a sure criterion by which to distinguish Etruscan and Greek productions.

5. The Romans

The Romans seem scarcely ever to have cultivated the higher branches of painting, though they were the greatest 'collectors' of 'old masters'— Marcellus taking the initiative. Fabius (Pictor[27]) is the earliest painter of consequence. At the end of the Republic, however, the art treasures of Rome rendered it 'one vast wonder,' and the city was full of artists, many of them Greeks, but nearly all portrait painters or decorators. Ludius was a very celebrated decorator of halls and corridors, and also a landscape painter, in the time of Augustus. These decorations were exceedingly arbitrary; architecture, figures, vegetable and other forms, being strangely combined with villas, gardens, streams, and all sorts of comic situations, producing a pleasing and light, though fantastic, effect. This is the origin of *arabesque* or *moresque.*[28] A picture of Minerva, by Fabullus, in Nero's Golden House, was admired, because the goddess appeared to look at every one from whatever situation the eyes were directed towards her. This effect might have been increased through the picture being in a dark situation; though many persons with a lively imagination fancy, whenever eyes are painted looking anything like straight out of the canvas, that the representation has this effect. It is very fallacious, however, to make this the great test of a good portrait, as is often done. Nevertheless, although fancy has frequently much to do with this impression, there seems to be a real optical and perspective phenomenon in this effect, and it has been explained by Dr. Wollaston in one of the papers of the *Philosophical Transactions.*

Pliny, in the time of Vespasian, justly regards painting as a perishing art. Painting was then only employed to minister to luxury or vanity. Their vanity the Romans gratified in portraiture, applying portraits painted or sculptured to many purposes since unheard of. At an early period it was usual, among both Greeks and Romans, for portraits of warriors to be carved on their shields, and dedicated in the temples either as trophies or memorials of the deceased. (See Appendix, note E.) But the Romans placed wax busts of themselves in the most conspicuous part of their own houses; and the custom obtained for some time for the relatives upon the decease of the original, to convert his bust into a full-length effigy, which they carried and deposited in the temple with great ceremony and state.

We have seen the estimation in which the Greeks held their artists, and Julius Caesar, Agrippa, and Augustus were also great patrons of art; but painting was, from the common decorative character it assumed, at length almost left to be practised by slaves, and the painter ranked according to the quantity of work he could do in a day. Now, as art is appreciated, so, naturally, is the artist held in estimation; the converse, likewise, no doubt, holds good; we may easily infer, therefore, the extent of the 'décadence des Romains.' In the age of Hadrian, painting must, however, have revived with the other arts. Ætion, who belonged to this age, is ranked by Lucian among the greatest artists, especially for his charming picture of 'Alexander and Roxana.'

From this time, however, painting continued steadily to decline, till all that in its prime distinguished it may be said to have ceased about the end of the third century of our era.

Upon the foundation of Constantinople (the ancient Byzantium[29]), Rome was in its turn despoiled to embellish the new capital, and nearly all of what was left was destroyed by the incursions of the barbarians. Everywhere, also, ignorance produced neglect and indifference, and religious fanaticism contributed greatly to the destruction of the remains of ancient art. The establishment of Christianity was, in addition, a great check to the practice of art; for the purity of the new religion contrasted so greatly with heathen corruption, that its professors naturally looked with little favour upon arts which were identified with pagan idolatry so intimately as to be scarcely possible to disunite them, not to mention that a branch of art had long been depraved to gratify the lowest sensuality. Moreover, cupidity had a share in the general destruction: things which could be melted down, such as the bronze statues, were thus disposed of; and, finally, numerous collections were destroyed by accidental fires.

6. Remains of Ancient Painting

We have incidentally mentioned some remains of ancient painting, but it has been remarked that the great works of painting of the best ages of antiquity are entirely lost to us: all that remains consists of mere decorative painting, and for the most part the commonplace productions in a second-rate city of the inferior artists of an inferior age. Yet it is to be suspected that from these works a false impression of the merits of the ancient painters has been conveyed to the popular mind. It should, however, be remembered that the style of the paintings to which we more particularly allude—those discovered in the excavations at Pompeii and Herculaneum—is condemned strongly by Pliny and Vitruvius. The designs on the ancient vases afford a greatly superior idea of the excellence of their more important works. Nevertheless, even in the remains at Pompeii and Herculaneum, modern painters see sufficient to confirm the probability of the justness of ancient criticism, which esteemed the works of their painters equally with those of their sculptors. From these remains Sir Joshua Reynolds himself formed a very high opinion of ancient painting. Many of the single figures, such as the floating forms of dancing nymphs, centaurs, and bacchantes, are indeed deserving of the highest praise; and in groups, the composition is frequently equally admirable. The mosaic of the Casa del Fauno, or House of the Great Mosaic, at Pompeii, discovered in 1831, and supposed to represent the battle of Issus, or some other of Alexander's battles, is the most important illustration of the *composition* of the ancient painters. It displays thorough understanding of perspective and foreshortening, and is probably the copy of some celebrated picture.

A painting found in the house of the Tragic Poet at Pompeii, and now deposited in the Museo Borbonico, is, however, considered the most beautiful specimen of ancient painting which has been preserved to modern times. The subject is 'Achilles delivering Briseis to the Heralds of Agamemnon.' 'The scene,' says Sir William Gell, 'seems to take place in the tent of Achilles, who sits in the centre. Patroclus, with his back towards the spectator, leads in from the left the lovely Briseis arrayed in a long and floating veil of apple-green. Her face is beautiful, and, not to dwell upon the archness of her eye, it is evident that the voluptuous pouting of her ruby lip was imagined by the painter as one of her most bewitching attributes. Achilles presents the fair one to the heralds on his right; and his attitude, his manly beauty, and the magnificent expression of his countenance, are inimitable. The tent seems to be divided by a drapery about breast high, and of a sort of dark bluish-green, like the tent itself. Behind this stand several warriors, the golden shield of one of whom, whether intentionally or not on the part of the painter, forms a sort of glory round the head of the principal hero.[30] It is probably a copy of one of the most celebrated pictures of antiquity. When first discovered, the colours were fresh, and the flesh particularly had the transparency of Titian. It suffered much and unavoidably during the excavation, and something from the means taken to preserve it, when a committee of persons qualified to judge had decided that the wall on which it was painted was not in a state to admit of its removal with safety. At length, after an exposure of two years, it was thought better to attempt to transport it to the Studj at Naples, than to suffer it entirely to disappear from the wall. It was accordingly removed with success, in the summer of the year 1826, and it is hoped that some remains of it may exist for posterity. The painter has chosen the moment when the heralds Talthybius and Eurybates are put in possession of Briseis to escort her to the tent of Agamemnon, as described in the first book of the *Iliad.* The head of Achilles is full of fire and animation.'

The sudden admission of the fresh atmosphere after it had been excluded for so many centuries, was the cause of a large number of paintings perishing immediately afterwards. Among these was a most curious representation of a painter's studio, in which all the figures were grotesques. Fortunately, however, Mazois the painter was present, and secured a copy with his ready pencil, which is included in his 'Pompeii.'

Several valuable and costly works have been published on the remains of Pompeii. Foremost is the great work of Zahn, containing coloured representations of the originals. Sir William Gell's *Pompeiana,* and the work on *Pompeii* published by the Society for the Diffusion of Useful Knowledge, may also be particularized.

Besides the very ancient paintings in the Etruscan tombs already mentioned, other works of this class, of the time of the Emperors, if not earlier, have been found in various parts of Italy. When Raphael and Giovanni da Udine saw the beautiful arabesques discovered in the Baths of Titus, which they imitated in the Vatican, they stood, it is said, motionless with astonishment. One of the most beautiful series of ancient paintings is the 'Life of Adonis,' discovered in 1668 in some ruins near the Coliseum. These pictures, admirable for their chaste simplicity, were engraved by Pietro Santi Bartoli, for his work, with text by Bellori, on the Subterranean and Sepulchral Paintings of Rome.[31] This work likewise contains engravings from the paintings of the tomb of the Nasoni (the family of Ovid), which are good examples of the decorative taste of the period.

The vase painting of antiquity may be studied to great advantage in the noble collection of vases in the British Museum.

7. Christian Art in Tempera and Encaustic

As Christianity gradually became in the third and fourth centuries dominant over paganism, so the prejudices against art became relaxed; but from apprehension lest Gentile converts should, if *images* were introduced, again relapse into idolatry, the early Christians, before the time of Constantine, used symbols only. Such were the cross, the monogram of Christ, composed of the two first Greek letters of the name X and P, but variously written; the alpha and omega, the fish (a curious, but favourite emblem of Christ and his disciples), the dove, the lamb, the cock, the phoenix, the peacock, the ship, the vine, the palm, the lyre, &c. To the not unreasonable dread also of approximating to the forms and appearances of the pagan idols which still existed in great numbers, may be attributed the very unnatural and purely representative style adopted when sacred personages were permitted to be chosen as the subjects of art.

Even when art was accepted, it was not accepted as such. The object was not to excite pleasure and produce effect, but to inculcate certain religious principles. Thus, as soon as the person of Christ was introduced, he was almost invariably depicted as the Good Shepherd. But He was not represented beautiful: for not only was it essential that the mind should not be led into idolatry by forgetting the *thing represented* in the representation, but in respect particularly to our Saviour, he was regarded as essentially differing in his earthly form from the ideal beauty of the heathen deities: they remembered how he was announced by the prophet: 'He hath no form nor comeliness; and when we shall see him, there is no beauty that we should desire him.' 'His visage was so marred more than any man, and his form more than the sons of men.' That a combination of outward circumstances led to a false view of the function of art, we need hardly stop to remark; for there is surely no reason why religion should compel us to do violence to that instinct of beauty which the Creator has implanted in us. However, the typical style, first adopted from religious prejudice, became sanctioned by use, and ultimately from habit regarded as almost sacred. A few of the pagan forms, and even some of their more negative and innocent legends, such, for instance, as that of Orpheus, and Cupid and Psyche, were, notwithstanding, introduced in early Christian paintings, and on the bas-reliefs of sarcophagi.

Nevertheless, the aversion to the arts continued very violent, first in the Western or Roman church, and afterwards in the Eastern or Greek church, long after the time of Tertullian (the second century), who wrote with great zeal against artists, as persons of iniquitous occupations. The carvers of graven images were looked upon as the servants and emissaries of Satan. Whoever carried on this hateful calling was declared unworthy of the cleansing waters of baptism; whoever, when baptized, returned to his old vocation, was excommunicated. The Gnostics appear to have been the first who had recourse to the use of images. A bishop of Pola introduced paintings into two churches, which he built at the close of the fourth century; and this must have been one of the earliest instances of the kind in Italy. In the fifth century the practice was common, and the general ignorance of this period favoured the commencement of the grosser form of Christian idolatry. From the fifth to the ninth century mosaics were, however, preferred for church decoration on account of their great durability. Encaustic painting had continued to be much practised in the second and third centuries; but, like tempera, though occasionally employed (the latter more particularly in missal painting), it was eventually superseded entirely by mosaic for wall painting.

Some extremely interesting remains of Christian wall paintings of the time of the Empire discovered in the Catacombs of Rome[32] require, however, to be noticed. The grandest and most impressive of these were found in the Catacomb of San Callisto, on the Via Appia, under the church of S. Sebastian, called after St. Calixtus, who was Pope from A.D. 219 to 223 One chamber contained an 'Adoration of the Kings;' but the Virgin and Child, and a town (Bethlehem) in the background, are all that remain. Lower down is a man pointing upwards, supposed by the late eminent German critic, Dr. Kugler, to be the prophet Micah, and to have reference to the words—'But thou, Bethlehem Ephratah, though thou be little among the thousands of Judah, yet out of thee shall *he* come forth unto me that is to be ruler in

Israel,' &c. Other subjects are, 'Moses striking the Rock;' 'Daniel in the Lions' Den;' the 'Ascension of Elijah;' 'Noah looking out of the Ark;' the 'Raising of Lazarus;' Orpheus (an emblem of Christ); besides single figures of Job, Moses, and several symbols. On the ceiling is a bust portrait of Christ, the neck and bosom uncovered, with the exception of some drapery hanging over the left shoulder, which is supposed to be the earliest portrait of Christ, and to indicate the type subsequently preserved for others.[33] The face is oval, the nose straight, eyebrows arched, the forehead rather high and smooth; the expression serious and mild; the hair parted on the forehead, and flowing curls on the shoulders; the beard not thick, but short, and divided.

In other of the Catacombs may also occasionally be traced the habits of the early Christians. They are seen assembled for their 'love-feasts,' celebrating baptisms and marriages, and congregating together for the purposes of instruction. We have noticed only some paintings of earlier times; but as the Catacombs for many centuries after Constantine the Great remained open to the public as places of veneration, and as such continued to be decorated in the taste of the day, it follows that the paintings extend to much later periods. 'The Virgin Mary,' says Kugler, 'occurs so seldom in the earlier paintings of the Catacombs, and then only subordinately, that in those times no particular type had been established for her,' this was reserved for the 'Mariolatry' of a later period.

It has been noticed that the grosser forms of Christian idolatry may be dated from the fifth century. The great mass of the people were unable to read, and sunk in ignorance. With the inseparable concomitant of ignorance —superstition—it was not surprising that they did not correctly apprehend the nature of the images, even if their bishops had a more intelligent intention in setting them up. Instead, therefore, of regarding them as exemplary records of fortitude and piety, or spiritual symbols incentive of devotion, they worshipped them as holy images, material saints, and mediators. Notwithstanding that this idolatry had been foreseen and warned against by the earlier prelates, resisted by contemporary dignitaries of the church, and forbidden by the edicts of several councils against the adoration of images, their use gradually prevailed; and, surviving all the efforts of the Iconoclasts in the eighth and ninth centuries, finally triumphed throughout the whole of Christendom, both in the Western and Eastern churches.

The Iconoclasts (or image-breakers) of the Eastern church commenced their systematic destruction of works of art in 728, and it was continued with slight interruptions for upwards of a century. The productions of ancient art were not directly involved in the general demolition — although they must have suffered: the zeal of the Iconoclasts was directed against Christian images, viz., the images of Christ, the Virgin, and the saints, as idols. The popes of the West, however, at this time encouraged their use; and the consequence was, that a contest arose which convulsed the whole Empire. Eventually the party in favour of the use of images triumphed through the influence of the Empress Irene, the widow of the Emperor Leo IV, though the contention still continued, and the Emperor Theophilus (829–842) protected the Iconoclasts. In the ninth and tenth centuries the images were finally tolerated in the Greek Church.

Yet, although the Greek artists were frequently persecuted and dispersed, Constantinople apparently remained throughout the whole of the Middle Ages the capital of the arts. The works of art here suffered, however, still further devastations by the Crusaders, and more especially in the great fires of 1203 and following year, when the city was taken by the Venetians. But to this Latin conquest, which opened an intercourse with the Venetians, has been generally attributed the first impulse towards the revival of the arts in the West. The Greek artists poured into Italy, at Venice, and Palermo, and also at Pisa, which was then a flourishing seaport. And to the schools thus established at Venice, Pisa, and Siena, although the Byzantine characteristics were for some time broadly preserved, has been referred the growth of modern Italian art; for it has been assumed that the seed sown in a fresh soil rapidly fructified in greatly increased luxuriance and beauty.

But Dr. Kugler is of opinion that the first germs of a purely Western mode of conception are discernible not only contemporary with the influence supposed to be traceable to the works of these last emigrants from the East, but at a considerably earlier period. 'After the close of the eleventh century, that epoch of national prosperity dawned upon the distracted country which, sooner or later, never fails to infuse into art a fresh and higher life. The Roman church arose from a long-continued state of degradation, for which she was herself partly accountable, to be mistress of the West. She reinstated Rome as the centre of the world, and restored to the Italians a sense of national existence . . . The Byzantine style was, at that time, so utterly sapless and withered, even in its native land, that it could as little resist as rival the innovating principle, though individual painters occasionally made the attempt.' The amalgamation, then, of the Byzantine style with the old native Longobardian of Italy, produced a new school, which is known as the '*Romanesque,*' or Romano-Greek.

However, to the Greeks the Italians were at least indebted for the methods of preparing pigments, and other technicalities. Byzantine art, we have seen, became a regular traditional system; technical methods descended as property from master to apprentice, and the manufacture of pictures was as regularly organized as that of any other article of constant and regular demand. In fact, in the Eastern empire, and even in Italy long after the revival of painting, the artist was generally confounded with the workman, and only the 'master of works,' or architect—who, however, was sometimes a painter—was held in esteem, or liberally rewarded. But where the higher qualities of art are neglected, and any innovation regarded as a species of heresy, we may yet easily imagine it possible for the mechanical departments to be very successfully cultivated. And that this was the case mediaeval manuscripts afford abundant and conclusive evidence. Of these we may mention two treatises in particular, *De Coloribus et Artibus Romanorum,* by Eraclius, and *Diversarum Artium Schedula,* by the monk Theophilus. These are well known to antiquaries; but respecting their date there is considerable diversity of opinion among their several editors, Raspe, Mrs. Merrifield, De l'Escalopier, and Hendrie. They are, however, certainly not later than the end of the twelfth, or beginning of the thirteenth century, The most complete copy of Eraclius is that transcribed, with, others, by Jehan le Begue, in 1431, and edited, together, with many other valuable MSS., by Mrs. Merrifield.[34] Nothing is known of the personality of Eraclius and

Theophilus; but it is highly probable they were of some country north of the Alps, and therefore represent the northern followers of the Byzantine school. All that is positively known of Theophilus is that he was a monk, and that Theophilus was not his right name. Lessing, one of his editors, in vain seeks to identify him with Tutilio (891–921), a famous painter, sculptor, and gold-worker of the celebrated monastery of St. Gall in Switzerland. In the treatise of Theophilus, amid many empirical formula and traditions, embodying, possibly, some of the symbols of alchemy, there is much that is interesting and important; and by it we obtain a curious insight into the various arts practised in the cloisters. After a kind of apostolic form of greeting common in such works, we have the following passage in an introduction, which concludes with a pious benediction and prayer:

'Should you carefully peruse this, you will there find out whatever Greece possesses in kinds and mixtures of various colours; whatever Tuscany knows of in mosaic work, or in variety of enamel; whatever Arabia shows forth in work of fusion, ductility, or chasing; whatever Italy ornaments with gold, in diversity of vases and sculpture of gems or ivory; whatever France loves in a costly variety of windows; whatever industrious Germany approves in work of gold, silver, copper, and iron, of woods, and of stones.'

The reader will remark the reference to Greece as the source of the 'kinds and mixtures of various colours;' and a further confirmation of the opinion that the Italian artists owed at least their knowledge of technicalities to the Greeks is afforded by the resemblance the contents of this treatise bear to the curious Byzantine MS. discovered by M. Didron in a convent of Mount Athos.

The knowledge of art being confined to the religious fraternities, we need not be surprised that the pilgrim monks carried in their various missions the practice of art into the remotest corners of Europe where they penetrated. Thus may England and Ireland, even as far back as the time of St. Augustine and St. Patrick, have gained a knowledge of art, in addition to the Roman or native traditions that might have been preserved. Certainly the Irish and Anglo-Saxon manuscripts of the seventh and eighth centuries display, though rude in taste, extraordinary elaboration. However this may be, certain it is that, after the year 1000, art made so sudden and simultaneous an advance throughout Europe, that the various countries were placed almost on a level.

The Roman and Byzantine influence is thus traced to England by Mr. Hendrie: 'We find that, previously to the edict by which Charlemagne resolved to encourage the various arts to the utmost of his power, Wilfred, Bishop of York, and Biscop, his friend, had already availed themselves of the assistance of foreign artists, in order to decorate the cathedral of St. Peter [York Minster], before the year 675. Biscop undertook a journey to the Roman States, and brought home many pictures with which the churches of St. Peter and Weremouth were ornamented. The second visit of Alfred to Rome with Ethelwulf, although undertaken at an early age, would, doubtless, not be without its influence on such a mind. The painted chamber at Westminster, in which Edward the Confessor died, the renown of St. Dunstan as an accomplished painter and a skilful contriver of instruments, the remains of the Saxon chased and enamelled work, which was esteemed on the Continent as early as the seventh century, and the manuscripts which are yet extant, prove that, in this country at least, the arts, as introduced by the Romans, were never wholly lost. Records exist of Alfred the Great having summoned workmen from all parts of Europe to assist in the construction of the edifices he proposed to erect, and it is probable many Byzantine traditions may thus have been acquired for England.'

We may now without further digression glance at the great revival of painting in Italy in the thirteenth century, which immediately followed two of the most important events in the history of the world—the discovery of gunpowder and the invention of printing—events which ultimately entirely changed the constitution of society. This revival consisted first, *objectively,* in a closer imitation of nature, although for nearly two centuries, till the time of Massaccio, there was little individuality in the imitation, and many (modified) Byzantine conventionalisms were for a considerable time preserved; and, secondly, *subjectively,* of a more earnest religious vitality and sentiment in the *'motives.'*[35]

At the head of this revival, which commenced in the Florentine or Tuscan school, the name of Cimabue has been usually placed; but artists preceded him who gave some indication of independent feeling. Of these, Guido da Siena and Guinto da Pisa may be named: Margaritone d'Arrezzo also preceded Cimabue; but his works are more purely Greek, and he murmured bitterly at the innovations of the latter. (See his picture in the National Gallery.)

Nevertheless Giovanni, of the noble family of Cimabue, was the first painter of renown (*b.* 1240, *d.* after 1300). One of his earliest and best-known works is the colossal Madonna, still in the church of Santa Maria Novella, to which it was carried in triumphal procession from the house of the painter—an event which gave the name of Borgo Allegro, or the 'gay quarter,' to that part of the city. But the talents of Cimabue are exhibited most conspicuously in the large distemper wall paintings ascribed to him in the upper church of S. Francesco at Assisi, some of which still exist. Giotto completed the extensive decorations both of the upper and lower church. This church is highly interesting for having been erected by foreign architects in the first half of the thirteenth century, in the 'Tedesco,' as the Italians called the German or Gothic style, then foreign to Italy; but more particularly for its connection with the Order of St. Francis, the first of the great artist orders. The Benedictines being chiefly engaged in literary pursuits, it remained for the Franciscans and Dominicans to inspire a new feeling for art in Italy. Some of the ornaments introduced in these paintings by Cimabue approach almost for the first time to the antique.

Duccio di Buoninsegna was somewhat younger than Cimabue, and advanced far more from the Byzantine traditions. He executed a large altarpiece for the Duomo (cathedral) of Siena, which is said to have been carried in triumphal procession like the picture by Cimabue. It was originally painted on both sides, but is now cut in two, and is a truly remarkable work for the period.

With the opening of the fourteenth century an original style is at length developed. The final enfranchisement of the artist from the trammels of Byzantine superstition, and the commencement of the first great epoch of modern painting, together with the establishment of the Florentine school, are to be ascribed to Giotto, who surpassed his master, Cimabue,[36] far more than Cimabue had surpassed his predecessors. It is true that the outlines of Giotto are hard, his light and shade flat and ineffective, and that perspective is little regarded; yet his expression is greatly superior, and, for the first time since the decline of ancient art, we observe a successful attempt at composition, or the regular disposal of the subject in the space allotted. His originality is further apparent in the introduction of portraiture, and the infusion of a didactic or allegorical spirit into his works. The latter is due, perhaps, to the influence of his friend Dante's great poem. We read of the general acquirements and character of Giotto in the works of Dante, Petrarch, Boccaccio, Sachetti, &c. Many stories are told of his humour, which he showed as a boy: that, for example, of the pupil painting a fly on the face of a picture in the master's absence, and the subsequent attempt of the master to brush it off, is first told of Giotto and Cimabue. There is a saying, Rounder than the O of Giotto, which originated thus: Boniface VIII wishing to decorate St. Peter's, sent an envoy to Florence and Siena for artists, of whom he required specimens. Giotto's specimen was a circle drawn without the aid of compasses, with a brush charged with red colour. This appeared more wonderful to the Pope than anything else sent to him, and in the event Giotto fully justified the preference in the eyes of the Roman Court. A peculiarity in the figures of Giotto is the long almond-shaped eyes set close together. The tempera vehicle he employed was more fluid than that hitherto used; it allowed greater freedom of hand, and has also darkened but little with time.

Many of the works of Giotto have disappeared; but a most interesting discovery, or rather recovery (for it was known to exist), of a youthful portrait of Dante by Giotto, was made in 1840, on removing the whitewash from the wall of a chapel at Florence. Giotto was sculptor and architect as well as painter: the elegant detached Campanile (or bell-tower) of Florence is his work. So many, it will be seen, besides Giotto, of the greatest masters have distinguished themselves in more than one branch of the fine arts, that the suspicion naturally suggests itself whether the modern custom among artists of confining the attention to one *specialité* is not a mistake. If technical superiority is in this way arrived at, are not the grander and broader principles of art left unattained?

The most exact idea of the style of Giotto to be gained in this country, may be obtained from the series of tracings and woodcuts published by the Arundel Society, taken from the paintings in the Chapel of the Arena at Padua, representing the life of our Saviour, and the life of the Virgin. The figures in the life of the Virgin, especially those in a 'sposalizio' (or espousals), possess considerable grace. In the church at Assisi, Giotto painted a series of subjects from the life of (the patron saint) St. Francis. The life of this saint, it has been well said, is 'One of those mediaeval melodramas (if the term may be used), in the form of biography, which furnish the most interesting and beautiful subjects a painter can desire. The curtain rises on the youth of St. Francis, and, as the plot thickens, his strange hallucination —his quarrel with his father in the market-place on account of his passion for poverty—his giving his cloak to a poor person on the wayside—his institution of the order—his appearance before the Pope—his ecstasy—his stigmatization, follow in succession, until the catastrophe is reached in the death of the saint.'

These and similar biographical and historical series, executed in the fourteenth and fifteenth centuries, had special uses among a people who, even to the present day, have comparatively little benefited by the invention of printing. It has been justly remarked that painting in the fourteenth and fifteenth centuries was at once a means of noble decoration and a manner of conveying information, thoughts, and ideas, not then, as now, to be got at through literature. Pictures were the books of the unlearned, and the unlearned were five-sixths of the people. The decorative purpose of pictures was effected mainly through colour. Hence it is that, apart from colour, we cannot estimate those early works aright as decoration; and apart from their sequence and connection in town-hall or chapel, we cannot read them book-fashion, or in any way comprehend the reality of their significance.

Giotto painted in various cities from Naples to Milan, and his works doubtless had an indirect influence in all parts of Italy. The scholars and imitators of Giotto are so numerous, that we can only mention a few of the principal. Among these, Taddeo Gaddi, the son of Gaddo Gaddi, the mosaicist, was one of the most important. The son of Taddeo, Angiolo Gaddi, was a good colourist, and the master of Cennino Cennini, who was apprenticed to him in 1375. In the *Trattato della Pittura* of Cennini, we accordingly find a description of the practice of the fourteenth century, although it would partly appear that the original MS. was not finished till 1437. Tommaso di Stefano was called Giottino[37] from his successful imitation of Giotto. The humorous Buffalmacco was a contemporary of Giotto.

For a century after the time of Giotto his followers did not considerably progress beyond the point he reached; and his influence is very perceptible in the paintings executed dining that period in the Campo Santo at Pisa. This celebrated cemetery takes its name from having, it is said, been filled with earth brought from the Holy Land. The walls of the arcaded building, which surround this sacred earth, are covered with paintings, quite invaluable as illustrations of the art of the fourteenth century, though now unfortunately greatly decayed. Among these, two of the most remarkable are by Orcagna, viz., the 'Triumph of Death 'and the 'Last Judgment.' The attitudes of Christ and the Virgin in the latter were afterwards borrowed by Michael Angelo in his famous 'Last Judgment.' Later painters have also taken Orcagna's arrangement of the patriarchs and apostles as their model, particularly Fra Bartolommeo and Raphael. Orcagna was a still greater architect and sculptor than painter. He designed the elaborate and beautiful Tabernacle of the Virgin in Or' San Michele at Florence.

Contemporary with Giotto, a celebrated painter, Simone di Martin (improperly called Simone Memmi), flourished at Siena. He is the subject of two of Petrarch's sonnets, and is said to have painted the portrait of Laura; but nothing is known of this picture. A small specimen of this plaster is preserved in the interesting collection of early works belonging to the Liverpool Institution. Painting made nearly equal advancement in other parts of Italy as in Tuscany; but the only names we need recall are those of Pietro Cavallini[38]: and Gentile da Fabriano, of the early Roman, or, as it was termed at this period, Umbrian school.

One Florentine painter, however, remains to be noticed; for although contemporary with the great innovations made by Massaccio early in the fifteenth century, he yet in essential points adhered to, or rather consummated, the types of the fourteenth century. We allude to the Beato Fra[39] Giovanni da Fiesole, or, as he has been generally called, Fra Angelico (the Angelic), from the great piety to which his life and works equally bear testimony. Fra Angelico never painted for money. He never began his work without prayer; and so entirely did his subject fill his soul, that he was frequently interrupted by tears when representing the sufferings of the Redeemer. It is not surprising that he considered what he painted with such intense feeling as a kind of inspiration, and therefore never ventured to retouch or attempt to improve what he had once finished. Profound serenity of feeling, confiding devotedness, a pure and holy frame of mind, form the never-failing characteristics of the paintings of Fra Angelico. 'He knew nothing of human anxieties, of struggles with passion, of victory over it; it is a glorified and more blessed world which he endeavours to reveal to our view. He seeks to invest the forms he places before us with the utmost beauty his hand could lend them; the sweetest expression beams in all their countenances; a harmonious grace guides all their movements, particularly where the action is expressed by the treatment of the drapery. The most cheerful colours, like spring-flowers, are selected for the draperies, and a profusion of golden ornaments is lavished over the whole: every auxiliary has been employed that could give a new glory to these holy subjects. With a peculiar religious awe, he adheres scrupulously to traditional types, and ventures on none of the innovations which were already introduced into art at Florence: these would have been a disturbing element to the child-like serenity of his mind. Of all artists, Fiesole is the most perfect example of this style; but in him likewise it appears most decidedly in all its restrictedness. He is inimitable in his representations of angels and glorified saints; weak, timid, and embarrassed when he introduces man in his human nature. Not merely the rancour and hatred of the foes of Christ, but all determined action is feebly expressed; his figures, even when in momentary repose, are deficient in apparent power to act, though the act to be performed may be the highest and the holiest. Thus, his representations of Christ, in whose form human power and divine sanctity should be equally prominent, are everywhere unsatisfactory, frequently unworthy. These faults are the result of a defective knowledge of the organization of the human body, the lower limbs of which are generally destitute both of that truth of action and position which Giotto especially had attained.'[40]

Fra Angelico's first efforts were in miniature illuminations, and the peculiarities of this style are apparent in his numerous small panel pictures, and also in those of his pupil Benozzo Gozzoli. But the large compositions with which he adorned the cloisters of his order, in the monastery of S. Marco at Florence, show greater freedom of execution, especially his *chef-d'œuvre,* the 'Crucifixion.'

'The taste for studying the history of early Italian art is not a recent development in our own country alone; it is a novelty even in Italy itself. A century ago the Italians seemed to regard Perugino, the master of Raphael, as the *Ultima Thule* to which point investigation might be carried; and even Ghirlandajo, the teacher of Michael Angelo, with his fine frescoes in the Sassetti Chapel of the Trinità at Florence, and compartments of the Sistine Chapel at Rome, was overlooked. Two energetic men, Ottley in England, and Lasinio in Italy, laboured hard to make the interest of this field of investigation more generally felt. Lasinio, the appointed *conservatore* of the Campo Santo at Pisa, exerted his utmost to save it from destruction during the revolutionary period, and removed coats of whitewash and mural tablets that even then, in classic Italy, obliterated the pictures and disfigured the walls. At the same time be published a magnificent series of large engravings from the paintings which decorate the ambulatories, as far as time had then spared them. The *conservatore* had in his youth spent years upon the study of these old neglected paintings; he recognised in them illustrations of former history, the past glories of his country, to which he was so attached, and which at that time lay so abased. He quoted the merry stories of Boccaccio about Buffalmacco, as he traced the few lines yet remaining from his pencil; and saw in Giotto's frescoes relating to the history of Job scenes of Italian life, with all the richness and festal luxury which distinguished the nobles in the days of Dante; and beheld also, in many of the priestly functions, the ecclesiastic paraphernalia of Pope Boniface himself. Lasinio, by his energy and industry, made these works known, and, in the capacity of cicerone to the English visitors, who always flocked to the Campo Santo, he contributed in no slight degree to the prevalence of the taste now so general among us. Ottley, the Englishman, at the same time enjoying a certain independence of means, imbibed from his intercourse with Lasinio a similar taste, and made careful drawings of the more important frescoes, both at Pisa, Florence, and Assisi. These he published in a series of bold engravings, but, from unavoidable costliness, they have never had any extensive circulation. D'Agincourt, in Paris, also did much to diffuse a wider knowledge of the history of Italian art by collecting drawings of all available "monuments," including the sketches of Ottley and Lasinio, and arranging them in chronological order. Lanzi, too, a writer of high order, contributed much to spread a taste for the study of the history of art by his delightful volumes upon the various schools in Italy; a work which has been made equally popular in England by the well-known translation of William Roscoe. It is not a little remarkable that seven years ago we had no translation of Vasari's *Lives of the Painters* in the English language. Mrs. Foster's version, therefore, published in Bohn's Series, in 1850, was of noteworthy importance; and the more remarkable, as Vasari had for many years been translated into almost every other European language.'—*Mr. Scharf, jun., on the Paintings by Ancient Masters in the Art Treasures Exhibition.*

The end of the fourteenth century is remarkable for the introduction of *genuine* fresco painting, and, as the most important works of immediately succeeding artists consist of wall paintings, we may examine them to greater advantage after some inquiry into the nature of 'fresco buono,' as it is termed. At the same time it must be remembered that many mural paintings were still executed in distemper, and panel pictures, of course, in the ordinary egg tempera, until the introduction of oil painting. To adhere, however, to chronological order, as nearly as our plan will permit, we must offer some account of mediaeval mosaics, miniatures, and glass painting before confining our attention to fresco painting. But, before concluding the present subject, we may mention that distemper was employed as complementary to fresco; and, that up to the present day, as will be seen in the next section, oil pictures are frequently executed partly in tempera —taking the word in its largest signification, and making it include water-colours, distemper, &c.

8. Tempera and Encaustic in Modern Times

Various attempts have been made to re-introduce wax painting; but the art of *pencillum-encaustic,* as practised by the ancients, seems to be lost. Wax painting, in the first centuries of the Christian era, appears to have superseded all other processes, except mosaic. In a manuscript of the eighth century wax painting, however, meets with little attention; and the art was almost forgotten during the twelfth, thirteenth, and fourteenth centuries, the original process being quite lost, judging from the slight descriptions in the extremely rare notices of wax painting known to exist. A document in the records of the Duomo of Orvieto mentions a wax vehicle or varnish as having been used by Andrea Pisano in 1345, but only for colouring marble statues of the Virgin. Mrs. Merrifield, however, mentions a picture, reputed to be painted in wax, of the 'Martyrdom of St. Simon the Younger,' by Andrea Mantegna, in the possession of Signor Vallardi, at Milan. 'The vehicle,' says Mrs. Merrifield, 'whatever it was, appeared to me to have been as manageable as that of Van Eyck.'

The same collection, we are told, contains a modern picture, which may also with propriety be said to be in encaustic, since the colours are melted in by the application of a hot iron. In the attempted revival of wax painting in France and Germany (more especially at Munich), the principle of dissolving the wax in an essential oil has been adopted, the vehicle being consolidated by the addition of resins. The efforts of Montabert were most prominent in introducing this method; but Taubenheim and others recommend the solution of wax in a drying oil.

A method of wax painting, invented by Count Caylus, about the middle of the last century, was highly extolled at the time, though beset by grave inconveniences. At Parma as well as Munich, a method of wax painting is now being practised, and, in repainting the pictures by Sir James Thornhill,

Mr. Parris, the artist, is represented to have used a wax vehicle, his own 'marble medium.'

We have said that oil pictures have been and are frequently executed partly in distemper. This partial use of watercolours, which is generally confined to the preparatory stages of the picture, recommends itself by enabling the artist to advance with greater facility through those stages, and also by the increased purity it secures in the superimposed colour. Nearly all the Venetian painters are believed to have used this mixed method. It is known that the invariably clear blues in the pictures of Paul Veronese were painted in distemper and afterwards varnished. Upon this subject we venture to quote, as the opinion of a practical authority, the following valuable passage from Burnet's *Essays on the Fine Arts.*

'Until the time of Correggio and Titian, the peculiar beauties of oil painting were unknown. The power of representing the variety of textures and surfaces in nature, the art of giving to the light the means of reflecting back that luminous body unimpaired, and the conduct in the shadows so as to swallow up and absorb all reflexion and refraction of light, were soon discovered to be its advantages over fresco; and Correggio and Giorgione availed themselves of such discovery: hence the impasto, and *absence of oleaginous substances* in the light portions of their pictures, and the unctuous and transparent properties in the shadows.

'The effect of such treatment can only now, in a manner, be guessed at; for though the lights remain in a degree unaltered, the rich glazings of the shadows have become dried up and blistered by the effects of time and heat. We can easily imagine that the watercolour, in the first instance, when the change took place, was not sufficiently charged with size or some resisting fluid; so that, on the application of oil glazings, the work darkened in a very great degree; and though colours laid on in distemper and glazed with oil pigments, will produce a much richer effect than either process separately, we trace a gradual approximation to the effect of water, or the luminous character of fresco painting, through the works of Titian, Tintoretto, and Paul Veronese.

'The truth and force of nature produced by a union of the peculiar properties of the two modes, have been felt and acknowledged by all painters up to the present time; and though Rubens, who laid the foundation of the art in Germany, finished his works principally in oil, yet, from adopting a white watercolour ground, he preserved in a high degree the fresh and brilliant effects of the Venetian mode of painting; and by Velasquez it was carried into Spain, and by Vandyke into England, but gradually sunk into a leaden and dull arrangement of colour, until revived by the indefatigable exertions of Sir Joshua Reynolds. So anxious was this celebrated artist to combine the luminous qualities of the Venetian style with the rich transparency of Correggio and Rembrandt, that half his life was spent in trying experiments on the various modes of producing this union, and which has occasioned the decay and destruction of many of his works; for though watercolour will support oil painting, yet, when washed over it, so as to recover the freshness of the original ground, it contracts and tears the work to pieces: hence the deep and multifarious cracks and fissures in the background of most of his best coloured pictures.'

Turner also carried this principle too far, combining and varying the two methods in the most reckless manner.

'In Etty,' Mr. Burnet continues, 'we have the true Venetian crackly substance of watercolour with the rich and transparent glazings of oil, and Wilkie had part of the quality for which we are contending in a very high degree. His pictures possess that peculiar stearine substance found in the works of Watteau, and which cost Reynolds a long life to acquire; but the other requisite is absent, the fresh watercolour look we find in Watteau.'

Since the introduction of oil painting, pictures have occasionally been executed with the old tempera egg vehicle. In the Colonna Palace at Rome there are several fine landscapes by Gaspar Poussin, said to be *à uovo;* and in the different collections throughout Europe tempera pictures may be found which have been painted as designs for fresco.

Chapter 5

Mosaic Painting

Few persons who have not seen any of the great mosaic works in the ancient churches of Italy could imagine the sumptuous effect produced by immense walls covered with figures, often of colossal proportions, coloured in variegated hues of crystalline brilliancy, set in backgrounds of gold and purple and azure, and surrounded with many-coloured marbles. If the intention of Sir Christopher Wren had been carried out, and the inside of the dome of St. Paul's Cathedral had been 'decorated with rich and durable mosaic,' like the cupola of St. Peter's at Rome, we should have had a higher idea of the capabilities of the art than can be formed from the inspection of snuff-boxes, or, at most, a few cabinet pieces. We are glad to know, however, that there is at length a prospect of the design of the great architect being completed.

A number of mosaics are among the decorations now proposed for St. Paul's; and a design for the first, to be placed in the three compartments of the half-dome of the apse at the end of the, choir, has been approved, and only awaits sufficient funds for execution. The subject is 'The Transfiguration,' and the designer was Baron de Triqueti. Mosaics are also to be placed in the Memorial (Wolsey) Chapel to the late Prince Consort, in St. George's, Windsor.

Mosaic, called opus musivum, musaicum, mosaicum (from *muson, musiæon,* polished, elegant, or well-wrought), and of which there are various kinds, is, in the widest sense of the word, any work which produces a design, with or without colour, on a surface by the joining together of hard bodies. Though, seemingly, too mechanical to rank as a style of 'painting,' yet it is generally and justly considered entitled to the distinction. For, it must be remembered, whatever may be thought of the means, that the principle of painting is involved, and it is as necessary to prepare a cartoon for an original composition in mosaic as for a fresco, or the most elaborate picture—in fact, it is not merely as necessary, but in this instance it is quite indispensable.

At the present day in Italy the most celebrated pictures are copied with perfect accuracy. And even this copying must require a very considerable knowledge of art, and a correct appreciation of the different schools, to do justice to works thus invested as it were with immortality. There is a studio expressly devoted in the Vatican to the manufacture of the beautiful mosaics of St. Peter's. The number of enamels of different tints and hues preserved for the purposes of the work, amounts to no less than 10,000; and many of the large copies from Raphael and Domenichino in various parts of the building have occupied from twelve to twenty years in their execution. The art having never been lost, we may best describe the more mechanical part by referring to the present practice in the establishment in the Vatican, especially as it is here more, conducted than it was among the ancients.

The method is simple enough. The slab upon which the mosaic is made is generally of Travertine (or Tibertine) stone. In this the workman cuts a certain space, which he encircles with bands or cramps of iron. Upon this hollowed surface mastic, or cementing paste, is gradually spread as the progress of the work requires it, this forming the, adhesive ground, or bed, on which the mosaic is laid. The mastic is composed of calcined marble and finely powdered Travertine stone, mixed to the consistence of paste with linseed oil. Into this paste are stuck the *smalti,* or small cubes of coloured glass, which compose the picture, in the same manner as were the coloured glass, stone, and marble *sectilia* and *tessera* of the ancients. These *smalti* are vitrified but opaque, partaking of the nature of stone and glass, or enamels; and are composed of a variety of minerals and materials, coloured, for the most part, with different metallic oxides. They are manufactured in Rome in the form of long slender rods, like wires, of different degrees of thickness, and are cut into pieces of the requisite sizes, from the smallest pin point to an inch. When the mastic has sufficiently indurated (and it acquires in time the hardness of stone), the work is susceptible of a polish like crystal. Care must be taken, however, that by too high a polish the entire effect of the work is not injured, as innumerable reflected lights in that case would glitter in every part of the picture. When the design is to be seen at a very considerable distance, as in cupolas or flat ceilings, they are generally less elaborately polished, as the inequalities of the surface are the less distinguishable, and the interstices of the work cannot be detected by the spectator. On ascending the dome of St. Peter's the visitor is invariably astonished at the coarseness of mosaics which appear from below of the utmost delicacy and finish.[41]

The age of a mosaic may be determined by the composition, the drawing, and the nature of the materials employed; and if of the Christian period, as a general rule, the more numerous these are, the more modern the mosaic. Many antique mosaics, which were supposed to consist of coloured stones, are found to be of glass, or vitreous.

ANCIENT MOSAICS

The employment of mosaics is traceable to the most ancient periods, and seems to have had its rise among the eastern nations. In the Book of Esther (ch. i. v. 6) we read of 'a pavement of red and blue, and white and black marble.' The invention appears to have been transmitted through the Egyptians to the Greeks, from whom it was stolen by the Romans, as they stole their arts, sciences, and gods.

Mosaic received its first great development in the sumptuous Alexandrian age, during which a prodigality of form and material began to corrupt the simplicity of Grecian art. At first small cubes of stone and terra-cotta were employed, but later, vitrified substances of various colours. Mosaic was first applied as an ornament for pavements, and commenced in the close imitation of inanimate objects, such as broken food and scattered articles lying apparently on the floor. It thence proceeded to large historical compositions. Splendid works were made of stone as well as clay cubes, as early as the Alexandrine period; and under the first Emperors the art attained the highest technical development and refinement. Mosaic pavements became general, and they were even made portable. Caesar carried the pavement as well as the canvas of his tent with him, whether from the love of the art or a dry floor is somewhat doubtful. Cicero caused such pavements to be placed in all the porticos of his house. Under the protection of the Roman dominion this peculiar art spread itself over the ancient world, and was executed in the same manner upon the Euphrates, on Mount Atlas, and in Britain. Wherever the Roman arms were carried the mosaics followed, and hundreds have been found in Gaul, Germany, and Britain.

There were several varieties of mosaic among the ancients, but the mention of the following may suffice:

1. Floors formed of pieces of stone of different colours, cut geometrically and cemented together—*pavimenta sectilia.*

2. Floors inlaid with small cubes of stone forming a coloured design, such as were usual in antiquity, not merely in rooms, but also in courts and terraces—*opus tesselatum, pavimenta tesselata* (tesselated pavement).

3. The finer mosaic, which essayed to come as near as possible to painted pictures, and usually employed coloured pieces of clay, or glass; but also the very costly material of precious stones, where the imitation of numerous local colours was required called *opus vermiculatum (majus* and *medium), crustæ vermiculæ.* In the time of the Emperors the employment of glass cubes in the decoration of apartments first made its appearance, and quickly came into great request. There are many remains of this kind of mosaic, of which a few may be pronounced artistically excellent. The art seems, however, to have long been employed principally for pavements, and till the end of the third century there is only slight mention of its having been transferred to the walls and ceilings. But historical mosaic painting of the grander style seems to have had a sudden development in the course of the fourth century.

4. Outlines and intaglios were, according to Müller, engraved in metal, or some other hard material, and another metal or enamel melted into it, so that figures in so-called *niello* resulted from the process.[42]

Besides these, the forming designs for windows with pieces of coloured glass appears to have been known at least to later antiquity, and this may be considered a species of mosaic. We find accounts also of what are called, though somewhat vaguely, mosaics in relief. These were thought to have been the invention of Pompeo Savini of Urbino, but they are considered by some to be of ancient date; and are supposed, under the Empire, to have superseded the bas-reliefs of painted clay, common in the times of the Republic. The practice, if it obtained, was borrowed from the Greeks; for, according to M. Raoul-Rochette, the Ionic capitals of the Erectheum at Athens were adorned with an incrustation of coloured enamel. The fountains discovered at Pompeii had a covering of mosaic in coloured paste. In the Villa Hadriana the entire vault of a crypto-porticus was covered with bas-reliefs in a very hard stucco, said to be incrusted with a paste of glass or enamel, in imitation of bas-reliefs of wax painted in natural colours.

The cubes employed were of every possible tint, and were set up by the workmen much as the types are by our printers, or rather, compositors. Many were gilt, and such were extensively employed afterwards in every description of mosaic by the Byzantines, who placed their figures on gold grounds. The gold leaf was applied at the back of the cube, where it was fixed by a mordant covered with pounded glass, and fired in a furnace.

Christian Mosaics: the Later Roman Style

It is in relation to the history of art, and especially of Christian and mediaeval art, that mosaics assume their extreme interest and importance. For nearly a thousand years—from the fourth century till the revival of tempera in the schools of Cimabue and Giotto—mosaic was most extensively employed for mural decoration, and during at least four centuries—viz., from the fifth to the ninth—seems to have almost entirely superseded other methods for such purposes. But for mosaics, then, the art of these long ages would be lost to us, saving and except the knowledge we might glean from missals. The loss of such art would possibly be, for its own sake, not much to be regretted, but with it would have disappeared a perfect epitome of the religious ideas of those ages; clues to innumerable symbols and legends; and much which throws light upon the introduction of some of the peculiarities of Romanism—such notably as the gradual elevation of the Virgin Mary to virtually divine honours.

Fortunately, however, of so durable a nature is mosaic, that from existing remains, not only is all this preserved, but every change of style in art, and every phase of manner, may be distinctly traced. There are mosaics near Rome of the fourth or fifth century in almost perfect preservation, and at Ravenna they are still as fresh as in the days of Justinian. Domenico Ghirlandajo might well say it is the only painting for eternity. St. Mark's at Venice is of itself a complete museum of the works of the *mosaicisti* for several centuries, commencing with the Greek artists of the eleventh century.

The Christian mosaics which decorated the 'triumphal arch' and apse of basilicas, the cupola of baptisteries, and other parts of the interior of buildings, consisted of cubes of coloured glass, the older specimens being generally inlaid either on a white or blue ground, as in the Roman school, or on a gold ground, as in the Byzantine school—at St. Sophia, Constantinople; at St. Mark's, Venice; at Rome, after the seventh century, and elsewhere. The only remaining specimen of Christian mosaic executed in the antique manner appears to be the curious incrustation on the waggon-roof of the ambulatory of Santa Constanza, the baptistery erected near Rome by Constantine. It represents a vine; it is, in fact, a *pergola,* and has, introduced among the leaves, many Christian symbols. The style is the mixed *opus tesselatum* and *vermiculatum (majus* and *medium)* of the ancients, and has none of the characteristics of the various kinds subsequently employed. This is believed to be the earliest and only Christian wall mosaic of the fourth century.

All other Christian mosaics may be included in three classes. 1. Glass mosaic, called *opus musivum*—pictorial and imitative, used for walls and vaulted ceilings. The Oriental taste for splendour had shown itself among the Romans, as we learn front the gold-ground mosaic of the late monuments of Pompeii; the transition was, therefore, insensible in this respect to this rich Christian glass mosaic, in which the ground is nearly always gold. The pieces of glass were of very irregular shapes and sizes, and of innumerable colours and tints. The execution is always large and coarse, and rarely approaches in neatness of joint and regularity of bedding to the larger style of the ancients, the *opus majus vermiculatum.* 2. Glass tesselation, called *opus Grecanium*—conventional, generally inlaid in church furniture. 3. Marble tesselation, called indifferently, *Grecanium* and *Alexandrinum*—conventional, formed into pavements.

The principal defect in mosaics, artistically speaking, is the general want of expression, although the faces frequently have a peculiar dignity. This defect is owing to the mechanical manner in which they are executed from the cartoon. Nevertheless, from the necessary restriction of this branch of art, as far as possible, to large and simple forms, in order to insure general distinctness, and the consequent renunciation of rich and crowded compositions, has resulted a certain breadth and grandeur of style which, no doubt, has exercised an important influence over the whole province of art, but manifested particularly in fresco.

In addition to the mosaic of the fourth century, already mentioned incidentally, there is another, which is said to belong to this early date. This mosaic was found originally in the cemetery of S. Callisto at Rome, and is now preserved in the *Museum Christianum* of the Vatican. Lord Lindsay, in his *Sketches of the History of Christian Art,* observes, that in it we find the first appearance of the peculiar Byzantine character of the head of the Redeemer, which for centuries after became the established type. 'This primitive type consisted of a half-length placed within a wreath, and generally in the act of blessing with the right hand [if in the Latin church, the thumb and the first and second fingers extended, symbolical of the Trinity], and holding the cross or the globe in the left,[43] and is to be often met with in the basilicas successively built at Rome, and elsewhere in Italy.' At a later period this arrangement became popular throughout Europe, the representations frequently including the whole figure of the Saviour placed upon a throne. Over the doors of Norman churches, for example, we find a bas-relief of this subject. The Virgin Mary is also shown similarly enthroned. The word *Maestà (Anglicé* 'Majesty') is applied to these representations.

In the fifth century we meet with a sudden and extensive adoption of mosaic in baptisteries and basilicas. The rite of baptism was anciently performed in a separate building, or baptistery, and this being generally circular or polygonal, and the decoration chiefly confined to the cupola, it was natural that the centre subject should represent the baptism of Christ, round which the figures of the apostles formed an outward circle. Of the basilica, and its decoration, we borrow the following description by Dr. Kugler: 'This form of church building had generally obtained in the East. It consisted in a principal oblong space, of three or five aisles, divided by rows of columns, the centre aisle loftier than the others, and terminating in one or three semi-domed tribunes or *apsides;* before which, in some instances, a transept was introduced [thus forming the Latin cross as distinguished from the regular Greek cross.]

'The chief apsis behind the altar, as the most sacred portion of the building, was almost invariably reserved for the colossal figure of the standing or enthroned Saviour, with the apostles or patron saints and founders of the church on either hand. In later times the Virgin Mary was introduced next to Christ, or even in his stead. Above the chief figure appears generally a hand stretching out of the clouds, and holding a crown, an emblem of the almighty power of the Father. . . . Underneath, in a narrow division, may be seen the Agnus Dei [Lamb of God], with twelve sheep, which are advancing on both sides from out the gates of Jerusalem and Bethlehem—a symbol of the twelve disciples, or the faithful generally. Above, and on each side of the arch which terminates the apsis, usually appear various subjects from the Apocalypse referring to the Advent of our Lord. In the centre, generally, the Lamb, or the book with the seven seals upon the throne; next to it the symbols of the Evangelists,[44] the seven candlesticks, and the four-and-twenty elders, their arms outstretched towards the Lamb.

'In the larger basilicas, where a transept is introduced before the apsis, it is divided from the nave by a large arch called the arch of triumph. In this case the subjects from the Apocalypse were usually introduced upon this arch. In addition to this, the clerestory of the centre aisle, and the spandrils of the arches over the columns, were seldom left in the larger and more splendid basilicas without decoration.'

The most numerous and valuable mosaics of the fifth and following centuries are found in the churches of Rome and Ravenna. Among the most remarkable mosaics of the fifth century are the following: the internal decorations of the baptistery of the cathedral of Ravenna; the numerous but now much restored mosaics in Sta. Maria Maggiore; the rich decoration of the monumental chapel of the Empress Galla Placidia (SS. Nazaro e Celso) at Ravenna, the harmonious effect of which is incomparable; and the mosaics on the arch of triumph in S. Paulo fuori le Mure, Rome.

Of the sixth century the finest mosaics of ancient Christian Rome are those of SS. Cosmo e Damiano; and although classical influence had almost died out, a figure of Christ may be regarded as one of the most marvellous specimens of the art of the Middle Ages. Countenance, attitude, and drapery combine to give him an expression of quiet majesty, which for many centuries after is not found again in equal beauty and freedom. Here, already, St. Peter is depicted with the bald head, and St. Paul with the short brown hair and dark beard, by which they were afterwards recognizable. At Ravenna, in the celebrated church of San Vitale, are two large processional and ceremonial representations, on a gold ground, of the Emperor and Empress, Justinian and Theodora, which, as among the very few surviving specimens of a style which preserved many of the higher features of pagan painting, are of great interest, and as examples of costume quite invaluable. In the mosaics of S. Apollinare Nuovo, upon a throne surmounted by angels, the *Madonna* is perhaps for the first time represented as an object of reverence. In the seventh century all appearance of life and more noble expression ceases; and with the general prevalence of the Byzantine style, a statuesque rigidity, a moroseness of expression, a settled traditional conventionality, and total absence of the plastic element (or modelling) succeed.

CHRISTIAN MOSAICS: THE BYZANTINE STYLE

The mosaics of S. Vitale above-mentioned have been claimed as Byzantine, front the circumstance of the occupation of Ravenna in 539 by the Byzantians; but they are clearly of the late Roman class, and there is no reason to believe that the artists belonged to a more Eastern school. The Byzantine style was in truth only a transformation of the Roman through succeeding stages; and till the seventh century the art of the East and the West was essentially the same, for the ancient Roman models had been carried eastward with the migration of the court. Local considerations, however, render it perhaps more convenient to treat of this style as if it could be originally identified with that Byzantium from which it derives its name; and where, after the city had received a new designation from Constantine, it was so extensively and systematically cultivated.

Constantine, the first Christian Emperor of the Roman race, when he removed the seat of empire from Rome to Byzantium, about A.D. 330, carried with him the arts of the former empire, and applied them to the enlargement and embellishment of the new city. From these arose, in process of time, that combination of Roman, Greek, and Oriental traditions which were united in the Byzantine style, and diffused proportionately with the extent and influence of the Eastern Empire. But of the period from the time of Constantine to the middle of the sixth century few examples remain. Most of the existing Byzantine monuments date from the time of Justinian to the eleventh century. After this period, till the final conquest of Greece by the Turks, in the fifteenth century, the influence of the style gradually decays, and a European, and more especially a Venetian, character is visible.

It is then, dating from the commencement of the sixth to the eleventh century, that we find those monuments of the Byzantine style which ultimately affected not only the styles adopted in Italy, France, Germany, and Great Britain, but penetrated widely among the Slavonic and Oriental races, and was carried by the conquering Arabs through all the north of Africa and the greater portion of Spain. In Italy this is precisely the period of the deepest decline of art. After the Ostrogoths had succumbed to the armies of Justinian, and Italy had submitted itself to the Eastern dominion, it was next invaded by the Longobards, who brought about the most singular division of the country; for while the great mass of the centre of the land fell into their hands, the important coast regions, such particularly as Ravenna, remained in the possession of the Byzantines.

The earliest as well as greatest example of Byzantine art and architecture is the celebrated mosque of St. Sophia at Constantinople, built by Justinian, who ascended the throne in 527. Contemporary with this was the erection at Ravenna, the capital of the Exarchate, of S. Vitale, founded by Julian, the treasurer of Justinian, about 530, and especially interesting as having furnished the model after which Charlemagne caused his cathedral at Aix-la-Chapelle to be built. We have already alluded to the remarkable mosaics of S. Vitale, but of the far more elaborate and sumptuous decorations of St. Sophia at this period, scarcely a trace has survived the effects of wars, fires, and Mahomedan fanaticism.

The natural desire of the Eastern church to convert the Jews and Mahomedans, both of whom reproached the Christians with idol-worship, led to the great Iconoclastic persecutions, and the final severance of the Eastern and Western churches, when Gregory II formally excommunicated all Iconoclasts, including the Emperor Leo III, himself, in the year 726. One effect of these persecutions was to drive out over Europe a multitude of artists, who thus planted a taste for art in districts in which it might otherwise not have taken root. In Germany, under Charlemagne, the Greek artists from Constantinople and their productions were in the greatest favour.

But one curious effect of this persecution upon the Byzantine style itself remains to be noticed. The Iconoclasts did not direct their zeal so much against pictures as against the more literal 'images' of sculpture. The consequence was, that the Byzantine artists, in order to give no offence, not only avoided the imitation of nature generally, and deprived their representation of all attractiveness, at least of form, but especially shunned any approach to the appearance of relief (particularly in the face), or anything that might recall the hateful modelling of the sculptor. Most of the other characteristics of the style have been already adverted to in various places. Byzantine painting, therefore, from various causes, ultimately lost every spark of vitality, and became as stationary as Chinese art. The causes similar to those which led to the settled character of Byzantine, and, as we have noticed, also of Egyptian painting, have probably produced the long-continued conventionality of the painting of the Chinese, Indians, Persians, and other Oriental nations. Indian painting, however, like the Egyptian, has constantly been declining, the oldest specimens being by far the best.

Thus, one portion after another of the Byzantine figures became rigid, and the countenance assumed a suffering, stricken expression. At the same time, a singular pretension to correctness of anatomy forms a more odious contrast to the departure from nature in all other respects. Figures, in which no one limb is rightly disposed, have still, as far as the forms is seen, the full complement of ribs in the body, and a most unnecessary display of muscle in the arm, such as could only be seen on dissection. The 'figure' sometimes measures in length no less than thirteen heads, which is five more than antique statues; and the classical proportions are somewhat taller than nature. Another peculiarity is, that the face is always represented in the full view, the profile being utterly unknown to this art. In fact, the Byzantine artist had sunk into a luxurious handicraftsman, who sought to make up for his incapacity for all original composition by the splendour of his materials. He rested satisfied with a mere conventional type; for we find it identical throughout Europe; and this, as soon as established and traditionally communicated, invariably comes to be regarded with superstitious reverence. Accordingly, in one of the arguments adduced by an advocate for images in the Nicene Council, A.D. 787, it is distinctly asserted that, 'It is not the invention of the painter which creates the picture, but an inviolable law, a tradition of the Catholic church. It is not the painters, but the Holy Fathers, who have to invent and to dictate. To them manifestly belongs the composition, to the painter only the execution.' The church, then, having once decided upon the most fitting representation of any sacred subject, there existed no grounds for ever departing from it; we need not, therefore, be surprised to find that the painters of the Greek church to this day scrupulously submit themselves to the 'dictations' of the 'Holy Fathers.' No church would, of course, have ventured to dictate to a really living art, whatever other persecution might be attempted; and the deadness of the Byzantine school was as much the cause as the effect of such ecclesiastical interference.

Perhaps the first mosaics in Rome which distinctly show Byzantine influence are those in the tribune of Sta. Agnese fuori le Mure (625–638);

but the style is still more evident in the very extensive mosaics in the Oratorio di S. Venanzio, a side chapel of the baptistery to the Lateran (640–642). To the latter part of the seventh century belong the last mosaic decorations of importance in Ravenna, viz., those in the splendid basilica of S. Apollinare in Classe. The Exarchate, upon which the Longobards had encroached, was now seized by the Franks under Charlemagne, and made over to the Papal chair. From this time Ravenna, sinking into insignificance, confined itself to a few solitary decorations and to repairs; and to this circumstance we are indebted for the preservation of some illustrations of the art of the early Middle Ages not to be equalled elsewhere in the whole world. In the eighth and ninth centuries Roman mosaic sank, as regards expression, almost into barbarism. Some extensive and splendid works were, however, executed, and among these the mosaics in Sta. Prassede, on the Esquiline Hill, are in remarkable preservation. After the close of the ninth century the art seems almost to have ceased in Italy.

Meanwhile, however, as the influence of Rome in matters of faith increased among the new nations, so some of her arrangements prevailed also, as, for instance, the plan of her churches, so different from the Eastern form; and this plan was assimilated, as the design easily could be, with the old Roman monuments still existing throughout Europe — monuments which would naturally be chosen as objects of imitation. Indeed, in many cases, the materials, columns, &c., of the ancient edifices were incorporated in the new structures in other parts of Europe as well as Italy. Nevertheless, the influence of Constantinople would be felt, if only commercially. From the sixth to the tenth century Constantinople was undoubtedly the capital of the arts of the world; and numerous works of ornamental art, such as wood and ivory carvings, richly woven and embroidered stuffs, illuminated manuscripts and panel-pictures, and ornaments in the base and precious metals, were carried by traders, as well as the pilgrim monks and others, throughout Europe. Then, again, from shortly after the death of Theodoric the Ostrogoth, in the year 526, till the conquest of Italy by Charlemagne, in 774, the kingdom of Italy, with the exception of the Exarchate of Ravenna, was held by the Longobard or Lombard sovereigns; and, although they invented an original style, which has deserved to be separately distinguished as the 'Lombard,' they certainly derived their taste in art rather from Constantinople than Rome. Moreover, Charlemagne, who put an end to the dynasty of the Lombards, adopted in a great measure their style and naturalized it, in connection with Byzantine models, in the buildings of Aix-la-Chapelle and along the banks of the Rhine. The Lombardic style received, however, its chief development in northern Italy, commencing with the remarkable group of ecclesiastical buildings at Pisa (1063), extending subsequently its influence to Lucca, and merging into the Romanesque during the thirteenth century at Florence, Siena, Parma, Modena, Piacenza, and Ferrara.

Retracing our steps, we find, in the tenth century, some activity in the arts, notwithstanding that they had arrived at the lowest point of degradation, in consequence of the disasters which had befallen them, and their neglect from a universal belief in the approaching end of the world; and the persecuted Greek artists were employed in various parts of Europe. In Sicily and Southern Italy, in Rome and Venice, they found a home. In France their style was spread through a Venetian colony at Perigueux, and afterwards at Limoges. Germany, also, and Greece itself preserves many monuments to recall the fact of their presence. Their influence, likewise, extended to Asia Minor, Armenia, the Caucasian provinces, and among all the Slavonic races. But in the eleventh and twelfth centuries a curious complication is brought about in Apulia and Sicily by the strange advent of the Normans. From the conquered Greek and Saracenic races the Normans adopted the arts those races (more particularly the former) cultivated; but at the same time blended with the Byzantine a character partly Lombard, yet still to some extent peculiar to themselves. Greek artists were, however, principally employed in Sicily, though the *pointed arch,* a feature then of common occurrence in Saracenic buildings, was appropriated by the Normans from the Saracens. The most splendid specimens of the Norman-Byzantine paintings are the very extraordinary mosaics in the Cathedral of Monreale at Palermo. The centre apse contains an unusually colossal half-length figure of Christ.

The Byzantine type is, however, preserved with far greater distinctness in the exceedingly elaborate and extensive series of mosaics in the church of St. Mark, Venice, the earliest wall and cupola pictures of which go back to the eleventh, and perhaps to the tenth, century. This unmodified preservation of the style is explained by the circumstance of the Venetian republic being under the nominal protection of Byzantium while the mart for the empires of the East and the West; and, even after all political connection with Constantinople had ceased, the active commerce which was maintained became a constant bond of union. We need not describe the gorgeous luxury of the mere materials employed in the construction of St. Mark's; sufficient for our purpose to say, that the upper walls, waggon-roofs, and cupolas, comprising a surface of more than forty thousand square feet, are covered with mosaics on a gold ground; a gigantic work, which even all the wealth of Venice spent six centuries in patching together. No consistent plan has been adhered to in these decorations; and every style of art, therefore, which flourished during these centuries, is recognisable in this edifice. Many of the mosaics were executed in the sixteenth century, and Titian supplied cartoons to one of the two celebrated mosaicisti—the brothers Zuccato; Tintoretto and other great painters likewise furnished designs for these works.

It has been remarked that the Byzantine style is preserved unaltered since the tenth century in the modern Greek church, and its important branch, the Russian. The traditional and religious superstition with which Greek pictures came to be regarded was likely to recommend them to a rude, ignorant people; and the imitative instincts of the Slavonic races were favourable to the dissemination of a purely mechanical art. The Russian churches of the present day are covered from floor to roof with paintings; but the chief splendour is concentrated upon the pictures of saints which hang on the high screen, or iconostasis, which separates the altar from the rest of the church. The artists are all monks and nuns. Thus the Russian peasant thinks this style of art something identified with and inseparable from Christianity, and the picture itself becomes sacred because its established forms are sacred. Pictures therefore take the place of charms, amulets, fetishes, and household gods. They are indispensable in every room, and the Russian thinks he can never have enough of them—rich peasants possessing whole collections. This explains why so many small Byzantine pictures were found upon the bodies of the Russian soldiers during the Crimean war.

The modern French archeologist, M. Didron, made some, very interesting researches in 1839 into the present Byzantine art of the East, particularly on the sacred Mount Athos (with its 935 churches, chapels, and monasteries), where the tradition of art, according to all evidence, has been preserved with Egyptian pertinacity in one unbroken course during thirteen hundred years. The object of the French traveller was to throw light upon the subject of early Christian symbolism and iconography; and this he attained in the discovery of a MS.[45] evidently compiled from the most ancient authorities, and copies of which were in use in all the convents. In this manuscript formal receipts are given for the designing, grouping, and distribution on the walls of every saint, symbol, or device which may either occur singly or compose the prescribed sacred subjects and scenes which alone admit of orthodox representation—these receipts being as strictly followed as the practical and technical formulae of the actual process of painting. Mount Athos, it appears, has been for the last few centuries a general academy of Greek art. Almost every Greek artist pursues his studies there; and thence innumerable pictures on wood are transported to Greece, Turkey, and Russia. Mosaic work, however, is now seldom heard of; but the quantity of frescoes is almost incredible. To show with what rapidity these are produced, M. Didron relates that he saw with his own eyes a monk and five assistants paint a Christ and eleven apostles, the size of life, within an hour, and without cartoons or tracings. To explain this apparent artistic feat, we are told that these painters bring no thought whatever of their own to the task. Not only the range of their subjects, but the mode of representation, even to the smallest details, is supplied them by tradition and old patterns. Their 'studies' begin by making tracings from the works of their predecessors, and by degrees they learn every composition and figure, with their accompanying accessories, so entirely by heart, that they work with the utmost rapidity and without the slightest exertion of thought. Individual genius or character would be only a hindrance, and neither appreciated nor understood. The painter being the instrument of one common process, is of course quickly forgotten in Greece, though his works may indeed be innumerable.[46]

THE ROMANESQUE STYLE; AND THE LATER HISTORY OF MOSAIC

We now return to the commencement of the twelfth century, when a strictly Romanesque style was eliminated in central Italy from the Byzantine traditions and the new life of the period. The origin of this style has already received some attention; and the reader will now be in a still better position to estimate the various elements which contributed to its formation. The two following instances show, perhaps, in the department of mosaic, most freedom from Byzantine influence; viz., the mosaics in the basilica of Sta. Maria in Transtevere (1139–1153), and the tribune mosaics of the basilica of S. Clemente in Rome. Wall painting reappears in this century: various specimens still existing. From these we find that the rise of mediaeval painting in Italy was not confined to Tuscany, as modern Italian writers on art, being chiefly Tuscans by birth, would lead us to believe.

Early in the thirteenth century the Italians in Florence and elsewhere began to execute mosaic work for themselves. Andrea Tafi, while residing in Venice, is said to have gained the goodwill of a Greek painter named Apollonius, so that he taught Andrea the art of mosaic, and accompanied him to Florence, where they executed in conjunction the mosaics in the tribune of the old church, now the baptistery of S. Giovanni. Tafi, alone, afterwards executed a figure of Christ fourteen feet high, which Vasari says spread his fame throughout Italy. Contemporary with Tafi was Jacopo da Turrita, who conducted some remarkable mosaics in Sta. Maria Maggiore at Rome. Cimabue directed several artists who worked upon a mosaic at Pisa; and Gaddo Gaddi, the friend of Cimabue and Tafi, and the father of a race of artists, executed, among other works, a 'Coronation of the Virgin,' over the principal door in Sta. Maria del Fiore, the *Duomo* or cathedral of Florence.

Giotto, also, as well as many, if not all, of the early Florentine painters, practised this branch of art. His celebrated *Navicella,* now in St. Peter's at Rome, was executed for the ancient basilica. It represents a ship with the disciples on an agitated sea; the ship denoting the church, according to the early Christian symbolization. The mosaic has been so frequently repaired that the composition alone can be attributed to Giotto. Alesso Baldovinetto, one of the last mosaic painters we have to mention, taught the art to Domenico Ghirlandajo, who executed, in conjunction with Gherardo, some mosaics in the Duomo of Florence.

Before concluding this subject, one or two varieties of mosaic deserve a passing notice. Several modern Oriental styles were probably founded on the art of Byzantium. Thus, the Arabs, having become possessed of the materials of mosaic, and pictorial representation being forbidden by Mahomed, they would naturally arrange the pieces of glass in geometrical patterns. Glass tesselation, of merely ornamental character, prevailed also over Italy for many centuries. Tesselated marble work, usually of porphyry and serpentine (reddish-purple and green-coloured), was used for church pavement for a still longer period.

Gradually the 'Florentine mosaic,' or *opera di commesso,* was introduced, and even pictorial representations in marbles were applied for pavements. In the Duomo of Siena the pavement by Beccafumi exhibits large and elaborate historical compositions in chiaroscuro, by means of the contrast of three marbles only.

We may likewise mention, as a species of mosaic, the gorgeous enamels upon gold which was an especial department of Byzantine art. One of the best existing examples is, perhaps, the Pala d'Oro, the altar-piece of St. Mark's, Venice, which was ordered to be the most costly that Constantinople could furnish. It consists of a number of delicate gold plates, upon which Christ and the saints, with biblical scenes, and the Life of St. Mark, are represented by engraving and in enamel of the richest and deepest colours.

Tarsia, or the art of inlaying woods, stained, or of different natural colours, so as to represent architecture, landscapes, and various ornamental objects, was much employed in Italy in the seventeenth century, and to a certain extent imitated by the French in their *marqueterie.*

Efforts have recently been made to introduce into this country an art new to England, called marble tarsia. The first specimen was sent to the International Exhibition of 1862, and was purchased by the authorities of South Kensington, and is now in the Museum of Ornamental Art. The subject is 'The Salutation,' and the designer is Baron de Triqueti. The lines of the composition and a few principal shadows are incised and removed from a slab of statuary marble, and the spaces filled in with black marble; the broader masses of half-tint are treated in a similar manner, and filled with grey Sicilian marble; and the white marble is left for the lights. Subjects in marble tarsia have already been placed in the church at Wilton, built by the late Lord Herbert of Lea, and in the neighbouring church of Teffont Manor. The art recommends itself for mural ornament by the durability of its materials and colours. But it has more analogy with the ancient 'marble chiaroscuro' than with the tarsia of wood from which it takes its name, as it is precisely like the pavement of the Duomo Siena already mentioned.

Chapter 6

Manuscript Illuminations and Miniature Painting

1. Missal and Other MS. Illuminations

For many centuries during the Middle Ages missals, *livres d'heures,* and other books of prayer were the only literature and the sole study of a great number of the people. The monk scholars and devotees especially delighted to embellish these books, which formed the charm and solace of their monastic existence, and supplied them with a kind of sacred occupation. The works of art in these books being of small dimensions, and, as part of MSS. which could not be multiplied by printing, having a value beyond their illuminations or miniature paintings, there was both greater facility and greater interest in their preservation. All the older specimens being also painted on vellum, there was little danger of their decay through time. Panels, canvases, and paintings on walls, on the other hand, independent of the difficulty of their removal and deposit in safe places in cases of emergency, were constantly exposed to injuries from which the illuminations of MSS. were preserved, from the habit of depositing them in places of safety, and from their being closed from the action of the atmosphere.

Hence, when a hiatus occurs in the history of the art of various countries, it can frequently be filled up by the miniatures in these books, which are generally to a considerable extent an index to the state of art in other departments. Thus, as Dr. Waagen[47] says, 'the English specimens supply the *only* means of tracing the historical development of English painting from the 9th to the 16th centuries.' Moreover, being painted for the most part with opaque colours, which, being of mineral or earthy extraction, are the most durable, the colouring is surprisingly pure and brilliant; and even when the more fugitive vegetable tints were employed, from the way in which they have been protected from light and damp, they have faded far less than if they had been exposed as in other pictures. The style of any particular period is, however, not always to be correctly appreciated from these performances; for, when the higher qualities of art are almost entirely absent, we sometimes find a remarkable development of the mere decorative portions of painting. For instance, there are in some Byzantine MSS. the most splendid arabesques of mixed foliage and animals, and the richest architectural fancies in the margins.

The study of the caligraphy, or penmanship, of ancient MSS. is replete with interest; and the art of deciphering ancient writings, or palæography, has received of late years some of the attention it deserves. We must, however, limit the few remarks our space permits to examples in the art of illuminating, or *limning,* as it was formerly called. But it may be remarked that we owe the preservation of some of the most precious works of classical authors to what are called palimpsest MSS. These are MSS. which have been twice written. From the difficulty of procuring vellum, the mediaeval caligraphers frequently erased the writing of some antique MS. to make way for their own; chemistry, however, has furnished us with the means of making the original visible.

The word 'miniature' derives its origin from the practice of writing the rubrics or initial letters, &c., with *minium,* or red-lead. The French term 'illuminer' is supposed to be derived from the custom of illuminating or heightening the lights with gold. 'The art of miniature painting was divided into two branches: the professors of the first were styled "miniatori," or miniature painters, or illuminators of books; and those of the second, "miniatori caligrafi," or "pulchri scriptores." To the first class belonged the task of painting the scripture stories, the borders, and the arabesques, and of laying on the gold and ornaments of the MSS. The second wrote the whole of the work, and those initial letters generally drawn with blue or red, full of flourishes and fanciful ornaments, in which the patience of the writer is frequently more to be admired than his genius.'[48]

That the miniature painter was generally distinct from the caligrapher, is evident from the fact that some MSS. want the initial letters altogether, the spaces being left to be filled in by the more strictly 'decorative' artist.

But Mrs. Merrifield tells us that the two branches were sometimes practised by the same person; whence the term 'writing' was also extended to painting, and the word was not confined to miniature painting only, but was applied to painting on glass, which was also called 'writing on glass.' Vasari intimates that the initial or large-letter writing was a distinct occupation about 1350; for he says, in the *Life of Don Lorenzo,* that the monk Don Jacopo was the most distinguished large-letter writer in Europe in the fourteenth century. This Don Jacopo 'wrote' for his monastery, Degl' Angeli in Florence, twenty folio choral books, the miniature illuminations of which were painted by Don Silvestro, a brother of the same monastery; and so highly was their skill esteemed by their brother monks, that they embalmed their right hands after their death, and preserved them in a casket with the utmost veneration. These large illuminated initials are ornamented with all kinds of fanciful objects and figures, as men, animals, birds, flowers, &c. They are called *lettres historiées,* because they generally illustrate the text. In English and French MSS. of the fourteenth century, initials in purple, red, and gold are very frequent, in which are disposed figures of men and animals. The ornamentation is usually extended in spiral scrolls along the upper and lower margins of the page; and these also support small groups or single figures of dogs, hares, apes, &c. These illuminated letters are said to have commenced with the Greeks in the seventh century; and they attained their utmost elaboration in the twelfth.

Among the more *celebrated miniatori* were Simone Memmi, Giotto, Fra Angelico da Fiesole, Franco Bolognese (mentioned by Dante in Canto XI of the *Purgatorio),* John Van Eyck, Squarcione, Girolamo dai Libri[49] Memling, Gherardo of Florence, of the school of Ghirlandajo, and Giulio Clovio. But most of these were equally, or still more distinguished in other branches of art. Mewling, the Flemish master, was perhaps the best of all illuminators. The Italian, Giulio Clovio, the pupil of Giulio Romano, produced, however, some extraordinarily elaborate and highly finished miniatures. According to Vasari, he spent nine years in executing twenty-six miniatures in a breviary of the Virgin for the Cardinal Alessandro Farnese, now in the Royal Library at Naples. And Mr. Humphreys tells us, in his *Illuminated Books of the Middle Ages* (with the beautiful illustrations by Mr. Owen Jones), that a medal was struck in his honour. Attavante, a Florentine artist of the fifteenth century, was a very celebrated illuminator of MSS. A magnificent missal which he illuminated for Matthias Corvinus, King of Hungary, is in the library at Brussels; and the former regents of Belgium used to take their official oath upon it.

The pigments employed were prepared with the greatest care; and were commonly preserved by steeping small pieces of linen cloth in the liquid dyes—hence called 'clothlet colours.' When the colours were required for use a small portion of the cloth was cut off and placed in a shell containing water, and the tints were generally converted into 'body-colours' by the admixture of white, for we seldom find the shading transparent. The vehicle was egg, gum, or glue, dissolved in water, but usually diluted sufficiently to leave the surface dull and unshining. D'Agincourt,[50] however, mentions some miniatures, the colours of which are insoluble in water; and Dr. Dibdin[51] states, in describing the illuminations of a MS. of the Codex Justinianus of the fourteenth century, that on close examination the colours appear to have been mixed up with a glossy material not unlike oil.

2. Historical Sketch of Ms. Illuminations

The taste for decorating manuscripts existed among the ancients. The Egyptian papyrus, with its coloured hieroglyphs, vignettes, and rubric-like initials, was a veritable illuminated MS. Greek and Roman MSS. likewise had their red titles, or commencements and initials. The portraits which Marco Varro enclosed in his books are thought by some to have been painted; but their number renders this almost incredible. Seneca, in his treatise *De Tranquillitate Animi,* speaks of books ornamented with figures. The most ancient specimen of caligraphy extant is probably the Virgil of the fourth or fifth century in the Vatican. It contains fifty miniatures, but design and execution are inferior. In the celebrated collection of the Vatican are some of the most valuable MSS. known. Among these is a very interesting MS. of the Book of Joshua, which, though, according to an inscription on it, not of earlier date than the ninth or eighth century, is doubtless from some work of the best early Christian time. It is a *volumen,* or roll of parchment of more than thirty feet long. The illuminations are executed in few colours, and differ greatly from the highly-finished splendour of later Byzantine miniatures; but, excepting in the extremities, it has few of the Byzantine defects; on the contrary, there is much classical spirit, and the costume and weapons are perfectly antique. In the Ambrosian Library at Milan, fifty-eight miniatures have been preserved, fragments of a manuscript Homer, which may also date from the fourth or fifth century, judging from the broad and solid manner in which the colours are applied and the treatment of the drapery. After the seventh century, while the Byzantine style was adopted in Italy for mosaics, a style of greater licence and degeneracy prevailed in Italian MSS., which may be called, from the ruling power, the 'Longobardian.'

We have already alluded to the splendid embellishments of the Byzantine MSS. The best miniatures of the Byzantine time do not, however, actually belong to the Byzantine school, but are copies of earlier Roman works. For instance, the most celebrated *Codices* of the time of the Macedonian emperors, now in the Bibliothèque Impériale at Paris, are copies and fac-similes of the best Romano-Christian works. The finest miniatures are contained in a codex of sermons by St. Gregory Nazianzen; and some of these are repetitions of compositions of the fifth and sixth centuries, representing the principal events from the creation of the world to the time of St. Gregory. A Psalter of the ninth century is still more interesting, from its numerous personifications of natural objects and abstract qualities in the manner of the antique; the invention of which the art of the time was totally incapable. Among works essentially Byzantine is the well-known costly Menologium, or calendar, executed about A.D. 1000, for the Emperor Basilius II. Though imperfect, there being but the months from September to February inclusive, it contains no less than 430 splendid miniatures on a gold ground, the work of eight artists, whose names recur at intervals. The subjects include scenes from the life of Christ, the lives and martyrdoms of the saints, and the history of the church, or rather its synods.

The more important Greek MSS. are, however, of the period of the

Comnene emperors—from 1056 till 1204. Of these *the Dogmatica Panoplia* or Complete Defensive Armour against Heresies, in the Vatican, is remarkable for its brilliant colouring and the stiff gold-embroidered garments; while a collection of sermons for the feast of the Virgin is noteworthy for the great beauty of decorative ornament in its initials. An *Evangelarium,* or the four Gospels, executed in the reign of Johannes Comnenus *(Biblioteca d' Urbino), is* also interesting; and a MS. of St. John Calimachus (in the Vatican), contains some very delicately-executed and curious designs. It is called *The Ladder,* from the favourite allegory of the Virtues as the steps leading to Heaven, and the Vices as those which lead to Hell. The Byzantine miniatures of the thirteenth century partake of the general degeneracy of the style.

In the West, Charlemagne and his grandson, Charles the Bald, greatly encouraged the transcription and embellishment of manuscripts, which are hence termed Carlovingian. The Bibles of Charles the Bald, preserved at Paris in the Imperial Library, and at Rome in the Benedictine monastery of S. Callisto, are very beautifully decorated. The series of illustrations in the latter (the so-called Charlemagne Bible), and which afterwards constantly recur with few variations, is known as the *Speculum Humanæ Salvationis,* and contain subjects from the Old and New Testaments which embrace the entire history of the fall and redemption of man.

The English MSS. are fully equal to the Continental; and at an early period the Anglo-Saxons were even surpassed by the Irish and the monks of Iona. The *Benedictional* of St. Ethelwold (963-967), in the Duke of Devonshire's collection, is the most complete example of early English art. It was executed by a monk of Hyde Abbey (then the most celebrated place in England for such works) named Godeman, for Ethelwold, Bishop of Winchester. An English Psalter, in the British Museum, of the early part of the fourteenth century, which was presented to Queen Mary by Baldwin Smith, represents the art of the period unusually well. The celebrated Bedford missal, now in the possession of Sir John Tobin of Liverpool, who purchased it for 1100*l.*, was executed in France for John, Duke of Bedford, in the reign of Henry the Sixth, and contains the only known portrait of the Regent of

France. The great majority of illuminated books were religious; some few, however, such as romances, were secular, and are particularly valuable for their illustrations of costume, &c. Of these, one of the most frequently decorated during the fifteenth century was the French *Romaunt de la Rose,* a poem of the thirteenth century. The British Museum copy is considered the most beautiful. Our national collection of MSS. is now very rich, and additional facilities for obtaining some knowledge of manuscript illuminations have been afforded the public of late by the exhibition of a few of the paintings in glass cases.

3. Miniature Painting on Ivory and Enamel

Miniature painting, popularly understood, has, since the invention of printing superseded the art of the caligrapher and illuminator, been confined principally to portraiture, and the ancient vellum has been discarded for ivory and enamel. This is the most convenient place to consider the modern art, still it must be borne in mind that in nothing except smallness of size have the works of the late Sir William Ross, and the still living Mr. Thorburn, any affinity with the illuminations of such famous 'limners' of old as Don Silvestro Camaldolese or Girolamo dai Libri.

Ivory is preferred in modern practice for the soft semi-transparency of its texture, which communicates a peculiar delicacy to the colours, especially the carnations or flesh-tints. The ivory being cut in thin sheets, requires, however, on account of this property, something perfectly white and not liable to tarnish at the back to serve as a foil, otherwise the effect of the painting might be quite destroyed by the darkness of the surface behind showing through. Ivory and enamel being quite smooth, and without texture or absorbency, it is impossible to spread a flat tint. With the most dexterous handling, a little heap of colour will collect where the brush first touches or leaves the surface, and the intervening space, which it may have been intended to cover with an even 'wash,' will present something of the irregularity of a flow of water on a greasy plate or polished table. Hence, it becomes necessary to fill up the interstices of these irregularities with hatchings and stipplings. The point and steel scraper are both used, to more rapidly procure the desired gradation, as well as to obtain mechanical regularity in the stippling, which has been much sought for, particularly by French artists. It is true that the labour thus involved may be avoided in certain parts by the use of body-colours—that is to say, colours rendered opaque by the addition of white. But body-colour washes, from their unmanageable nature on ivory, can only be used in portions which can be covered at once, or do not require much finish, such as backgrounds and draperies; and here the surface of the ivory is, of course, sacrificed. Body-colour applied in this way will give an even, flat gradation in a background, and impart a *cloth-like* effect to the representation of the modern male costume; but, from the difficulty of calculating when 'wet' the difference of tone the body-colour will assume when dry, it is useless for flesh-painting, if spread in coats so as to cover the ivory. Opaque and semi-opaque pigments, of earthy and mineral extraction, were, we know, used in the flesh by the ancient painters on vellum, but then they were in general lightly stippled, not loaded; and such pigments may be worked transparently in the same way on ivory, though the modern miniature painters prefer the more transparent colours. Where body-colour, therefore, is laid on in certain parts, so as to cover the surface, and the ivory shows through in other portions, the work can scarcely be harmonious. For this reason the use of body-colours, which were extensively, and are still, employed by French miniature painters, has been discontinued by the English artists of the present century. Gum-water is the only vehicle besides simple water employed with the transparent or body-colours.

The large size of modern miniatures may excite some curiosity as to how a sheet of ivory can be obtained so much larger than the diameter of the largest elephant's tusk, especially when it is known that the sheet is not joined, as might be supposed. The tusk is simply sawn circularly in other words, round its circumference; the ivory is then steamed, and flattened under hydraulic pressure, and finally mounted with caoutchouc (rubber) on a mahogany panel.

Enamel painting has the great recommendation of being perfectly indestructible. Specimens of this art applied to pottery are now in existence which have not changed their hues during 3000 years. The enamel tints on Egyptian idols, scarabei, necklaces, &c., are precisely similar to the colours now produced by the enameller. The difficulty of handling the brush is quite as great as in painting on ivory. But a far greater technical difficulty is that of calculating the exact effect of the process of firing the enamel, in altering the hues of the several applications of colour. Fine colouring is therefore rarely found in enamels.

Moreover, the enamel painter's list of pigments is limited to those prepared from metallic oxides, and many metals are perfectly useless on account of the high degree of heat to which enamel paintings are subjected. Modern science has, however, done much to supply this deficiency. The colours are mixed with oil of spike or lavender, or with spirits of turpentine. These essential oils volatilize rapidly under the effect of heat, but the fixed oils would cause the enamel to blister. The ordinary brushes of the painter in watercolours are used.

We extract the following valuable remarks on enamel painting, and account of the process employed by the artists of the present day, from a communication to the *Art Journal*, in 1851, by Mr. W. Essex, himself (as well as his brother) an enamel painter of reputation. He says:

'Pictures in enamel of any importance as works of art have been very rarely produced until within the last eighty or ninety years;[52] for, although Petitôt, in the reign of Louis XIV, drew with exquisite neatness, he seldom produced enamels which aimed at more than microscopic finish, and accurate drawing of the human head. His works generally measure from about an inch and a half to two inches in diameter, and are usually either circular or oval. It was reserved for modern times to try a bolder flight, and the result has been that enamel paintings are now produced with every possible excellence in art. The rich depth of Rembrandt and Reynolds can be perfectly rendered, together with all their peculiarities of handling and texture; and the delicacy of the most beautiful miniature on ivory may be successfully competed with. As regards size, enamels are now painted measuring as much as 16 inches by 18, and 15 inches by 20. The kind of enamel used for pictorial purposes is called "Venetian white hard enamel:"

it is composed of silica, borax, and oxide of tin. The following is a brief description of procedure in the art of enamelling:

'To make a plate for the artist to paint upon: A piece of gold or copper [usually gilt] being chosen of the requisite dimensions, and varying from about an eighteenth to a sixteenth of an inch in thickness, is covered with pulverized enamel, and passed through the fire until it becomes of a bright white heat; another coat of enamel is then added, and the plate again fired; afterwards a thin laver of a substance called *flux* is laid upon the surface of the enamel, and the plate undergoes the action of heat for the third time. It is now ready for the painter to commence his picture upon. "Flux" partakes of the nature of glass and enamel it is semi-transparent, and liquefies more easily in the furnace than enamel. When flux is spread over a plate it imparts to it a brilliant surface, and renders it capable of receiving the colours: every colour during its manufacture is mixed with a small quantity of flux; thus, when the picture is fired, the flux of the plate unites with the flux of the colour, and the colouring pigment is perfectly excluded from the air by being surrounded by a dense vitrified mass. From this will be understood the indelible (and we might almost say eternal) nature of enamel.

'The plate undergoes the process of firing after each layer of colour is spread over the whole surface. This process corresponds to the drying of the pigments in oil or watercolour painting before the artist ventures to retouch his work. Sometimes a highly-finished enamel requires fifteen or twenty firings. Great care must be taken to paint without errors of any kind, as the colours cannot be painted out or taken off (as in water or oil) after they have once been vitrified without incurring excessive trouble and loss of time. If the unfortunate artist miscalculates the effect of the fire on his pigments, his only alternative is to grind out the tainted spot with pounded flint and an agate muller; and so hard is the surface that a square inch will probably take him a whole day to accomplish.'

Silver is very seldom used for the substratum of the plate (or *plaque)* of enamel for painting, because liable to blister, and brass is too fusible. Enamels are produced in great variety, but all are of a vitreous nature, although either opaque or transparent. White opaque enamel, we have seen, is used for painting on, but enamels of various colours are used, so to speak, for painting with. Of the latter, which is a species of mosaic, some description of one or two varieties has already been offered in our account of ancient and Byzantine mosaics. Then, again, the painting on or with these enamels, which are all applied to metals in various ways, is to be distinguished from painting on pottery, porcelain, and ceramic works generally.

Painting on ivory, to which in ordinary usage the word 'miniature' is especially applied, and the species of enamel painting, the process of which is above described, ranking high in public estimation, we shall give a slight glance at these arts and their history.

Miniature portraits may, in historical interest, often challenge comparison with large oil portraits.[53] They are equally valuable as records of costume; and the portable size of miniatures frequently alone secures their preservation, so that often they are all we have to enable us to recall the lineaments of the illustrious dead. Not only also is the work historically valuable, but we all know that a diminished resemblance of an object affords a special pleasure and illusion. Who has not looked, for instance, through an inverted telescope with almost childish delight? When, too, a miniature is painted on ivory, the warm, delicate, semi-transparent surface renders it susceptible of a certain polished beauty unattainable by other means. The minuteness of such works does not preclude the possibility of their possessing qualities of high art. In proof of which, we might adduce the small picture of 'The Three Graces,' by Raphael himself, or his sublime 'Vision of Ezekiel' in the Pitti Palace, Florence, as well as remind our readers of small pictures by Correggio and other of the greatest masters, not to mention most of the Dutch painters. If, indeed, smallness of size were any objection to a work of art, we should not esteem some of the most exquisite remains of antiquity—Greek glyptics—nor modern cameos, intaglios, and medallions.

Miniatures have, moreover, tender and romantic associations seldom attached to larger pictures. Many a miniature has been kissed by dying lips. These humble performances entwine themselves with human emotions, hopes, and regrets, perhaps more intimately than any other of the productions of genius. The mother treasures the resemblance of her lost son, and sheds tears over it in secret. They nestle in fair bosoms—sometimes lying unconsciously near breaking hearts. And many a manly breast has had no other consolation in danger or trial, on the battle-field or in exile. What strange and secret passages in the lives of the highborn and eminent, the worthy or infamous, would be disclosed could each little portrait tell its own tale! What extraordinary inedited materials for biography would be furnished, or *Mémoires pour servir* be supplied! The mere discovery of some of them having been worn would have involved loss of life or proscription, as, for example, under certain circumstances, the numerous lockets of the Pretender and Prince Charles.

It is a matter for some national gratulation that this charming branch of the fine arts has always been successfully practised in England; indeed, we excelled in it long before we obtained distinction in any other. We had Nicolas Hilliard, Isaac and Peter Oliver, when we were indebted to the foreigners, Holbein and Vandyke, for larger portraits. And although Petitôt and his brother-in-law, companion, and fellow-enameller, Bordier, were patronized by Charles I, they were quickly obliged to leave on the fall of their master, and their loss was more than compensated by our native miniature painters, Samuel Cooper and Hoskins; when, too, we were again obliged to employ for larger works the foreigners Lely and Kneller. Even up to the present time, with the exception of our own Samuel Cooper, few miniature painters of any country can compare with old Isaac Oliver. His execution is principally distinguished from that of our other great miniature painter, Cooper, by its patient and minute stippling; whilst that of Cooper has more the character of hatching, the 'drag' of the brush being evident. The latter is, therefore, more suggestive and descriptive. We must remember, however, that Cooper lived in an age of greater facility, and had the advantage of studying and copying the works of Vandyke (Cooper was called 'Vandyke in little'); yet the boldness and freedom of his style is scarcely more admirable than the delicate fidelity and truth to nature which distinguish the best pictures of Isaac Oliver, and which give them, together with their rarity, so great a value among collectors. His son, Peter Oliver, approaches very near his father in mere finish. The works of these artists may be studied to advantage in the fine collections of the Dukes of Portland and Buccleugh.

From the time of Hoskins and Cooper,—near which time also flourished Zincke, the enamel painter, Flatman, Gibson 'the dwarf,' and other inferior artists, — miniature painting continued to be cultivated, though met with so much success, down to the time of Cosway; and although his beautiful works are now considered wrong in method, and we have had within the present century quite a new style—we may almost call it a new school; still we asserted our superiority in this branch of art at the Exposition des Beaux Arts at Paris — a fact admitted even by French critics. Dr. Waagen, who states that he has been 'engaged for many years in compiling the materials for a history of miniature painting of various periods and countries,' says, that 'in no department have the English artists attained so high a state of perfection as in this.' We cannot but regret to find that since the introduction of coloured photographic portraits[54] the demand for this branch of art in its only tasteful and valuable form has become almost extinct.

The oldest miniatures have generally a brilliant ultramarine background, and gold is used in representing itself, as in other contemporary paintings, and also in modern Indian and Persian miniatures. Miniatures have, however, generally had a style of their own, not usually resembling closely that of other works of the same period. In respect to the practice of Sir William Ross, Mr. Thorburn, and other artists of our own time, whatever may be thought of its legitimacy, it must be confessed that qualities of richness, force, and depth are attained which were formerly looked for only in the oil pictures of Titian, Vandyke, and other such masters. Greater structural knowledge is also now displayed, which is probably due to the fact that most of the best miniature painters of this century have paid more attention to drawing in large than the earlier artists. For, as Haydon says, 'When a man who draws in large comes to paint in little, he compresses his knowledge; but a man who draws in little, when he paints in large, but enlarges his ignorance.'

The French have had several excellent miniature and enamel painters since Petitôt (whom Louis XIV welcomed from England and loaded with honours), more particularly during the time of the Empire—of whom may be mentioned Isabey, Augustin, Guerin, and Saint.

4. The Earlier Kinds of Art—Enamels and Enamel Painting

Both the application and composition of enamels are extremely diverse. But, in speaking of 'enamels,' we commonly understand the word as restricted to vitreous substances, either transparent or opaque, and white or variously coloured with metallic oxides, applied to a metallic recipient, and fused and fixed in a furnace. Painting on pottery, although claiming to be considered a variety of enamel painting, will be treated separately. We have already described, on account of its connection with miniature portrait painting, the most perfect form of enamel painting—a form however which it only assumed after passing through several gradations of inferiority; we may, therefore, now glance at the consecutive stages of development *seriatim.* And although the earlier varieties have, as already stated, a greater affinity with mosaic, their classification here will be more convenient, because the modern method of enamel painting has been derived step by step from the more mechanical operations of the mere enameller.

Enamels, then, have been applied to metals in three different ways, corresponding to three distinct periods; and they are thus distinguished, as forming three separate classes. 1. Incrusted; 2. Translucid upon relief; 3. Painted. In the first kind, the colours are divided from each other by thin lines of gold, the pattern or object represented being defined and mapped out into so many cells, by means of slender walls or partitions of gold filigree, before the colouring matter is inserted and fired. The appearance, therefore, is that of a kind of mosaic, each colour being enclosed in a case or setting of gold. Sometimes, however, the ground only is coloured. These enamels all partake of the Byzantine style, and this, together with the cumbrous process, however delicate the mere workmanship, combine to give almost unmitigated ugliness to the representations attempted. In the second kind, the design is delicately chiselled in relief upon the metal, the surface of which is then covered with translucid enamels. In the third, or most artistic kind, the use of the metal corresponds to that of the canvas or wood in oil painting: vitrifiable colours are laid on with a brush, either on the surface of the metal, or more generally upon a layer of enamel with which the metal has been previously coated, so as to produce at once the design and the colouring.

The first kind, or 'incrusted enamels,' is subdivided into two classes, and bear names given them by French antiquaries, viz., the *cloisonné* (partitioned), or, *à cloisons mobiles* (with moveable partitions), and the *champlevé* (cut or carved-out ground). We shall confine ourselves, in the first place, to the *cloisonné* enamels. In these the metal is first cut into the requisite shape, and provided with a little rim for the purpose of retaining the enamel. Thin strips, or fillets of the metal of the same width (or, we may say depth, supposing them measured vertically, as placed to receive the enamel), were then bent and fashioned in such a manner as to form the outline of the pattern or representation, and frequently even the most minute portions of the figure. These strips were next joined and fixed in an upright position upon the plate, thus forming a continuous metal outline. Each little bed or partition was then filled up with various enamels, reduced to a fine powder and moistened into a paste, and the piece finally underwent the firing process in a furnace. Sometimes the metal formed the ground out of which the space for the figure was scooped, the figure being then executed in the manner described. The colours used by the enameller were very rich: white, black, and lapis-lazuli (ultramarine) blue are always opaque; the other colours are sometimes opaque, sometimes semi-translucent. These enamels were also occasionally executed on copper. These *cloisonné* enamels are commonly of small size, and were chiefly used for ornamenting shrines, vases, crowns, and other objects; and when so employed they were fixed in a projecting setting, like precious stones. From having been executed upon a groundwork of gold, few have escaped the crucible of the goldsmith, and they are, therefore, very rare.

The crown of Charlemagne, preserved at Vienna, is ornamented with enamels of this description, representing Solomon, David, King Hezekiah,

Isaiah, and Christ. The workmanship is Greek; but, though retouched, it is believed the enamels must belong to this early period. The largest and finest known works of this process are, however, the famous Pala d'Oro at Venice, and parts of the shrine of the Three Kings at Cologne. The celebrated and much-revered relic, the Dagmar Cross of Denmark, a copy of which (as a pendant to a necklace) was given as a wedding-present to our Princess of Wales by her uncle the late King of Denmark, is a *cloisonné* enamel. The most curious specimen in England is the Alfred jewel in the Ashmolean Museum; and this is still more remarkable if, as is supposed, it was wrought by a British artist in the Byzantine manner. A pectoral cross in the possession of Mr. Beresford Hope also deserves mention. Sometimes, though rarely, the enamels were executed without a metal ground; that is to say, the colours were set clear in the metal network, like transparent precious stones, without foils. The *cloisonné* method is decidedly Byzantine, and the Greek artists appear to have derived the process from the Oriental nations, who practised the art in remote antiquity. If the classical nations were acquainted with enamelling, the methods were entirely lost in Italy and Greece. These *cloisonné* enamels came to be in very general use in the twelfth century; but in the fourteenth they were superseded by translucid enamels upon relief.

The second kind of incrusted enamels, it has been said, are called *champlevé*—cut or carved—out ground. In these, as in the last, a slender line of metal describes on the surface of the enamel the principal outlines of the design. But, instead of applying thin fillets of gold, the cells or cavities were scooped out of the substance of the groundwork, and thin walls of the metal left to form the outline and contain the vitreous matters. The flesh, and even the whole figure, were, however, not unfrequently represented by the metal, the outlines and the portions in shade being very finely engraved, or chiselled in bas-relief. The metal was almost always copper, the cheapness of the material admitting the use of plates of larger size. The *champlevé* enamels are generally complete works of art in themselves: unlike the former, which were usually attached as ornaments to pieces of jewellery and plate. The vitreous matter was commonly employed in the thirteenth and fourteenth centuries to colour nothing but the ground, and thus form a border round the figures in gilded metal. The practice of representing the flesh tints by enamels approaching the natural colour, and of using colours in the draperies, is peculiar to the eleventh and twelfth centuries. But when the figures were very minute the enamellers of this period expressed the carnations by lines incised on the gilded metal, and the draperies are then coloured by enamel; but if the whole of the little figures are engraved on a metal plate, the incisures are always filled with enamel.

The *champlevé* enamels were extensively applied from the eleventh to the fourteenth centuries to a variety of copper utensils for secular life, such as coffers, candlesticks; arms, rings, and jewels; but more especially to objects used for ecclesiastical purposes, such as crosses, sacramental vessels, pastoral staves, and book covers. The shrines which enclosed the reputed bones of saints and martyrs were in particular enriched with this beautiful incrustation, and even monuments of a larger size, such as tombs and altars. It is not surprising, therefore, that specimens of this manufacture are, comparatively speaking, common in public and private collections.

M. Labarte states, in his valuable article on enamels,[55] that these enamels are always distinguishable from those incrusted by the *cloisonné* process, although the earlier *champlevé* enamels could not escape the prevailing Byzantine taste. The French archaeologist and others claim for the *champlevé* process a strictly Western origin at a period when the art of enamelling did not exist in Italy and Greece, and long before, as he asserts, the Byzantines borrowed the *cloisonné* method from the Orientals. There is in the *Treatise upon Images* by Philostratus, a Greek by birth, but who afterwards established himself at Rome, an allusion to enamelling as an art known only to 'the barbarians living near the ocean, who pour colours on heated brass so that these adhere and become like stone, and preserve the design represented.' Specimens of enamel[56] have actually been found of the Gallo-Roman period, which agree perfectly with the narrative of this writer as regards the materials of their composition, and the localities in which they have been discovered. It may then, M. Labarte infers, be considered as established that the art was unknown in Italy and Greece at the beginning of the third century of the Christian era, but that it was practised at this period in the industrial cities of Western Gaul. Limoges, albeit a Roman colony, may be presumed to have been one of these cities.

Be this as it may, the enamellers of the school which began to flourish at Limoges in the eleventh century, though preserving their own method of fabrication, owed much, at least, of their style to the establishment of a Venetian colony of merchants, who made Limoges a kind of depôt for the supply of central France with the articles they imported at Marseilles, and at the same time introduced some of the Greek artists who had been received with favour at Venice from the Iconoclastic persecution. This explains how the earliest Limousin enamels may be easily mistaken for Byzantine. From the twelfth century the Limousin enamellers acquired great celebrity; and till the end of the fourteenth, Limoges continued to be the head-quarters of the art; and the comparative cheapness and durability of the process caused a regular demand for Limoges work, not only in France but throughout Europe. The Limousin artists during the thirteenth century were sometimes sent for at great expense from various parts of France; and their own enterprise probably carried them to more distant regions. To this is perhaps ascribable the establishment in some town on the Rhine of what has been claimed as a distinct school of enamelling on copper by the *champlevé* process. The productions of this school cannot, however, be distinguished by ordinary observers from the manufactures of Limoges, except where the character of the design is clearly German.

But this rude, mechanical, and mosaic-like method of encrustation could not satisfy a more artistic age, and accordingly a new style of enamelling was introduced into Italy towards the close of the thirteenth century. This, the second of the methods of applying the enamel to metal we have enumerated, is that of 'translucid enamels upon relief.' In this process the metal surface itself was engraved, or chased, into bas-relief, and then a translucent coating of coloured enamels fused over the whole, through which the design below was visible. The higher skill of the goldsmith's art at its most glorious period being here brought into operation, such works became the vehicle of the most beautiful designs of the most accomplished artists.

Nevertheless, there are fine specimens of Italian metal work and enamelling which nearly resemble mechanically one description of *champlevé* enamels. These consist in figures or ornaments engraved upon silver, and executed in niello work, with a ground of opaque blue enamel. Many examples might be mentioned, but those of the celebrated silver altar at Pistoia and that of the Baptistery of S. Giovanni at Florence will suffice. The enamels upon these altars present, at first sight—setting aside the metal employed and the style of the figures—a great analogy with the later Limousin enamels, in which the figures are expressed by a fine engraving upon metal, and the background alone enamelled. But, upon close examination, it is found that in the enamelled portions the metal was not scooped out deeply as in the *champlevé* enamels; the space is only very slightly depressed, and the enamels have been laid on according to the process adopted for translucid enamels.

In the early part of the fourteenth century this style of translucid enamelling was brought to great perfection, and one of its greatest masters, Benvenuto Cellini, has left, in his *Trattato sopra l'Orificeria,* a minute description of the improved methods. Antonio Pollajuolo greatly distinguished himself in his chasings covered with enamel. 'The most delicate pencil,' says Vasari, 'could not have finished them more exquisitely.' But Francesco Francia, as famous a goldsmith as a painter, surpassed all his contemporaries in his enamelling on silver. Niccolo Pisano has the credit of the first discovery of this method. The new style was not practised long before it was imported from Italy into France, and there the enamels of this kind received the name of *émaux de basse taille.* The well-known pastoral staff of William of Wykeham, and the famous cup from King's Lynn, are ornamented with enamels of this description.

The artists of Limoges, finding the Italian process had, at the close of the fourteenth century, superseded all others in public estimation, would of course be desirous to discover a still further improved method. In this it has been thought they succeeded by the invention[57] of the third kind, or true 'painted enamels,' which differed essentially from all hitherto described. The gold and copper outlines were dispensed with altogether; as also the use of the graver to express the design—this was now executed with the brush, so that great freedom was attained, and an unlimited variety of treatment rendered possible. The metal was either entirely concealed under a coat of enamel, or, if left uncovered, served as a subjectile to the opaque painting in the same way as wood, canvas, vellum, or ivory. It was probably the modifications introduced in the fourteenth century in the art of painting upon glass, which suggested this new style of enamelling. Mosaic grounds of coloured glass were at this time almost entirely discontinued, and artists had begun to paint superficially upon glass with enamel colours. It became then evident that what was done upon glass might also be done upon copper, with the difference only of giving, either naturally or artificially, complete opaqueness to the colours. Lucca della Robbia, it is true, produced a kind of enamelling; but he was a sculptor belonging to the fifteenth century, and his works are only reliefs in clay enamelled in white or colours; there is in them no painting properly so called. Painting on majolica in Italy also commenced some considerable time after the Limoges artists had produced their first painted enamels. We cannot do better than quote the concise description given by the French antiquary, M. Labarte, of the various processes successively adopted in an art peculiarly French, and which contributed so much to mark the Renaissance.[58]

'The first attempts at this new kind of painting were, of necessity, very imperfect . . . The Abbé Texier has an enamel representing St. Christopher, which he considers one of the earliest specimens of the art. The enamel colours are applied upon the metal in layers sufficiently thick to admit of the movement of the drapery which covers the shoulders of the saint, and the agitation of the waves which bathe his legs being expressed by inequalities of the enamel paste, which is of a uniform colour. The drawing of these first attempts is always very defective, and the enamel colours are applied immediately to the metal itself.

'Towards the middle of the fifteenth century painting in enamel had made great progress, and, with the specimens now before us,[59] we are enabled to explain the processes employed in making them. On an unpolished plate of copper the enameller traced with a style *[stylus]* the outline of the figure or subject to be represented. The plate was then overlaid with a thin translucid flux; after which the enameller began to apply his colours. The outlines of the drawing traced by the style were first covered over with a dark-coloured enamel, which was to give the outline upon the surface of the picture; the draperies, the sky, the backgrounds, and accessories were then represented by enamel colours in tolerably thick layers, filling up the spaces intervening between the dark-coloured outline, which, as it were, performed the same office as the lines of metal in the process of incrusted enamels. There was, therefore, a total absence of shadow in this painting, in which the first design was expressed by thickness of colours. The space for the flesh tints was filled with a black or deep violet enamel; they were then rendered upon this ground by white enamel, applied in layers more or less thin, in order to preserve the shadows, and thereby indicate, very lightly in relief, the principal bony and muscular parts of the face and body; consequently in this process all the carnations have a bistre or violet hue, by which they may be easily recognised.

'In order to produce effect in the rest of the painting in which the shadows were entirely wanting, the light parts of the hair, draperies, and background were most frequently indicated by touches of gold. The imitations of precious stones applied upon the mantles of the saints and upon the draperies are peculiar to this description of enamels, which are generally painted upon flat pieces of copper, rather thick and coated with a thick enamel at the back, presenting a vitreous appearance.

'In the beginning of the sixteenth century, when the arts of design were making such rapid progress, so imperfect a process as the first attempts in enamel painting could not long be sustained in practice. Accordingly, about this period, we find a great change in the processes employed by enamel painters. Before beginning their painting they covered the plate of copper with a thickish layer of enamel, either black or of a deep colour. Upon the ground thus prepared, they executed the drawing by means of different processes with white opaque enamel in such a manner as to produce a *grisaille*,[60] of which the shadows were obtained, either by laying on this white enamel less thickly in some parts than in others, or by scraping it away to let the background reappear; which latter operation was to be performed before the firing of the piece. A few heightenings of white and gold were added to increase the effect. The carnations continued, as before, to be lightly laid on in relief, but were almost always expressed by a flesh-coloured enamel.

'If the piece, instead of remaining in grisaille, was to be coloured, the different colours of a semi-transparent enamel were spread over the grisaille. In the coloured enamels of this class the sky and some portions of the ground were often represented by thick layers of colour. The piece was of course placed several times in the furnace during these operations, which could only be done in succession. Thus, by adding an enamel ground to the plate of copper, before beginning the painting, the colours were rendered capable of being worked with freedom and at different times, and became susceptible of every kind of combination and of every gradation of tint resulting from this fusion. The drawing and painting were also rendered more perfect from the facility of re-touching. The Limousin enamellers possessed a great many other processes and resources.' One of these in particular they frequently made use of. 'In different parts of the draperies and accessories,[61] a leaf of gold or silver, called *paillon* or *clinquant,* was fixed upon the enamel ground; upon this thin leaf of metal the shadows were painted; it was then covered with a coloured translucid enamel; the lustre of the metal gave a brilliant effect, which the artist knew how to turn to advantage.

'The talents of the enamel painters of the sixteenth century were exercised on a vast number of objects, and present a great variety. Until towards the end of the first third of this century, painting in enamel was employed almost exclusively for the representation of sacred subjects, of which the German schools supplied the models; but the arrival of the Italian artists at the court of Francis I, and the publication of engravings of the works of Raphael and other great Italian masters, gave a new direction to the school of Limoges, which adopted the style of the Italian Renaissance. Cartoons for the Limousin enamellers were painted by Rosso and Primaticcio; a circumstance which has given rise to the idea that they themselves painted in enamel. The delightful productions of the engravers, to whom have been given the name of "Petits maîtres," furnished also excellent subjects for the artists in enamel. Dating from about the middle of the sixteenth century, the enamellers no longer confined themselves to the production of small pictures; they created a new style of metal-work. Basins, ewers, cups, plates, vases, and utensils of every kind, formed of thin sheets of copper, and most elegant in design, were overlaid with their rich and brilliant paintings.'

The names of numerous Limousin enamellers have been preserved; of whom may be mentioned Leonard Limousin (the latter name conferred upon him by Francis I to distinguish him from Leonardo da Vinci); Pierre Raymond; four artists of the name of Pénicaud; numerous painters of the Courteys family; Jean Limousin, Pierre Noalher; and Noël Laudin.

The last great improvement was the discovery by Jean Toutin of the present mode of painting, already described in the notice of miniature, and in which a set of vitrifiable and opaque colours were laid upon a white enamel ground, gold being employed to receive the enamel on account of its bearing a higher temperature. Toutin was not exactly the inventor of this new method, for Leonard attempted several times to paint with enamel colours on a white ground; but the coloured enamels employed were not adapted for the purpose. In the execution of the new enamel paintings, Toutin was assisted by Isaac Gribelin, a celebrated crayon painter. But these were far surpassed by the famous artists Petitôt and Bordier, of whom we have already spoken.

A remarkable exhibition of the works of the Limousin artists of all periods took place in 1858 at Limoges itself.

5. Painting on Pottery and Porcelain

Painting on pottery usually bears something of the same relation to the more delicate enamel painting that watercolour bears to miniature painting. In our account of Greek painting some few notices of antique vase painting have already been given. Mr. Birch, in his learned *History of Ancient Pottery,* tells us that there were competitive exhibitions, among other works of art, of clay figures also, and that the method of colouring them was extensively practised by artists who were solely employed in painting statues, bas-reliefs, and other architectural accessories. The famous sculptors Phidias, Polycletus, and Myron did not disdain to furnish designs of vases for the potters of their time; from which it may reasonably be inferred that some of the painters of the figures on these vases also ranked high as artists. In almost every age pottery has been a favourite vehicle for the display of art. Yet the art of *decorative* pottery, which is alone that with which we are concerned, was entirely lost in Europe during the Middle Ages. The process of the lustrous *glazing* of the Roman pottery appears to have been lost about the third century of our era. The first reappearance of the art was in Spain, whither the Moorish invaders had carried with them the manufacture of the enamelled tiles with which the mosques of Persia, Arabia, and the African sea-board were adorned. This kind of tile is of a pale clay coated over with an opaque white enamel, upon which are traced elaborate patterns in various colours, chiefly blue and brown, and sometimes iridescent, or resembling mother-of-pearl. But this Moorish pottery of Spain was by no means confined to tiles, for jars and vases of great beauty are known to exist. It appears, however, from a passage in the 10th chapter of the second book of the treatise by Theophilus, that in his time the Byzantine Greeks possessed a method of decorating pottery both with colours fixed by the action of fire (which can be no other than vitrifiable colours—true enamels), and with gold and silver leaf. Damascus was the great seat of this as well as other manufactures. Nevertheless, to the celebrated Italian majolica, universal tradition has assigned a Moorish origin. This much is certain, that an opaque stanniferous enamel was known to the Arabs of Spain, at least from the end of the thirteenth century; and consequently more than one hundred years before Lucca della Robbia produced in Italy his enamelled earthenware bas-reliefs.

The first introduction of the Moorish pottery into Italy is attributed to the following circumstance: The Republic of Pisa, after a long siege, conquered in 1115 Nazaredeck, the Mussulman corsair of Majorca, and among the spoils carried back to Italy were numerous plates or *bacini of* the painted Moorish pottery. Many of these trophies may still be seen incrusted in the walls and towers of the Pisan churches, and, indeed, in other parts of Italy. It was traditionally believed in Italy that the process of manufacture was imported from the same place; and being adopted by the Italian potters, was named majolica, after Majorca, the island, whence the original specimens were obtained.

Majolica, heretofore more commonly known in this country as 'Raphael ware,' or 'Faenza ware,' has always been held in some estimation from the universal belief that Raphael himself had, in the outset of his career, condescended to paint plates and dishes of this ware. During the last few years, although stripped of the interest conferred upon it by this reputed association, it has met with more intelligent appreciation, more particularly since the exhibition of the Soulages collection. Majolica is now recognised as an important development of industrial and decorative art, as excellent in its degree as the great works of painting and sculpture of the age in which it arrived at perfection, and worthy of imitation by the art-manufacturers of the present day.

In tracing the history of this important description of pottery, we find Pesaro was the first place in Italy to improve upon the Hispano-Arabic process. Here a method was practised as early as 1300 of imparting an iridescent metallic glaze to an opaque white enamelling. More than a century after this Lucca della Robbia discovered his stanniferous enamel for application on terra-cotta. After 1450, the Lords of Pesaro gave great encouragement to the manufacture of earthenware. The productions of this period, which reached considerable perfection, are called *mezza majolica.* There are comparatively few specimens; but the drawing in them is tolerably pure, though hard and dry. The outlines of the figures are black or blue, the white ground is left for the flesh, and the draperies are coloured. But the greatest peculiarity is the iridescent metallic lustre, and especially a beautiful ruby-red colour employed in the draperies and decorations. This colour was subsequently in use at Gubbio in 1518; but the secret of its preparation was completely lost about thirty years afterwards. An iridescent yellow also occurs, which has all the appearance of gold.

About the middle of the fifteenth century the practice of artistic pottery had extended to Faenza—whence is derived the French name *faïence* (which is now used by English writers in place of the old Anglicised word 'fayence')—a name which has been generally, though without strict propriety, given to all the enamelled earthenware of Italy. The manufacturers of Faenza and Florence were the first to cover their pottery with a white enamel glaze. Towards the end of the century the manufacturers of a number of towns in central Italy—of Urbino, Gubbio, Castel-Durante, and Pesara—had adopted the improvement. This process constitutes true majolica, the *majolica-fina*. The method of fabrication was simple and rapid; the pieces receiving a vitrescent opaque coating, which entirely concealed the dirty colour of the paste. The paintings were then executed in vitrifiable colours, and the fusion of these completed the firing.

The painters were no longer contented with mere decorative painting of arms, foliage, ornaments, or, at most, single figures, but attempted historical subjects and copied cartoons furnished for them by painters of reputation.

From 1530 the art rapidly progressed. A very celebrated artist of this time was named Giorgio Andreoli: he signs his fine paintings on dishes 'M° G°' (Maestro Giorgio). His colouring is extremely rich, and in his works we find the golden yellow, the ruby red, and the brilliant iridescent lustre of the early majolica. Guidobaldo II, Duke of Urbino, was the great patron of the ceramic artists. He collected for them a large number of original drawings by Raphael and his pupils. Some majolica compositions seem evidently to have emanated from Raphael himself, though they have neither been painted nor engraved. There are also what we should suppose at first sight copies of his large well-known works; but, from differences in details, these paintings must have been executed from sketches now lost. All this might naturally lead to the belief that the great master himself painted in enamel on majolica; but no pieces in which his compositions may be traced bear a date before that of his death.

The majolica painters copied the engravings of Marc Antonio as well as drawings by the best masters, but they had also original artists of their own, and the art was carried to perfection by Orazio Fontana. A short quarter of a century embraced the beginning and the end of the period of highest perfection. From 1560 the art rapidly declined, although the processes were imitated with more or less success in other parts of Italy. An attempt to revive the manufacture at Pesaro, in 1763, was unsuccessful.

It is, of course, not within our province to describe the various kinds of earthenware, the ornaments of which are coloured reliefs, but which contain no artistic painting strictly speaking—no painting on a flat surface with shading colours. We must, therefore, pass by the fine French faïence, so mysterious and unique in its kind, called Henry II ware, and also the enamelled earthenware now so familiar to us in the form of green dishes, bristling all over with contorted eels, snakes and reptiles, cray-fish and shells, and the discovery of the fabrication of which gave such a romantic colour to the life of Bernard Palissy. It requires, also, only to be remarked of the stonewares of Flanders and Germany, that some specimens have polychromatic enamels upon relief.

Nor need we recall how artificial, or soft porcelain *(pâte tendre),* was first made at St. Cloud; or how Böttcher, in Saxony, became a life-long prisoner through his undertaking to imitate Oriental porcelain; how be at length succeeded, through the accidental discovery of kaolin, or the white earth, which forms the principal base of true porcelain; or, finally, how this natural or true porcelain was at length made at Sèvres. For the true understanding of ceramic mysteries, are there not such books as Marryat's *History of Pottery and Porcelain, Mediaeval and Modern?* Suffice it to say, that painters, as well as sculptors, were engaged to bring the Saxon porcelain (or, as it is called, 'Dresden china') to perfection, and that the still more artistic porcelain of Sèvres, especially the costly 'old Sèvres,' with its beautiful *bleu de roi,* and *rose Dubarry* grounds, has been ornamented with paintings by some of the best miniature painters of France.

6. Glass Painting

Some account of Glass painting (properly so called), which is believed to have originated from the tenth to the twelfth century, will be necessary, in order to give a complete view of the applications of painting in the Middle

Ages, before directing our attention to fresco and the improved oil painting of the Van Eycks.

Stained glass must not be confounded with *painted* glass. In stained glass the colouring is either a superficial layer, or pervades the substance of the glass, and is obtained by applying a layer of metallic oxides in the process of manufacture, or by mixing them with the glass in a state of fusion. The art of joining small pieces of stained glass together, so as to form a coloured design or species of transparent mosaic, was, it is believed by many, practised in classical times. Although, however, panes of glass and window-frames have been found at Pompeii and Rome, and although the ancients were perfectly acquainted with the art of colouring glass, as is evident from the Portland and other vases, &c., yet the fragments of ancient window-glass hitherto discovered are all white. But in the first ages of Christianity, when the ancient basilicas were converted into Christian temples, it is certain that windows in these new churches were adorned with stained glass. Nevertheless, throughout the dark ages, it is equally certain that windows of any kind were far from common, even for churches. A window filled with slabs of a transparent kind of alabaster is still preserved in the church of S. Miniato at Florence; which was built in the commencement of the eleventh century. The use of glass windows in private houses was extremely limited during the Middle Ages. In France they were not employed till the close of the fourteenth century, and then very rarely; while in England they were not in common use till the reign of Henry the Eighth. The ordinary substitutes were parchment and linen; and in France, paper, rendered more transparent by oil or grease, was much employed in domestic architecture, even at a late period.

The brilliancy of the early glass mosaics would naturally induce a wish to trace upon them figures and subjects. The origin of painting on glass is, however, involved in obscurity. There are no existing specimens to which can be assigned with certainty an earlier date than that of the eleventh century; but mention is made in 949 of 'a portrait of King Constantine (VII), admirably executed on stained glass.' The earliest painted glass in York Cathedral was executed about 1200.

The first attempts at glass painting were made by forming pieces of stained glass into figures, and painting the shadows of the draperies and other parts with a brush and a vitrifiable or enamel black, reddish or bistre colour, which was fixed in the furnace. The painted windows of the twelfth and thirteenth centuries are all executed in this way, and have in other respects a general resemblance. The ground of the window consisted of mosaic work, arranged in squares or lozenge-shaped compartments, and filled with quatrefoils, trefoils, and other ornaments. Over this were symmetrically distributed little medallions of various forms, containing painted historical subjects, the whole design being surrounded with borders of varied patterns. The subjects of the medallions are taken from the legendary history of saints more frequently than from the Old or the New Testament. The principal outlines of the design, both of the medallions and the grounds, are formed by the lines of lead used for holding the different pieces of glass together. Subsequently, the little medallions were replaced by isolated figures of a larger size, on a mosaic background. These windows have a pure decorative character, invariably harmonizing with the architectural effect of the edifice to which they belong. And, notwithstanding the general brilliancy of the colours, from the pieces of glass being rarely plain, these windows shed a very impressive 'dim religious light.'

This kind of semi-painting — for it is to be remembered that the local colours were given by the several pieces of various coloured glass — was afterwards superseded by painting on glass, in the fuller signification of the words. This, however, was executed in various ways. Sometimes the colours were diluted with a tempera medium, namely, white of egg; and sometimes they were mixed with oil, and afterwards varnished in both cases. One of the earliest applications in Italy of transparent oil colours was for this painting on glass.

But the varnish did not long protect the paintings executed by either of these methods against the action of damp and sunlight. Vitrifiable colours were therefore introduced, and from time to time increased in number, till the glass painters of the middle of the fifteenth century were enabled to give up entirely glasses stained in the mass, and to paint upon a single piece of white glass with enamel colours laid upon one or both surfaces, the glass answering the same purpose as wood or canvas in oil painting. This, then, was enamel painting on glass; the colours were true enamels, coloured by metallic oxides; the vehicle was a vitreous compound, or 'flux'; and the painting was fixed upon the glass, and incorporated with it by firing the plate of glass in a furnace.

The invention of this glass enamelling has been ascribed to the Flemings or Germans; but Le Vieil, a celebrated French writer on glass, claims the honour for France, giving it as his opinion that painting on glass, properly speaking, took its rise in that country in the eleventh century. From the celebrity of the glass works at Murano, it might be supposed that the Venetians would have excelled in the art of painting on glass; but this has not been the case. The art was but little practised by them, and the glass manufactured at Murano was found too opaque for this purpose. The art has, however, been practised in other parts of Italy, and Vasari has given a lengthened description of it; but it appears that the Italians procured much of their coloured glass *(smalti)* from Germany, and if they did not thence obtain all their glass for painting, they sometimes employed German glass makers, or Italians who had been in Germany. The glass, for example, in the windows of the Duomo of Florence (which were painted by the famous Lorenzo Ghiberti) was made by a Tuscan who had learnt the art in Lubeck —contrary to Vasari's assertion that the glass was Venetian. The most distinguished painter on glass of the fifteenth century, in Italy, was a native of Ulm in Germany—Beato Giacomo da Ulmo. The discovery of the art of staining glass a transparent yellow with silver has been ascribed to Van Eyck; but it is attributable with greater reason to this Fra Giacomo. Another, also, and the greatest of all the artists who practised painting on glass in Italy, was not a native—as, indeed, is implied by his name, Guglielmo de Marcillat—that is to say, if the usual interpretation of this name, as 'William of Marseilles,' is correct, of which, however, Mrs. Merrifield shows there is some doubt: at all events, there is no doubt he was a Frenchman. Vasari mentions the great dexterity of Guglielmo in applying different colours to the same piece of glass. This was effected by using a white glass coated or cased with red; certain parts of the red glass, which formed the local colour of the draperies, were ground away, and in these parts new layers of glass variously coloured were introduced, which were fixed by firing under the muffle.

In the fourteenth century the glass painters already began to copy nature with some success. The light and shade become more vigorous, and the flesh, instead of being represented by violet-tinted glass, as in the oldest specimens, is painted on white glass with a reddish-grey colour. The pieces of glass are larger, the strips of lead are placed at wider intervals, large single figures occupying a whole window become more common, and these figures are placed under elaborate canopies, and on a plain blue or red, instead of mosaic ground.

From the beginning of the fifteenth century the tendency of the artists to produce individual works is more and more observable. The decorations which, like frames, surround the figures and subjects, and which always are borrowed from the architecture of the time, are increased from day to day, and present a great complexity of lines and ornaments, which have often a very beautiful effect. During the greater part of the fifteenth century, the legends painted upon the phylacteries explain the subjects most commonly by a verse of Scripture. The blue or red hangings introduced behind the figures are of damasked stuff's of great richness. Borders are rare, and when found consist of branches of rather meagre foliage, painted upon long strips of glass. The artists make frequent use of grisailles, which admit a great deal of light into the edifices, but produce none of those fine effects of the old coloured mosaics. In the second half of the fifteenth century, buildings and landscapes in perspective were first introduced.

In the sixteenth century, artists showed great skill in producing graceful compositions, depth of background, trees, fruits, and flowers. Claude, Bernard Palissy, Guillaume, Jean Cousin, Pinaigrier, and many others, distinguished themselves in this style of painting, and produced works of great correctness of drawing and remarkable execution.[62] But the era of legitimate glass painting was at an end. From the moment that it was attempted to transform an art of purely monumental decoration into an art of expression and full pictorial character, its intention was perverted, its true principles were violated, and this led of necessity to its ruin. The resources of glass painting were more limited than those of oil, with which it was unable to compete, and in the attempt to do so it lost much of its own peculiar charm. From the end of the sixteenth century the art was in its decline, and towards the middle of the seventeenth was entirely given up.

In Germany and Switzerland, from the beginning of the fifteenth century, painted glass was very much used in the decoration of private houses as well as for religious purposes. There has been an attempt of late years to revive the art of painting on glass, both at home and abroad: but too often we find the misconception of its proper function alluded to above. In the window, for example, from Milan, in the Great Exhibition of 1851, the chiaroscuro was so powerfully expressed, that some of the shadows were quite opaque, which can scarcely be allowed as a legitimate effect, whatever the abstract merits as a work of art, in an object primarily intended for the transmission of light. The colours of modern glass appear, also, comparatively poor; but may not this be partly the result of age, as well as manufacture or method of painting? We all know the purifying as well as the bleaching effect of light; and may we not reasonably suppose that, during the long ages the old glass has been permeated and saturated by floods of sunlight, that the colours have been chastened, purified, and exalted in brilliancy?

Chapter 7

Fresco Painting

The fact that the grandest works of human genius in painting have been executed in fresco, not to speak of the great development in our times of fresco painting in Germany, and the revival of this style of art in England for the decoration of the New Palace at Westminster, will justify our treating the subject at some length; especially as the details are interesting, and there appear to be frequent misconceptions in reference thereunto.

Painting in fresco—in Italian *al fresco*—takes its name from being executed upon the last coat, while it is *freshly* laid and still wet, which the plasterer puts on when finishing a room. This last coat, called by the Italians *intonaco, is* composed of finely-sifted river-sand and lime mixed in certain proportions. The well-known tendency of lime thus used to imbibe water and harden, gives its peculiar character and durability to fresco. The colours being ground in water and mixed with lime when applied to this absorbent surface, become incorporated with the lime-water and sand of the plaster;[63] and in drying a crystallization takes place over the surface, and the colours (if wholly applied while the plaster remains wet) are not to be dissolved again by water externally applied, although internal damp will in time, even when every precaution may seem to have been taken, have the most injurious effect. The basis of fresco and the colours become, then, under favourable circumstances, inseparable and positively harder than stone. The compound resulting simply from the mixture of the sand and lime is indeed one of the most durable and changeless with which the chemist is acquainted, namely, silicate of lime. The rapidity with which this coat of plaster dries, presents to the artist one of the greatest difficulties of the process. Only so much of the plaster must be laid on as the painter can cover and complete as a portion of a picture in one day. Joinings are therefore unavoidable, and some ingenuity is necessary to conceal them by making them coincide with lines in the composition, or take place in shadows.

Only those colours can be used which light will not act upon or lime deteriorate.[64] The fresco painter is therefore limited to a few pigments, which are principally natural colours or earths, and consequently sober in hue. The blue is the only brilliant colour in fresco; but the old masters rarely employed either the cobalt or the still more beautiful ultramarine used in modern frescoes; probably on account, partly, of the expensiveness of those colours. Their blues, therefore, being generally imperfectly prepared mineral compositions, have commonly faded; the frescoes by Guercino being one of the rare exceptions. The blacks and greys, which are nearly all derived from animal and vegetable substances, have also proved very fugitive. Lime is mixed, as we have said, with the colours; but lime itself is also used alone as a pigment for the lights, the presence of sand with the lime rendering the plaster ground a delicate half-tint. The German fresco painters consider it indispensable that the lime should be slaked and kept buried underground several years before it is used, either as a pigment or for coating the walls. Early authorities do not, however, insist upon the necessity of keeping the lime for a very long period, and there is no apparent scientific reason for doing so.

From the power of absorption, little force of shadow is attainable in fresco compared to the depth and transparency of oil painting; but this deficiency is more than compensated, for internal decoration, by the far greater luminousness of colour in fresco and its breadth of bright pearly effect. The colours assume, as it were, crystalline brilliancy; yet with none of the glare of an oil painting, which prevents, if the picture be large, a great portion being seen; the colours, moreover, do not become embrowned with age, like those mixed with oil. Some of the disadvantages of oil painting for large monumental and decorative works here alluded to may be observed in the Whitehall ceiling painted by Rubens. And, although the style itself of fresco is more brilliant, in early frescoes the colours were, in addition, actually used pure and unbroken. These frescoes, it should, however, be remembered, were executed in chapels always pervaded by solemn twilight; the colours, therefore, would not appear at all gaudy; the gloom was, in fact, provided against by this extra brightness and crudeness of colour. The same remark applies to the ancient remains at Pompeii and elsewhere. Houses in such a climate were naturally kept dark, to exclude the summer heat; the crudest tones were, therefore, harmonized, and became almost necessary.

'The power of fresco,' Haydon says, 'lies in light — the power of oil in depth and tone. A mighty space of luminous depth and "darkness visible" gives a murky splendour to a hall or public building. A mighty space of silvery breadth and genial fleshiness—with lovely faces, and azure draperies, and sunny clouds, and heroic forms—elevates the spirits, and gives a gaiety and triumphant joy to the mind. The less shadow in decoration the better.'

The material limitations, then, of fresco, and its being restricted from the resources of other kinds of painting, compel greater attention to the higher and more essential qualities of art. Its immediate and necessary connection with the highest aims of art precisely fits it, therefore, to embody those inventions which belong essentially to the domain of thought. It thus becomes a great test both of artistic knowledge and conception; and hence it is very generally acknowledged to be the noblest style of art.[65] An intimate acquaintance with everything represented is 'essential by compulsion.' Defects in composition, form, action, expression, and the treatment of drapery may be redeemed in an oil painting by various technical merits; not so in fresco.

Here we have not, generally speaking, the allurements of transparency, depth, richness, showy handling, texture, and other of the more material characteristics of oil painting; which, though not the grand essentials of art, may yet please and form the principal excellence of pictures worthy of commendation; but, here, there is no evading such things as anatomy, drawing, and expression.

Fresco (and of course the less durable methods of oil and distemper) is very much affected in time by the nature of the wall upon which the plaster is spread. The following are the conclusions on this subject given in the various reports of the Royal Commission on the Fine Arts, having reference to the decoration of the New Palace, Westminster. Ashlar walls, that is to say, walls composed of freestones as they come out of the quarry, are objectionable, because they become very wet in warm weather, from the condensation of the damp in the atmosphere on the cold wall. Rubble walls are worse; from the loose, incongruous materials employed: many of the most precious works of the great masters owe their destruction chiefly to the circumstance of being painted on walls of this description. Frescoes may be safely executed upon lath (strip or sheet of wood). But brick walls are, upon the whole, the most eligible.

The following is a sketch of the method employed: It is assumed that it is impossible to retouch a fresco painting to any extent. The portion of work undertaken in the morning must be completed during the day. Hence every part of the design must be defined in preparatory studies. The fresco is, in fact, a copy from these, the former being traced on the wall from a finished drawing or drawings of the same size. Such large preparatory drawings are termed *cartoons*. A cartoon, when of the kind prepared for tracing a fresco, is a simple black and white drawing without colours: such, for example, as the two large charcoal drawings by Agostino Carracci in the National Gallery. But an additional coloured cartoon was also prepared to serve as a study of colour, and a guide during the execution of the fresco. Such cartoons for fresco are preserved in the different collections throughout Europe. Similar finished cartoons were also designed for tapestry; the well-known series of cartoons by Raphael at Hampton Court affording a notable instance. The worker in tapestry traced the outlines, and matched as nearly as possible the colours; frequently, however, introducing, in the lights, heightenings of gold and silver threads. (For a few words on what we may call painting in embroidery, see note F in Appendix.)

The cartoon for a fresco is generally enlarged from small drawings of the whole composition, with the aid of careful separate studies for the more important parts. As an assistance in these drawings, several of the greatest masters (many of whom were sculptors as well as painters) modelled their figures in wax or clay, and arranged draperies on them composed of linen or muslin saturated in clay-water. These models were disposed according to the intended arrangement, and from them the incidental effects of light and shade were studied. They were especially serviceable also in enabling the artist to conquer the difficulties of foreshortening; and it was by such means that Correggio painted his wonderful foreshortened figures in the cupolas at Parma.

When the fresco is to be very large, and it is found inconvenient to prepare a cartoon of the same size, the drawing may be made less in some proportionate degree, fractional or integral, and afterwards enlarged by squares to the full dimensions, portion by portion; or the whole composition of the full size may be divided into two or more cartoons. Raphael's cartoon for the 'School of Athens' was divided in this way; and the portion preserved in the Ambrosian Library at Milan contains the figures only without the architecture.

A finished drawing of the full size (or a portion) being ready, a part of this 'working' outline, as much as can be finished in a day, is now nailed to the wall, and transferred by tracing, or, as it is also called, *tallying*. This is effected either by pricking through the lines into the wet wall, and pouncing the holes with red or black dust, or by tracing the outline with a sharp point, which leaves slightly indented lines on the plaster. Besides the cartoon in which the forms and general light and shade are determined, it is desirable, for reasons already given, to have a coloured sketch of the whole composition. This is frequently prepared by the oil painter, but it is ordinarily found almost indispensable in fresco, in which, when once finished, it is as impossible to change colours as forms. Some few, it is true, of the great Italian fresco painters commenced at once upon the wet wall, merely marking the relative position of the figures with a few strokes of the point; but fresco painting has so many unavoidable difficulties, that the modern artist finds it necessary to anticipate as many as possible. He has, moreover, the example of the two very greatest masters of fresco to keep him in countenance: for even the impatient genius of Michael Angelo condescended to the tedious process of pouncing, and Raphael's cartoons are likewise covered with pin-holes. When any defect in the painting is irretrievable, the spoiled portion is carefully cut out and replaced by fresh plaster.

When the outline is secured on the wall, the artist can derive little assistance from any source other than his own experience. The tints, when first applied, look faint and spectral, and sink in like vanishing spirits; so that it is necessary to go over the surface repeatedly before the full effect appears. From this tendency to sink in, it must not, however, be concluded, as it is commonly, but erroneously, that fresco painting is perpetual glazing like watercolour tinting. On the contrary, we find on the surface of old frescoes a gemmy body of colour, or *impasto*. An example of this may be seen in the 'Vision of St. Catherine,' by Giulio Romano, in the National Gallery: the lights on the edges of the clouds glisten from their actual relief. Mr. Wilson, in his 'Continental Report' to the Fine Art Commission, goes so far as to say: 'We find in the frescoes of the old masters every quality of execution that has a name in oil painting, although those qualities are necessarily exemplified in different degrees; we have transparency, opacity, richness; we have thin and thick painting, nay, loading, and that to an extent which cannot be contemplated in oil. We have the calm, transparent, elegant painting of the Florentines and Romans; the rich variety of the Venetians; and there are cases in which the well-nourished brush of Rembrandt seems represented in the works of the fresco painters of old Italian times.'

It night be supposed impossible to remove frescoes from the walls on which they are painted. But this is easily effected if the works are in true fresco; but is attended with great danger, if they should happen to have been finished in tempera. In this case the touches applied subsequently to the drying of the fresco are destroyed: an accident which also frequently occurs when frescoes are cleaned in an ignorant and careless manner. The method adopted for removing frescoes is to apply upon the face of the painting a linen cloth, covered with a kind of glue. The 'intonaco,' or last coat of plaster, is then carefully detached from the wall with a knife. The rough surface at the back having been rubbed down with pumice-stone, until the plaster is reduced to the thinnest state consistent with the preservation of the painting, canvas is fastened upon the back, and the cloth in front moistened and removed. The detached fresco may then almost be treated like a common oil picture, if this operation has been skilfully performed. The removal, by this method, of frescoes of interest, for sale, or for preservation in public museums, has now become of frequent occurrence in Italy.

Other Kinds of Painting Allied to but Mistaken for Fresco

As a consequence of misconception of the true nature of fresco, there are other kinds of painting mistaken for it; some of which have little in common with that manly art. The method hitherto described is called by the Italians *buon* (good, genuine, or true fresco), and is stated by Vasari to have been adopted by the great masters. 'Buon fresco' does not, however, appear to have been in use till near the close of the fourteenth century.

One substitute for genuine fresco is termed *secco* (dry), or 'fresco secco,' or, as it is otherwise called, 'mezzo' (half) fresco, or Florentine fresco; for, like persons as well as things of doubtful reputation, it has many *aliases.* This method of lime painting has been described by Theophilus. The following will explain in what it differs from the former process:

The plastering having been completed in the ordinary manner, it is *allowed to dry* thoroughly. The surface is then rubbed with pumice-stone, and the evening before the painting is to be commenced it is thoroughly wetted with water in which a little lime has been mixed. The wall is again moistened the next morning, and the artist then traces his outline, and commences to paint in the usual way. If the wall should become too dry, a syringe is used to wet it; and thus he can always keep the plaster in a good state for working on. He can therefore quit or resume his work at pleasure; he need not rigidly calculate his day's work; and no joinings in the painting are observable. 'Work done in this way will bear to be washed as well as real fresco, and is as durable; for ornament it is a better method than real fresco, as in the latter art it is quite impossible to make the joinings[66] at outlines, owing to the complicated forms of outlines in ornament [the joinings are particularly observable in the Loggie of the Vatican]. But whilst it offers these advantages, and is particularly useful where mere ornamental painting is alone contemplated, it is in every respect an inferior art to real fresco. Paintings executed in this mode are always heavy and opaque, whereas fresco is light and transparent.'[67]

This process appears to have been common in Italy during the thirteenth century, and till the introduction of true fresco. The head by Giotto in the

National Gallery, from the Brancacci Chapel of the Carmine at Florence, is in fresco secco.

A nearer approach to the effect of buon fresco is, how ever, made by roughly commencing the design, and hastily laying in the forms and masses of colour while the plaster is still wet, and then finishing when dry in fresco secco or tempera. The mixing lime with the colours in true fresco occasions a want of force, which it was sought to remedy by these 'retouchings.' This last method of finishing by retouching in tempera is certainly a very illegitimate process, although, from the facility it affords of concealing defects, and the tempting means it presents of giving depth and force to shadows, it has been employed more or less by nearly all the great masters; if not so much at Florence, certainly in the other Italian schools. Retouchings without lime are, however, altogether useless when aa fresco is intended for exterior decoration; simply and literally because they will not wash, for the first shower would remove all such additions.

These retouchings may be easily detected, for they soon become darker, and present a dim, smoky surface. Indeed some modern frescoes in the Vatican have, more particularly in what should be their high lights, become quite black from these touches having been added as described. Vasari—who himself painted numerous works in fresco—says, 'He who cannot finish his work in one day is obliged to retouch when the fresco is dry, which in time brings on patchings, stains, retouchings, colours one upon another, and brush marks, after the colour is set, which is the vilest thing in the world, because it is evidence of the shallow power of the artist.'

These are the distinctions, then, between the three chief processes employed in wall painting. Fresco is executed with lime colours on the wet plaster; secco, also, with lime colours, but when the plaster has dried and been re-moistened; and tempera, or, as we now commonly call it, distemper, without lime at all, and on a dry wall.

1. Did the Ancients Paint in True Fresco?

Having become acquainted with the principal modes of mural painting which are either possible or probable, we are in a better position to ascertain the answer to this inquiry; for, as we have no satisfactory ancient authority upon the subject, we must be guided by artistic and chemical examination of the remains of ancient paintings. It has, in the first place, been discovered that, in the paintings at Pompeii, with very few exceptions, lime was mixed with the colours, whether employed as the general tint of a compartment, or in the painting of figures and ornaments. A drop of diluted sulphuric acid produced an effervescence, indicating the presence of a small, and often invisible, portion of carbonate of lime, even on the deepest black. The exceptions are where some portion must have been executed in tempera. Some colours on walls,—for instance, vermilion,—are protected with a wax varnish. Winkelmann and others, deceived by this circumstance, have erroneously maintained that the paintings of Pompeii were executed in wax.

From the use of lime in nearly all the colours, we might infer that these paintings were executed in fresco. But the joinings in the plaster are at too great intervals for the work included to have been executed before the plaster would dry; and, moreover, these lines do not coincide with the outlines of the design. In most of the walls two horizontal joinings only in the plaster are to be detected, and the painting, in either of the three divisions, is much more than could be executed in a day. The method, therefore, could hardly have been 'buon fresco,' but was, in all probability, that of 'secco.' The Pompeiian paintings consist almost entirely of ornamental work, and the peculiar fitness of 'secco' for this purpose has already been pointed out. It is, of course, possible that the general groundwork may have been executed in true fresco, and secco, and, as it appears, even tempera occasionally, may have been employed in finishing. Not only the presence of lime in the colours supports this view, but the fact that many of the walls exhibit indented outlines, sometimes indicating the process of tracing, renders it extremely probable.

From observing these marks of tracing, some have inclined to the opinion that the paintings may have been executed even in 'buon fresco;' but the suggestion they offer to get over the difficulty of the quantity of work, that the numerous layers of mortar in the wall may have kept the surface moist for many days, is scarcely sufficiently probable. It appears, then, most reasonable to conclude that the wall paintings of the ancients were executed by the method known as 'fresco secco,' and it is not at all unlikely that the mediaeval painters derived this process, as they did many others, directly from antiquity.

2. Fresco Painting in the 15th Century

By far the noblest works in painting of the fifteenth century were executed in Italy on walls, and, for the most part, in fresco. These works, too, are most distinctly representative; so that we shall review the Italian art of the period with especial reference to mural decoration, including works in oil as well as frescoes. But, in order to render our notice as complete as our limits permit, we shall also mention incidentally the most important works on panel. Many wall paintings, we may remark, to prevent misconception, were still executed in the older methods.

The fifteenth century, or, as the Italians term this remarkable era, the *quattrocento,*[68] is memorable for what is termed the Renaissance or new birth of art. This was effected chiefly by the genius of the great fresco painter Masaccio, and by the collection and study of the remains of ancient art. Masaccio, although not quite free from the fourteenth century naïveté, was the first to look at nature for himself; and thus, being scarcely at all prejudiced by education and convention, of necessity he developed truth and individuality of form. Art, though it does not lose the internal life of preceding periods, is at length emancipated in its external relations. Florence, now established as the capital of Tuscany, under the powerful family of the Medici, has the honour of taking the lead in this great revival of sculpture as well as painting.

The introduction of 'buon fresco' slightly preceded the Renaissance. The earliest works are supposed to be some subjects from Genesis, painted by Pietro d'Orvieto in the Campo Santo at Pisa. Other circumstances were favourable to the advancement of art. Perspective was cultivated by Pietro della Francesco and Ucello. The former has the credit of being the first to reduce perspective to a practical system; and the latter distinguished himself by foreshortenings not hitherto attempted. Masolino da Panicale, also, advanced the knowledge of chiaroscuro.

But the frescoes of Masaccio (the contracted form of Tommasaccio, which means Slovenly Thomas) in the Brancacci Chapel of the Carmelite Church at Florence, form the great landmark of the art of this century. In expression and composition, in truthful imitation and selection of forms, in modelling and knowledge of the naked or nude, and in the disposition of drapery, these works show a vast improvement; and for nearly a century, even to the time of Raphael, they, together with the frescoes by Filippino Lippi in the same chapel, formed the school of the artists of Florence. One of the most celebrated figures by Masaccio is that of a naked boy trembling with cold in the fresco of 'Peter baptizing the People;' and a figure of St. Paul by Filippino Lippi was exactly imitated by Raphael in his well-known cartoon of 'Paul preaching at Athens.' The works of this chapel escaped in the fire which destroyed the works of Giotto in the same church; fortunately, however, the paintings by Giotto were engraved by Thomas Patch the works in the Brancacci Chapel are engraved, and are also now in course of being published in chromolithographic facsimile by the Arundel Society.

Benozzo Gozzoli, the pupil of Fra Angelico da Fiesole, though he studied the works of Masaccio, did not equal him in design. The pictures of this artist are light and cheerful in colouring. There is a small example in the National Gallery. But by far his most important works—and one of the most interesting monuments of the art of the fifteenth century—is the series of frescoes with which he adorned the whole of the north wall of the Campo Santo at Pisa.

Fra Filippo Lippi is named as a scholar of Masaccio. This worldly monk presents a strong contrast in his attention to the external or sensuous qualities of art, as well as in his life, to his contemporary and spiritual brother Fra Angelico. Fra Lippi painted a few pictures in oil, but his most important works are the frescoes in the choir of the Duomo at Prato.[69]

Sandro Botticelli was one of the most distinguished pupils of Fra Filippo Lippi. He executed many circular pictures of the Madonna and Child, of which there are two in the National Gallery. He also began to introduce classical myth and allegory into modern art. The son of Fra Lippi, Filippino Lippi, inherited more than his father's talents, and he likewise surpassed his master, Sandro Botticelli. His finest works in the Carmine we have already mentioned. These and other of his frescoes in Florence and Rome are remarkable for dramatic power. About 1474 the Sistine Chapel at Rome was built and named after Sixtus IV, and its walls were decorated with frescoes by all the most celebrated painters of the time, including Sandro Botticelli, Luca Signorelli, Perugino, Cosimo Roselli, Domenico Ghirlandajo, and Cecchino Salviati. The ceiling and altar-wall subsequently received the great frescoes of Michael Angelo.

Conspicuous among other Florentine painters of this time was Domenico Ghirlandajo, the master of Michael Angelo. His most excellent frescoes are in the Sassetti Chapel in Sta. Trinità and in the choir of Sta. Maria Novella; and in them he introduced portraits of many of his contemporaries. There is great elevation and admirable execution in these works. His finest easel pictures are also still at Florence. The study of the nude was advanced chiefly by two celebrated sculptors, who handled the pencil as well as the chisel: Antonio Pollajuolo and Andrea Verocchio (or 'the keen-sighted'). The former is said to have been the first artist who studied the dead subject for the purposes of design. But Luca Signorelli carried this difficult department of art to still greater perfection. The correctness of his foreshortening, and his masterly drawing of the naked figure in his frescoes, representing the 'Last Judgment' and the 'History of Antichrist,' in the cathedral of Orvieto, distinguish him as the true precursor of Michael Angelo; and Vasari says that Michael Angelo observed that 'all may see he made use of the invention of Luca in his own "Last Judgment" in the Sistine Chapel.'

In the school of Padua we find a similar tendency to the study of form; but, instead of referring to nature, the painters of this school devoted themselves to the reproduction of the ideal beauty of antique sculpture. This is visible even in, the architectural and ornamental accessories of their pictures; in the frequent imitation, for example, of ancient bassi-relievi, and the introduction of festoons of fruit. Squarcione is the founder of this school. While travelling in Italy and Greece he formed the first great collection of antique sculpture. This collection be opened in Padua, and it is said to have attracted no less than one hundred and thirty-seven scholars. Among these, the most important was Andrea Mantegna, the founder of the school of Mantua. The plastic, or sculptural element, and antique severity of form, predominate in the works of this great master. Yet these characteristics are united with great originality of invention and much feeling for nature and reality. The nine coloured cartoons in Hampton Court Palace of the 'Triumphal Procession of Caesar,' are excellent examples of Mantegna; and his frescoes in the church Degli Eremitani of Padua display a technical skill far surpassing anything hitherto known. Like other Paduan masters, he painted pictures in chiaroscuro.[70] With the mention of Melozzo da Forli we must pass by other less important artists of Padua, Ferrara, Milan, and other parts of Northern Italy, with the exception of those of Venice.

The school of Padua exercised an important influence on the earliest art of Venice, especially on the Vivarini family, of whom Luigi Vivarini was the best painter. But the chief characteristic of the Venetian school—love of colour—soon manifested itself and quickly became paramount. The introduction and adoption of oil painting in Venice long before it prevailed generally in Italy, was highly favourable to the development of this peculiar charm of painting. In the account of oil painting, we shall, however, have to recur to this subject more at large.

Giovanni (John) Bellini is the head of the Venetian school, in virtue of his transparent, gem-like colouring, although his outlines are hard, and his stippled touch has nothing in common with the bold sweep of later Venetian masters. His works are in oil, and his subjects chiefly Madonnas and portraits. Gentile, the elder brother of Giovanni, is a less important artist. Cima da Conegliano, a follower of Giovanni Bellini, was an admirable painter, and has not been sufficiently appreciated in this country.

The region of Umbria, a retired valley of the Upper Tiber, was for ages remarkable as a peculiar seat of religious enthusiasm. This gave a severity (sometimes bordering on asceticism) to the style of some remarkable painters of this district and those who came under their influence: among whom was Raphael, all his earlier pictures having this character. Pietro Perugino (so named from Perugia, the place where he established himself, and opened a large studio and school), is one of the most distinctive exponents of this style, as may be seen to advantage in the noble example of this master in the National Gallery. There is not only a tender earnestness and dignity about his figures, but some of the more youthful: have the most refined and saint-like beauty. 'Christ's Charge to Peter,' in the Sistine Chapel, is one of the best of his numerous frescoes. But Perugino's greatest glory was, that he was the master of Raphael. Pinturicchio (of Perugia) executed some fine frescoes in Rome, and also adorned the walls of the Libreria, attached to the Duomo of Siena, with a series of historical representations. The youthful Raphael assisted in these compositions; and some of his drawings still in existence are said to be much more beautiful, more full of mind, than the large pictures executed from them. LoSpagno (the Spaniard) was, next to Raphael, the most distinguished of Perugino's scholars. The father of Raphael, Giovanni Sanzio, of the neighbouring Urbino, was by no means an inferior painter. But an artist of far more importance than the last was Francesco Francia, of Bologna. The fine specimen of this master in the National Gallery proves he is entitled to rank with Perugino, with whom he has considerable affinity. He has the same delicate sentiment; but his type of countenance is less peculiar and unearthly. The best of Francia's works are the frescoes in Sta. Cecilia at Bologna.

Lastly, we find the early Neapolitan school greatly influenced by the importation of Flemish oil pictures. Colantonio del Fiore is the first name we meet with; but the school was principally established by Antonio Solario, surnamed Lo Zingaro, from having been a Gypsy in early life. He is said to have been a smith, and to have learned the art out of love for Colantonio's daughter. His frescoes are remarkable for their fine landscape backgrounds.

3. FRESCO PAINTING IN THE 16TH CENTURY

Pursuing our plan, we still give to fresco painting the prominent (though not exclusive) consideration to which the grand productions of the schools of Central Italy, in the early part of the sixteenth century, entitle it.

Hitherto, in the progress of painting, we have chiefly seen, on the one hand, the attainment of pure sentimentality in art, and on the other the development of individuality and ideality of form. We now arrive at the most glorious climax of modern painting, in which, during little more than a quarter of a century, all the most intellectual, and also the more fascinating qualities of art, were carried to a point of almost the highest conceivable perfection. Still, as if to show the infinite capabilities of art, each of the great masters of this age exhibits individual characteristics in his works. The universal genius, Leonardo da Vinci, was the first in a measure to unite the separate excellences of preceding painters; yet he was chiefly distinguished for expression and chiaroscuro. Raphael united still more of these excellences, and also carried them to higher perfection; yet his chief glory will ever be, that he was the painter of purity and loveliness. Michael Angelo was essentially and remarkably individualized in style, having constructed, upon profound anatomical knowledge and diligent study of the remains of antique sculpture, an ideal of the human figure, which for sublimity has never been surpassed. Correggio's peculiar merit was the delicacy of his gradations of light and shade; and lastly, Titian and the other great Venetians wrought out the richness and grandeur, no less than the subtler harmonies and less palpable beauties there are in colour. Our space will, however, not permit us to enumerate more than the most memorable works of these great men; our object being less to trace the general history of art than to give the history of the origin and progress of methods, and an explanation of technicalities. For the rest, the sources where further information may be obtained are at once ample and accessible.

Leonardo da Vinci (1452–1519) probably derived his inclination for the study of sculpture as well as painting from his master Andrea Verocchio. Unfortunately his greatest performances in both these arts are either entirely destroyed or irreparably defaced. One of these, the model for a colossal equestrian statue of Francesco Sforza, to be cast in bronze, and erected in Milan, was accidentally broken while being carried in triumphal procession. The other is, or rather was, for the original can scarcely be said to exist, the world-famous 'Last Supper.' This work, which far surpassed anything hitherto produced in painting, was executed for the refectory of the convent of Sta. Maria delle Grazie, Milan, on a wall twenty-eight feet long, the figures being larger than life.[71] Leonardo was an extremely painstaking and conscientious painter, and, in order to do justice to the greatness of his subject (the painting of which occupied him two years), he adopted oil instead of fresco, because in this medium he would have greater facility of retouching. To this circumstance, and the imperfect preparation of the wall, is to be attributed the early decay of this noble work. In a great inundation at Milan it was partially submerged. In 1545 it was already in a ruined state. The lower part of the figure in the Saviour was destroyed to make a door in the wall, and it has been twice completely repainted by impudent and incompetent bunglers. Some of Leonardo's cartoons for single heads, including that of the Saviour, are, however, preserved.

Great uncertainty prevails about the majority of the paintings ascribed to Leonardo da Vinci: the stiffness and edginess in his earliest pictures are totally unlike the melting softness of the outlines in his more mature style; and his very able scholar Luini, in particular, frequently very nearly approaches the master. Sometimes, also, the composition is attributed to Leonardo, and the execution to Luini, as is the case with the picture of 'Christ disputing with the Doctors,' in the National Gallery. The following give most distinct evidence of the master: 'La Belle Ferronière,' and 'Mona Lisa,' both in the Louvre, two exquisitely beautiful heads, full of intense 'expression, and marvellously finished; the so-called Modesty and Vanity,' at Rome; 'La Carità' (a female, with several children), at the Hague; and his own portrait in the collection of portraits of artists by themselves at Florence. There are several repetitions of the famous 'Vierge aux Rochers,' among the best of which is one in Lord Suffolk's collection, and another in the Louvre: they all, however, betray more or less the hand of scholars. At Florence Leonardo competed with Michael Angelo for the intended decoration of the Palazzo Vecchio with paintings, but the cartoons they produced are lost. A group of four horsemen 'Fighting for a Standard,' from Leonardo's cartoon, has, however, been preserved in a copy by Rubens, engraved by Edelinck: the cartoon of his young rival, Michael Angelo, represented some Pisan soldiers suddenly called to arms while bathing in the Arno. Parts of this are also preserved in engravings. Leonardo accepted the invitation to France of the great patron of art, Francis I, and died in that country three years after his arrival.[72]

Lorenzo di Credi copied some of the works of Leonardo very successfully; but the painter who partook most of the spirit of the master was Luini, the scholar of Leonardo, already mentioned. This great artist is seen to most advantage in his frescoes preserved in the Brera Gallery and elsewhere in Milan. Gaudenzio Ferrari, another Milanese, has also left a number of frescoes, which are distinguished for freshness and purity of colour.

The cartoon by Michael Angelo, alluded to above, was executed when he was only twenty years of age; yet his contemporaries said he never afterwards produced anything so perfect. The exhibition of this cartoon, more than the competing work of Da Vinci, is believed to have considerably advanced the art of this period. Like Leonardo, the great talents of Michael Angelo Buonarotti[73] (1474–1563) were universal: he was equally great as architect, sculptor, and painter; he was, besides, an excellent musician and poet; conversant with most sciences, and a profound anatomist. As architect, he carried the building of St. Peter's, more especially the construction of the great dome, almost to completion, after every previous attempt had miscarried. In sculpture, his David, his Moses, and the monuments of the Medici family, with their grand allegorical figures in the sacristy of S. Lorenzo at Florence, are still generally ranked as the finest works of the kind produced since classical times. In painting, the noblest monument of his genius is the fresco decoration of the ceiling of the Sistine chapel. Yet there also the genius of the architect and sculptor, as well as the painter, is exhibited in the admirable adaptation of the painted compartmental framework to the proper display of the principal masses of the composition, and to convey the appearance of support, which is so often neglected in ceiling decoration; and in the sculpturesque character of repose, so essential in the numerous merely decorative figures, coloured to imitate stone or bronze.

Pope Julius II conceived the idea of employing Michael Angelo, whom he had previously invited from Florence to Rome, to paint this ceiling: the artist at first wished to decline the commission, recommending Raphael, then already occupied in the Vatican Stanze, as a more fit person for such a task; but the Pope earnestly insisted, and Michael Angelo was therefore constrained to charge himself with this immense undertaking. The great painter was still so diffident of his own powers, that he engaged some of his old Florentine companions to execute the frescoes from his cartoons; he was not satisfied, however, with what was done by these painters, and he accordingly knocked down their work, and executed the whole with his own hand. This he is said to have accomplished in the incredibly short space of twenty months; but this cannot possibly include the preparation of the cartoons.

The frescoes represent the 'Creation' and 'Fall of Man,' with its immediate consequences in the early 'History of the World.' The ceiling forms a flattened arch in its section. The upmost flat surface is divided into nine compartments, the centre of which contains the 'Creation of Eve;' the 'Creation of Adam' (a very sublime conception) is next to this on the one side; and on the other the 'Temptation, Fall, and Expulsion from Paradise,' in one composition. The remaining six compartments contain the following representations: the 'Separation of Light from Darkness;' the 'Gathering of the Waters;' the 'Creation of the Sun and Moon;' the 'Deluge;' the 'Thanksgiving of Noah;' and the 'Drunkenness of Noah.' At the four angles of the ceiling are 'David beheading Goliath;' 'Judith with the Head of Holofernes' (the two last, it would seem, accepted as typifying the fulfilment of the prophecy—'It shall bruise thy head'); the 'Punishment of Haman' (suggesting Esther as a type of the Madonna); and the 'Brazen Serpent.' In the soffits of the window recesses, and on the wall above the windows—of which there are six on each side—are introduced many figures and groups, illustrating the genealogy of Christ. Between these recesses, on the triangular vaulted portions of the roof, are painted, in a larger size than the other figures, the most famous single figures of modern painting, the Prophets Jeremiah, Ezekiel, Joel, and Isaiah, alternating with the Sibyls Persica, Erythræa, Delphica, Cumæa, and Libyca,[74] the Prophets Jonah and Zachariah being one on each end, between the composition of the four angles. The 'Creation of Eve,' we have said, is in the centre of the ceiling. It is always made thus prominent in the early cycles of scriptural types, in allusion to the Messiah being born of a woman alone. But, whatever the incidents of the Old Testament introduced into early MSS. and pictures, it appears they were intended to be understood as pregnant with typical signification far beyond what the most fanciful modern theologian would conceive. The series of subjects on this ceiling, for instance, in which the Fall and its consequences are depicted, have each direct reference to the paintings on the upper part of the walls beneath, in which the argument of the Redemption was anticipated by the painters who preceded Michael Angelo in the decoration of the Sistine Chapel; and these, again, are mutually associated and related to the tapestries which were designed to hang between them and the floor, and of which we shall have again to speak. Michael Angelo, like Luca Signorelli, whose works in the cathedral of Orvieto he so much admired, did not, it appears, display any originality in his choice of subjects for the decoration of this ceiling. Sir Charles Eastlake, in his notes to Kugler's *Handbook,* says that the usual biblical and theological subjects, which appear to have been authorized during the Middle Ages, were adopted by the great painters with no other change than that of superior treatment. These illustrations existed originally in MSS. (for example, in the *Speculum Humanæ Salvationis,* alluded to previously); and when wood engraving was invented, the same subjects, and sometimes precisely the same designs, were repeated.

In his sixtieth year Michael Angelo commenced, with characteristic energy of will, his second great work in painting, the 'LAST JUDGMENT,' on the end wall of the Sistine Chapel. The dimensions of this fresco are 47 feet in height by 43 in width. The opinions of this vast work, which occupied the artist seven years, are very various. The majority, however, agree that it is inferior in purity and majesty to the frescoes of the ceiling. The idea of the 'Last Judgment,' as the great 'Day of Wrath,' is considered to be insisted upon too much. Even in the upper portion, containing the assembly of the blessed, there is no joy and peace; but, on the contrary, nothing but doubt and dread; while Christ, the principal figure of the composition, wants every attribute but that of the Judge fulminating the last sentence of the wicked. The absurdity of the martyrs holding up the sickening instruments, and proofs of their martyrdom, is also complained of; it is also objected that many of the figures are coarse, mannered, and overcharged, and that the attitudes of the two groups of angels under the two arches of the vault, bearing the instruments of the passion, are violent and fantastic. The lower half, however, deserves and has received the highest and unmingled praise. The slow rising of the dead, the first anxious expression of awakening consciousness, and the ascent of the pardoned, are contrasted with the anguish, rage, and despair of the condemned, some of whom are convulsively struggling with evil demons, and descending headlong in knotted groups. Altogether, the number of figures in this stupendous work, the awe-inspiring boldness of the conception, the masterly drawing (particularly of the very extraordinary and difficult foreshortenings), and the startling and dramatic delineation of human passions, place this work alone in the expression of superhuman power and grasp of mind.[75]

Michael Angelo painted two other excellent frescoes in the Pauline Chapel in the Vatican. His easel pictures are very scarce—a circular 'Holy Family' in tempera in the tribune of the Uffizj at Florence being perhaps the only perfectly authenticated specimen. Another and a more remarkable unfinished picture in the possession of the Right Hon. H. Labouchere, has however, as already observed, been attributed to him by the best authorities. Foremost among the scholars of Michael Angelo, or artists, who painted in his style, may be named Marcello Venusti, Daniele da Volterra, and Sebastiano del Piombo. The masterpiece of Daniele da Volterra is the 'Descent from the Cross' in the Church of Trinità de' Monti at Rome, executed with the assistance of Michael Angelo, and considered by Poussin to be the third greatest picture (not fresco) in the world, inferior only to Raphael's 'Transfiguration,' and the 'Communion of St. Jerome,' by Domenichino. One of the finest works of Sebastiano del Piombo is the 'Raising of Lazarus,' in the National Gallery, in the design of parts of which Vasari says he was assisted by Michael Angelo. This, joined to his own powerful colouring, which he had acquired in the school of Giorgione, led some to prefer this work even to the 'Transfiguration' of Raphael, when they were (when finished) publicly exhibited together at Rome. The 'Scourging of Christ,' in S. Pietro in Montorio at Rome, is a famous fresco. This painter was also eminent in portraiture.

There were several artists in Florence contemporary with Leonardo and Michael Angelo, but comparatively independent of their influence, who yet displayed great and peculiar the honour of teaching Raphael the softness and sweetness of colouring in which the *frate* excelled. A large and grand figure of St. Mark, in the Pitti Palace at Florence, by this painter, is very celebrated. Fra Bartolommeo introduced the use of wooden 'lay-figures' (which will be described later), and thus advanced the study of drapery. Albertinelli, a friend of the last painter, produced a very celebrated picture of 'The Salutation' in the Uffizj. Andrea del Sarto, with less religious earnestness, but more simplicity and nature, yet followed the general style of Fra Bartolommeo. The best works of Andrea are his frescoes in the court of the SS. Annunziata at Florence. In the centre court of the adjoining convent a 'Holy Family,' in which Joseph is represented leaning on a sack—hence known as the 'Madonna del Sacco'—is the most celebrated fresco of the master.

We now approach the greatest name by general concession in modern painting. Yet the greatness of Raphael[76] (1483–1520), to whom we of course allude, is not so much in kind as in degree. In separate, and those the highest, qualities, he may have been equalled by some contemporary painters; while in colouring and the technicalities of oil painting he was certainly surpassed by the Venetians; but no painter, although be died at a comparatively early age, has left so many truly admirable and original works, in which there is so little that is unpleasing; but, on the contrary, which invariably reflect his own peculiarly pure, noble, and affectionate character, and exquisite feeling for all that is beautiful and lovely.

The first traces of Raphael's exertions are believed to be observable in some pictures by his master Perugino, under whom he was instructed from twelve to twenty. One of his first independent works was the altarpiece 'Crucifixion' in Lord Ward's collection. Much of the stiffness and constraint of the Peruginesque school are preserved in the early works of Raphael, and constitute his first manner, as it is called. The following are examples: 'The Marriage of the Virgin' (Lo Sposalizio), in the Brera, with a temple placed symmetrically in the background; the 'Vision of a Knight,' a small picture, in the National Gallery; and the 'Agony in the Garden,' in Mr. Fuller Maitland's collection.

Gradually, in the works we are about to mention, the master acquired more freedom of execution and greater cheerfulness of conception, till, in the last two or three enumerated, his second or Florentine manner is fully developed. An improvement in the colouring of Raphael at this period was due to his acquaintance with Fra Bartolommeo. We cannot particularize all the subsequent representations of the Madonna—representations in which Raphael so peculiarly excelled; but the celebrated 'Madonna del Granduca' may be mentioned, because, in the words of Kugler, 'We feel that no earlier painter had ever understood to combine such free and transcendent beauty with an expression of such deep foreboding.' An altar-piece for a convent in Perugia is now at Naples, but the small pictures of the Predella (see note D in Appendix) are dispersed among different collectors in England. Raphael's first fresco in S. Severo at Perugia is a grand composition. The 'Madonna del Cardellino' (so named because the little St. John presents a goldfinch to the infant Christ), in the Uffizj; 'La Belle Jardinière' (the Madonna seated in a garden), in the Louvre; the 'St. Catherine,' in the National Gallery; the larger altarpiece, 'Madonna del Baldacchino' (taking its name from the canopy over the throne) in the Pitti Palace, Florence; the 'Entombment,' in the Borghese Palace, Rome; the small picture of the 'Three Graces,' in Lord Ward's collection; and Raphael's own portrait, by himself, in the Uffizj—all belong to this period.

In 1508 Raphael, then in his twenty-fifth year, was invited to the court of Pope Julius II to decorate the state apartments of the Papal residence in the Vatican. The great frescoes he executed in these apartments or *stanze* (with the partial exception of the first—the so-called 'Disputa'), together with other cartoons and pictures painted up to the period of his death, at the early age of thirty-seven, develop the third or Roman manner of the master, and at the same time embody the highest dramatic and general characteristics of the great Roman school. The frescoes by Raphael in the Vatican cover the ceilings and walls of three chambers, and a large saloon (Sala di Constantino), now collectively called the 'Stanze of Raphael.' These and other works in which Raphael was engaged were, however, so numerous and extensive, that he was obliged to invite a number of artists to share his labours; and such was the influence of the amiable character of Raphael upon these assistants and scholars, that all professional jealousy was forgotten, and the highest ambition of these men was to make the style of their master their own. The first chamber painted by Raphael was the Camara or Stanza della Segnatura (of the Signature); and all the frescoes of this apartment were finished in 1511, about one year before Michael Angelo finished the ceiling of the Sistine Chapel; a fact which tends to disprove the assumption to which Sir Joshua Reynolds has given currency, that Raphael was indebted for the general superiority of his works to these frescoes by Michael Angelo.

The first frescoes executed in the Stanza della Segnatura appear to have been the eight small medallion pictures of the ceiling, representing personifications and illustrations of the subjects of the great frescoes on the wall beneath.[77] Of these small pictures a 'Fall of Man' is especially admired. The subjects of the great frescoes beneath are Theology, Philosophy, Poetry, and Justice, Law or Jurisprudence; the two first being the more important paintings. The 'THEOLOGY,' or, as it is sometimes erroneously called, the 'Dispute of the Sacrament,' is in two principal parts, or large groups: the upper portion represents, in the symmetrical and conventional manner of the early painters, above, in the clouds a heavenly assemblage of saints and angels, with the three persons of the Trinity; in the lower portion there is a council or synod of the great dignitaries and teachers of the Church on earth. The other great composition of this chamber is 'Philosophy' or the 'School of Athens.' Here the grand Roman style of Raphael is matured, with no reminiscence of earlier art or individual tentative effort. The two principal figures in the centre are Aristotle and Plato, supposed to be disputing on the merits of their respective systems. Plato points upwards, indicating in the attitude his own spiritual doctrine; while Aristotle points to the earth, signifying that all practical philosophy must be deduced from the investigation of nature. Socrates, Pythagoras, Archimedes, Zoroaster, Ptolemy, and Diogenes, are also variously characterized. The rich architectural background of this fresco is believed to be from a design by Bramante. 'POETRY' is an assembly of the great Greek, Roman, and Italian poets of all ages up to that time on Mount Parnassus, with Apollo and the Muses under laurel-trees in the centre. 'JURISPRUDENCE' is divided into three distinct compositions on account of the window which occupies the middle of the wall. Above are three female personifications of Prudence, Fortitude, and Temperance. At the side are incidents suggesting Ecclesiastical and Civil Law —'Gregory XI delivering the Decretals to a Consistorial Advocate,' and the 'Emperor Justinian delivering the Pandects to Tribonianus.'

The works in the Stanza of Heliodorus, so called from its principal picture, appear to have directly followed those above-mentioned. The 'Expulsion of Heliodorus from the Temple,' one of Raphael's grandest frescoes, represents Heliodorus, when, as treasurer to the Syrian king Seleucus, he attempted, at his master's command, to plunder the temple, but was prevented: 'For,' quoting the Second Book of Maccabees, 'there appeared to them a horse with a terrible rider upon him, adorned with a very rich covering; and he ran fiercely and struck Heliodorus with his fore-feet: and he that sat upon him seemed to have armour of gold. Moreover, there appeared two other young men, beautiful and strong, bright and glorious, and in comely apparel, who stood by him on either side, and scourged him without ceasing with many stripes.' The subject is said to have been chosen to commemorate the deliverance of the States of the Church from foreign enemies through Julius II. Julius himself is represented borne into the temple to point the allusion; but the absence of interest and emotion in the group around the Pope disturbs the fine dramatic effect of the other portion. The 'MASS AT BOLSENA' represents a miracle pretended to have been performed to convince a doubting priest of the truth of the doctrine of transubstantiation—blood is said to have flowed from the Host he was consecrating. The 'ATTILA' represents St. Leo turning Attila from his design of plundering Rome; supposed to have reference to the expulsion of the

French from Italy by Leo X. The richness of the colouring in this fresco—as well as we can infer of its original condition—has never been surpassed in this style of art, although all who have visited the Vatican must confess that the first impression of all the frescoes in their present condition is greatly disappointing. The *'Delivery of St. Peter from Prison'* is a night-scene with three lights, viz., from torches, the angel, and the moon, admirably and beautifully arranged.

Raphael had now so many commissions, that the decoration of the next chamber, the Stanza dell' Incendio, was almost wholly entrusted to his scholars. This chamber takes its name from the painting of the *'Fire in the Borgo;'* but all the paintings are inferior. The frescoes in the Sala di Constantino were painted after the death of Raphael, from his drawings, and under the direction of Giulio Romano. The principal work is the 'Battle between Constantine and Maxentius,' at the Ponte (Bridge) Molle near Rome. It was executed by Giulio Romano, after a drawing of Raphael, with scarcely the slightest alteration: the design is therefore Raphael's, and it is certainly one of his most important compositions. We have already alluded to the arabesque fresco decorations of the open-air corridors, or Loggie of the Vatican, by Raphael and Giovanni da Udine: we have only to add that the extensive cycle of Scripture events represented on the ceilings is known by the name of 'Raphael's Bible.'

It has been mentioned that it was intended to embellish the lower portion of the walls of the Sistine Chapel with tapestries. The designs for these were made by Raphael; and seven of them—the famous 'CARTOONS'—are preserved at Hampton Court. The tapestries were worked at Arras their complete number was ten, divided into two series; they are now preserved in some rooms of the Vatican, but are greatly faded. The seven coloured distemper Cartoons at Hampton Court are also very much faded, from long-continued ill-usage and repeated removal; yet these great works will always rank as Raphael's noblest productions, most completely characteristic of his fully developed style, and among the grandest monuments of the *cinque-cento.* The first cartoon, the 'MIRACULOUS DRAUGHT OF FISHES,' or the 'Calling of Peter,' appears to have been painted by Raphael's own hand, with the exception of the fish and herons, which are assigned to Giovanni da Udine. The keeping and repose in this cartoon are inimitable; but the straight line of the boats has a singular effect, and the boats are obviously too small to contain the figures placed in them. But, in reference to this, it has been remarked that, 'had Raphael made the boats large enough for those *figures,* his picture would have been all boat, which would have had a disagreeable effect; and to have made his figures small enough for vessels of that size, would have rendered them unsuitable to the rest of the set, and have made those figures appear less considerable—there would have been too much boat and too little figure. It is amiss as it is; but would have been worse any other way, as it frequently happens in other cases.'[78] The other subjects of the Cartoons at Hampton Court are—'Christ's Charge to Peter;' 'The Healing of the Lame Man at the Beautiful Gate of the Temple;'[79] 'The Death of Ananias;' 'Elymas the Sorcerer Struck Blind;' 'Paul and Barnabas at Lystra;' and 'Paul Preaching at Athens.'

A few other important works by Raphael remain unmentioned: viz., the fresco of four Sibyls in Sta. Maria della Pace, Rome; the circular 'Madonna della Sedia' (of the Chair), in the Pitti Palace; the grandly composed 'Holy Family,' known by the name of the 'Pearl,' in the Gallery at Madrid; the large 'Madonna di Fuligno,' in the Vatican (with a very beautiful boy-angel holding a tablet); the 'Madonna del Pesce,' at Madrid; the indescribably lovely 'MADONNA DI SAN SISTO,' in the Dresden Gallery, the most important picture of this class; the 'Archangel Michael,' in the Louvre; and the famous 'Transfiguration on Mount Tabor,' in the Vatican. This was the last work of the master, and not quite finished till after his death. It was suspended over his corpse. Opinions are diverse respecting this celebrated picture. The incident of the possessed boy certainly did occur in the absence of Christ, but objection is made to the licence of bringing it and the actual transfiguration, on a mere improvised hillock, in such direct proximity; still, the composition was, without doubt, intended to symbolise the source of consolation and redemption from evil as immediately above the calamities and miseries of human life; and, artistically considered, the picture is grand in the extreme.

Finally, Raphael designed some mythological frescoes in the Farnesina Villa at Rome; but, with the exception of a fresco known as the 'Galatea,' the cumbrous forms and heavy execution of these compositions betray the hand of Giulio Romano. There are full-size copies of these works in Northumberland House, Charing Cross. Raphael's portraits of the Popes Julius II, Leo X, the 'divine' Joaña of Aragon; his own mistress, the 'Fornarina,'[80] &c., are fully equal to his other works; and he has left at least one excellent statue—that of Jonah—in marble.

Many of the numerous scholars and imitators of Raphael quickly degenerated into a heavy, sensuous, mannered style; and, like all copyists, in imitation of the letter, forgot the spirit. Giulio Romano, the most eminent of these, painted a number of vigorous frescoes representing the 'Fall of the Giants' in the Palazzo del Tè, at Mantua, and established a school in that city. A large 'Holy Family,' in the Dresden Gallery, is his most celebrated picture. Other distinguished artists who came under the influence of the Roman school were Primaticcio (who subsequently went to France), Perino del Vaga, Gianfrancesco Penni (Raphael's confidential scholar), Polidoro, Andrea da Salerno, Caravaggio, Dosso Dossi, L'Ortolano, and Garofalo, who executed some excellent frescoes in Ferrara, and whose colouring is remarkably vivid. Gianantonio Razzi, a Sienese artist, who appears, however, to have formed his style chiefly under Leonardo da Vinci, painted some frescoes in Siena, the extraordinary beauty of which, especially of the single female figures, scarcely seems to us to have been sufficiently recognised.

The schools of Lombardy continued, during this period, to preserve a comparatively independent character. Correggio (1493–1534), in particular, seems to have obtained his first instruction from Mantegna, and to have been subsequently influenced by Leonardo da Vinci. But, while remarkable for sensibility and animated life-like conception, Correggio will ever be distinguished as the greatest master of chiaroscuro—for his peculiar ability in knowing how to 'anatomise light and shade in endless gradation.' Correggio appears to have arrived at excellence even earlier in life than Raphael. He had painted several large altar-pieces at Carpi and Correggio (the place whence he derived his name) before he was twenty-five. Two of these are preserved—a 'Holy Family,' in the Dresden Gallery, and a picture of four Saints in Lord Ashburton's collection. The first of his celebrated ceiling frescoes was painted in the cupola of S. Giovanni in Parma. But this gland style was carried to perfection in the large frescoes in the cupola of the Duomo at the same place, representing the 'Assumption of the Virgin.' Above this dome there is no window or lantern, the light being admitted from long oval windows in the lower part. Correggio has taken advantage of the consequent convergent rays to place Christ, who descends to meet the Virgin, in the strong light of the centre. Around are saints, and the Virgin borne by angels, all wonderfully foreshortened. Lower down, between the windows, stand the Apostles gazing on the ascending Madonna; and in the four pendentives under the cupola are the four patron Saints of Parma. The effect of the whole is indescribably rich; but, as all the figures are foreshortened, and therefore more limbs than bodies are visible from below, the artist was jestingly told that he had painted a 'hash of frogs.' The easel pictures of Correggio are highly esteemed. In the gallery at Dresden there is a series of altar-pictures, among which the *'Notte,'* or 'Night of the Nativity,' is the most famous. The 'Ecce Homo,' the small 'Holy Family,' and the 'Education of Cupid by Venus and Mercury,' in the National Gallery, together with the 'Agony in the Garden,' in the Duke of Wellington's collection, of which there is a repetition in the National Gallery, are also celebrated pictures of this great painter.

Parmigiano is the next most distinguished master of this school. This painter displayed, with grandeur of design, a peculiar grace, which, in some of his works, borders on affectation; particularly in the unnaturally lengthened proportions of his figures. In the frescoes he left unfinished in the Steccata at Palma there is a figure of Moses which has been very much lauded. Parmigiano, it is said, was engaged upon the large picture of St. Jerome, now in the National Gallery, during the sack of Rome in 1527, and that some soldiers actually surprised him while absorbed in his work; but they were so overawed with admiration, that they protected him against their comrades.

The only remaining quality of painting not entirely developed by the great masters of design of the Roman and other schools was colouring; but this their contemporaries at Venice carried to the utmost perfection, in works full of the evidences of material wealth, and all the accessorial draperied pageantry of a most luxurious civilization. The Venetians painted comparatively little in fresco; but attained such command of the vehicle of oil, that they executed works of equally gigantic proportions in this medium. However, to complete our view of Italian art, we may include a general notice of the Venetian school in this section, although we shall have again to refer to the introduction of oil painting into Italy. Some account of the Flemish and Dutch schools, in which fresco painting was scarcely heard of, will naturally find a place in a description of that method which was originated and brought to perfection in those schools.

Giorgione (1477–1511) was the first to throw aside the dry manner of his master Giovanni Bellini. His works are remarkable for a rich, internal glow, which contrasts in a remarkable manner with the noble sternness or melancholy romantic beauty of his portraits and ideal heads. A very celebrated poetic composition, representing a 'Sea-storm raised by Demons,' is in the Venetian Gallery; and there is an extremely fine picture, now in the possession of Mr. Alexander Barker, entitled 'Giorgione, his Mistress and Pupil,' about which Byron raved when it was in the Manfrini Gallery at Venice. Among the scholars of Giorgione, Palma (Vecchio) successfully imitated the master.

The great Titian (1477–1576), also a pupil of Bellini, owed, no doubt, something of his golden glow to Giorgione; but he soon manifested his own originality. Titian has proved himself the first of colourists in historical or religious compositions, in landscape, and indeed in every department of art; but in portraiture he is, by universal consent, considered the greatest master of modern times. The quiet, conscious vitality, the 'senatorial dignity,' and essential beauty of his portraits have never been equalled. The number of these, painted during a life-time which was only terminated by the plague, at the age of 99, is, however, far too great to particularize. The following are some of Titian's most famous works: 'An Entombment of Christ,' in the Manfrini Gallery; 'Christ crowned with Thorns,' in the Louvre;

the dubiously named 'Sacred and Profane Love,' in the Borghese Gallery; the 'Bacchus and Ariadne,' in the National Gallery; the 'St. Peter Martyr,'[81] in S. Giovanni e Paolo, at Venice, a colossal altar-piece, considered by many Titian's *chef-d'oeuvre;* the 'Assumption of the Virgin,' in the Academy of Venice; and the 'Martyrdom of S. Lorenzo,' at Madrid, and of which there is a repetition in the Jesuits' Church, Venice; also, very large and celebrated pictures. Titian painted important frescoes in the Ducal Palace, Venice, but they were destroyed by fire, with the exception of a fresco of St. Christopher.

Of all Titian's masterly representations of the naked female form, the two so-called 'Venuses,' in the tribune of the Uffizj, and that at Dresden, are among the most celebrated. Titian painted the portraits of many of the greatest historical and literary personages of his time, including his great patron Charles V, Francis I (probably from a medallion), Pope Paul III, and no less than five Doges. His most important family group is that of the Cornaro family, now in Northumberland House. His daughter Lavinia is often painted, holding up a plate or casket. But his most admired female representations are known as 'Titian's Mistress,' a dark-eyed beauty, with dusky golden hair, of the ripest womanly fascination, yet withal somewhat serious in expression. The portrait in the Louvre (with the mirror), the so-called 'Flora' in the Uffizj, and those in the Pitti and the Sciarra Gallery at Rome, are the most famous repetitions.

Some of the most celebrated painters who imitated Titian were Bonifazio, Veneziano, Schiavone, and Dom. Campagnola. Other masters were distinguished by a style peculiar to themselves. Such were Semolei, Pordenone (celebrated for the softness of his flesh-painting), Paris Bordone (whose lovely red-haired 'Female Figure' was not long since placed in the National Gallery), Il Moretto di Brescia, and his pupil Moroni, who rivals Titian in portraiture, and whose portrait of a Jesuit, better known as 'Titian's Schoolmaster,' is the gem of the Sutherland (Stafford Rouse) collection. Il Bassano was, perhaps, the earliest Italian who may be called a *genre* painter.

In the latter half of the sixteenth century two great Venetian painters, Tintoretto and Paul Veronese, carried the practice of painting on the most stupendous scale to the extreme of daring. Tintoretto was one of the most vigorous and rapid painters who ever wielded a brush, which obtained for him the name of 'Il Furioso' from his contemporaries. His style he described in the inscription placed over his studio—'The drawing of Michael Angelo, the colouring of Titian.' His picture of 'Paradise,' fixed to the ceiling of the library in the Ducal Palace, Venice, is the largest oil painting in the world, measuring 74 feet by 34. There are numerous works by Tintoretto, in oil and fresco, at Venice; among the most celebrated of which are the 'Miracle of St. Mark,' in the Academy of Venice (the saint is represented to have made a Venetian, who had become a Turkish slave, invulnerable when sentenced to be tortured), and a' Crucifixion,' in the Scuola di San Rocco.

Tintoretto's colouring, notwithstanding that in it he professed to rival Titian, is, however, generally cold and heavy. The pure Venetian principles of colour, but in a light scale, and a pervading silvery tone, were carried to perfection by Paul Veronese. 'Never had the pomp of colour been so exalted, so glorified, as in his works; his paintings are like full concerts of enchanting music.' In one of the chief characteristics of the Venetian school, namely, the imitation of different stuffs and textures, Paolo greatly excelled. The magnificent architectural backgrounds, for which some of the works of this master are so conspicuous, are said to have been painted by his brother Benedetto Cagliari. In many of the works of Paul Veronese, the evidence of the accomplished *artist,* in the more decorative and material sense, is the paramount impression. The 'Family of Darius at the Feet of Alexander,' in the National Gallery, is a moderately good specimen of the master; but a far more renowned oil picture is the well-known gigantic 'Marriage of Cana,' in the Louvre. The Doge's Palace and other buildings in Venice, particularly the Church of S. Sebastiano, where the painter lies buried, contain innumerable works by this painter.

Fresco Painting in Italy in the 17th and 18th Centuries

Various causes led to the general decline of painting in Rome and Florence, even more than in Venice, towards the end of the sixteenth century; but chiefly the universal mannerism consequent upon the rapid productiveness aimed at by artists in order to satisfy the demands of patrons who esteemed art chiefly as a means of sumptuous architectural decoration. To check this deteriorating tendency, it seemed necessary, since individual originality and genius were not forthcoming, to introduce and establish rules founded upon the practice of the generally recognised greatest masters. The school of the Carracci, founded by Ludovico Carracci (1555–1619), at Bologna, was the first to professedly adopt this principle. Ludovico was supported by his nephews Agostino and Annibale Carracci; and a sonnet by Agostino defines their general aim. The sonnet may be thus rendered: 'Let him who wishes to be a good painter acquire the design of Rome, Venetian shade and action, the terrible manner of Michael Angelo, Titian's truth and nature, the sovereign purity of Correggio's style, and the just symmetry of a Raphael; the decorum and well-grounded knowledge of Tibaldi,[82] the invention of the learned Primaticcio, and a little of Parmigiano's grace; but, without so much study and toil, he need only apply himself to imitate the works which our Niccolino (dell' Abbate)[83] has left its here.' This system of selecting various excellences obtained for the great academy founded by the Carracci the title of the Eclectic school; but the study of nature was not excluded. It has been remarked that this endeavour to unite characteristics essentially different, at once implies a contradiction; and the Carracci themselves certainly did not reduce their theory to practice.

Among others, Denis Calvert, the Fleming who had established a famous school at Bologna, at first violently opposed the Carracci; the school of Calvert was, however, quickly superseded by that of the Carracci, and all detraction appears to have ceased after the execution of the celebrated frescoes of the Carracci, in the Magnani Palace. Ludovico's engagements as a teacher, perhaps prevented his being a prolific artist; but Agostino (although with his brother Annibale only the son of a tailor) was a learned man, and being profoundly acquainted with the principles of his art, he undertook the chief superintendence of the instructions of the academy; his pictures are, consequently, still more rare. He is, notwithstanding, particularly celebrated as an engraver. The best known works of the family are by Annibale. In 1600, Annibale was invited to Rome, to decorate the Farnese Gallery with frescoes. These famous works he completed, with the assistance of his brothers Agostino, Domenichino, Albani, and Lanfranc, in four years. For technical excellence, correctness, and external artistic qualities, these frescoes have never been surpassed. The most renowned oil picture by Annibale is unquestionably the 'Three Maries,' at Castle Howard. Annibale was one of the first Italian artists who practised landscape painting as a separate branch of art. The best frescoes, by Ludovico, were in the convent of San Michele, in Bosco; but they have long since perished. The oil pictures of Ludovico are highly eulogised by Sir Joshua Reynolds in his *Second Discourse,* especially for, as he says, 'The solemn effect of that twilight which seems diffused over his pictures, and which appears to me to correspond with grave and dignified subjects better than the more artificial brilliancy of sunshine, which enlightens the pictures of Titian.'

The Eclectic, or, as it was also called, the Academic style, was developed, with, however, certain peculiarities and much originality, by the following very distinguished painters of the Carracci school. Domenichino, perhaps, makes the least parade of what is rather unreasonably called academic mannerism; unreasonable, we say, because this mannerism is generally the result of the painter's native incapacity, quite as much as it is a necessary product of systematic instruction. Domenichino's 'Communion of St. Jerome' is placed opposite Raphael's 'Transfiguration,' in the Vatican picture gallery, and has been considered, next to the latter, the greatest picture in Rome. Some frescoes near Rome, and at Fano, are among Domenichino's best performances.

Guido, another pupil of the Carracci, ranks next to Domenichino. Guido's masterpiece is the ornamental fresco of 'Aurora preceding the Chariot of Phœbus,' drawn by piebald horses, and accompanied by the Hours in rapid flight, in the Rospigliosi Palace, Rome. Guido painted in three manners: his first was distinguished for breadth and power of light and shade; his second, for a rich mellow tone of colouring; his third, for a pale, silvery-grey tone of colour. His numerous 'Madonnas,' 'Cleopatras,' 'Sibyls,' &c., are chiefly in the latter manner. These generally flat and empty representations were painted rapidly to retrieve his losses at gambling, and he even farmed himself out for the same purpose. Guido had a fine feeling for abstract beauty, that is to say, beauty with little individual character or anything like Raphaelesque expression; his ideal appears to have been taken from antique sculpture: many of his female heads resemble the Niobe.

Albani is chiefly distinguished for his highly finished cabinet oil pictures; the subjects of which, though mythological representations, and generally naked figures, are full of charming natural fancy. The landscape backgrounds are always admirably painted; but still more so the numerous chubby little *amorini,* or, as they are popularly called, 'Cupids,'[84] which are almost invariably introduced.

Among other less important artists who formed their style immediately under the influence of the Carracci, or belonged to the general Eclectic school, may be named Guercino, whose works display considerable force and a happy union of chiaroscuro and colour; Lanfranco, remarkable chiefly for vigorous handling; Sassoferrato and Carlo Dolci, generally pleasing, and always smooth in execution, but the latter frequently degenerating into affectation; the Procaccini; Cigoli; Andrea Sacchi; Jacobo da Empoli; Pietro da Cortona (the painter of the ceiling of an immense saloon in the Palazzo Barberini); Allori, whose beautiful and sumptuously dressed 'Judith' is one of the most striking works in the Pitti Palace; and Carlo Maratti, remembered principally as the restorer of the frescoes by Raphael, in the Vatican.

The opposition to the Eclectics of those painters who adhered entirely to the study of nature was extremely violent, particularly in Naples, where a 'cabal' of artists was formed, who conspired to have recourse even to poison and the dagger, should any unfortunate Academic painter attempt to establish himself in Naples. Domenichino is said to have been one of their victims. The style of these *Naturalisti*—as, from their unselected imitation of nature, these painters were called—reflects all the savage passion and dark criminality of their nature: the style has been called the 'poetry of the repulsive.' The violent contrasts of light and shade in their works are perfectly congenial with the horrible or ghastly scenes of suffering, sorcery, murder, and robbery they delighted to represent. The most powerful painter of this school was Caravaggio; though Ribera, the Spaniard, hence called Spagnoletto, might be more properly entitled to rank as the head of the Neapolitan school. Salvator Rosa, though a remarkably original genius both in his figure pictures and landscapes, usually carried a similar feeling into landscape painting; his favourite scenes being storm-frequented and bandit-haunted mountain gorges. Salvator was himself, though probably involuntarily, associated with bandits in his youth. Luca Giordano, a later Neapolitan artist, appears to have sacrificed extraordinary natural gifts to a rapidity of execution which obtained for him the title of *Fa Presto.* The similarity in the temperament of the Spaniards and Neapolitans will readily explain why this style prevailed also extensively in Spain. Padovanino, and some other Italian artists of consequence in the seventeenth century, and Raphael Mengs, the German fresco painter of the eighteenth century, might be named; but our intention has been fulfilled if we have described the rise and progress of painting in that country where it has received its highest development, and if we have indicated some of the leading causes which effected its deterioration and hastened its decline.

Fresco Painting in the 19th Century

In the present century there has been a great revival of fresco painting in various countries of Europe, more especially in Germany. The movement commenced with the decoration of the Chevalier Bartholdy's house at Rome, by Cornelius and some other then unknown young German artists. The success of this attempt induced that most munificent patron of modern art, the ex-king Ludwig, of Bavaria, to invite the ablest of these young artists to Munich, and guarantee them a salary for ten years, in order that they should embellish with frescoes the numerous magnificent public, ecclesiastical, and regal edifices in course of construction under his auspices in that capital. Here, and somewhat later at Berlin and Dusseldorf, these and other German artists formed academies and schools; and one by one the names of Overbeck, Veit, Cornelius, Schnorr, Schadow, Hess, Kaulbach, and Rethel, and for large works in oil, Menzel, Lessing, &c., had acquired European reputation. The style adopted by several of these painters was that of the severe early Italian Christian art, thus committing the grave mistake of believing that art can be transplanted from one period to another differing greatly in its wants and sentiment; with strange perversion of taste, also, the Germans rejected the rich positive colouring of these early masters, substituting cold, insipid, half-tints.

The most important fresco in Munich is the 'Last Judgment,' by Cornelius, in the Ludwigs-Kirche. The figure of Christ in this fresco is much admired, though the whole composition is but a varied repetition of Michael Angelo.

Two large apartments in the Glyptothek, or Sculpture Gallery, are also covered with frescoes by Cornelius and his pupils. The halls and loggie of the Pinakothek, or Picture Gallery, are decorated throughout with arabesques by Neureuther and others, and with historical and other frescoes in the lunettes and cupolas. These frescoes, which have all some reference to the history of art, were designed by Cornelius, and executed by Zimmermann and others. The walls of the interior of the splendid Basilica of St. Bonifacius are adorned with frescoes by Hess and his pupils. The Köninsbau is decorated with frescoes by Zimmermann and Kaulbach, and the state apartments of the king and queen with encaustic paintings by Schnorr, the subjects of which are from Greek and German poets. The Festbau contains battle-scenes by Hess and Adam, and German historical subjects by Schnorr. Lastly, in the sumptuous Allerheiligen-Kapelle, Hess and his pupils have revived the mediaeval practice of painting frescoes on a gold ground.

In Berlin some very noble works in fresco have also been executed in our own time. The illustrations of the *Niebelungen Lied,* by Cornelius and others, in the palace of the King of Prussia, compose a fine cycle of epic representations. The 'Battle of the Huns,' by Kaulbach, in the gallery of M. Raczynski, is also a great work; but still more celebrated are the great frescoes illustrating the 'Races of Man,' by this very eminent painter, in the entrance-hall of the new Museum.

In Paris, of late years, mural decoration has been extensively employed for the embellishment, in some instances, of the exterior porches and porticoes, as well as the interior of the churches and public buildings. The 'Hemicycle' of Paul Delaroche, in the Palais des Beaux Arts, is deservedly the best-known wall painting in Paris; but other public buildings, as the Louvre, the Bourse, the Elysée, and the churches of St. Eustache, St. Vincent de Paul, Notre Dame de Lorette, St. Germain L'Auxerrois, the Madeleine, St. Severin, St. Germain des Près, &c., are enriched with frescoes and oil paintings by Delacroix, Flandrin, Ingres, Ary-Scheffer, Cabanel, and other of the most distinguished modern French artists. Added to these, many of the great military oil pictures at Versailles by Horace Vernet, Yvon, Pils, &c., are on the scale of the largest mural works. The famous 'Hemicycle' is painted in oil, but it has all the breadth and freedom of fresco. In this masterpiece of Delaroche the most celebrated artists of every age and country are assembled, and disposed in groups round the semicircular wall. Presiding over them, and elevated on thrones in the centre, are Phidias, Ictinus, and Apelles — the greatest sculptor, architect, and painter of antiquity. Below these are four female figures (one of which was the artist's wife), allegorical representations of the chief epochs of art; and in the immediate foreground is a female stooping to gather wreaths, which she seems preparing to scatter out of the picture. In the amphitheatre which contains this noble work of art, and immediately in front of it, the prizes are distributed to the students of painting, sculpture, and architecture: this, therefore, explains the intention of the painter's composition. In Belgium, some fine frescoes and other works in the nature of monumental paintings have been executed by Baron Leys, Gallait, &c.

In England, Sir Joshua Reynolds proposed, in the last century, that certain members of the Royal Academy should fill with paintings the spaces in St. Paul's which Sir Christopher Wren had intentionally left for that purpose; but public opinion was not then ripe for an innovation which the great architect believed would sooner or later take place. The first serious effort to elevate painting in this country to its highest office, that of mural decoration, was made by Barry; and the unhappy result to the starving artist of his attempt to introduce 'high art' is well known. And to this day the great qualities in his oil paintings of 'The Progress of Civilisation,' in the Hall of the Society of Arts in the Adelphi—though, we admit, ill-adapted to the purpose, and containing palpable defects—are not adequately recognised. The decoration of the New Houses of Parliament afforded the best possible opportunity for the revival of fresco painting. That English artists felt the grandeur of the occasion, they sufficiently proved. None will forget, who saw the exhibitions of cartoons in Westminster Hall in 1843 and 1845, the noble response they made to the invitation of Government; although there were abundant proofs of want of practice, and of a just conception of the requirements of fresco decoration; for hardly one, probably, of those artists had ever before drawn upon the 'scale of those cartoons, and very few had even attempted to treat subjects similar to those proposed.

The year 1841 will be memorable in the history of English art for the appointment of the 'Select Committee to take into consideration the promotion of the Fine Arts of this country, in connection with the re-building of the new Houses of Parliament.' During the year the Committee examined many individuals well acquainted with the progress and position of the arts, both at home and abroad; and the result of the inquiry tended to direct them to select fresco as best adapted for the decoration of public buildings. This was, however, as we have said, a style of painting then hardly known in this country. It was therefore proposed to invite artists to furnish cartoons, coloured sketches, and specimens of fresco painting, in competition for several premiums, varying in amount from one to three hundred pounds. The general excellence of the cartoons, &c., sent in and exhibited in Westminster Hall in 1843, and again in 1845, surpassed expectations, and so far fully confirmed the Committee in their preference of fresco.

The House of Lords was the first portion of the New Palace chosen for decoration. It was decided that six compartments, three at each end, should contain subjects by artists who obtained the highest premiums, illustrative of the functions of the House of Lords, and of the relation in which it stands to the sovereign. Three of these were to personify, in abstract representations, Religion, Justice, and the 'Spirit of Chivalry,' and the remaining to correspond with such representations, and express the relation of the Sovereign to the Church, to the Law, and to the State. These frescoes have long since been completed, according to this intention. Those over the Throne are, 'Edward III conferring the Order of the Garter on the Black Prince,' by Mr. Cope, R.A.; the 'Baptism of Ethelbert,' by Mr. Dyce, R.A.; and 'Prince Henry acknowledging the Authority of Judge Gascoigne,' by Mr. Cope, R.A. Those over the Strangers' Gallery are the corresponding personifications: the 'Spirit of Justice,' by Mr. Maclise, R.A.; the 'Spirit of Religion,' by Mr. Horsley, A.R.A.; and the 'Spirit of Chivalry,' by Mr. Maclise, R.A. Other parts of the palace, including the corridors and the Upper Waiting Hall, or Hall of the Poets (so named from the illustrations of our great poets, supplied by the Paintings), have subsequently been decorated with wall paintings by these artists and Messrs. Herbert, R.A., Ward, R.A., Tenniel, Watts, and Armitage. In five of the compartments of the Peers' Corridor the following subjects have been executed by Mr. Cope, namely, 'Charles I erecting his Standard at Nottingham,' 'Basing House defended by the Cavaliers,' 'The Burial of Charles I,' 'The Parting of Lord and Lady Russell,' and 'The Embarcation of the Pilgrim Fathers for New England.' The subjects intended for the vacant spaces are (on the Royalist side) the 'Expulsion of the Fellows of a College in Oxford for refusing to sign the Covenant,' and (on the Parliament side) 'The Train-bands of London setting out to relieve Gloucester,' and 'Speaker Lenthall asserting the Privileges of the Commons when Charles I attempted to seize the Five Members.' In the corresponding Commons' Corridor Mr. Ward has completed 'The Execution of Montrose,' 'The Last Sleep of Argyle,' 'Alice Lisle assisting the Fugitives to escape after the Battle of Sedgmoor,' and 'Jane Lane assisting Charles II to escape after the Battle of Worcester;' and is now engaged upon 'The Landing of Charles II at Dover,' 'The Trial of the Bishops,' 'William and Mary receiving the Lords and Commons at the Banqueting House, Whitehall,' and 'Monk declaring for a Free Parliament,' are to follow from the same painter. Mr. Maclise has executed in the Royal Gallery a most remarkable work, the 'Interview between Wellington and Blucher after Waterloo,' in the new material of water-glass, for further particulars of which we refer the reader to our article on the process. Mr. Dyce is advancing, though very tardily, with, as they will doubtless be deemed, his very remarkable frescoes relating to the legend of King Arthur. In the Peers' Robing Room or Chamber of Appeal, Mr. Herbert was, at the date of our going to press, on the point of finishing his great picture, in stereochrome, of 'Moses bringing down the Tables of the Law to the Israelites,' which will, we believe, be considered one of the most elevated and original works of modern art. Of this, with Mr. Maclise's gigantic works, also in stereochrome, in the Royal Gallery, we shall speak in our description of the water-glass process. An opinion seems to prevail among architectural purists that some of the works already executed are unsuitable in character, because they have no relation whatever to the architectural features of the place.

Mr. Watts has decorated one end of the beautiful hall of Lincoln's Inn with a large fresco entitled, 'The School of Legislature'—an ideal representation of the great lawgivers of the world. In All Saints, Margaret Street, the east wall of the choir is painted by Mr. Dyce, with frescoes in the style of early Christian art. Besides these, we may mention the following important mural decorations: the 'Illustrations of Northumbrian History,' painted (in an oil medium, though without gloss) by Mr. W. B. Scott, in Sir Walter Trevelyn's mansion at Wallington; the roof-paintings of Ely Cathedral, left unfinished by the death of Mr. L'Estrange, and to be completed by Mr. Gambier Parry; Mr. Armitage's frescoes in the Roman Catholic Church of St. John's, Islington; oil paintings by Mr. Watts in Little Holland House; Mr. Rossetti's Altar-piece, at Llandaff Cathedral; and Mr. Leighton's at the Church of Lyndhurst, New Forest; the distemper paintings by Mr. Rossetti, and other pre-Raphaelites, in, the Union Rooms, Oxford; and the decoration of Mr. Holford's Mansion, Park Lane, now in course of execution, by the distinguished amateur Sir Coutts Lindsay.

Chapter 8

Oil Painting

The practice of art, it has been seen, was confined throughout the Middle Ages to the cloisters. This circumstance explains at once the religious character of art, and also—from the sphere of its cultivation being so contracted—that numerous branches were practised by the same individual. Learning and science were similarly confined and centralized, so that the artist, if not absolutely compelled to do so, had every facility for acquiring the chemical and botanical knowledge necessary to enable him to prepare his various pigments and vehicles. In such study the painter would be greatly assisted by the *spenseria,* or dispensary, generally attached to, and even sometimes now connected with, the convent in Italy. In mediaeval ages the tradition indeed obtained that St. Luke, the patron of artists, was a physician as well as painter; and many a *frate* seemed to have emulated the presumed example of the Evangelist, by uniting the two professions in his own person. And even when, at a later period, the artist became independent, his monk employers still frequently supplied him with his materials. But the artists of early times generally, and almost of necessity, were acquainted with the various methods of preparing these materials themselves—indeed this knowledge was considered an essential part of artistic education.

Thus the acquisition of the knowledge of painting entailed not simply the study of an art, but also the drudgery of learning a business. Like ordinary handicraftsmen, the Italian painters had their *botega* or shop—for 'studios' were then unknown—and the artists of both the North and South of Europe had their guilds; the rules of which define, among other privileges, the number of pupils which the masters in certain grades were permitted to instruct each master, of course, taking as many pupils, to increase his profits, as these rules would permit. The pupils were duly and formally apprenticed, generally, at an early age, and the term of their apprenticeship was in some cases protracted till long after they had arrived at manhood. Cennini fixes the period of apprenticeship at thirteen years, six of which were to be given exclusively to the manufacture of colours, the composition of tempera vehicles, the laying on plaster for fresco, the preparation of panels, &c. For more than a century after the time of Cennini, the practice regularly obtained; the introduction of oil painting involving the necessity for giving still more attention to the properties of media and varnishes, and their effect upon pigments.

These, then, were the material conditions, so to speak, of the practice of painting which obtained in the North as well as in Italy, and at the beginning of the fifteenth century, when the Van Eycks introduced the improved vehicle of oil painting—an improvement, without doubt, due to their possessing a more than ordinary amount of this practical and chemical knowledge. Some of this knowledge the reader may think it desirable to be put in possession of before we attempt to ascertain the precise nature of the discovery of the Van Eycks. Various other technicalities and artistic appliances may also be explained, and will not be out of place under the present heading; because, although not always peculiar to 'oil painting,' the impression will naturally be induced, that all practical details common to painting generally should be included in an account of the method which is at the present time most extensively practised. We commence then with—

THE PAINTING-ROOM

The source, not only of the effects in the works of individual painters, but of the characteristics of whole schools, will hardly be apparent without reflecting upon the difference between painting in the open air and in a confined room. The quantity of light admitted into the artist's studio, or *atelier (Fr.* workshop), as it is sometimes called, is also a material consideration. Before attempting detailed description, we cannot refrain from giving the first 'peep behind the curtain,' at an artist *chez lui,* afforded by Mr. Thackeray,[85] in the following beautiful passage from *The Newcomes:*

'The palette on his arm was a great shield, painted of many colours; he carried his maul-stick and a sheaf of brushes along with it, the weapons of his glorious but harmless war. With these he achieves conquests wherein none are wounded save the envious; with that he shelters himself against much idleness, ambition, temptation. Occupied over that consoling work, idle thoughts cannot gain the mastery over him, selfish wishes or desires are kept at bay. Art is truth, and truth is religion, and its study and practice a daily work of pious duty. What are the world's struggles, brawls, successes, to that calm recluse pursuing his calling? See, twinkling in the darkness round his chamber, numberless beautiful trophies of the graceful victories he has won—sweet flowers of fancy reared by him, and shapes of beauty which he has moulded.'

The first requisite of a painting-room is, that its dimensions should be adequate to allow the artist space to retire from his work to the distance at which the picture will be conveniently viewed when placed in its destination. For large decorative paintings, the room must therefore he very spacious. We find accordingly that the studios of some of the Italian painters were immense.

An inventory, which has been preserved, of the effects of Rembrandt when he was declared insolvent,[86] furnishes a most interesting sample of the incongruous contents of a painter's studio.

There is, as might be expected, a large collection of pictures by Rembrandt himself, and a number by other Dutch painters. There are also several Italian pictures, including specimens of Raphael and Michael Angelo, and many volumes of prints, after Flemish, Dutch, and Italian masters. The stock of furniture includes some picturesque Spanish chairs, in leather and green velvet; but the quantity of *bric-à-brac is* quite enormous, comprising columns and china, globes and minerals, busts of Roman emperors and ancient philosophers, helmets and armour, stuffed beasts, birds, and fishes; plaster casts, including a Sibyl and the Laocöon, walking-sticks and bamboo pipes, musical instruments, bows and arrows, and a metal cannon; heads and hands moulded from nature, stag-horns and Indian armour, fragments of antique dresses and draperies of diverse colours, halberds and swords, a wooden trumpet, and the skins of a lion and a lioness. How the motley contents of a painter's workroom throw light on his studies and tastes, and how curiously they may be combined in his works, we need not attempt to point out.

Painters generally prefer a window with a northern or eastern aspect, because the light from those quarters is least affected by the direct rays of the sun, and therefore less variable; but a southern light is undoubtedly more beautiful, and is likely to conduce to an agreeably warm tone of colouring. The size and altitude of the window is of extreme importance. The more contracted the opening, the broader and more intense will be the shadows; while the higher the aperture through which the ray penetrates, the longer will be the descending shadows, and the more abrupt the downward diminution of brilliancy. The colouring will be likewise affected, necessarily in tone, and generally in hue. With sombre shadow the colouring may be deep and rich, but it will more frequently be sad and broken; but in cheerful light it will usually be pure as well as pale. The early painters commonly gave an open-air effect to their pictures. Leonardo da Vinci was the first to show extreme partiality to indoor effects and powerful shadows; he has, therefore, been considered the inventor of *chiaroscuro.* The confined light breaking through the rocks, which give the title to the celebrated Leonardo in the Collection of Lord Suffolk, 'La Vierge aux Rochers,' illustrates the impressiveness of lighting figures in this way.

Correggio, also, another and the greatest master of chiaroscuro, being, perhaps, still more admirable in this treatment of light and shade than for his proverbial *grace,* often introduces a very small proportion of the luminous element. We may instance the 'Magdalene Reading,' at the mouth of a cave, in Lord Ward's collection (a repetition of the Dresden picture), and the supernatural light in the famous 'Notte,' in the Dresden Gallery. The effect in this last picture, though often spoken of as original, has been employed before and since. The promised 'Light to lighten the Gentiles' seems to be rendered literally. From the body of the new-born infant Saviour emanate rays symbolical of Divine enlightenment and revelation dissipating the world's outer midnight darkness, and as they diverge they beam on the Madonna's enrapt features, and compel the worshipping shepherds to shade their faces from the miraculous splendour. There is a striking effect, also, in the *replica (Ital.* repetition or copy) in the National Gallery, of the 'Agony in the Garden,' in the Duke of Wellington's collection. The principal charm of the chiaroscuro of Correggio is, however, the melting softness of the transitions from light to shade, and the sweetness of the intervening pearly half-tints. The Bolognese school, with the exception of Guido in his third manner, generally inclined to the profound shadows and background which a darkened studio so naturally suggests. The very impressive picture belonging to Lord Carlisle, 'The Three Maries at the Sepulchre,' by Annibale Carracci, owes as much to the congenial solemnity of its shadows as to the appropriately sorrowful expression of the figures. The 'cloistered tone,' the effect of a 'dim religious light through storied pane,' in the pictures of Ludovico, is, as we have already remarked, greatly admired by Sir Joshua Reynolds in one of his *Discourses.*

To Rembrandt it was reserved, however, to show the full poetry and mystery of shadow. Though not born in a mill, as was long believed, it is more than probable that his father's mill was his first painting-room, and that in it he acquired something like a feline power of dilating the pupil of his eye to see into shadowy corners, and learned how vividly a pencil of concentrated light from a high-up window-slit will 'pick out' points of detail from the surrounding breadths of half tone. The strange witchery which Rembrandt's chiaroscuro has over the mind is partly ascribable to the quantity of reflected light in his shadows, by which objects are not fully 'made out,' as it is called, but seem to float in phantom indistinctness.

One of the most delightful prerogatives of the painter, in contradistinction to the photographer, is the power of representing reflected light. Compared to the range in nature from sunlight to midnight, the artist's scale is extremely limited, from his most brilliant white to his most intense asphaltum; but he can to a certain extent compensate for this by dwelling on the exquisite phenomena of reflected light, so often overlooked by the uneducated eye. Various expedients are adopted in the studio, by adjusting sheets of white or coloured paper, to obtain much coveted particular reflections. Caravaggio and Spagnoletto (Ribera), and other Neapolitan and Spanish painters, gave the appearance produced by confined light, but omitted these reflections; hence their shadows are repulsively heavy, wanting in transparency, and dark rather than deep. Caravaggio was said by his contemporaries never to emerge from his cellar. Pictures painted on these principles convey the impression of having been executed by lamplight. In many schools the drawing and painting are conducted entirely by gaslight;[87] and many writers on artistic education recommend the practice as favourable to the attainment of vigour, richness, and breadth of light and shade. Tintoretto is said to have drawn by lamplight from casts from the Florentine and antique sculpture, in order to obtain forcible relief; and the blackness of his shadows bears witness to the practice.

The effects represented by such means are, however, so artificial, or at least so unlike the ordinary aspect of the fair daylight face of nature, that two great factions have always existed, which, as Mr. Frank Howard says, in *Colour as a Means of Art,* rival in fierceness, as in name, the feud of the Bianchi and the Neri of Italy. The inadequacy of his means compels the artist in some way to select or force his effects; and 'the Neri, apparently, give up all hope of rivalling the brightness of nature; but, by forcing the shadows and general tone of the whole picture, they endeavour to produce the same gradation of light and shadow as in nature, but on a lower scale. The Bianchi party, on the other hand, endeavour to compensate for the want of positive brilliancy by refining or increasing the delicacy and beauty of the tints. Light is the origin, or immediate cause of colour, and the brighter the light, the greater variety of tints will be found or displayed. As we cannot rival the cause, the Bianchi contend that we must increase the effect by introducing colour in lieu of those tints which in nature appear neutral, and thus conceal the weakness of our imitation of the cause by making it apparently produce greater effects. Thus, all the greys are rendered by pure ultramarine tints or delicate pearly purple, and the greatest possible variety of beautiful and delicate colours is introduced in the light; while the shadows are generally of a neutral colour, the most decidedly contrasting with the tints in the light. But sometimes the [complementary] colour is carried through the shadows as well as the lights; positive crimson being introduced into those of leaves of grass, while those of flesh are rendered by a dull red, and those of a sandy bank by pure glue. The main difference lies in the different treatment of the atmospheric influence and association.'

On the other hand, to again quote Mr. Howard, 'certain tones of colour have been found to be almost universally recognised as agreeable, and by the mass of artists and critics called the Neri, it is held to be fine colouring to reduce every representation, without consideration of propriety, to these conventionally agreeable tones. Sir Joshua Reynolds commends a picture of a moonlight scene by Rubens, which is so rich in colour, that if you hide the moon, it appears like a sunset. The background of the far-famed "Mercury, Venus, and Cupid," in the National Gallery, and the sky of the "Bacchus and Ariadne," are instances of this practice. It would be difficult to say what the former was meant for except *background* to the figures, and no one ever saw a sky such a blue as the latter.' It must always be remembered, however, that there are many influences which have very greatly obscured nearly all old oil paintings, especially in the shadows. The modern pre-Raphaelites have, several of them, returned to the light tones of the early fresco and tempera painters, and thus rushed to the opposite extreme; but perhaps no artists of the present day have united more truth of colour to open-air effect than Mr. John Lewis and the late Thomas Seddon, in their Eastern subjects.

Painters, if practicable, or unless there is a special reason to the contrary, work with the light on the left, to prevent the 'cast shadow'[88] from the brush falling inwards; it follows, therefore, that pictures are nearly always seen to the greatest advantage with the light on the left of the spectator; but we shall return to this again in our remarks on Watercolour Painting.

It remains to be noticed, that the light may occasionally be modified by some semi-transparent medium with the happiest result. It was, we have seen, by very slow degrees that glass was substituted for the parchment and linen windows of the Middle Ages; and (oiled) paper windows were retained in domestic architecture even at a late period. Le Vieil, the French writer on glass of the eighteenth century, says, these paper windows were found, in his time, only in the studios of painters and engravers, who preferred them because the light which passed through them was more equal and less fatiguing to the sight, and they were useful in diminishing the noise in the street. But such windows have a far greater recommendation, namely, the delicate breadth of transparent half-tint they spread over objects, by which minute blemishes are softened and effaced. Mr. Burnet, in his *Practical Hints on Portrait Painting,* alludes to the charming effect of a portrait, by Phillips, of a lady 'seated out of doors with the light coming through on the countenance, interrupted by a white parasol.' The 'Nelly O'Brien,' by Reynolds, in the Marquis of Hertford's collection, which made such a sensation in the Manchester Art Treasures Exhibition (1857), owes its fascination to a similar effect; but the white parasol is replaced by a mushroom straw hat. 'But,' again quoting Mr. Burnet, 'the strongest proof of the influence of delicate shadow in refining the asperities of nature was in a portrait of old "Sir Isaac Heard," by Devis. While talking of the harsh lines often observable in the countenances of old people, he drew the muslin curtain across the painting-room window, which in an instant produced the most delicious grey and pearly tones over the shadows, and removed the whole appearance from common nature to the most finished work of art.'

THE IMPLEMENTS, ETC

Brushes are used for the application of 'wet' paint, and are thus distinguished from the 'dry point.' The latter (though usually confined to the engraver's art) is a convenient term to avoid the ambiguity which has resulted from the use of the word 'pencil,' both for a small brush and a stick enclosing blacklead, &c. Painters prefer long handles to their brushes for large works because they enable them to approximate to the distance at which such pictures should be viewed, and because they favour that masterly execution whereby a few touches, apparently coarse when seen near, yet convey the impression of perfect finish at the proper distance. Velasquez and our own Gainsborough are said to have worked with brushes six feet long; and the latter placed the model at the same distance, so that the subject, the painter, and the picture occupied an equilateral triangle. Vasari recommends that the cartoon should be drawn with a piece of charcoal fixed into along cane. From the desirability of seeing the effect of each touch at a greater distance than that at which it is convenient to place it on the picture, artists contract the habit of swaying backwards and forwards, like so many Mandarin images, and in a manner that to the uninitiated must appear somewhat affected. Sir Thomas Lawrence used to go so far as to place portrait and sitter side by side towards the finishing, then retire to a distance to compare both, and work upon the picture while so situated.

The larger brushes are made of hog-hair,[89] and are called 'tools.' The word 'pencil' is still sometimes applied to the smaller sable brushes. These are either round or flat: the latter, though Haydon expressed great contempt for them, certainly contribute to a squareness of marking greatly admired in the works of many masters. Most artists also use a brush made of badger's hair, something like a shaving-brush, only that it is kept dry, and the hairs diverge more. It bears the significant names of 'softener' and 'sweetener,' and is used to blend the colours and remove 'edginess,' by being swept to and fro over them while freshly laid. Its use is very tempting to tyros; but it is apt to produce a 'muzzy,' feeble, unpleasant appearance, by no means uncommon, technically called 'woolliness.'

The Maul (or *Mahl) Stick,* is used to steady the hand holding the brush. It is held in the other hand, and the end of the stick is enveloped with a pad to prevent indentations when it may rest on the canvas. The old painters never used a maul-stick when working on large pictures, considering that the practice interfered with freedom of hand. Rubens mentions being obliged to have recourse to one in his old age and in declining health.

The Palette, 'set' with its little heaps of pigments—'the shield of many colours,' and the 'sheaf of brushes' through the thumb-hole,—are the most common symbols of the genius or muse of painting. The 'thumb-hole' is, however, of recent introduction, and replaced projecting handles. The latter is the form in Sir Joshua Reynolds' early portrait of himself; and such is the form of the palette which belonged to the great English master, and is preserved, together with that of Hogarth, in the Royal Academy.

The Palette-knife, or Spatula, has a pliable blade, and is used to temper colours and mix tints on the palette, and also frequently takes the place of the brush in the actual application of colour, more particularly in the early stages of a picture, and in fact whenever a solid body of colour is required. The colour is, as it were, trowelled on, leaving a smooth pleasant surface for subsequent operations. It was a favourite instrument with Turner. Artists differ greatly in the number of tints they arrange on the palette: some preparing a great number, and others mixing them at the end of the brush from a few simple colours. Great authorities on art have said that the surest road to fine colouring is through a simple palette.

The Easel is a frame which supports the picture during its progress; the commoner description is triangular, and supplied with pegs for the adjustment of the height of the work. Of a better and more convenient form is the square 'rack' easel, which allows the painter great facility in raising or lowering his picture. Wilkie's first easel was a chest of drawers, one of which be pulled out, and inclined his panel against another. Pictures whose dimensions are so moderate as not to require a special scaffolding are classed as 'easel pictures,' the smaller of which are called 'cabinet pictures.' The easel of Sir Joshua Reynolds is preserved in the Royal Academy.

The Slab and Muller, for grinding pigments, figure in a painter's paraphernalia far less frequently now than formerly.

The Throne is the name portrait painters give the chair provided for their 'sitters,' from the circumstance of its being placed on a raised daïs, covered usually with red cloth. The 'patients' are thus elevated on a 'monument' of convenient height for the operation or taking the likeness. And not only is it desirable to have the sitter nearly on a level with the eye of the painter when standing, for the sake of its mere convenience, but, as may be seen in the works of the old masters, it communicates a superior air to the bead if painted as it appears, looking at it rather from below than above. Nothing, in fact, requires greater artistic knowledge and taste than the choice of the most characteristic and agreeable carriage of the head, and the best view of the features. In these essential particulars photographic portraits chiefly fail, in consequence of the innumerable bad habits of sitters. Reynolds, though of low stature, is supposed to have brought the 'throne' and standing at the easel into fashion; but Vandyke was also a little person, and painted standing. Velasquez we know did, as he is thus represented in the picture where the children of Philip IV are in his painting-room. Titian was of small stature, yet he is said, on the contrary, to have generally painted sitting, as we learn from an anecdote told by Vasari; for, while once painting the Emperor Charles V, a friend of his, a sculptor, stood behind his chair and made a model of the Emperor at the same time. But of course all artists sit when they paint small pictures.

The Mirror is the painter's most valuable councillor, though a severe critic. If anything is 'out of drawing' in the picture, but to which the artist is blinded by the defect having, as it were, grown into the eye from gazing and peering at the work too long—by placing the picture before the glass and looking into its honest face, not only is the 'fresh eye' instantly restored, and the fault consequently detected, but from the error being reversed, it will actually appear greater than it really is.

The Lay Figure, or Mannikin, is a wooden or stuffed doll, usually of life size (though smaller sizes are used for some purposes), so ingeniously constructed that it can be made to assume and retain any posture the artist may desire for the adjustment of his drapery. The introduction of the use of the lay figure is ascribed to Fra Bartolommeo. It is very serviceable in painting elaborate dresses and draperies,[90] when, if a living model wore them, it would be impossible for the model to remain still sufficiently long without disturbing the arrangement, to enable the artist to paint every fold in detail. Nevertheless, the use of the lay figure as the original model is attended with great danger. The awkward, unnatural postures, the strange and unaccountable lifelessness, observable in so many pictures, may be traced to the lay figure. The most elegant disposition of drapery is almost always the result of accident, and to be caught, like the expression of the face, in a moment. The course adopted, therefore, is to make a rapid sketch of the folds which seem most happy from the drapery placed on the living figure; and when the lay figure is used, the folds should be adjusted by means of a slender stick, or a still more slender wire, or such a thing as a knitting-needle.

VEHICLES

Since the properties of vehicles materially influence the character and styles of execution in a picture, and affect its subsequent appearance and preservation, the description of their properties is an essential branch of our subject. The term 'vehicle,' which is borrowed from pharmacy, we have already mentioned, is applied in art to the fluid employed to bring pigments into a proper working state. The vehicle gives the name to the mode of painting—directly in oil and water, and indirectly in tempera or distemper, and fresco. As in water various substances are held in solution, so in oil various ingredients are combined.

One of the most important points for the general reader to bear in mind, in reference to 'oil' painting, is, that a varnish which might be spread over a picture when finished may be used as a vehicle with the colours in the actual process of painting. The colours of pigments 'bear out'[91] (assume their full force) with effects differing according to the liquids with which they are combined: in some instances they obscure or depress by their tinge and opacity, in others they enliven or exalt the colours by their colourless transparency, or, much more so, by a refractive power, as in varnishes made of resinous substances. The peculiar exalting effect of varnishes upon colours continues when they are dry, because resins form a glossy, transparent cement, while the media afforded by expressed oils become 'horny,' or semi-opaque. This principle of the heightening or depressing power of vehicle applies also to water painting, according to the substances (gums, &c.) held in solution.

It is objected by some to the ingredients which impart a gloss to vehicles that their use is illegitimate because nature is not varnished, but rather presents the appearance of fresco. To this it may be replied, that every mode of representing *space* must be conventional; and if the glazed transparency of oil-varnish more forcibly or illusively represents *shadowed space* than fresco—which it unquestionably does—why seek to deprive oil painting of its peculiar characteristic and distinctive merit? Certain of these objectors at the same time, with much inconsistency, recommend placing pictures under glass; forgetting that the effect of glass, under such circumstances, is simply that of a perfectly colourless varnish.

The tendency of all oil vehicles, and varnish, to darken more or less in the course of time, is inevitable. Oils, like wax, after having been bleached in a strong light, become again more or less yellow-coloured, or, as it is called, 'rancid,' according to the degree in which the situation where they are kept or exposed is badly ventilated, or deprived of light. Even the clearest resinous substances are, after a certain period, found coloured, varying in degree according to their hardness: thus the soft mastic is most affected, but the hardest, viz. amber and copal, are ultimately obscured. For this reason so many old pictures present an appearance vastly different from what they bore when fresh from the painter's hand. In the very lightest portions they are considerably embrowned; but where a much greater quantity of vehicle is used, as in the glazed shadows, the obscuration must, of course, be greater.

Some idea may, nevertheless, be formed of the original brightness of the colouring of such works by examining then upon the principle applied in copying—at least when copying is conducted with intelligence; namely, selecting some point of 'highest light,' which must have been originally white, and observing how much it is lowered, and with what it was, in imagination, comparing the rest of the picture. Perhaps there is nothing which has produced so much empiricism and quackery in practice, and elicited so much affected and simulated admiration in theory, as the accidental darkening of the vehicle of oil painting. The 'brown tone' of the old masters, which has been raved about so senselessly, is, however, now better understood; and the 'brown demon' which possessed the old-fashioned *dilettanti,*[92] to the great detriment of the living artist, is at length pretty nearly exorcised.

On comparing water, as a vehicle, with oil or varnish, we find it is of simple and easy use, and dries readily. It will not protect and preserve colours like the oleo-resinous vehicles, by 'locking them up' (using the painter's phrase); but it is subject to little alteration of colour or effect subsequently. For, notwithstanding that oils and varnishes are less chemically active upon colours than aqueous fluids, the vehicles of the oil painter subject him to innumerable perplexities by their bad drying, change of colour, cracking, and 'blooming,'[93] and by 'habits' varying with a variety of pigments. They are required, moreover, to possess almost a contrariety of qualities—to unite tenuity with strength, and to be fluid without 'flowing' (that is to say, being discharged freely from the brush without flowing or spreading on, the canvas); of being used either with sufficient body to give an embossed effect to the touch, or sufficiently diluted to permit the most rapid execution, and of being spread in the thinnest possible film.

It is natural, therefore, that painters should differ in nothing more than in the vehicle they employ. Some use oil only, and others a peculiar compound of their own to which they attach importance. Volatile oils, we have said, are useful diluents of the thicker oils; but they weaken the body of the vehicle, and occasion it to flow or spread so much as to render the touch of the pencil spiritless and uncertain. These properties give occasion for the introduction of resin or varnish, to restore the required consistence. Various vehicles have been compounded on principles derived from a knowledge of these properties of the oils and resins which are in great favour with artists. They are called 'Meguilps,' from the inventor of a particular kind: one variety receives the name of 'Gumtion.' Meguilps possess a gelatinous texture which enables them, while flowing freely from the pencil, to keep their place in painting and glazing. Varnish, when used in inordinate quantity, or applied as a final coat too soon after a picture is finished, is sometimes, though not always, the cause of the cracks we see in pictures. These constantly occur also from sufficient time not being allowed for each coat of colour to become perfectly dry before subsequent applications: the consequence being, that the oil is absorbed from the upper into the lower coat; the superficial colour being therefore charged with little oil, and exposed to the action of the atmosphere, dries more rapidly than that beneath it; and should the atmosphere be warm enough to allow the under colour to dilate, it will necessarily rend the upper in every direction. The use of incongruous vehicles, in successive couches, as water and oil, varnish and wax, in the same picture, bituminous glazings, imperfectly-prepared grounds, and improper primings, are, as we shall endeavour to show, other fertile causes of 'cracks.' Haydon and other writers on art advocate the use of pure oils in painting, and assert, without sufficient authority, that such were the only vehicles of the Venetian painters. The late Mr. Leslie in his *Handbook for Young Painters,* p. 213, gives it as his opinion, 'after more than forty years' experience,' that vehicles are of little consequence except in so far as it is desirable to ascertain if they are one of the causes of premature decay in some modern English pictures; and that the 'Venetian secret,' as it is called, has little to do with chemical secrets: 'I am persuaded that Titian would have coloured as finely as he did with the materials used by any school, while the colours or grounds of Titian would not have enabled David [the French painter] to imitate flesh.'

Oils

Oils are distinguished into *fat, drying,* and *volatile oils:* the two first are also called *fixed* and *expressed oils;* the latter, *essential oils.*

The Fixed Oils are viscous and greasy to the touch, and are so called because they do not almost entirely evaporate in drying, like the volatile oils (which leave only a small residuum of solid resin); and they are termed 'expressed 'oils because they are not extracted by distillation, like the essential oils. Of the fixed oils, *linseed* has been in most general use in painting. It is by far the strongest oil, and dries best. *Nut oil,* the oil expressed from walnuts, was much used by the Italian painters. *Poppy oil* was introduced latest; it has the reputation of keeping its colour better than linseed, and it is on this account generally employed in grinding white and most of the light pigments. It is said to have been first employed by the flower painters of the Netherlands, about the end of the sixteenth century. A Dutch writer of the period mentions 'mancop olie'—mancop (moon-head), the poppy.

Preparation of Oils. The oils are few; but they have to undergo certain processes before they are fit for the painter's purpose, and the nodes of purifying and bleaching them are very various. The clarification of oil from its mucilage is of the first importance. This maybe effected merely by repose; but it requires considerable time: this is why Reynolds esteemed so highly a present of some very old nut oil. All watery particles have also to be removed, and the oil to be freed from its (oleic) acid. Apropos of the purification of oil, we may recall Titian's remark, that 'With good oil you can make a good picture, and with *bad oil* you can still make a good picture.' To one defect in the vehicle all the great painters were, however, far from indifferent. The care taken by them to render their oils as colourless as possible, to prevent their subsequent yellowing, or 'rising,' in pictures, and forming what is called a 'horny surface,' is not a little remarkable. This is entirely opposed to the dilettante ideas of the desirability of yellow lights and green blues, which originated chiefly from the study of altered pictures; and it is no less contrary to the opinion of some modern writers, that, as the alteration of oils is unavoidable, it is better to use them at first in the coloured state, which they must ultimately attain. Numerous processes are described in old treatises on painting (many of them troublesome and tedious in the extreme) to secure perfect and stable clearness in the vehicle; and the effect of the altered oil is, of course, most dreaded on pale and cold colours. The Italians generally mixed a colourless essential oil with their delicate tints, including flesh tints; but essential oils cannot be used extensively in northern climates, because they do not fix and protect the colours against damp. Paul Veronese painted his blues in tempera, and then varnished them. Several of the Flemish painters practised the same method, or sometimes—as also did the Italians—strewed the blue pigments on fresh white lead, or made some provision for the absorption of the oil. Rubens expresses great anxiety, in one of his letters, lest any of the whites should have become yellow in some pictures that had long remained packed up; and he requests that they might be exposed to the sun, to cure this 'disease of the heart,' if it occurred.

The Drying of Oils. When oils are expressed without heat, or, as it is termed, 'cold drawn,' they are less drying than when subjected to warmth, or boiled. And, although the three oils previously named have a natural tendency to dry, yet this quality is not sufficiently strong to prevent some colours retarding it in various degrees: a circumstance which has led to the addition of other siccative ingredients, or 'dryers,' to the oils. Whatever contributes oxygen to oil dries it, as is the case with pure air, sunshine, &c. Hence, also, all the perfect oxides of metals dry oils, and the best dryers are those that contain oxygen in excess, such as litharge, sugar of lead, minium (red lead), umbers, sulphate of zinc or white copperas, and verdigris. All dryers, however, have in some degree a pernicious influence on colours: they increase the yellowing tendency of oils on blue, and, most of them being salts, diminish transparency or actually cover the surface with a white efflorescence. Verdigris becomes in time black, and, as it was common as a dryer in Italy and Spain in the sixteenth and seventeenth centuries, to its immoderate use may partly be attributed the blackness of the shadows in some of the Spanish masters, and in Tintoretto. There is, moreover, no doubt that by working more leisurely, and not overloading the colours, or by proceeding with more than one picture at a time, so as to allow sufficient intervals, artists might dispense with dryers of every description.

The Volatile or *Essential Oils* are destitute of the strength of the fixed oils, having scarcely more adhesiveness or cementing power in painting than water alone; but, owing to their extreme fluidity, they are useful as diluents of the thicker oils and varnishes, and are still more serviceable as solvents of the resinous and other substances introduced into vehicles and varnishes. Naphtha, called also oil of petroleum, or 'rock oil,' is collected among the rocks in Italy and other places. It is the oldest essential oil, being, as is believed, the oil used in painting by the ancient Egyptians, and the solvent used by the ancients in snaking their varnish. Other volatile oils are obtained by distillation from various vegetable substances; of these the rectified oil, improperly called *spirit of turpentine, is* now most commonly employed. Its great use among house painters, under the name of 'turps,' is to thin and assist the drying of oil paints, and in larger quantity to 'flatten,' or produce a dull, unshining surface on white and other colours. The English *oil of lavender,* or the inferior foreign *oil of spike* (a larger species of lavender), is preferred in enamel painting.

Varnishes

Every liquid or substance may be considered as a varnish which, when applied to the surface of a solid body, gives it a permanent lustre. The last operation of painting is *varnishing,* which completes the intention of the vehicle, when this either has not enough of the nature of a varnish, or is not used in sufficient quantity to cause the design and colouring to bear out with their fullest freshness, force, and keeping.[94] Varnishing supplies, as it were, a transparent atmosphere and natural moisture, while it forms a glazing which secures the object from injury and decay.—*Field's Grammar of Colouring.*

Varnishes are prepared from an immense variety of substances, of which the *resins,* improperly called gums (see an article by Mr. Hunt in the *Art Journal* for Dec. 1858), afford the best, and those principally used. These substances usually give the name to each particular varnish, as 'copal,' or 'mastich' varnish; but varnishes are also classed, according to the solvents of these substances, as essential oil varnishes, (fixed) oil varnishes, and spirit (spirits of wine or alcohol) varnishes (which last afford the 'French polishes' for cabinet work), and water varnishes. The (fixed) oil varnishes are called 'hard' varnishes.

The Resins and *Balsams*[95] are very numerous; but it will be necessary to describe the qualities of those only which have been most generally used in the composition of varnishes for painting.

By *Turpentine* and Terebinthina is understood the generally light-coloured resinous liquid which flows from many kinds of trees; when hardened by the sun, or by fire, it is called concrete or solid turpentine, to distinguish it from the essential oil of turpentine. The following are some of the varieties: *Venice turpentine,* obtained from the larch; *Strasburg turpentine* (the Italian 'olio di abezzo '), which exudes from the abete; *Pine-resin* (the incense usually burnt in churches is this produce of the Pinus abies); *Pece Greca (Greek pitch, Colophony,* or the *Pégoula* of old MSS.); and the *Frankincense* of works on art.

Mastic. This soft resin flows from a species of lentil tree. It has been extensively used in modern times in the composition of vehicles, and is now the usual varnish for pictures when finished.

Sandarac. The fluctuating significations of the word sandarac show how commonly this resin has always been confounded with amber, which it resembles in appearance; and it is still more difficult to distinguish the one from the other in the old words common to both—*glassum, glassa, grassa, &c.* It was, as it has been observed, the usual substitute for the more costly amber, in the composition of the Italian 'vernice liquida' of the tempera painters. In the Middle Ages the word 'vernix' was also applied indiscriminately to these substances, but by degrees to sandarac alone. This resin flows from the African 'arbor vitae,' which abounds in Barbary, on the sides of Mount Atlas; but it is also obtained in various parts of the East. When fresh, sandarac is light in colour, and transparent; but, as it acquires age, it becomes red. It probably, Sir. C. Eastlake tells us, obtained its name from this circumstance, for 'sandaracha,' with the Greeks and Romans, meant a red pigment (in Dioscorides, red orpiment). 'The word sandarac, when applied to the substances named, had various modifications. The Sanskrit form was the compound "chandarasa," which literally means moon-juice.'

Amber.[96] Some of the most interesting investigations in relation to painting have (as we shall see) had reference to the accredited use of amber in the vehicle of the first oil painters, dissolved and rendered colourless by a method now generally believed to be lost. Little doubt, however, can be entertained that modern chemistry could supply an amber varnish, equally eligible with any used by the old painters. We know that, as regards its purification, amber has been so clarified in recent times as to be employed as a substitute for magnifying glasses; and these lenses are stated to have been more powerful than those made of glass in igniting gunpowder. This remarkable substance is now universally admitted to be of vegetable origin. Humboldt remarks that, 'all the Baltic amber is derived from a coniferous tree; but the amber-tree of the former world had a richness in resin with which none of the coniferous tribes of the present world will bear any comparison.' The best kind of amber is imported from Russia and Poland.

Copal forms the substitute for amber in the modern vehicle of painting. It is a very light-coloured, transparent resin, obtained from various parts of the world. The word 'copal' is, however, derived from the language of the aborigines of South America, who applied it to this resin, which they burnt as incense, and also to resins generally. Under this name, therefore, it cannot be found mentioned before the introduction of American produce. The Oriental variety was, however, known before this period, and was no doubt sometimes confounded with amber and sandarac in the old MSS. It has a tendency to crack, which has to be counteracted by the admixture of linseed oil.

Benzoin and *Copaiva Balsam* have also been used as ingredients of varnishes.

Lac. White Lac Varnish was introduced by Mr. Field, author of *Chromotography, &c.;* and is prepared by dissolving in alcohol, or spirits of wine, the lac resin of India deprived chemically of all colouring matter, and purified; without which the varnish is opaque and of the dark colours of the japans and lacquers of the East. By passing lac over an oil ground, or painting, the artist is enabled to work in watercolours; and thus a multitude of minute details and fine markings, such as architectural lines, branches, and thin, light foliage, may be rapidly struck in, which, when covered with a little lac varnish, becomes a component part of the picture.

OF THE USE OF VARNISH WITH THE COLOURS; AND ON VARNISHING

The oil painting of the early Flemish masters, who first perfected the art, was, we shall find, more strictly speaking, (oil) *varnish* painting; in other words, an oleo-resinous vehicle (such as amber varnish), of sufficient consistency, was mixed with the colours to render final varnishing unnecessary. The Venetians adopted this vehicle; but it was soon diluted, for larger work, by the Italians generally, the requisite protection being song ht in the application of a final coat of varnish. As the northern artist also gradually thinned their vehicles they likewise required the same defence for their works—with this difference always, that greater solidity, both of vehicle and varnish, was indispensable in the more humid climate of the north. Leonardo da Vinci is the first Italian writer who mentions amber oil-varnish. The Italians, however, introduced essential oil varnishes at an early period, commencing by substituting a liquid resin for the oil, and employing finally a balsam liquefied in essential oil without other resinous ingredient. A varnish of this character, the 'olio di abezzo,' already named, thinned with naphtha, is stated by Armenini to have been used by Correggio and Parmigiano. Such compositions last perfectly well in Italy, when well prepared; and to the qualities of this particular varnish described by Armenini has in a great measure been attributed the preservation of Correggio's pictures, and the clearness of the tints. From some interesting experiments by Mr. Sheldrake, published in the *Transactions of the Society of Arts, 1801,* it would appear we may broadly infer that, when an old picture is found possessing evidently superior brilliancy of colour, independent of what is produced by the painter's skill in colouring, that brilliancy is derived from the admixture of a resinous substance in the vehicle. Among Venetian pictures, while some are so tender that it is almost impossible to clean them without injury, others offer great resistance to the most powerful solvents, and consequently must contain amber or copal. With regard, therefore, to the comparative durability of varnishes under ordinary circumstances, it is certain that those composed of amber and oil should be placed first; next those containing other resins and oil, or copal or amber dissolved in a liquid resin; and those must be considered the least durable which consist only of resins dissolved in essential oils. In proportion, however, to the hardness and perfection of these varnishes is the difficulty of using them as vehicles. It is to be observed, in conclusion, that not only were Italian pictures generally varnished, but the use of varnish with the colours, and more especially in glazing, and with the shadow-colours, was very extensive: the darks of a picture by Correggio are represented to be of the thickness of a five-franc piece above the rest of the picture.

As many persons are fond of what is termed 'doctoring' pictures, which generally includes loading them with varnish, we may add a few remarks on the subject of *varnishing.*

Although the hard varnishes are more durable, the soft mastic varnish (dissolved in spirits of turpentine) now commonly used may be removed and renewed with less risk to the picture. And notwithstanding the necessity that a picture should be thoroughly dry to prevent subsequent cracking, varnishing over colours and tints newly laid has the important advantage of preserving the colour of the vehicle used from changing . Early varnishing is, however, as just intimated, always at the risk of cracking; and with soft varnish, dries slowly and is more disposed to bloom. Mr. Field says, 'the saving grace of early varnishing appears to arise from the circumstance that they attract oxygen, by the power of which they entirely lose their colour; but, after becoming dry, they progressively acquire colour. It is at the mediate period between oils thus losing and acquiring colour, which commences previously to the oils becoming perfectly dry, that varnish preserves the colour of the vehicle, probably by preventing its farther drying and oxidation, which latter may in the end amount to that degree which constitutes combustion, and produces colour: indeed, it is an established fact that oils attract oxygen so powerfully as in many cases to have produced spontaneous combustions and destructive fires. It is eminently conducive to good varnishing, in all cases, that it should be performed in fair weather, whatever varnish may be employed, and that a current of cold or damp air, which "chills" or "blooms" them, should be avoided. To escape the perplexities of varnishing, some have rejected it altogether, contenting themselves with "oiling out" [spreading a thin coat of oil, as already explained]; a practice which, by avoiding an extreme, runs to its opposite, and subjects the work to ultimate and irrecoverable dulness and obscurity.'

From a published *Report of the Select Committee of the House of Commons,* it appears in evidence, that very many pictures have had a small proportion of fixed oil mixed with the mastic varnish with a view to prevent blooming. The practice (long since discontinued) has been much deprecated, as oil varnish becomes very yellow, can hardly ever be totally removed, and will never afterwards admit but of its continuance; for varnish subsequently applied, without the addition of the oil, would cause the picture to crack all over.

'About the beginning of the present century,' says Mr. Leslie, in his excellent *Handbook,* 'it was not unfrequent for the possessors of old pictures to have them toned, as it was called. The noble landscape by Rubens [containing a view of his "Château near Mechlin"],then the property of Sir George Beaumont [now in the National Gallery], was saturated with linseed oil to prevent its scaling from its panel; and this was suffered to dry on its surface. There is, therefore, under the deep yellow coating that now covers it, a fresh and natural picture—the picture Rubens left—and which the world may never be permitted to see again. The St. Nicholas of Paul Veronese has been, happily, relieved from the brown glaze, or oil, bestowed on it forty or fifty years ago; but Sebastian del Piombo's Raising of Lazarus remains under the gradually-deepening obscurity it was consigned to about the same time; and so do the large landscape by Salvator Rosa, the landscape called "Phocian," by Nicolo Poussin, and others, which, taking these as guides, will easily be discovered as involved in the same misfortune. Goldsmith, in the *Vicar of Wakefield,* tells us, what no doubt he himself had seen, that a would-be connoisseur in an auction-room "after giving his opinion that the colouring of a picture was not mellow enough, very deliberately took a brush with brown varnish that was accidentally lying by, and rubbed it over the piece with great composure before the company, and then asked if he had not improved the tints." I have myself seen a common workman in an auction-room smear a thick coat of varnish over a fine picture, in the most hurried and careless manner, to make it look well at the sale; and I am sorry to say that even respectable dealers are apt to load with varnish, to an injurious degree, pictures they are anxious to sell.' Picture-purchasers should always be on their guard against highly-varnished paintings. Do we not say of everything meretricious, 'Oh, it has been varnished over?' Do we not talk of a 'varnished tale?'

CANVAS, PANELS, ETC

The materials, or subjectiles, upon which paintings have been executed, have been very various. Besides wood and canvas, silk (as in many of Guido's pictures), slate, stone, copper, slabs of marble, &c., have been employed. Titian used various textures; sometimes merely fine linen stretched, without any preparation; at other periods, very coarse Italian canvas, or, as Haydon calls it, 'table-cloths;' and some of his pictures are painted on leather—for example, the 'Loves of the Gods' at Blenheim.

Canvas is the material now in general use. It is kept in rolls of various widths and of three qualities—'plain cloth,' 'Roman,' and 'ticken.' There is a series of regular portrait sizes—as 'bead size,' 'three-quarter,' 'Kit-Cat,' 'half-length,' 'whole length,' &c. The following is an account of the origin of the word Kit-Cat as applied to a particular portrait size.

'The Kit-Cat Club was a society of thirty-nine noblemen and gentlemen zealously attached to the Protestant succession in the House of Hanover. The club is said to have originated about 1700, in Shire Lane, Temple Bar, at the house of Christopher Cat, a pastry-cook, where the members dined: he excelled in making mutton-pies, always in the bill of fare, and called Kit-Cats—hence the name of the society. Jacob Tonson, the bookseller, was secretary. Among the members were the Dukes of Somerset, Richmond, Grafton, Devonshire, and Marlborough; and (after the accession of George I) the Duke of Newcastle; the Earls of Dorset, Sunderland, Manchester, Wharton, and Kingston; Lords Halifax and Somers; Sir Robert Walpole, Garth, Vanbrugh, Congreve, Granville, Addison, Maynwaring, Stepney, and Walsh. Tonson had his own and all their portraits painted by Sir Godfrey Kneller: each member gave him his; and, to suit the room, a shorter canvas was used (viz., 36 by 28 inches), but sufficiently long to admit a hand, and still known as the Kit-Cat size. The pictures, forty-two in number, were removed to Tonson's seat at Barnes Elmes, where he built a handsome room for their reception. At his death, in 1736, Tonson left them to his grand-nephew, also an eminent bookseller, who died in 1767. The pictures were then removed to the house of his brother, at Water-Oakley, near Windsor; and, on his death, to the house of Mr. Baker, of Hertingfordbury, where they now remain.'—*Curiosities of London,* p. 195.

For small cabinet pictures, *panels* of well-seasoned mahogany are prepared. *Oiled paper* is serviceable for sketching and trying the effects of any work previous to its commencement. *Academy board* is a thin millboard, on which most of the studies (Etty's, to wit) made at the Royal Academy are painted. *Millboards* are thicker than the last, and are well adapted for sketching in oil colours from nature.

The Van Eycks and their followers in the Netherlands painted on panels, the solidity of wood being essential to the durability of tints spread thinly, as were those of the older Flemish masters. Pictures by the Venetian painter in oil, Giovanni Bellini, are also executed on wood; but the Venetian painters from the first commonly preferred cloth, the oldest using it fine in texture. This preference may have originated from the known introduction into Venice of the thin German tempera painting on cloth already described. The Venetian painter Giorgione, however, like many artists of the period, was in the habit of painting panels for the *cassoni* or great chests in which Italian ladies kept their wardrobes, and for various other articles of ornamental furniture. In the Italian schools generally, white poplar or chestnut was employed. The Flemish selected oak, because seldom injured by worms. Wood liable to throw out unctuous exudations (odours), such as fir, is obviously unfit for the purpose.

Several precautions were adopted by the old masters to prevent the wood warping or splitting, but time has shown with little success, particularly in large pictures consisting necessarily of several pieces. The best contrivance to preserve wood flat and sound is to strengthen the back with 'battens,' or ledges. For large works (called by the Italians *tavole,* from *tavola,* a tablet or table), the planks were joined by a strong glue made from the insoluble parts of cheese, which has been proved to be far more powerfully adhesive than the glue in ordinary use. The wood (probably chestnut) is always so thick in Raphael's altar-pieces as to be more properly considered timbers than planks. In some large altar-pieces each separate plank has become slightly convex in front. This is distinctly observable in the 'Transfiguration,' by Raphael, and many have supposed it to have been caused by the heat of the altar-candles;[97] but there is little doubt that heat, if sufficiently intense to have any effect, would produce the contrary appearance, by causing concave contraction. The explanation is to be found in the paint with its 'ground,' which prevents the wood shrinking on the front. It would seem that this was understood by the Flemish painters, but not by the Italians. The former, apparently to equalize the tendency to warp on both sides, painted the back of the panel. The fact that this contributes to protect the wood from being worm-eaten, may, however, suggest the original motive of the practice. The oak panel on which is painted the principal specimen of Van Eyck in the National Gallery, is protected in this way at the back by a composition of gesso, size, and tow, over which a coat of black oil paint was passed: the panel is, notwithstanding, split.

GROUNDS

Upon nothing, perhaps, does the durability of a picture so much depend as the quality of the ground, or substratum, and its priming, or the preparatory couch of size or oil colour. To the use of white-lead in the priming is attributed, for example, the large cracks observable in many pictures otherwise in good preservation. The habitual use of a light or dark ground may also have a diverse influence, analogous to that we have traced to painting in the open air or in a darkened studio; the painter, on the first, being insensibly led to prefer a broad and bright, or, on the second, a dark, scenic, and partial chiaroscuro. The grounds employed by the first oil painters were identical with those of tempera. The surface of the panel was first prepared with two or three coats of size; a layer of coarse gesso *(gesso grosso)* was then applied; and on this at least eight layers of a finer description *(gesso sotile)* was spread; and the surface was finally carefully scraped, till, in the words of Cennini, it was as white as milk and as smooth as ivory.

In the Italian school of the time of Raphael the grounds were generally composed of pipe-clay mixed with chalk; and such are decidedly the most durable. Claude frequently used a similar composition; and the consequence is, that we find the skies, distances, and delicate passages as clear as the day they were painted. Nothing, indeed, is better established than that white grounds are in every way preferable. Sir Charles Eastlake observes (in a note to Goethe on *Colours,* p. 378), 'the secret of Van Eyck and his contemporaries is always assumed to consist in the vehicle he employed; but a far more important condition of the splendour of colour of the works of those masters was the careful preservation of internal light by painting thinly, but ultimately with great force, on white grounds.' It matters not, however, whether the brightness reside in the ground, or is reproduced at any stage of the work. Titian, for example, frequently obtained the effect of *luce di dentro* (light within), so much extolled by the Italians, by painting with white opaque colour over the dark or red grounds he frequently employed, and then glazing over this opaque colour.

The greatest demerit of dark grounds is, that they tend ultimately to show through and obscure the superimposed colour. Gaspar Poussin's grounds are of this description; and there is little doubt that the examples of this master in the National Gallery are from this cause lower and more gloomy in tone than was originally intended. Velasquez and Murillo painted upon the red-earthy preparations with which the Spanish canvas has almost uniformly been charged. The Carracci, and W. Vandevelde, likewise painted on a dark ground.

Canvases were prepared, in the earlier periods of the art, like the panels, with the distemper (size and plaster, or chalk) grounds we have described. Generally the pictures of Paul Veronese were painted upon cloths, with this composition thinly spread: it was necessary to take this precaution on canvas to prevent cracking, to which the ground was especially liable if the picture was rolled up for the greater convenience of removal. The thickness and composition of the original ground was, moreover, subject, under all circumstances, to be softened by moisture; and it would be obviously more so when on linen, through the back of which damp would readily penetrate. Even in Italy, in certain situations, the porous white poplar imbibed sufficient moisture to cause the destruction of several oil pictures mentioned by Vasari.

The intention of priming the ground with size or oil is to prevent the very rapid absorption of the colours, which would impede the free motion of the brush. When the ground is prepared with the power of partially abstracting the oil from the first lay of colour, it is called an 'absorbent' ground; but if it has a 'hard' or 'oil priming,' it is termed 'non-absorbent.' The gesso ground has been generally supposed to have been preferred, from its being absorbent; but this we shall prove to be a mistake. In Venice, however, some artists used grounds possessed of this property.

The Colours

Much has been written on the subject of colouring, and various elaborate and fanciful theories have been propounded; but, with the exception of M. Chevreul's discoveries, they are found to be of no great use to the artist, and would be of still less service to the general reader. By practice and observation, the sense of harmony in the association, and fitness in the sequence of colours, may be refined; just as by the same means our perception of harmony in the combination, and melody in the succession, of sounds may be improved. But what is called an 'eye for colour,' is as much a natural gift as an 'ear for music.' It is not the product of civilization, for savages are excellent colourists. Nor is it effected by climate, for the Dutch and Flemish surpass the French and Spanish. The English school, despite our clouded skies, is essentially a colourist school. That altogether exceptional people, the Chinese, are perhaps the best colourists in the world. The 'eye for colour' is seen to gladden the cottage home as well as the palace. The simple rustic maiden frequently sets off her charms to far greater advantage than the most aristocratic beauty; and the cheap nosegay of native wild flowers is often arranged with better taste than the costly bouquet of exotics.

The theory of colouring most reducible to practice is that of M. Chevreul. This is founded not upon any supposed occult properties of the colours themselves, but upon their demonstrative physiological effect upon the eye. The sight of colours is not so simple an affair as might be supposed. The eye passes through certain successive stages while viewing a coloured object; an effect due to the physiological fact of the eye being constructed for seeing *white* light; and these stages or conditions of the eye give rise to various kinds of contrast. Thus, there are influences at work which cause the colours with which the artist is painting, or those at which the spectator of a picture may have long been gazing, to look different from what they really are. From a knowledge of this fact, the painter learns that to imitate his model faithfully he must copy it differently from what under such circumstances it appears to him. And this knowledge is also of the highest importance in a picture gallery, in order to make due allowance for the mutual influence resulting from the juxtaposition of pictures differing greatly in their general tone of colour.

Light, we know, is resolvable into three primary colours; and the colour required with another colour to form *white* light is called the *complementary* of that colour. Whenever we look long at one particular colour, the eye gradually, but unconsciously, supplies its complementary colour. This phenomenon is the foundation of M. Chevreul's first great law of *simultaneous* contrast. Other laws of contrast are *successive* or *mixed:* there are likewise contrasts of 'tone;' but we must content ourselves with indicating the direction of the researches of the celebrated French chemist.

As regards the properties of the material pigments, we have not much to add likely to be of service to others than artists to what is said in other parts of this work. It must be remarked, however, that the vehicle of oil and the ultimate varnishing has a very considerable effect upon the preservation of certain colours. Some colours, for instance, are affected only by exposure to the atmosphere, and therefore quickly fade in watercolour painting, while they are perfectly permanent when 'locked up' in oil. Other colours, on the contrary, such, for a more particular example, as blue, are very obviously changed in hue by the yellowing of the oil. This defect of the vehicle is so unpleasantly apparent in the colour blue, that the early oil painters were induced (as already mentioned) to try to obviate it by various devices; such as using essential oils, and sprinkling the colour in a dry state on freshly laid white paint. The yellowing effect of the oil is increased by the tendency some colours have, in certain circumstances, to what is called 'sink-in,' and leave a shining surface formed by the surpernatant oil. This was sought to be counteracted, among the Flemings, by painting quite up to the brightness of nature, and, among the Italians, by the admixture of essential oils; and these oils, though used in quantities sufficient to work pleasantly with, would yet leave a surface dull and unshining, that would reader final varnishing desirable.

Some persons have imagined that the excellence of the colouring in the works of some of the 'old masters' arose from their employing colours with which we are unacquainted; or from their preparing them in a vastly superior manner. So far from possessing colours unknown at the present day, the early painters used no colour of any importance with which we are not familiar, and some beautiful and otherwise eligible pigments have been discovered by the moderns of which those painters were ignorant. We think it possible, however, that we may still find we have something to learn respecting the derivation or preparation of certain very beautiful colours used in China and Japan. Haydon says, 'Titian got his colours from the colour-shops on the Rialto, as we get ours from Brown's;' and adds quite truly that, 'if Apelles or Titian were living now, they would paint just as good works with our brushes and colours, as with their own.' There is no doubt, however, that the final preparation of the materials for oil painting was more carefully attended to by the generality of the early oil painters themselves, or their immediate assistants, during their long apprenticeship, than at the present day. The early oil painters appear to have been indebted to the colour-merchant for materials only, and, as remarked elsewhere, they spared no pains to obtain them of the best quality, considering it a moral and religious obligation to do so, and also to prepare them with scrupulous care and attention, in order to ensure the durability of works which represented all that in the heart of the people was held sacred.

Nevertheless, there appears no sufficient evidence to prove that the more respectable artists' colourmen of the present day injure the beauty or diminish the durability of the colours by carelessness or dishonesty in their preparation. The chief fault lies with the artists themselves, who, for the sake of procuring a meretricious brilliancy, which they know will last only a few years at most, and perhaps only during 'the Exhibition,' sacrifice the lasting effect of their works, and with it much of their fair fame. Turner was a most lamentable instance of this: many of his finest effects have already disappeared, evaporated, dried up, and vanished; and many others are being spirited away in the broad glare of day or the thick gloom of night—crumbling off in the dry, or becoming darkened and obscured in the damp. With the utmost admiration for Turner, one can hardly help feeling that a satire upon human vanity is now pointed by the Turner and Claude (which, according to the wish of our great master, are placed side by side in the National Gallery), owing principally to the frightfully altered colour of the sky (chromate of lead) in the one, and the pure limpidity preserved in the other.

The permanent colours are the earths and ochres, and those mineral colours which bear the test of fire and lime. Unfortunately, these colours, with the exception of ultramarine and one or two others, are at first less brilliant and more difficult to work and mix to the requisite hues than the fugitive colours prepared from lead, animal, and vegetable substances: hence the temptation to use the latter. A few notes upon the more important colours may be offered. Previous to which we may remark that the pigments were originally kept in a dry state, and, when used, placed in saucers, shells, and pots; subsequently the colours were kept ready prepared in small bladders: now they are enclosed in very convenient collapsible metal tubes.

White. White-lead prepared with extreme care is the only white pigment used in oil.

Yellow. The ochres are the most permanent yellows, and were chiefly relied upon by the old masters for the flesh. Iron is the principal colouring matter in them all. Other yellows are prepared from arsenic, lead, and vegetable substances. Some of these being transparent, were glazed over blue to produce a green; but they have frequently turned black. This is the cause of the heavy greens we see in some Italian pictures. Other yellows used in this way have faded, leaving the blue plants and ivy, so observable sometimes in Dutch pictures. The extreme richness and glow of the browns of Rubens has been attributed, not to the use of any particular brown earth, but to the addition of a transparent yellow.

Red. Iron is the great colouring principle of red in nature. Vermilion: this celebrated red is found in a native state (then called cinnabar), and produced artificially. The Chinese possess a native cinnabar so pure as to require grinding only to become perfect vermilion. Vermilion is an ancient pigment. The artificial was called in early MSS. 'minium,' a term now confined to red-lead. The word vermilion, in its older form, *vermiculus,* referred formerly to the insect called kermes by the Moors, which furnished the colour and name of crimson *(Kermesino, cremèsino).* Rubens used this colour (i.e. vermilion) with remarkable boldness in the flesh, particularly the reflections.

Lake is a name (derived from the *lac,* or *lacca,* of India), common to a variety of red (and a few other coloured pigments) of great beauty, prepared for the most part by precipitating coloured tinctures of dyeing drugs upon alumine and other earths. They are all more or less fugitive. Sir Joshua Reynolds, in his early pictures, used them freely in the flesh, and to heighten the lips; and to this is referable the pale, faded carnations of many of his female portraits. The common lake is prepared from Brazil wood. The finer lakes are prepared from cochineal, kermes or grana, lac, and rubric or madder. Kermes, or grana (called grain from the prepared material), are the dead bodies of the female insect of the Coccus ilicis, which lives upon the leaves of the prickly oak. The colour obtained from them was the purple and scarlet dye[98] known from the time of Moses. The cochineal insect is produced on different species of cactus. The colours (scarlet, crimson, and carmine or rouge) which it supplies are extremely beautiful, but not durable. These colours were unknown before the conquest of Mexico: the Spaniards learnt the method of their extraction from the American aborigines. The preparation of colours from the madder-plant appears to have been known by the writers of the early treatises on painting, yet for some two centuries we have no written traces of it. Madder is, however, stated to have been used by the great Venetian painters. In our own time improved methods of preparing from madder various beautiful rose-tints of extreme transparency have been introduced. These colours are of especial value to the painter in watercolours, and they have the recommendation of being more durable than the lakes.

Blue. Blue alone possesses entirely the quality technically called *coldness* in painting: yellows and reds partaking more or less of the opposite quality of *warmth.* Ultramarine (blue), or azure, is the most deservedly celebrated, and the most perfect of all modern pigments; and, from its name and properties, is probably the same as the no less celebrated Armenian blue, or Cyanus, of the ancients. It is prepared from the lapis lazuli, a precious stone found principally in Persia and Siberia. It furnishes the most beautiful pearly atmospheric greys in flesh painting. Ultramarine has always been occasionally used in painting; at least from the thirteenth century. It was so highly esteemed that, in the early periods of art-history, it was frequently the subject of a particular stipulation in contracts. Ultramarine, and also the gold, were generally supplied by the person who ordered the picture, but in some cases the artist himself supplied it. It was considered an act of criminal dishonesty for the painters of early Italian frescoes to employ any colours but those of the best quality; and this applied—on account of its extremely high price—most especially to ultramarine, if it had been agreed that that colour should be used. In the statutes of the painters' guilds it was provided that fines should be imposed for every offence of this kind. Cennini insists upon the use of good colours as a religious obligation, and most especially in portraying the Virgin. If the painter, he declares, be even underpaid for his work, God and our Lady will recompense him in the soul and the body. An anecdote is told of Pietro Perugino, who, when watched by a stingy abbot, for whose convent he was painting a fresco, lest he should steal the ultramarine, continually washed his brushes, and asked for fresh supplies of the pigment. At the end of the day, exhibiting the deposit that had accumulated at the bottom of the basin, he remarked that, had he desired to cheat his employers, he should have had no difficulty in accomplishing his purpose. Many noble frescoes have been almost entirely destroyed by greedy priests and friars for the sake of their ultramarine and gold.

Copper supplies a number of beautiful blues. Cobalt is a name now applied to the modern improved blue prepared with metallic cobalt, or its oxides. Prussian blue takes its name from the country where it was discovered by accident, in 1704.

Yellow, Red, and Blue cannot be composed, and are hence called *primary* colours. The union of two of these, in the three combinations of which alone they admit, produces *secondary* colours. Thus the mixture of yellow and red gives Orange; red and blue, Purple; blue and yellow, Green. Ultramarine is the only pure primary colour; the finer specimens having neither a tinge of green on the one hand nor purple on the other. Purple is a term frequently employed very indefinitely; for example, we talk of '*purple* hills' when we may mean blue alone, or slightly modified with red, and 'Imperial *purple,'* when we may mean red, scarlet, or crimson. The mixture of two secondary colours successively produces the *tertiaries* Citrine, Olive, and Russet. These colours, for the most part, are known as *Browns.* Asphaltum, or bitumen, is a species of pitch or mineral oil solidified. Bitumen is collected on the surface of the lake Asphaltites (the Dead Sea), and is called 'Jews' pitch;' but there are several kinds of asphaltum and bituminous earths used in the arts. The power and intensity of asphaltum, when employed for glazing shadows, render its use very tempting. To its use, however, is attributed the innumerable cracks and constantly widening gashes in the works of Sir Joshua Reynolds, Wilkie, and so many other English artists. Asphaltum is, therefore, now generally discarded. And yet it would appear that the mischief must have arisen partly from impure or adulterated specimens having been chosen, or from some mistake in their preparation or use, for it is certain that this pigment was used by the old masters of every school and climate.

Vandyke Brown — hardly less celebrated as a pigment than the great painter whose name it bears — is a species of peat or bog earth of a fine, deep, semi-transparent brown colour. Mr. Field says, that 'the pigment so much esteemed and used by Vandyke is said to have been brought from Cassel; and this seems to be justified by a comparison of *Cassel-earth* with the browns of his pictures. The Vandyke browns in use at present appear to be terrene pigments of a similar kind, purified by grinding and washing over.'

PROCESSES AND MANIPULATIONS

Glazing. A glaze is a film of transparent colour which is in general so clear as to have the effect, when spread, of a sheet of tinted glass held before the picture. All colours which, when mixed with suitable vehicle, are transparent, are termed glazing colours. In considering simply what constitutes the true manner or scheme of effect of each school, and of the several masters, so far as regards merely their technical process, we perceive that the entire code may be reduced to two points, viz., *transparent* and *opaque* painting. The Venetians, Titian especially, carried transparent glazing to the highest perfection. They advanced their pictures as far as possible with pure red, white, and black only, and upon this preparation they glazed repeatedly the richest and purest colours. To the extreme facility of glazing, oil painting owes its supremacy over tempera, though glazing was to a certain extent practised in the latter.

Glazing forms a distinct series of tints, without which it is impossible to represent transparent objects. By it shadows are strengthened, and warmth or coldness given to their hue; by it also lights that are unduly obtrusive are subdued, or additional colour and tone given to those that are deficient in force and richness. The process of glazing, we have observed, is generally effected by the application of diluted transparent colour; but occasionally semi-transparent colours are used, when rendered sufficiently transparent by the admixture of a large proportion of vehicle. Such glazings are useful to modify parts of the picture, or produce particular effects, such as representations of smoke, dust, mists, and the like. Glazing, when used injudiciously or in excess, produces that 'horny' uniform dulness of surface and 'leathery' discoloration so offensive to the eye, which till recently was the common characteristic of the modern Continental schools.

Impasting (Ital. *impastáre,* to knead, cover with plaster) is the opposite of glazing. The shadows or dark portions of a picture are thinly and transparently painted, but the lights are 'solidly' painted with opaque colour—that is to say, with colour mixed more or less with white. Impasting gives 'texture' and 'surface.' In the foreground, and in parts not intended to 'retire,' the 'impasto' should be bold; but in the more brilliant lights it can scarcely be 'loaded' too much. This loading of thick masses of colour upon the picture, so as to make them project considerably from the surface, is done with a view to their being strongly illuminated by light impinging on these prominences, and thus mechanically to aid in the production of roundness and relief; or to give a sparkling effect to polished objects or glittering points. Reynolds greatly admired and imitated the gem-like impasto and textural richness of the old masters, comparing its appearance to cheese or cream. There is, however, a reasonable limit to the practice of loading: for actual protuberances of solid paint will in certain lights project a false shadow, and therefore give an unnatural effect. These protuberances also produce a coarse and vulgar air, and defeat their own object by affording in the inequalities a lodgment for dirt and varnish, which appear the more conspicuous for occurring in what should be the brightest and most unsullied passages.

Pictures in oil, as in tempera, may, of course, be *thinly* painted throughout, or they may be executed with a considerable body of colour; impasto is therefore in all cases relative and comparative. But a picture, especially if on cloth, is, as may be supposed, more liable to change, when thinly painted, from the effects of air, damp, and dust, on both sides. Thin painting was very generally preferred in the early Flemish school; but that pictures so executed are calculated to retain their freshness much longer on panel than on cloth, the following may be considered to prove, if it were not in itself apparent. In thinly painted oil pictures, which have not been lined, the colours are sometimes in a very perceptibly better state of preservation where the bars of the stretching-frame behind afford a greater protection to the cloth, the better condition of the surface frequently corresponding exactly with the form of the wood-work. And when the picture is varnished, the portions thus protected 'hear out,' while the rest of the picture becomes comparatively dead.

Scumbling resembles glazing in that a thin coat is spread lightly over the work; but opaque instead of transparent colour is employed. It is used to modify certain portions of a picture which may require to be rendered cooler, greyer, and less definite; and it gives air and distance to objects which seem too near. An excess of stumbling produces a 'smoky' appearance. After a time the scumble partially sinks into the colour over which it is laid, and this is calculated upon by portrait painters to produce some very charming effects. Thus a pearly grey passed over a carnation will ultimately permit the warm colour to show through just as the blood blushes beneath the semi-transparent and downy epidermis. When colour is spread thinly and rapidly, it is occasionally said to be 'driven.'

Dry Touching, or *Dragging,* is the addition, when the picture is dry and in other respects finished, of a few feathery touches, on lights which have sufficient texture to retain the colour only on the projecting points. By this process spirit is communicated, but its abuse produces what is technically called 'mealiness,' the colours appearing as if sprinkled with meal.

The Dead-colouring is the first or preparatory painting, and is so termed because the colours are laid cold and pale to admit of the after-paintings, which gradually enforce the effect, establish the character, and discriminate the expression; and the final glazings, which impart the full warmth and animation of colour. The first painting of some of the old masters was more properly speaking 'priming,' as understood by house painters; thus, flesh colour was in the first instance primed with a full deep green, and parts intended to be green were laid in with a reddish colour. When the painting of a picture is divided for convenience into certain stages, they are sometimes called the first, second, third paintings, and so forth.

On comparing the different modes of painting, the simplest are decidedly the most durable. Mr. Leslie says, 'it is evident that by methods extremely simple many of the great colourists have produced their finest works, and among these may be named Titian himself. I have seen exquisitely coloured pictures by Jan Steen, as perfect in their surface and as free from the slightest change as if they were painted but yesterday, evidently from the use of virgin tints only, tints not produced either by glazing or scumbling. And the same simple method seems to have been the general practice of Paul Veronese. Not that transparent colours were excluded, but that a thin filmy method of obtaining the tints was avoided.' We may add that Mr. Leslie has illustrated his opinion in his practice: most of his numerous works in the Sheepshanks' collection are executed in the manner he has eulogized.

We have already explained the method of *transferring* by tracing or calking. In *copying*, when the copy has to be made larger or smaller than the original, the reduction or diminution is frequently effected by a scale of reticulation, the squares being proportionately larger or smaller. Some of the drawings of Raphael are covered with squares.

Handling is that part of the mechanical 'execution,' or 'manipulation,' of a picture which exhibits the pencilling or play of the brush, and is most essential in the foreground representation of the various different textures of objects, such as foliage, wood, water, &c. The first principle in the application of paint is to avoid unnecessarily mixing, or, as it is called, 'troubling,' 'saddening,' or 'tormenting,' the tints: the inevitable consequence of neglecting this precaution being a spiritless effect, a waxy surface, and muddiness of colour. When these defects are avoided, the touches are bold and distinct, the peculiar idiosyncrasy of the artist is indicated, and his particular handling is as certainly recognizable as is almost every person's handwriting. This individual character constitutes 'style;' but the abuse of facility of handling degenerates into 'manner,' as a free and ornamental handwriting may be merely a vehicle for nonsense. 'Manner' takes refuge in generalizations and ideals, which are not the product of independent and original thought, but the convenient screens for want of observation and hasty execution. Pre-Raphaelism, though open to the charge of mannerism, was a revulsion and protest against the unmanly conventionalisms into which a portion of the English school had fallen. The want of character in the foliage of even such masters as Gaspar Poussin and Gainsborough we may select as instances of mannerism. The various styles and manners of artists enable us to discriminate an original painting from a copy. 'Every touch of a great artist on the leading points of any object is a separate thought. A copyist, not being inspired by original thinking, cannot give to his chisel or pencil that air of the touch accompanying the thought which an original work always has.'—*(Haydon.)* Some painters are, however, naturally deficient in the freedom of hand which gives individuality. The execution of Leonardo da Vinci is very laboured, and it is related that his hand shook so much on setting to work that he could not paint for some time. In truth, nothing is more treacherous than the power of rapidly placing conventional lines and touches; yet this is often all that is taught by ordinary 'drawing masters.' What, however, would be thought of a child who had been taught to run over the keys of a pianoforte without any definite meaning?

Style is an elevating and invaluable attribute of art, which in some measure compensates for her inability to represent the infinity of nature. Style is a highly suggestive epitome; manner is a plausible but empty symbol. At the same time it must be remembered that the meaning of the word 'style' is frequently indefinite, and 'manner' is often convertible with 'style.' Thus we often speak of the different descriptions or modes of painting as so many styles; and yet we talk of the first, second, and third manner of Raphael. Smooth painting is perhaps less apt to be mannered than 'loading,' yet the latter is far more stimulating to the imagination; and this was probably the reason why it was more generally adopted by the Italians, who were in their conceptions far above the mechanical unimaginative Dutch. Again, in the unfinished drawing chance strokes are evidently intended to play their part in the effect. In the work that is obviously hastily performed, whatever appears wrong is very readily construed into a *lapsus pennæ*. But the unfinished sketch derives its principal merit from the fancy of the observer. Some of the appearances of nature, such as gleams of light, and gentle gradations of sky and cloud, are so vague and so indeterminate in their character, as to admit of frequent and even striking instances of resemblance from purely accidental causes.

In the works of some artists we find a breadth of handling, apparently utterly oblivious of form, and as incomprehensible as so many chance blots and blurs when viewed near; yet, owing to the truth of the general effect, and the wonderful power of our binocular vision—so beautifully illustrated in the stereoscope—assume at the proper distance a startling appearance of reality, almost of relief. But such artists are often betrayed into making their pictures merely coloured hints, too slightly indicative of natural facts. They consequently acquire meaning only in proportion to the degree of knowledge and vividness of imagination of the spectator. This, taking the spectator, as it were, into partnership, however, very subtly flatters his *amour-propre* (self-esteem), and hence the frequent affectation of pretending to see more in such performances than there really is. Who has not, in a similar manner, amused himself by making out objects and 'faces in the fire?' Who has not felt vain at deciphering a handwriting not legible to others? It must never be forgotten, however, that the handwriting is none the better for being illegible to many.

An excess of handling is, moreover, an evidence of bad taste. What is called 'spirited execution,' carried throughout a picture, is like the great drum and trumpet in full play all through a musical performance. In the thinly painted works of Teniers we see, perhaps, the happiest union of hard and soft markings. The style will, however, vary, according as the subject is grave or gay, lively or severe.

Reynolds calls execution, very finely, 'the genius of mechanical performance.' 'Yet,' says he, 'he that does not express particulars expresses nothing.' This leads us to the vexed question of the degree of *finish* proper to a work of art; and the great problem of the union of breadth and finish. The degree of finish will be regulated by the size of the picture, the nature of the theme, the character of the object imitated, and, above all, by the distance at which the representation should properly be viewed. True finish does not consist in any kind of smoothness, nor in minute detail, but in the complete expression of character. And there is a legitimate charm in the use of apparently inadequate means, provided the effect is entirely satisfactory upon lengthened examination.

'There are,' says Haydon, 'in all objects great characteristic distinctions that press on the senses and affect the imagination; these the man of comprehension views, sees, transfers, and hits off by touches, leaving the aggregate of useless particulars to the imagination of the spectator: while the man of narrow understanding dwells only on the aggregate of particulars, deceiving himself that the leading points will come. Never was a greater delusion. . . . Painting is an optical delusion, acting on the eye through the medium of atmosphere, which softens, flattens, and unites the pores of surfaces. In looking into the face of the greatest beauty, it is anything but smooth; but at the given distance, the pores of the skin are united; and the skin has the look of the polished pearl-like cheek, soft, tender, and beautiful. Ivory is the reverse of flesh—it is smooth near, but hard at a distance: the atmosphere has nothing to act on, therefore the invisible pores are rendered still more invisible, and the effect is one of a smooth hardness; while skin, having something for atmosphere, has the real look of softness. Vanderwerf, Denner, Mengs, and David are instances of this laboured smoothness, looking anything but fresh, on the above principle. One of the greatest evidences of genius is the use, more or less, a man makes of atmosphere. A power of calculating the effect of atmosphere is one of the great attendants of the highest genius. It was the characteristic of Phidias in sculpture; and Michael Angelo, Titian, Rubens, and others in painting . . . In Rembrandt and Reynolds surface is too artificial; in Rubens it does not predominate; but in Titian it is perfection; unobtrusive, but existing—relishing, but retiring. There it is, nobody knows how; but take it from Titian, half the charm goes with it; and yet it is hardly perceived except by its consequences.'

'The touchers'—to again quote the same writer — 'Michael Angelo, Raphael in his cartoons, Titian, Bartolommeo, Giorgione, Tintoretto, Veronese, Rubens, Velasquez, David Teniers, Rembrandt, Reynolds, Wilson, Wilkie, Gainsborough, Vandyke, are the great men who had discovered the optical principles of imitating nature to convey thought. The polishers are the little men who did not see a whole at a time, but only parts of a whole, and thus vainly essayed to make up the whole by a smooth union of parts.' To these graphic passages we may add, that there are many phenomena in nature, as a storm, which it is impossible to represent otherwise than suggestively. Among the masters most remarkable for precision or rapidity of handling are Rubens, Tintoretto, Teniers, and Velasquez. Rubens painted his very celebrated work, the 'Descent from the Cross,' in nine days. The change from Leonardo da Vinci to Titian was great; but the rapid and dexterous movements of Rubens' pencil rendered nearly everything apparently stationary that had preceded him. 'Rubens,' says Sir Joshua Reynolds, 'was, perhaps, the greatest master in the mechanical part of the art, the best workman with his tools that ever exercised a pencil.' Tintoretto, from the rapidity of his execution, received the nickname of *Il Furioso;* Sebastiano del Piombo said, that Tintoretto could paint as much in two days as would occupy him two years. Mengs, speaking of a picture by Velasquez, executed in his later style, says that be appears to have painted it with his *will* only, without the aid of his hand. Of the important branches of execution, *stippling* and *hatching,* we have already treated in the article on Tempera.

A few remarks on the distribution and care of paintings, and on picture-cleaning and restoring, are offered in the Appendix, note B.

1. OIL PAINTING PRACTISED BEFORE THE VAN EYCKS

Probably every person who sees for the first time a picture by Van Eyck, if not at all surprised at its antiquated treatment or quaintness of expression, will be very much astonished to find that the work of the reputed inventor of oil painting has preserved its brilliancy of tone after the lapse of more than four centuries far better than most pictures executed within the last hundred, or even the last fifty years.

By 'brilliancy of tone' we do not mean the force and depth, the luscious richness of colour and fulness of effect, which are the principal charms of painting in oil, as exhibited particularly in the Venetian school; but that the colour of Van Eyck, though quiet, will still be vigorous and fresh; that it will have limpid transparency, and an almost illusive vacuity of space. In addition to this, it will exhibit an amount of truthful realization of the most minute and exquisitely delicate details which is scarcely ever found united with the same imperishable durability elsewhere.

These characteristics distinguish more or less all the early Flemish pictures; and from persons habitually engaged in restoring them we learn that the colours of these pictures are mostly of a harder body than those of a later date: they resist solvents much better; and if rubbed with a file, they show a shining appearance, resembling a picture painted in *varnish*. Examination of the pictures themselves, and the researches of several learned writers within the last few years, leave no room to doubt that their durability is attributable chiefly to the vehicle employed, and that the colours were used not simply with oils, but with an oil varnish of the kind we call 'hard'—or, in other words, an oleo-resinous vehicle, such as might be employed strictly as a varnish over a picture when finished. Our immediate object, however, is not to discover the nature of the vehicle, but to ascertain what claim the brothers Van Eyck have to be considered as the absolute inventors of the art of oil painting.

If the vehicle, the use of which they were long reputed to have introduced, had been merely oil, popularly understood, with no native properties prejudicial to its employment—had been easy of preparation, simple in its composition, and affected by few conditions in its mixture with different colours, and without any inherent qualities tending to restrict its application to any surface or extent—we could without difficulty suppose that the Van Eycks might have stumbled on the discovery, and quickly realized in a more eligible medium, what would still have been, though in an inferior degree, the distinctive artistic qualities of their painting, had they continued the practice of tempera, glass painting, or illuminating. But we have already seen that the vehicle of oil painting is precisely the reverse of what might be considered possible or likely to have been suddenly discovered.

It is now known, from the frequent allusions to them, that, during three centuries antecedent to the technical perfection displayed in the works of the Van Eycks, there were what we may consider tentative efforts in oil painting. So distinct is the evidence of the practice of oil painting long before the beginning of the fifteenth century, that the invention or discovery of the Van Eycks, even understood restrictedly, has been denied altogether. Dr. Raspe published, as early as 1781, a dissertation, maintaining the attribution of the discovery to the Van Eycks as erroneous, and only allowing the possibility of their having introduced amber varnish and poppy oil. Haydon makes some sweeping observations to the same effect, and with less reservation, in his *Lectures,* published as late as 1844.

There must, however, be some foundation for the traditional ascription of an honour no rival schools have opposed, and which Vasari, the sufficiently vain historian of the great Italian painters, has not merely not disputed, but, on the contrary, acknowledged—confessing that his own countrymen failed in their efforts to improve the vehicle of tempera. As might therefore have been expected, recent research has shown that the Van Eycks are entitled to our gratitude, not indeed for having created the art, but for removing disqualifications which unfitted it to compete with, much less supersede, the ordinary tempera. It has been remarked, that it may be considered fortunate that the process of the Van Eycks was not altogether their own discovery; for had it been so, the method which has stood so well the test of time might still have remained a subject of conjecture; but as such is not the case, if we ascertain the principles commonly acknowledged before their time, it will be comparatively easy to trace the direction of their inquiry and the nature of their improvements.

The total absence of all even incidental reference among classic authors to oil painting may be considered conclusive evidence that they were unacquainted with the art. We have seen, however, that oils of some kind entered into the composition of varnishes from the remotest antiquity; and this is all which can be established. Oils having drying properties (which are indispensable in the practice of oil painting even in the warmest climates) were also probably known. Olive oil, so plentiful in Greece and Italy, never dries; but several 'drying' oils, such as walnut, poppy, and castor oil (used by the painters of the twelfth century as a varnish), together with modes for their preparation, are mentioned by the writers of the first three centuries of the Christian era — as for instance Dioscorides (who is supposed to have lived as early as the time of Augustus), Pliny, and Galen. These notices, however, occur only with reference to medicinal or culinary purposes. The first mention of a drying oil in connection with works of art is made by Aetius, a medical writer of the fifth century. Sir Charles Eastlake was the first to point out this interesting passage, which runs thus: 'Walnut oil is prepared like that of almonds, either by pounding or pressing the nuts, or by throwing them, after they have been bruised, into boiling water. The (medicinal) uses are the same [alluding to a description of linseed oil]; but it has a use besides these, being employed by gilders or encaustic painters; for it dries, and preserves gildings and encaustic paintings for a long time.'

On the evidence of a MS. at Lucca, we are to refer the important introduction of linseed oil into the arts to the eighth century: the oil principally used centuries after by varnishers and decorators, and later by painters, especially of the north of Europe.

It is certainly surprising that, although the modes of bleaching and thickening oils in the sun, as well as the siccative or drying power of metallic oxides, were known to classic writers; and though there is evidence of the careful study of these authors soon after the tenth century, yet that oil painting was not suggested for so many ages. The monks, who explored the buried knowledge and arts of antiquity, finding the great reputation which tempera and encaustic enjoyed, would, however, at first rather labour to restore these methods than invent a new one.

No record is preserved of the first immixture of solid or opaque colour with oil or varnish; but about the time of Cimabue, that is to say the end of the twelfth century or beginning of the thirteenth, the process is frequently mentioned in MSS. which are certainly of this date. From these and similar later sources, it is perfectly demonstrated that oil painting, at least in the lower sense of applying colours mixed with oil on surfaces of wood and stone, was common in Italy, France, and England in the thirteenth and fourteenth centuries. That the progress of the arts at this period was nearly equal in this as in other countries of Europe, is to be explained by the intercommunication and the bond of union which subsisted between the members of the different monastic orders.

In the records of Westminster and Ely, which are full of reference to decorative operations, oil is frequently mentioned in connection with painting. A mandate in the account-rolls of the decoration of the Queen's Chamber at Westminster, commissioned by Henry III, and originally published by Walpole, refers to the purchase of 'oil, varnish (vernix), and colours,' and this mandate bears date 1239. It was imagined by Walpole that this mandate alone furnished conclusive evidence that oil painting was practised in England at this early period. But such is not the case; for already it has been remarked that where the word 'vernix' occurs alone, it simply means dry resin;[99] requiring, therefore, to be dissolved in oil before it would furnish a varnish: the oil and 'vernix' mentioned in the monk's Latin of these rolls might, consequently, hate been employed merely for varnishing tempera pictures.[100] The records in connection with the decoration later in this reign of the celebrated Painted Chamber at Westminster, are also not clear as to whether the oil mentioned was used for mixing with the colours or to make a varnish for the tempera wall painting. The coloured remains of the Painted Chamber yielded easily to the sponge, when examined in 1819; it may therefore be inferred that they were size paintings, and that the varnish had possibly become decomposed by the damp of ages. Nearly the same obscurity exists even in reference to the splendid embellishment, in the reign of Edward III (1352–1358), of St. Stephen's, Westminster. But there are other proofs that oil painting of some kind was employed at Westminster. Methods of oil painting are also particularly described by Theophilus and Eraclius. The records of Ely, of the same date, mention the same materials; and are almost conclusive as to the immixture of oil with the colours.

The gradual improvement of the early oil process may be distinctly traced. Stone surfaces were primed[101] with white-lead mixed with linseed oil, applied in successive coats and carefully smoothed when dry. Wood was planed smooth, or, for delicate work, covered with leather made from horse-skin or parchment, then coated with a mixture of white-lead, wax, and pulverized tile, on which the oil and lead priming was laid. In the successive applications of the coats of this priming the painter is warned by Eraclius of the danger of letting the superimposed coat be more oily than that beneath, the shrivelling of the surface being a necessary consequence.

This is certainly one of the causes of a wrinkled and shrivelled surface, but it is also so common an effect of the use of an oil varnish that the appearance is considered sufficient evidence of its employment. Mérimée says: 'I have had occasion to examine closely the fine picture by Giorgione which is in the Museum [of the Louvre], No. 1011. This work is drawn into wrinkles in several places, which proves that the artist employed an oil varnish, for it is the constant effect of this vehicle to run into wrinkles in drying.'

The difficulty encountered by the early painters in rendering their oil paint sufficiently drying is evident from the directions which follow those already given by Eraclius that before the application of the second coat, and also before the varnishing, the first coat should be carefully dried in the sun, or by the aid of heat. Messrs. Crowe and Cavalcaselle, in their valuable work on the *Early Flemish Painters,* speak of a *bouche-à-ardoir* as used for this purpose. Hence painting in oil was frequently limited to wood, because moveable panels could be dried in the sun. It was necessary to dry even the varnish for tempera pictures in the sun; and the consequent splitting of a panel is said to have led to the improved oil painting of the Van Eycks. The practice of carefully drying each coat of paint was, it is true, continued in the best periods of art; but with a view to check the yellowing tendency of the oil, as well as to secure perfect dryness before varnishing. In the MS. of Eraclius, and the records of our English cathedrals, no restriction, however, in the employment of oil paint is implied. Oil is mentioned as used for the painting or varnishing of columns and interior walls. And, in one copy of Eraclius, a distinct description of a drying oil, as understood in the mature practice of oil painting, occurs; white-lead and lime being added, and the oil thickened by exposure in the sun, as was also the universal practice in Italy. The drying, or siccative ingredients ultimately employed in oil painting, were however originally used in mordants only.

It remains to inquire the kind of works in which and with what degree of refinement the system had been applied. The mere process without reference to its application was undoubtedly more successfully employed in England than elsewhere during the fourteenth century. The passages in Eraclius refer to ornamental work, imitations of marble, &c. In the records of Ely Cathedral, however, occur the words *pro ymaginibus super columnas depingendis,* which has been supposed to refer to painting figures pictorially. But the figures were no doubt only painted reliefs; and all that can be clearly determined from these and other English (and also foreign) documents is, that these applications of oil painting were merely decorative. The largeness of the quantities of oil supplied is very remarkable, and indicates the coarseness of the operations. Theophilus, indeed, mentions tints for faces—*mixturas vultuum;* but we have seen that the liquid oil which he used required to be dried in the sun, and it is expressly stated that he was dissatisfied with the process for pictorial purposes (on account of the slow drying of the vehicle) in the words which follow the directions given—*quod in imaginibus et aliis picturis diuturnum et tædiosum nimis est* (such a process is too slow and too laborious for painting pictures). The tints for faces it is, moreover, to be observed, are only mentioned in a passage describing a method in use of depicting various objects on a gold, or imitation gold, ground—the *pictura translucida* of the Middle Ages. The usual auripetrum ground (tinfoil lacquered yellow), for such works, was varnished, and the superadded painting must consequently have been in oil. For the subordinate, complementary, and decorative parts of pictures—such, for instance, as draperies and accessories—oil painting was, however, adopted. But no examples of figures or pictures, in the modern sense of the term, entirely executed in oil before the time of the Van Eycks, can be proved to exist; nor is there a distinct record of such works having been executed.

The process of oil painting was also used for the purpose of colouring standards, banners, and pennons, on which were represented the heraldic devices and arms of those for whom they were prepared. It was customary in Flanders, and even in the best periods of art in Italy, for the painter to be engaged in the court or suite of monarchs and princes, and to receive a stated salary. The colouring of the armorial bearings and devices of his patron was then the remains of feudal suit and service.

The painters in the pay of the Dukes of Burgundy were classed as 'varlets,' though their duties were not menial; for, on the contrary, they were served in their own persons by domestics in livery. Art in Flanders in various other of its applications rose from the requirements of luxury as much as from those of religion; and this partly explains, as Messrs. Crowe and Cavalcaselle have shown, why the pictures of the Flemings lack that elevated sentiment which can arise alone from the deepest fervour and a strong religious sentiment.

The oil generally employed was, as we have said, thickened to the consistence of a varnish, 'equally applicable,' in the words of a Venetian MS., 'to pictures, or for varnishing crossbows.' Delicacy of execution was therefore entirely precluded. Eraclius tells us, the longer the oil remains in the sun the better it will be. In Italy the process was always less complicated, fewer precautions being necessary in such a climate to ensure the drying of the oil; yet Cennini directs that it should be kept in the sun till reduced one-half. Colours in such a vehicle must have been almost unavoidably spread in flat tints only. The probable reason why the vehicle was not thinned with essential oils (the art of distilling which was introduced in the thirteenth century) was that, if used in sufficient quantity for the purpose, the essential oils would have produced a' flatted,' dull, or unshining surface, which would not only have rendered the picture more liable to harbour dust, but also have destroyed the glossy appearance which was considered the peculiar merit of the vehicle. This thickened oil had, however, merits which recommended its use for certain purposes, even in the best ages of painting. It was well calculated to exclude the air from colours which would rapidly change if exposed to damp. Its greater drying tendency rendered it fit for the generally slow-drying, dark pigments, whose hue would not be materially affected by the darker tint oil acquires in the process of boiling or thickening. This explains the prominent 'darks' in early Italian oil pictures.

2. The Improvement of Van Eyck: in What it Consisted

There has been much controversy in respect to which of the brothers Van Eyck, Hubert or John, should be awarded whatever honour is due for the improved oil painting they both illustrated in their practice. Van Mander, in his *Lives of the Painters,* gives 1366 as the date of the birth of Hubert; and the painter's interesting epitaph, formerly preserved, together with the bones of the artist's right hand and arm, in the church of St. John (now St. Bavon, the cathedral), Ghent, determines that of his death:

'Take warning from me, ye who walk over me. I was as you are, but am now buried dead beneath you. Thus it appears that neither art nor medicine availed me. Art, honour, wisdom, power, affluence, are spared not when death comes. I was called Hubert Van Eyck—I am now food for worms. Formerly known and highly honoured in painting; this all was shortly after turned to nothing. It was in the year of the Lord one thousand four hundred and twenty-six, on the eighteenth day of September, that I rendered up my soul to God in sufferings. Pray God for me ye who love art, that I may attain to His sight. Flee sin; turn to the best, for you must follow me at last.'

The younger brother, John, appears by sufficient evidence to have been born between 1390 and 1395, and as all writers agree that the improved oil painting was introduced about 1410, the probability is greater that the system had been discovered by Hubert, who was the elder by at least twenty-four years, than by a youth of between fifteen and twenty. No works by Hubert alone are, however, in existence whose execution by known priority of date would fix the discovery upon Hubert. The only undoubted specimen of painting by the elder brother is the upper portion of the celebrated great altar-piece at Ghent, of the 'Adoration of the Mystic Lamb.' The lower portion was finished by John. That Vasari should attribute the invention to John (Giovanni) is accounted for by the circumstance, that the works of the younger brother, which were in technical merit equal, if not superior, to those of Hubert, were alone known in Italy. Antonello da Messina, who communicated the Flemish process to the Italians, had known John Van Eyck only. It appears that Hubert (whom John survived nearly twenty years) he had never seen.

However, it is a much more important question what the improvement actually was which permitted a degree of technical perfection in many respects not since surpassed.

We may premise that there exists a *primâ facie* probability that the greatest improvements in the materials of painting would be made where, as in the Netherlands, it was most necessary to counteract the effects of a humid atmosphere on painted surfaces by hydrofuge or waterproof preparations. To the influence of climate may be attributed the greater prevalence, mentioned by Cennini, of oil painting in the north than in Italy; and likewise that the northern artists seldom attempted mural painting. Even the tempera vehicles used in the north of Italy itself were less thick in consistence than those used in the south. Climate, also, no doubt, induced the readier adoption of oil painting in Venice than in southern Italy, and caused the preference for canvas of thin and pliant texture.

Vasari, who was born nineteen years after the death of Antonello, and who wrote about a century after the death of John Van Eyck, could necessarily give only traditionary information respecting the actual improvement of the Van Eycks; yet he supplies the most direct evidence which can be adduced. It is to be remarked, however, that, although frequently incorrect in dates, Vasari, from having been a painter himself, is generally to be relied on in practical matters. Notwithstanding this, the description he gives of the improvement of Van Eyck is, if not carelessly worded, certainly more embarrassed and meagre than might have been expected, making every allowance for 'Time's effacing finger.'

The account referred to occurs in Vasari's life of Antonello da Messina. The Italian biographer assumes, in the first place, that painters were universally desirous of discovering some method which would admit of blending the tints with greater facility than could be effected in tempera by hatching with the point of the brush. But in this assumption he forgets that the union had been effected with the medium of the later tempera painters, and that the Italian painters generally were very tardy in adopting the new system. We are then told that Giovanni da Bruggia (John Van Eyck), being fond of alchemy (as chemistry was then called), made experiments to prepare various oils for the composition of varnishes and other things. That, having finished a tempera picture on panel, varnished it, and placed it in the sun to dry as usual, the heat opened the joinings; and that the artist, provoked at the destruction of his work, 'began to devise means for preparing a kind of varnish which should dry in the shade, so as to avoid placing his pictures in the sun. Having made experiments with many things, both pure and mixed together, he at last found that linseed oil and nut oil, among many which he had tested, were more drying than all the rest. These, therefore, boiled with *other mixtures of his,* made him the varnish which he—indeed, which all the painters of the world—had long desired.'

Messrs. Crowe and Cavalcaselle justly remark that a it would be wrong to infer from this passage that the drying qualities of linseed and nut oils were unknown to Van Eyck and the world previous to the experiments here referred to; and it is almost impossible that Vasari should have intended to convey such a meaning, when we know that he was perfectly acquainted with the treatise of Ghiberti *(vide* "Ghiberti" in Vasari), in which it is affirmed that "Giotto painted on the wall, painted in oils, and painted on panel." Nor can we consider him to have been ignorant of Cennini's *Treatise on Painting,* in which so many chapters are exclusively devoted to the subject of oils, used in colours, though evidently without any knowledge of Van Eyck's discoveries. He must have intended to express, not that Van Eyck discovered the qualities of linseed and nut oils; but, after repeated experiments, found that none were more drying than these—a fact of which he was not previously certain. His efforts would, therefore, be at first in one particular direction; namely, to make linseed and nut oils as siccative as possible. When he had obtained this, he mingled these oils with certain mixtures, and he obtained a more drying varnish. Thus the first grand step was gained.[102]

Vasari proceeds with the following words: 'Continuing his experiments with many other things, he saw that the immixture of the colours with these kinds of oils[103] gave them a very firm consistence, which when dry was proof against wet; and, moreover, that the vehicle lit up the colours so powerfully, that it gave a gloss of itself without varnish; and that which appeared to him still more admirable was, that it allowed of blending [the colours] infinitely better than tempera. Giovanni, rejoicing in this invention, and being a person of discernment, began many works.'

The whole of this description is sufficiently indefinite, for we are only informed of what led to the new and more important of Van Eyck's discoveries in the evasive words, 'other mixtures of his.' The incongruities in Vasari's statement may be partly explained by the fact of the Flemish system of painting having become obsolete in Vasari's time; the great Italian painters finding that oils and vehicles of less body than those used by their northern brethren favoured the rapidity of execution desirable in the larger scale of their works.

The importance of Vasari's description consists, however, in the one fact of which it puts us in possession, and with respect to which there is every reason to believe it trustworthy—viz., that it was in search of a varnish to cover pictures when finished, which would dry in the shade, that Van Eyck not only succeeded in his immediate aim, but also in rendering the varnish he had obtained more suitable for mixing with his pigments in the actual process of painting than any vehicle hitherto known. This last, then, is the great discovery, and its importance cannot be too much insisted upon. The new vehicle was not only recommended by its improved drying properties; but, as the works of the Van Eycks and their scholars prove, it was thinned at will by a diluent, so as to allow of infinitely greater precision of execution than the thickened oil previously in use. It was not so dark as to sully the colours with which it was mixed, as would the customary varnish for tempera pictures; and it gave not only extraordinary durability to the colours, from being so intimately combined with them, but also communicated a transparency and lustre, without any subsequent operation, unattainable by the ordinary vehicles of tempera, with all the assistance of the final coat of varnish.

We have remarked, that fixed oils alone, when thickened, become half resinified, and may be used as varnishes; but that, when oils so prepared are sufficiently thinned with essential oils to serve as vehicles, they lose the gloss upon their surface. But varnishes can also be made of fixed oils combined with resins, which may be thinned without this effect, provided the object of hastening the drying of the oils is attained by other means than the excessive thickening of the oils. This, it is found, may be effected by the addition of what are called 'dryers.' The 'other mixtures of his,' then, no doubt point to the discovery of a good dryer; and this was, therefore, one important part of Van Eyck's improvement.

That Van Eyck's vehicle also contained a resin, we shall find yet additional proof to that already given. But it will be desirable previously to ascertain the nature of the varnish *(vernice liquida)* in use for protecting tempera pictures, and which the Flemish painter spread over the memorable panel. Upon referring to an earlier section, the reader will find it stated that the finer description was made with amber or copal, but that sandarac was commonly employed. There were, however, in Flanders, local facilities for obtaining amber; hence the varnish containing this ingredient was called German varnish. This is a very firm resin, and the most competent judges have concluded, from examination of the works of Van Eyck, that such a resin was used. And varnish, made with amber, is mentioned in the oldest documentary evidence relating to the practice of early Flemish painters. There is, notwithstanding, every reason to suppose that, among these painters, the quantity of the resinous ingredient was varied for various purposes. Other resins, such as copal and sandarac (the substitute for amber and copal), mastic and purified (dry) turpentine, also, no doubt, in many instances replaced the amber; for the dissimilar appearances of the works of the earliest masters of the school point to this conclusion.

The natural inference is, that there was no 'secret' in the school that would infallibly produce, without the requisite intelligence, the same result. It may be assumed that Van Eyck was acquainted with the best processes for rendering the amber varnish as light in colour as possible; but we have the important conclusion arrived at by Sir Charles Eastlake, after the most patient and lengthened investigation, that 'it is not to be supposed that modern chemists would have any great difficulty in obtaining results as successful; nor is it imagined that there was any' particular secret in the operation which has been lost; or for which, if lost, an equivalent could not be found.' By known means, a varnish may be made from amber firmer than any prepared with the ordinary resins, and equally light in colour.

One reason why Van Eyck retained amber as a constituent part of the new vehicle, arose probably from observing that it imparted the same polished appearance to the surface of the painting as when used for a varnish. The gloss communicated to pictures by the lustrous varnishes of the Middle Ages, was considered an essential quality, and may have been traditionally admired from the estimation in which it was held among the ancients. At all events, this recommended encaustic and mosaic in the early periods of Christian art; thickened oil was no doubt chosen in the first attempts at oil painting with a view to this same effect; and it has ever remained a characteristic of the works of the Dutch and Flemish masters.

Van Eyck did not, we may reasonably conclude, at once succeed in properly thinning as well as lightening his vehicle. He would, therefore, probably, in the first instance, mix his vehicle with the dark and more flowing transparent colours, thus carrying a step further the tinging of varnishes already practised by tempera painters. The great leap (though timidly made) by which Van Eyck cleared the conventional bounds imposed on painting, was, however, the substitution of opaque for transparent colour on the lights; and this affords the final test and evidence of his improvement, implying, as it does, that the varnish was entirely changed both in colour and consistence.

By recapitulating, we arrive, then, at the following inferences: First, that Eyck, seeking for a varnish that would dry in the shade, perfected the methods of dissolving amber in oil, and then discovered a good dryer.[104] In this consisted a great part of the material improvement. Secondly, that, as the varnish obtained, having been subjected to no long process of boiling, was nearly colourless, he might not only use it with the transparent colours, but cautiously and gradually mix it with the opaque ones also — finding their purity little affected by this transparent vehicle, especially when thinned, as, from the appearance of his works, it probably was for the lighter colours, in order to prevent their yellowing. And, finally, as the thickness of the varnish was an obstacle to precision of execution, he would increase the proportion of its oil to its amber, or add a diluent, as occasion required.

The protection afforded by oleo-resinous media has, subsequently, always caused then to be held in greater favour in the humid climates of the North than in Italy. The lighter-bodied mastic varnish was, however, used by later Flemish painters—Vandyke in particular.

3. Oil Painting: Early Flemish and German

Greater obscurity exists respecting the early history of the art of Northern Europe than that of Italy; and the panel pictures of cis-Alpine countries probably fared worse at the hands of the iconoclasts of the Reformation, than would have fared wall paintings if mural painting had flourished as extensively in those countries as it did in Italy. The Carlovingian missals are, however, preserved; though no remains of the mural paintings which adorned the palace of Charlemagne at Aix-la-Chapelle have descended to our own time. The Byzantine trammels, judging from MSS., seem to have been thrown off in the North earlier in the thirteenth century than in Italy. But the earliest distinct development of the German style occurred towards the end of this fourteenth century, in the school of Cologne. William of Cologne is the earliest (tempera) painter of this school, and the oldest German painter to whom existing panel pictures are attributed. Meister Stephan is a more distinguished (tempera) painter, and his celebrated altarpiece in the Cathedral at Cologne is considered the masterpiece of the school. A later master of this school has been, on insufficient grounds, confounded with *Israel von Mechenen,* a contemporary goldsmith and engraver. The chief work of this painter is a representation of the 'Passion,' which was in the now dispersed collection of Herr Lyversburg, at Cologne; and the painter is known from this circumstance as the 'Master of the Lyversburg Passion.' This and other pictures of the school have gold backgrounds; but the characteristics are in other respects those which for ages we observe with remarkable uniformity in northern art. The northern artists imitated nature earlier than the Italian; but they never succeeded, like the latter, in the representation of the beautiful and the ideal. They never 'disclosed the one great mystery, and placed before us the inward sentiment and the outward form as one and indivisible.' Their faces are nearly always full of character, but their drawing and modelling of other portions of the figure, particularly of the extremities, exhibit structural ignorance. They never generalize; but concentrate their attention upon the minutiae of detail, and the accessorial ornaments they delight to introduce; imitating them with illusive faithfulness, but leaving an impression of stillness and lifelessness, which is aggravated by the stiffness and angularity of their draperies. Yet in all technicalities they, preeminently excel, and they are almost invariably fine colourists. In composition they are inventive, but their creations are singular and fantastic, and full of that *romantic* element which finds expression in their so-called Gothic architecture, and which is attributed to the influence of climate and the great features of northern nature.

The school of Westphalia, a similar school to that of Cologne, produced a painter known as the Meister Von Liesborn. There are specimens of the works of this artist, and also of Meister Stephan, in the National Gallery. But the most celebrated northern school of the fifteenth century was the Flemish school of Bruges, established by Hubert Van Eyck, and upheld by his brother John after the death of Hubert. There is little known of these masters beyond what has already been given. The whole of the tipper portion of the celebrated altar-piece in the cathedral of St. Bavon, at Ghent, was by Hubert; the lower portion was completed by John. The entire altar-piece was a polyptych[105] (consisting of several panels), and comprised two principal pictures, one above the other, each with double wings painted inside and out. When the wings were opened, which occurred only on festivals, the subject of the upper centre picture, consisting of three panels, was the Triune God, with the Virgin on one side and the Baptist on the other. On the adjoining wings were angels, who with music celebrate the praises of the Most High. At the extremities were Adam and Eve, the representatives of fallen man. The lower central picture shows the Mystic Lamb (Agnus Dei) of the Revelation, whose blood flows into a cup; over it is the dove of the Holy Spirit; angels who hold the instruments of the Passion, worship the Lamb, and four groups of holy martyrs, male and female, and priest and laymen, advance from the sides.

On the wings are coming up other groups of soldiers of Christ, righteous judges, hermits, and pilgrims. When closed, the upper part represented the Annunciation, and on the lower were single figures in chiaroscuro. The two central panels are all that now remain in St. Bavon. The celebrated copy made by Michael Cocxie, for Philip II of Spain, is likewise dispersed.[106] The finest of John Van Eyck's own works is the altar-piece of the Santa Trinita, in the Museum of Madrid; but the style of the master can scarcely be seen to greater advantage than in the picture in the National Gallery, containing, probably, the portraits of the artist and his wife.

The following are among the principal scholars or painters of the school of the Van Eycks: Van der Meire, Hugo Van der Goes, Justus of Ghent, Antonello da Messina (who introduced oil painting into Italy), and Van der Weyden of Brussels (Roger of Bruges). The existing masterpiece of the last painter is the very large altar-piece of the 'Last Judgment,' in the hospital at Beaune, in Burgundy. A picture by Antonello da Messina, representing the 'Crucifixion,' is in the museum of Antwerp. Hans Memling (formerly improperly spelt Hemling and Hemmelink), is, however, next to the founders, the most celebrated master of the school. His most important works are the 'Vision of the Apocalypse,' and the paintings on the reliquary or châsse of St. Ursula, in the hospital of St. John at Bruges; and the 'Joys and Sorrows of the Virgin,' and the 'Journey of the Three Kings from the East,' at Munich. At Louvain Dietrich Stuerbout painted two remarkable pictures, now at the Hague. The influence of the school extended over Germany and Holland.

Martin Schön, of Colmar, was an excellent painter, and also a distinguished early engraver. His most celebrated work is the 'Virgin in the Rose-bush,' preserved in the cathedral at Colmar. Hans Holbein the elder, of Augsburg, was a younger contemporary of Schön.

At the end of the fifteenth and beginning of the sixteenth century, the peculiar character of Northern art was carried to its highest perfection by Albert Dürer, as that of Italy was at the same time by Raphael. Albert Dürer was born at Nuremburg, in 1471, and in 1486 was placed with Michael Wolgemuth, the best artist of his native city; in 1538 he died. Albert was the most celebrated German artist of his age, and almost equally distinguished as painter, sculptor, and engraver. Raphael and Dürer exchanged drawings, to show each other their respective styles. Albert visited Venice, and complained that the Venetian painters abused his style, because it was not after the antique, although they subsequently praised his colouring. Among the most celebrated of Dürer's paintings is the 'Trinity surrounded by the Saints and Spirits of the Blessed,' at Vienna; but the artist's grandest work is his representation, in two companion-pictures, of the four apostles, 'John and Peter,' 'Mark and Paul.' These figures form perhaps the first complete work of art produced by Protestantism. Albert died shortly after their completion, and Kugler says: 'Well might the artist now close his eyes—he had in this picture attained the summit of art; here he stands, side by side, with the greatest masters known in history.'[107] Albert Altdorfer, also distinguished alike in painting and engraving, was the most original of all Dürer's scholars and imitators. A picture by this artist, of 'Alexander's Battle of Arbela,' at Munich, contains a countless number of figures all painted with marvellous minuteness and finish.[108]

Lucas Cranach headed the contemporary school of Saxony, and enjoyed almost as great a reputation as Albert himself. One of his masterpieces is the 'Mystical Crucifixion,' in the church at Weimar. He was an excellent portrait painter, and this altar-piece contains an admirable portrait of his intimate friend Luther. Cranach frequently painted mythological subjects, and also studies of the female figure-representations we seldom find in early northern art. He also executed numerous woodcuts and some engravings. Another contemporary school, that of Holland, produced Lucas Van Leyden, a very excellent enagraver; but not to be ranked with Albert Dürer, or the Italian Marc Antonia.[109] Lucas was also a painter of great merit; but his pictures are very rare.

Germany at this time gave us Hans Holbein *the younger,* the son of, and a far more important artist than, the Hans Holbein already named. This very distinguished portrait painter was honourably received and patronized by Henry VIII, and spent the latter portion of his life in England. The finest portraits by Holbein are in Windsor Castle, and at Longford Castle. The large composition by Holbein, in the Barber Surgeons' Hall, represents 'Henry VIII presenting to the Company of Barber Surgeons their New Charter.' There is another picture of the same kind in Bridewell. The most beautiful specimen of Holbein is the 'Virgin as Queen of Heaven,' in the Dresden Gallery. The woodcuts which form the celebrated 'Dance of Death,' by Holbein, are too well known to require description. Quintin Metsys, the blacksmith of Antwerp, who turned from the anvil and taught himself painting in order to win the hand of a painter's beautiful daughter,[110] is another remarkable artist of this period. The so-called 'Two Misers,' at Windsor, of which there are several repetitions and copies, is universally known; but the most important work by Metsys is an altar-piece in the Academy at Antwerp. The talent of Mabuse is illustrated to advantage in the great picture at Castle Howard, of the 'Adoration of the Kings,' which formed one of the prominent attractions of the Art Treasures Exhibition at Manchester, 1857. Other artists of some consideration were Schoreel and Antonio More (who was employed to paint Queen Mary of England before Philip's marriage); but northern artists, in the second half of the sixteenth century, gave themselves up to the imitation of the great Italian masters, whose fame had extended beyond the Alps; and, as an inevitable consequence, painting lost not only its national features, but other also of what should be its best characteristics. A few additional remarks upon the technical characteristics of the Van Eycks and their scholars may be added before we conclude this part of our subject.

Upon the pure white ground of the tempera painters the design for the oil picture was traced in a similar manner, and then *fixed* by being retraced with the brush. The light and shade of the picture were also usually expressed with the pen, and with the greatest possible care. Over this a coating of size was applied, thus rendering the ground non-absorbent, contrary to the universal opinion of writers upon the processes of painting; for it has been supposed that the use of the gesso ground was, by absorbing the oil, to remove in some degree the cause of yellowness in the colours. That the ground was not absorbent is proved by various circumstances; but especially in the ingenious process employed of late years for transferring pictures from panel to canvas. This is effected upon a principle similar to that described as employed for fresco: the panel is planed away, and when the ground is arrived at, it is found to be not in the least stained with oil. The true function, then, of the white ground was, by shining through, to impart the freshness and transparency we so much admire in the works of the early Flemish painters.

With a view to the preservation of this transparency, a warm, transparent, oleo-resinous priming was passed over the design—the ground being thus cut off from contact with the oil. The shadows of the picture were next strengthened to their full force, and the half-shades indicated with a uniform, rich, transparent brown. In modern practice the shadows have been frequently painted in colours complementary to the lights. The more solid or opaque, but still thinly-painted portions, were added last. Every precaution was, therefore, taken not to neutralize the effect of the ground by the careless embroilment of transparent and opaque tints. In the later practice of oil painting, lights were more and more loaded, and afterwards occasionally glazed; white was also introduced into the cool, grey half-tints, the shadows being still left in untouched transparency; but, contrasted as they were with the more solidly painted lights, they acquired much greater depth and beauty. This is the superior method of Rubens, and also of Teniers, particularly in his more sketchy style.

Rembrandt, likewise, with all his loaded colour, leaves in some portions the ground partially apparent. The methods of the great Venetian colourists afforded a still wider scope for diversifying effects, for they laid opaque colours even into the shadows, and recovered transparency by ultimate glazings.

The Van Eycks, Sir C. Eastlake thinks, adopted their principle of colouring from their practice as glass painters. 'They knew the value of light behind colours, and that the foulest mixture through which light penetrates is more brilliant than the purest colour lighted superficially. The most essential attribute of the mere materials of oil painting being *depth,* they secured this quality in the very highest degree by preserving internal light.' Their fine feeling for aerial perspective contributed also to the same result. The analogy between a glass painting and an oil painting is not, however, complete, and the highest lights of the Van Eycks fail to tell as such, and to give the full attainable relief, from not being sufficiently loaded.

The superiority of later practice consisted, among other merits, in permitting a suggestive freedom of handling, and the display of power of drawing in the touch itself in the opaque lights, which we do not find in the dry inlaid and minute detail of the earliest masters. The hand was, however, disciplined in the school of the Van Eycks to great correctness and exactitude of drawing in the preparatory 'study.' Indeed, in many instances of unfinished pictures, the design was wrought out with a care and finish which might seem altogether supererogatory. The fact that the most important part of the picture was executed with the point and not with the brush explains the partiality for etching and engraving in this early school.

4. Introduction of Oil Painting into Italy

The method of the Van Eycks was, according to Vasari, made known in Italy by Antonello da Messina.[111] Vasari's relation, which appears to be true in the main, is as follows Antonello saw, in the possession of the king Alfonzo I of Naples, about the year 1442, when he was twenty-eight years of age, a picture of the 'Annunciation' by John Van Eyck, which so struck him by the vivacity of its colouring and the beauty and harmony of the painting, that he set out immediately for Bruges, in order to discover by what means it was produced. He obtained the secret from John Van Eyck, and remained some time in Flanders until he had perfected himself in the method. He returned to Italy, and arrived in Venice about 1445, where be communicated his secret to Domenico Veneziano, who in turn confided it to Andrea dal Castagno 'the Infamous;' so named, because he murdered Domenico, as it is said, to become the exclusive possessor of the secret. After two visits to his native Sicily, Antonello finally settled in Venice till his death, about 1493.

The first oil pictures known to have been executed in Italy by Italian artists were those by Domenico Veneziano and Andrea dal Castagno on the walls of the Portinari chapel in Sta. Maria Nuova at Florence: they are no longer in existence. Other of the first Italian oil painters were Giovanni Bellini, Giorgione, Leonardo da Vinci, Perugino, and Francia. Little credit can, by the way, be given to the story that Giovanni Bellini introduced himself into the house of the Messinese disguised as a Venetian cavalier desirous of having his likeness taken, and that Antonello mistook the artist for the character he assumed, and thus betrayed his secret. The Flemish system was quickly modified in Italy, the works of one master—Titian, for example—frequently exhibiting a great variety of technical methods, and it was not long before the northern process was forgotten altogether. As Italian influence also became felt in the north, many of the southern technicalities were adopted some of the original materials and processes (such, for example, as the white ground and the use of varnish with the colours) were however preserved in the works of Rubens and Teniers; and it may be said that many of the Van Eycks' principles were carried to perfection by the former.

The following is represented and, partly from unfinished pictures, ascertained to have been Titian's method of conducting a picture in his mature style. The subject being drawn, the effect was wrought out as far as possible with pure white, red, and black only, the shades being left very cold. To check the yellowing of the oil, and to anticipate every contracting or expanding influence, the picture was then exposed to the sun and dew until perfectly dry and hard. Many months were generally allowed to elapse before the surface of this dead or first colouring, or *abozzo,* as it is called by the Italians, was rubbed down with pumice-stone, until quite smooth. This being done, the first painting was examined and corrected, fresh colours and the glazings were then applied, and these additions and glazings were frequently repeated seven, eight, or nine times, until the master was satisfied with his work. But, however numerous these repetitions, a long period was suffered to elapse between each fresh application of colour, and in the interval the picture was exposed to the sun and the dew.

Titian is said to have constantly laid on the paint with his fingers, particularly on the flesh and in glazing. When a broad glaze, or, as the Italians term it, *velatura,* had to be spread, the colour was, in order to cover the surface thinly and evenly, frequently rubbed on with all the fingers or the flat of the hand. When a smaller space had to be glazed, as the soft shadows of the flesh, the finger or thumb only was dipped in the colour and drawn once along the surface to be painted with an even movement. Such touches were called *sfregazzi.* It has been believed that Titian frequently glazed the whole surface of the picture, except the white linen, with asphaltum; but many maintain it was a yellow varnish; while others, again, attribute the yellow tone of his works to the use of oil in the glazing.

The method of Paul Veronese is opposed to that of Titian. Veronese usually painted 'alla prima,' that is to say, sought almost the full effect at once by direct means and simple mixture of tints, seldom repeating his colours, and using few glazings. He, however, employed a generalizing colour for all the half-tints, as well of the draperies and the architecture as the flesh. When the picture was advanced this way, he covered the whole with a thin coat of varnish, to bring out the colours, and then retouched the lights, and enforced the shadows with the boldest and most dexterous touches.

5. The Later German, Flemish, and Dutch Schools

In the north a revival of painting in the seventeenth century, not very dissimilar to that in Italy at the same period, was effected chiefly by the great artist of Antwerp, Peter Paul Rubens (1577–1640). Yet we find in this movement no very strikingly original characteristic; for the style of Rubens was derived principally from his study in Italy of the Italian, and especially the Venetian, masters. Rubens had one set palette for every kind of subject, grave or gay, sacred or savage, mournful or mirthful. Fuseli justly observes: 'What has been said of Michael Angelo in FORM, may be said of Rubens in COLOUR: they had but one. As the one came to Nature and moulded her to his generic form, the other came to Nature and tinged her with his colour —the colour of gay magnificence.' The earlier works of Rubens are the best: the later works attributed to him are more mannered; the result, probably, of having been generally executed in great part, if not entirely, by scholars from small coloured sketches by the master. Our limits will admit of a mere enumeration of only a few of the prodigious number of pictures in the various galleries which bear the name of Rubens. Antwerp still possesses his greatest, or at least his best known work—the 'Descent from the Cross.' The original of the copy in the National Gallery, by Vandyke, of 'St. Ambrose refusing to admit the Emperor Theodosius into the Church,' is in the Gallery of the Belvedere, Vienna. At Munich the small sketchy 'Battle of the Amazons,'—a wild host of Amazons pursued by Greeks, pouring over a bridge —and a small 'Fall of the Angels,' are highly extolled. In allegory Rubens chiefly fails—his 'History of Marie de' Medici' in the Louvre, to wit. Perhaps the most celebrated of his portraits is the 'Chapeau de Paille,' in Sir Robert Peel's collection. The almost unequalled portrait (or study of a head), known as 'Gevartius,' in the National Gallery, and called a Vandyke, is considered, with apparently good reason, to have been painted by Rubens. In landscape Rubens is also seen to great advantage. For the 'Rainbow Landscape,' Lord Hertford gave, five years since, 4,550*l.*

Rubens visited England, and undertook the great paintings for the ceiling at Whitehall, which were finished after his return to Flanders. The 'Rape of the Sabines,' in the National Gallery, is a perfect nosegay of colours, and a fine illustration of Rubens' technical principles and luxuriance of conception. The larger works of Rubens are especially remarkable for the boldness with which pure colours are placed side by side and left for distance to blend.

Vandyke (1599–1641) is the most celebrated of the scholars of Rubens. In his early works Vandyke even exaggerated the peculiarities of his master; but he afterwards adopted a less cumbrous type of form, and formed a style peculiar to himself; in which the tasteful, the exquisite, the refined, and the sentimental, sometimes border on the affected. Vandyke is chiefly distinguished as a portrait painter, and in this difficult branch of art is scarcely inferior to Titian. The last nine years of Vandyke's life having been spent in England, this country is very rich in portraits from his hand; the principal collections are the Royal Collection, and those at Blenheim, Althorp, the Grove, Gorhambury, Worksop, Petworth, and Wilton. Perhaps the best known single picture is the 'Charles I on Horseback,' at Windsor.

In Holland, a reaction against Italian influence set in about the beginning of the seventeenth century, and became very distinctly developed in every branch of art. In portraiture this was first evidenced by extreme faithfulness and literal resemblance, as in the portraits of F. Hals and B. Van der Helst, although the latter inclined rather to Vandyke's manner.

But this movement, or rather an entirely new style, is most peculiarly identified with Paul Rembrandt van Ryn (1606–1674, or more probably 1664). He certainly, in his portraits, could never have flattered—could never have 'treated,' as it is called, the peculiarities of his subject; but in historical painting he evinces a positive predilection for imitating vulgar nature, and seems to have chosen the most ill-favoured models in order to show how much he could effect by rich impasto and texture, masterly handling, and above all, by the magic of chiaroscuro and its effects upon colour. In all, indeed, that relates not to form, Rembrandt was, perhaps, the most original and creative genius in the history of painting. The striking effects of Rembrandt are obtained by concentration of light; contrasted with large masses of shadow, which are broken up with the utmost subtlety of graduated shade and reflected light.

Among Rembrandt's finest works must be ranked a portrait composition in the Museum of the Hague. The subject is the celebrated anatomist, Nicholas Tulp, 'demonstrating' on a dead body in the presence of several hearers. The private collection of Van Sixt (a descendant of the burgomaster of that name, Rembrandt's friend and best patron) at Amsterdam contains other excellent works of the same kind. The 'Woman taken in Adultery,' in the National Gallery, is one of the best of Rembrandt's earlier performances on a small scale. A famous picture of his later time is the so-called 'Night Watch,' a colossal work in the museum at Amsterdam, representing a party, with their arms, marching out to fire at a mark. The same museum contains the Staalmeestres (a council of one of the guilds of Amsterdam), which is considered by some as Rembrandt's masterpiece. Rembrandt applied his principles of light and shade to his very celebrated etchings,[112] and also to landscape: the landscape in Lord Lansdowne's collection, known as 'Rembrandt's Mill,' is a notable instance of the latter. The most distinguished of Rembrandt's pupils was Gerard Douw; but he afterwards abandoned the manner of the school for 'genre.' Other distinguished scholars were Eckhout, F. Bol, G. Flink, P. de Koning, S. Van Hoogstraten, and N. Maas.

In the subordinate branches of painting, classed together as *genre,* and which were generally pictures of a small size, the Dutch painters so greatly excelled, that *genre* and the *Dutch style* are almost synonymous. Minute and exact imitation—even to the point of illusion—of familiar and frequently vulgar subjects, is at once the principle and the characteristic of these artists. Only actual acquaintance with these works of the masters will, however, afford the power of discriminating their great artistic and various technical and mechanical merits; we shall, therefore, content ourselves with recalling the following names only of the most important. Peter Breughel, called 'Peasant Breughel,' on account of the scenes he represented, and to distinguish him from his son, known as 'Hell Breughel,' from the subjects he delighted to paint; David Teniers, the elder, who also painted 'Temptations of St. Anthony,' and the like; his son, David Teniers the younger, the head of the *genre* painters, and who, besides similar scenes of *diablerie,* represented tavern subjects, guard-rooms, &c.; Adrian Van Ostade, second among the low humorous painters; Adrian Brouwer, and Jan Steen, also very able masters in this style; Jean le Ducq, distinguished for his pictures of soldier life; Terburg, who painted the life and manners of the upper classes;[113] Gerard Douw, the painter of simple domestic life, artists' ateliers, &c.; Gabriel Metzu; F. Mieris; Netscher; Schalken, who excelled in lamplight scenes; and Peter Van Hooghe, remarkable for the effects of light in his interiors.

Landscape, also, is a department in which the northern painters, and especially the Dutch, greatly distinguished themselves. John Breughel, generally called 'Velvet' Breughel, from his high finish, or 'Flower' Breughel, from the quantity of flowers, fruit, &c., 'picked out' in his landscapes, is the representative of the first style. This style was, however, superseded by that of Rubens. Some northern artists, such as Paul Bril and Adam Elzheimer, caught the Italian spirit from painting in Italy. The most important Italian impulse communicated generally to landscape painting originated in the school of the Carracci; but is only fully apparent in the finely composed and classical landscapes of Nicholas Poussin, in the stormy, aerial effects in the works of Gaspar Poussin, and in the serene beauty and sunshine of Claude —all three, painters of French extraction. This ideal or poetic style had considerable influence on the artists of the north. Claude, in particular, found imitators (with a difference) in Both, Pynacker, and Cuyp. Berghem and his pupil, K. du Jardin, usually preferred the forms of southern nature; Adrian Van der Velde generally depicted pastoral subjects; Philip Wouverman found in the representation of hawking scenes subjects almost peculiar to himself. Many, however, of the northern artists do not display any of the romantic element in their landscapes; but adhere to the imitation of the features of nature around them, with generally only the ordinary effects of daylight upon them. Among these artists Hobbema is entitled to special mention; Paul Potter's men and cattle are also equally simple and faithful. Other painters chose the grander forms of nature, or communicated a peculiar feeling to their representations; as Ruysdaal, in his storms and solitudes, and Van der Neer in his twilights. The greatest of all Dutch marine painters is William Van der Velde the younger; Backhuisen is also distinguished in this department. Among architectural painters, Peter Neefs and Van der Heyden may be instanced. Of all the animal painters, Snyders, the friend of Rubens, is decidedly the greatest. Hondekoeter excelled in poultry; and Ridinger, of Augsburg, in hunting scenes. Dutch artists delighted likewise in representations of still life, and especially of eatables. Flowers, also tastefully arranged, were admirably painted by Seghers, de Heem, Rachel Ruysch, Weenix, and Van Huysum.

6. THE SPANISH SCHOOLS

John Van Eyck was sent upon an important mission to Portugal, and the earliest development of Spanish art was due to the political connection of Spain with the Low Countries. The 'German style,' as it is called by the Spanish, did not, however, long prevail. Italian taste, as represented more particularly by the Venetian masters of colour and execution, and the Neapolitan naturalisti, was diffused throughout the Peninsula, and continued paramount till rendered subordinate by the native characteristics exhibited in the seventeenth century in the works of Zurbaran, Velasquez, and Murillo. But the influence of religion upon art was felt in Spain more in every way than in Italy. The jealous bigotry and intolerance of the Inquisition prescribed the exact manner in which sacred personages should be depicted, and forbade any approach to representations of the nude — a restriction which accounts for the comparative weak drawing of most of the Spanish painters. A certain sternness in the Spanish character, joined to religious enthusiasm in most of the artists themselves, combined also to give a peculiarly sombre and ascetic, and, from the subjects chosen, a frequently repulsive, character to Spanish art.

Until within the last few years great ignorance existed in respect to Spanish art generally. This has been dissipated, however, by the excellent *Handbook for Spain,* by the late Richard Ford, and by the works of Mr. Stirling and Sir Edmund head. But — although the subject is attractive — as the Spanish practice exhibits very few original features, we shall curtail our remarks.

Titian spent a few years in Spain in the reign of Charles V; his pictures seem, however, to have had no great influence. The principal existing works in Spain date from the time of Philip II: many were executed by Italians, and the best Spanish painters studied in Italy. We shall confine our attention more particularly to the truly national painters. Antonio del Rincon (about 1446–1500) is the first distinguished Spanish painter; but a somewhat later artist, Luis de Morales, belongs to an equally early period, in virtue of the sentiment in his works—which has led to Morales being called the 'divine' and the Spanish Perugino. Luis de Vargas (1502–1568) was the founder of the higher school of art in Seville. He is said to have been a pupil of Perino del Vaga, and he certainly imitated the style of the Italian. Vicente Joanes (1523–1579) is, similarly, the *caposcuola,* or head of the school of Valencia. Joanes is sometimes called the Spanish Raphael. A. S. Coello was a distinguished portrait painter of this school; a branch of art in which he was instructed by Antonio More while this artist was in Spain. In what is called by Sir Edmund head the middle period of Spanish art—'when the Italian character was giving way to a certain national feeling, but the full power of Murillo and Velasquez had not yet burst forth' there were some distinguished masters of the school of Castile; among whom one of the most eminent was Juan Fernandez Navarrete, surnamed *El Mudo,* or 'the Dumb.' An attack of disease deprived this artist of hearing at the age of three; he consequently never learned to speak, hence his name. Theotocopuli, commonly called 'El Greco' (the Greek), 'a strange but admirable master,' is said to have been a pupil of Titian: his great study was colour. Federigo Zuccaro was one of a number of masters who were brought from Italy to assist in the decoration of the great Escurial Palace erected under the auspices of the gloomy bigot Philip II.

The prominence (compared with those of Aragon and the north of Spain) of the schools of southern Spain—viz., of Valencia and Seville—was still, in the latter part of the sixteenth century, supported by the following artists.

The great painter of the Valencian school was Ribalta, whom Mr. Ford describes as the Spanish Domenichino and Sebastian del Piombo combined. J. G. de Espinosa was an excellent painter, and is said to have studied under Ribalta. Josef de Ribera, or Lo Spagnoletto, though born in Spain, may more properly be said to belong to Italy. He went to that country very young, adopted the style of the powerful works of Caravaggio and the naturalisti, and died at Naples.

The school of Seville had several great masters. Pablo de Cespedes studied at Rome, and was considered one of the best fresco painters there in the time of Gregory VIII. He returned to his native Cordova, and distinguished himself as 'a great imitator of the beautiful manner of Correggio and one of the best colourists in Spain.' Juan de las Roelas has left works in Seville which prove him entitled to rank as a great painter, yet he is scarcely known out of his own country. Some of his works are considered equal to Domenichino and others to Guido. 'No master,' says Mr. Ford, 'ever painted the sleek grimalkin Jesuit like Roelas.' Francisco de Herrera *el viejo (*the elder) is said to have been the vigorous and sparkling touch adopted by Velasquez. Alonzo Cano was eminent as sculptor, painter, and architect. As a painter he is soft, rich, and pleasing. His works somewhat resemble those of Correggio, and form a singular contrast to the hauteur and violence of his character as a man.[114] By Sebastian de Llanos y Valdes, who was wounded by Cano in a duel, there are only two known pictures; but these are of great excellence. Pedro de Moya was a successful imitator of Vandyke.

Francisco Zurbaran (1598–1662) is one of the greatest names in Spanish art. He has been called the Spanish Caravaggio; but Mr. Ford says, with truth, that he was 'a far greater and more Titianesque painter.' He excelled in the 'cast' of his draperies—a rare merit in Spanish pictures. Philip IV is said to have stooped one day to look at him whilst at work in the Buen Retiro; and laying his hand on the artist's shoulder, saluted him as *Pinter del Rey y Rey de los pintores* (Painter of the King, and King of the Painters). A Franciscan monk kneeling in prayer and holding a skull, in the National Gallery, is a fine example of this master. Francisco Pacheco, though not a remarkable painter, is deserving of conspicuous mention as the best writer of his country on the art he practised, and as having established the school in Seville, from which came Alonzo Cano and Pacheco's great son-in-law Velasquez.

Diego Velasquez de Silva (1599–1660) is the most original of all the Spanish artists. The boldness of execution for which he is chiefly remarkable he learnt from Herrera, his first master; from whose school, however, he quickly removed to the more peaceful and orderly school of Pacheco. But, as Mr. Stirling says in his valuable life of the great painter, 'he discovered that Nature herself is the artist's best teacher, and industry his surest guide to perfection. He very early resolved neither to sketch nor to colour any object without having the thing itself before him.' The early manner of

Velasquez, which was formed before his first visit to Italy, and seems not to have been influenced by the journey, is harder, especially in the outlines, than the style of his later works: The 'Adoration of the Shepherds,' in the National Gallery, is in this early naturalistic manner. As a portrait painter Velasquez ranks with Titian and Vandyke. It is to be regretted that we have no authentic portrait by Velasquez in the National Gallery; the 'Boar Hunt,' however, gives a good idea of the painter's later handling; and at Dulwich there is one of the small repetitions of the celebrated portrait of the Infant Don Baltasar Carlos on horseback. Few painters had so prosperous a career as Velasquez. Of his great patron Philip IV there are numerous portraits by him. Velasquez had his studio in the royal palace, and the king kept a key by means of which he had access to it when be pleased. Nearly every day Philip used to come and watch him at work. All the stiff Spanish etiquette was relaxed in favour of the artist; he had all sorts of honours and emoluments conferred upon him, and received the most extravagant encomiums in the verses of contemporary poets. He was the only artist with whom Rubens became intimate on his visit to Madrid. Velasquez was commissioned by Philip to make a second journey to Italy to collect works of art; and while at Rome he painted a noble portrait of Innocent X. The Royal Gallery at Madrid contains no less than sixty-two pictures by this great master. His historical *chef-d'oeuvre is* the 'Surrender of Breda;' 'Velasquez painting the Portrait of the Infanta Margarita' is a celebrated portrait composition; and the 'Borbedones,' or 'Drinkers,' is another very fine work.

Murillo (1618–1682) is beyond all comparison the best-known Spanish painter. His simple, unaffected imitation of nature, the presence of no recondite artistic quality in his execution, and the softness and beauty of his colouring, have gained him universal popularity, and even a large share of admiration from artists; although the latter are generally disposed to prefer the more learned style and brilliant handling of Velasquez. The early works of Murillo incline, like those of his great contemporary, to the manner of Caravaggio, but later in life he adopted a softer outline and more mellow colouring. Most of his great pictures were painted after he was fifty years of age. In his own Seville there are still many of his finest works. England is very rich in Murillos; and the well-known pictures in the National Gallery are fine specimens of the master. The 'Flower Girl' at Dulwich is also a genuine specimen of a class of works (beggar boys, &c.) which in many cases are only the productions of pupils. In the Spanish Gallery of the Louvre the Murillos are very excellent; but the most famous work of the master is the great picture of the 'Immaculate Conception' (a very favourite subject with Spanish painters), from the Marshal Soult's collection, and now in the Old Gallery of the Louvre; for which it will be remembered the Emperor of the French paid 23,000*l*. In the Lansdowne collection there is an admirable portrait by Murillo.

Iriarte is one of the best landscape painters; but landscape never acquired much development in the art of Spain. Juan de Valdes Leal is the best painter after the death of Murillo. The Italian Luca Giordano, who came to Madrid in 1692, is charged with corrupting Spanish art by his able but specious facility of execution. Palomino is remembered far more as a biographer of Spanish artists than as a painter. Mengs, the tame academical Saxon painter, is the last name which need be particularized in the degeneracy of more modern Spanish art.

7. THE FRENCH SCHOOL

French art, viewed historically, is a branch of the Roman school. Giotti and Memmi, though they painted at Avignon, left no trace of their influence. Nor did Jean Fouquet of Tours, the miniaturist; nor Ring Rend of Anjou, who painted in the Flemish manner; nor François Clouet and Jean Cousin, who had similar characteristics, leave any impression, although the last has been termed the founder of the French school. The true Italianized French school dates from the time of Francis I, who invited the Italians Il Rosso *(Maître Roux,* as the French call him), Primaticcio, and Niccolo dell' Abbate, to decorate the gallery at Fontainebleau.

Simon Vouet was the first distinguished native artist of this school. He was a painter of naturalistic tendency, but he is chiefly remembered for having had as scholars Le Brun, Le Sueur, and other of the most eminent French painters.

Nicholas Poussin (1594–1665) has exerted a most important influence upon the arts of his country, although not immediately apparent in the decorative theatrical age of Louis XIV, or the tawdry and heartless times of Louis XV. Much of the stilted extravagance, the classical affectation, and disagreeable colouring of David and his school, may be traced to Nicholas Poussin. Unquestionably, however, Nicholas was a genius, and a painter of refined taste; yet it is not a little remarkable that Sir Joshua Reynolds should have so highly praised his works, and those of similar French painters, at the expense of the great Venetians, when, at the same time, his own practice was opposed to the principles which would be consistent with this admiration; and when Englishmen in general find so little in French art down to the time of David that is congenial to their feelings and natural predilections, and that they can unconstrainedly relish. Nicholas Poussin lived and painted almost entirely at Rome. There he formed his style upon the antique bassi-relievi and the ancient painting known as the 'Aldobrandini Marriage.' He has been styled the 'Learned Poussin,' from the knowledge displayed in his compositions, and the familiarity with ancient customs shown in his favourite mythological subjects.

Besides the excellence of his composition, Poussin's design is very correct, though monotonous, from uniform imitation of the antique; and his attitudes are frequently theatrical. His colouring has generally a brick-like tone, arising partly from the darkened red priming showing through; and the red and blue draperies in his pictures have a spotty effect. His constant study of bassi-relievi caused the general want of unity in his light and shade. In landscape Poussin holds a most distinguished place: his 'classical compositions' have, however, little in common with contemporary English landscape art. The characteristics of this master may be seen to almost as great advantage in the National Gallery as in the Louvre. Two sets of the 'Seven Sacraments,' one at Belvoir Castle, and the other series, together with 'Moses striking the Rock,' in the collection of the Earl of Ellesmere, and the 'Plague of Athens,' in the possession of Mr. Miles, of Leigh Court, are famous works of the master.

Gaspar Dughet, the great landscape painter, was a pupil of Nicholas, and is generally known by the name of Gaspar Poussin, which he adopted after the marriage of his sister with his master. He was born of French parents at Rome, and lived and painted in Rome. We have alluded to this master elsewhere. In his earlier works he adopted the severe forms of his brother-in-law, but a more genial feeling pervades many of his later landscapes. He paid especial attention to what we may call meteorological rather than aerial effects. Aerial perspective, that is to say, the true influence of atmosphere in conveying the impression of space and distance, was first interpreted by his great countryman, Claude (Gelée), the humble pastry-cook of Lorraine, who, some very few years only after being engaged at Rome as servant to the landscape painter Agostino Tassi, appears to have far surpassed his master in Tassi's own profession. Claude's landscapes are less severe in character than those of Gaspar Poussin, and are distinguished by their pure and beautiful, though somewhat mannered, luminousness. Pierre Mignard, surnamed 'le Romain,' also spent the greater part of his life at Rome. He has been called by Dr. Waagen 'the Sasso Ferrato and Carlo Dolce of the French school united in one person.' His portraits, particularly that of Madame de Maintenon, are well known. Nicholas Mignard d' Avignon, the elder brother of Pierre, is also celebrated as a portrait painter. Sebastian Bourdon was another artist who visited Italy, and became an imitator of Poussin. He returned, however, to France. In genre, portraits, and landscape Bourdon is, perhaps, seen to greater advantage than in historical works.

Eustache Lesueur is the greatest master who can be strictly claimed as French: yet, though he never went to Rome, it is remarkable that he is one of the most Italian of the French painters. He has been called the French Raphael 'much as Klopstock has been termed the German Milton.' His great work is the series of the 'Life of St. Bruno,' now in the Louvre. Jacques Callot is better known by his prints of the 'Miseries of War,' and the 'Temptation of St. Anthony,' than by his pictures. Philippe de Champaigne evinces clear perception of character and fidelity in his portraits. Antoine and Louis Lenain show a feeling for nature in their works, which is rare among the French.

Charles Le Brun is the generalissimo of the host of French artists (query in many instances) who have painted the acres of battle-pieces which cover the walls of that palace at Versailles with the modest inscription 'A Toutes les Gloires de la France.' Le Brun's chief performances are the five vigorously composed 'Battles of Alexander,' painted in direct adulation of his master Louis XIV. Jacques Courtois ('Il Borgognone'), and his pupil Joseph Parrocel, are also distinguished battle painters.

Other artists of the Louis-Quatorze era were Dufresnoy,[115] Michel Corneille, Claude Lefévre, Bon Boullongne, Noel Coypel, Jean Jouvenet, De Largillière, Hyacinthe Rigaud (the portrait painter), Jean Baptiste Monnoyer (the flower painter), and Louis Laguerre, who came to England, and is immortalised in Pope's line:

'Where sprawl the saints of Verrio and Laguerre.'

Antoine Watteau, the painter of Louis XV frippery, affectation, and false refinement, stands at the head of the painters of what were called *fêtes galantes;* and whatever may be thought of the subjects, the style of this painter is exactly suited to their characteristic expression, and first-rate of its kind. But Boucher is the most notorious painter of the tinselled debauchery and indecency of his time. Diderot thus characterizes him: 'I know not what to say of this man. The debasement of taste, colour, composition, character, expression, and drawing has followed step by step on that of morals.' Jean Baptiste Vanloo came to England, was patronized by Walpole, and became a fashionable portrait painter. Joseph Vernet, the prolific and excellent painter of sea-pieces and views of French ports, was the grandfather of the celebrated French painter, Horace Vernet, who recently died. Greuze, despite enamelled surface, and a certain taint of conventionality, is deservedly a favourite in this country, in virtue of the simple homeliness of his themes and his careful study of nature. 'L'Accordée de Village,' the subject of which is a father who has just paid the dowry of his daughter, is an admirable picture by Greuze, in the Louvre. Perhaps the most remarkable painting of the eighteenth century, in France, is the 'Apotheosis of

Hercules,' by François Lemoine, on the ceiling of the Salon d'Hercule, at Versailles.

Anticipatory of, and corresponding with, the gigantic and tempestuous political reaction of, the Revolution, was the revulsion in art, initiated by Vien, the master of David, but effected chiefly by the latter and his scholars. By strict adherence to the outward forms of the antique, by correctness of design and composition, and severity of colour, these artists believed they should embody the stern virtues and classical spirit of the ancients; and thus forcibly, though tacitly, protest against the unmanly degeneracy of a nearly effete age. But the general result, although in many respects more healthy and indicative of a purified atmosphere, was repulsiveness of colour, a pedantic display of drawing and classicalisms, a want of genuine natural feeling, and a fresh development of the besetting national vice of theatrical exaggeration. The most celebrated of David's works are 'Le Serment des Horaces,' painted for Louis XVI; the 'Sabine Women' and 'Léonidas,' purchased by Louis XVIII; the 'Serment du Jeu de Paûme;' the 'Death of Marat;' the great picture of the 'Coronation of Napoleon,'[116] for which the Emperor paid 105,000 f.; and the portrait of 'Napoleon crossing the Alps' on a white horse. The last is, of course, a fictitious representation, for the First Consul really, and could indeed only, have ridden over St. Bernard on a donkey or mule. David excelled, however, in portraiture, and his portrait of 'Pope Pius VII' is a much finer work of art than any of his historical pictures.

Gerard was a prominent follower of David: he was an excellent portrait painter, and his 'Entry of Henry IV into Paris,' now at Versailles, is a remarkable picture. Gros, Abel de Pujol, Drolling, and Drouais were also distinguished painters of the same school: the masterpiece of the last artist is 'Marius at Minturnæ.' The most coldly classical, but at the same time, however, the most elegant painter of the school, was Guérin. The 'Shipwreck of the Medusa,' by Géricault, the initiator of 'romanticism,' and Girodet's still more horribly detailed picture of the 'Deluge,' leave an indelible impression upon all visitors to the Louvre. The great merits of the Italian scenes by Leopold Robert, and of the works of Granet, Horace Vernet, Paul

Delaroche, Ingres, Delacroix, Ary Scheffer, Decamps, Gerome, Meissonier, Flandrin, Edouard Frère, Breton, Henriette Browne, Auguste and Rosa Bonheur, and many other of the more recent painters of the present century, are too well known to require note or comment.

8. The British School

The most important early works of painting in England were those executed in the reigns of Henry III and Edward III, in the Painted Chamber and St. Stephen's Chapel, Westminster. These are noticed in several parts of this volume, and may, therefore, with simple mention, be passed over in our slight sketch of painting in this country. The zeal of the Reformers and Puritans has deprived us of nearly every vestige of early English painting and sculpture; yet the beautiful monument to Richard de Beauchamp, Earl of Warwick, in St. Mary's Church, Warwick, proves that in the reign of Henry VI we possessed in William Austen, its designer, at least one native artist hardly inferior to his famous Italian contemporaries, Donatello and Ghiberti. The very remarkable sculptures in the west front of Wells Cathedral are also believed by Flaxman, Cockerell, and the best authorities, to be the work of native artists, though contemporary with Nicolo Pisano, the restorer of sculpture in Italy. We have, however, scarcely any record of English painters previous to the reign of Charles I. Foreigners were engaged for every important work in painting; and, in fact, foreign artists were preferred even down to the time of Hogarth and Sir Joshua Reynolds—from whose time the English school properly dates. During several successive reigns chiefly German and Flemish masters were patronized in this country.

Henry VII employed, among other foreign artists, the distinguished painter Jan Mabuse. The despotic successor of this monarch displayed a comparatively enlightened appreciation of art. The visit of Hans Holbein to the court of Henry VIII, in 1526, has already been mentioned. This eminent artist remained in this country until his death in 1554, painting numerous portraits remarkable, evidently, for unflattering fidelity.[117]

The Flemish master Sir Antonio More, as elsewhere stated, painted the portrait of Queen Mary. Queen Elizabeth employed Federigo Zuccaro and

Lucas de Heere, and also the celebrated native miniature painters Sir Nicholas Hilliard, and his far more eminent pupil, Isaac Oliver. Peter Oliver, the son of Isaac, was likewise distinguished in this branch of art. In the reign of James I, we have to chronicle the foreign names of Van Somer, Cornelius Jansen, and Daniel Mytens—the last an admirable portrait painter. The best English artist of this reign was Nicholas Stone, the sculptor.

Charles I was the most intelligent collector of pictures, and the most liberal patron of art, of all our English sovereigns. To him we are indebted for the possession of Raphael's cartoons, and of several fine works of art, notwithstanding that many pictures were dispersed at the Revolution, and many destroyed in the fire at Whitehall. In this reign the principal native painters were William Dobson, some of whose portraits are equal to Vandyke; Robert Walker, also scarcely inferior to the Flemish painter; George Jameson, called the Scottish Vandyke; Francis Barlow, known by his pictures of hawking; Gibson the dwarf; and Henry Stone, the son of the sculptor already named, and commonly called *Old* Stone, to distinguish him from his brother Henry. Old Stone was an excellent copyist of Vandyke. The foreign artists are still more numerous, including Rubens, Vandyke, Mytens, Petitôt, Honthorst, Abraham Diepenbeck, Sir Balthazar Gerbier, Abraham Vanderdort, keeper of the king's collections, and many others—the list, it will be perceived, comprising some of the greatest painters of the age. Until the painting of the Whitehall ceiling, it is a significant fact that nothing but portrait painting had found any encouragement in this country since the time of Edward III; and after the death of Charles I, there long continued to be scarcely any demand for other branches of art.

Sir Peter Lely succeeded Vandyke, and imitated his style, though with far more affectation and much less ability. Lely painted first in the reign of Charles I; then veering with the times, be took the portrait of Cromwell; and lastly became the favourite painter of the frail beauties of the dissolute court of Charles II.

Other foreign artists employed at this period were Antonio Verrio, Gerard Zoust, and the two Van der Veldes, the excellent marine painters. The only native artist of very great merit was Samuel Cooper the miniature painter.

Following in every sense in the wake of Lely, as Lely did of Vandyke, came Sir Godfrey Kneller, in the times of William III and George I. John Riley was the most distinguished English contemporary of Kneller.

From the long-continued neglect of using any means for fostering native talent, art in England had sunk about this period to apparently the lowest point to which it can descend in a civilized nation. A better era, however, dawned with the Georges, although certain stories are told betraying the utter want of taste of especially the first George. At all events the immigration of foreigners was checked by finding that the market was forestalled by Englishmen with whom they could not compete. Almost the last foreign artists we have to mention, or worth mentioning, as visitors, are Denner, Canaletto, Zincke (the enamel painter), Laguerre, Vanloo, Michael Dahl, Giacomo Amigoni, and Bernard Lens, the miniature painter. The following British artists flourished in this age of bigwigs: Charles Jervas, Thomas Flatman, William Aikman, Sir James Thornhill, Joseph Highmore, Thomas Hudson (the master of Reynolds), and Jonathan Richardson.[118] The first grand monumental work of painting entrusted to a native artist was the decoration of the interior of the dome of St. Paul's by Sir James Thornhill. But for the patriotic interference of the Earl of Halifax, this commission would have been given to Sebastian Ricci. The Italian would, in all probability, have produced a finer series of paintings; but the Englishman succeeded as well as might have been expected, and it was necessary to make a bold effort of this kind in order to remove prejudice and turn the current of patronage into its natural channel. No immediate effect, it is true, succeeded, simply because the effort was not consistently followed up. The best of Thornhill's decorative works are the well-known paintings in Greenwich Hospital.

William Hogarth (1697 -1764), the son-in-law of Sir James Thornhill,[119] is the first great name in the history of British art. Unlike his great contemporary, Sir Joshua Reynolds, he had, however, little direct influence upon the artists of his time; to Sir Joshua, therefore, has long been assigned the honour of being the head of the British school. Yet we are very much disposed to think that posterity will recognize in that indomitable genius,

William Hogarth, the real founder of our school; insomuch as he is the great and as yet in some respects unequalled exemplar of its most prevailing characteristics. For, while the influence of the style of Reynolds's painting, and the high-art doctrines propounded in his *Discourses,* have already comparatively died out, an entirely new and essentially national description of *genre* was originated by Hogarth, and may fairly be considered to have been derived from him through Wilkie, Leslie, Mulready, and many more, by the host of living painters of domestic incident. The very extraordinary originality and the wonderful satirical and humorous invention displayed in the works of Hogarth, and the acknowledged value of his pictures as records of life, manners, and costume, have led many to depreciate his very high technical merits as a painter. Against this unjust estimate he has, however, been ably vindicated by the kindred spirit, Mr. Leslie, and by a concurrence of recent critical opinion.

Hogarth was bred an engraver of crests and ciphers on silver salvers, sauceboats, and spoons; but be preferred to gain a scantier subsistence by engraving prints for booksellers, and he often sold his plates for little more than the value of the copper. As a portrait painter, however, he was more successful. His own portrait in the National Gallery, that of Captain Coram in the Foundling Hospital, and Garrick as 'Richard III' in Lord Feversham's collection, prove his ability in this department. But his fame will rest as long as good painting is appreciated, wholesome satire relished, unequalled originality esteemed, or reverence entertained for one, at least, of the great founders of the British school, and one of the most courageous champions of 'modernism' on the great series of 'Marriage à la Mode' (in the National Gallery), the 'Rake's Progress,' the 'Harlot's Progress,' and the four 'Election' pictures in the Soane Museum.

Owing, perhaps, to his defective education under Hudson, Sir Joshua Reynolds (1723-1792) never distinguished himself in his drawing of the human figure; but after his three years' residence in Italy, he displayed on his return to England qualities of colour and effect and a technical originality then unknown in this country; — where, with the single exception of Hogarth, mannerism universally prevailed, and where Kneller in painting was placed on a level with Shakspeare in poetry. These qualities, as beautiful as they were new, but still more his brilliant success as a portrait painter, and his subsequent elevation as first President of the Royal Academy, founded under the auspices of George III—an elevation which the painter justified equally by his pencil, his admirably written *Discourses,* and the general urbanity with which he upheld the 'dignity of the dying art,'—obtained for Reynolds so much consideration with Burke, Johnson, Goldsmith, and many other of his chief contemporaries, and secured him so many followers, that to him, as already remarked, has been assigned the honour of being head of the British school.

It is not all the works of Sir Joshua which justify the encomiums of his biographer Northcote. Though Titian and Rembrandt were his models in colour and chiaroscuro, he very rarely united so much richness with breadth as did the great Venetian, and he did not equal the force and effect of the Dutch master. His most successful (at least his best preserved) effort in colour is the portrait of 'Nelly O'Brien,' in Lord Hertford's collection; other masterpieces are the magnificent portrait of 'Mrs. Siddons as the Tragic Muse,' in the Grosvenor collection, an inferior replica of which is in the Dulwich Gallery, and the portraits of Lords Heathfield and Rodney, the former in the National Gallery, the latter in St. James's Palace. The taste and fancy of Reynolds are seen to especial advantage in his portraits of women, and of the children whom the old bachelor loved so well—and painted as they have never been painted; as, for example, in the large-portrait composition in the National Gallery, representing three sisters decorating a terminal figure of Hymen; in the 'Strawberry Girl,' 'Puck,' 'Miss Boothby,' and other portraits of children, familiar from having been in the International Exhibition of 1862. For the beautiful glazes, and the rich and creamy impasto he so much coveted, Reynolds paid dearly. Half his life was spent in experiments; and Northcote tells us that he deliberately scraped away and destroyed Venetian pictures of value in order to discover their technical secrets. He endeavoured to unite the best methods of the Flemish and Venetian masters; but his practice usually inclines, like that of the English school generally, to the traditions of the former. The decay of so many of his works is attributed to his introduction of wax and other incongruous ingredients and mixtures; to the use of lakes, (yellow) orpiment, and other fugitive colours; and to the varnishing of glazes of asphaltum which were not dry—cracking being the inevitable consequence. This last practice is, unfortunately, apparent in its results in most of Wilkie's pictures. The use of wax to gain substance and texture was a novelty which has found very few imitators. It is probable, however, that the vehicle of Reynolds had little to do with the rapid deterioration of many of his works. At all events, it will not explain the destruction of so many modern pictures; for, as Mr. Redgrave remarks, in his *Notes on the Sheepshanks Collection,* 'there are numerous pictures in a perfectly sound state, though known to have been painted with totally different media. In our own time we believe Mulready paints with copal, Landseer with a mastic maguilp, Leslie with the same [using freely, it would appear, essential oil diluents]; and other media are employed by artists whose works show no incipient flaw or defect.'

In one of his *Discourses,* Reynolds eulogizes Gainsborough (1727–1788) as a landscape painter; but seems hardly ever to have fully recognized his very high and rare merit as a portrait painter. Now, however, public opinion has placed the famous 'Blue Boy,' the 'Mrs. Graham,' 'Lady Ligonier,' 'Mrs. Siddons,' and other well known portraits by Gainsborough, on a level with anything produced by the President himself. In pictures of rustic children, and in landscape, Gainsborough has also left some works of almost incomparable sweetness and beauty. Romney superseded Reynolds as a portrait painter for a short period, even in his lifetime; but Romney's very great excellence in this branch of art seems to us not to have received due recognition since his death.

Benjamin West, as an historical painter, is already comparatively forgotten; and if he deserves to be remembered it is chiefly for the courage he displayed in the picture of the 'Death of General Wolfe,' in breaking away, even against the advice of Sir Joshua Reynolds, from the absurd practice then prevalent of representing the actors in modern events in ancient costumes. Barry's efforts in high art, in the Adelphi, we have already mentioned. His writings on art, together with those of Fuseli—another wayward genius—are, notwithstanding occasional extravagance, valuable. Other deceased historical painters were Opie, an almost self-taught Cornish artist; Northcote, the pupil and biographer of Reynolds; Copley (father of the late Lord Lyndhurst), the painter of the admirable 'Death of Major Pierson, at Jersey, 1780;' Harlowe; Westall; Briggs; Hilton, the painter of large religious works; Haydon, an artist of great but very irregular powers; and Etty, a splendid colourist, and our first historical painter in the 'high classical' sense. To these may be added the name of the promising young painter, Cross, who died a few years since. Martin, the inventor of the 'material sublime;' F. Danby, who painted similar subjects; Fuseli; and poor Blake—a painter of rare genius, but genius 'to madness near allied'—may be placed in a group apart.

Besides the foundation of the Royal Academy, other important encouragement of the higher branches of art was afforded about the end of the last century, by the formation of the Society of Dilettanti, by the private enterprise of Boydell in the Shakspeare Gallery, and by the establishment of the British Institution.

Sir Thomas Lawrence took the place of Reynolds in portraiture, and, though a painter of far less genuine ability, was equally successful. Compared to Reynolds, the taste of Lawrence, especially in expression, is decidedly meretricious, and in Colour he is poor and cold. Nevertheless, the portrait of 'the beautiful' Duchess of Devonshire, and some others, have a certain grace which lifts them much above the mere flimsy prettiness of many of his followers. Hoppner, Owen, Raeburn, and Jackson were also distinguished portrait painters. Raeburn has been called the Scottish Velasquez, and he founded the manly Scotch school of portraiture, at the head of which now stands Sir Watson Gordon.

In *genre,* Bird, Smirke, Stothard (chiefly known, however, as a designer), Collins, and Newton deserve respectful mention; but their contemporary Wilkie is, of course, pre-eminent. Wilkie's 'Blind Fiddler' and the 'Village Festival,' in the National Gallery—the 'Village Politicians,' the 'Rent Day,' and 'Blindman's Buff'—will bear comparison with any productions of the Dutch school. The genial and charming Leslie, and the recently deceased patriarch of English art, Mulready, some few of whose works are unsurpassed in exquisite perfection of execution, bring the list of deceased English genre painters down to the present day.

In landscape the English school, taking into consideration merely the works of deceased masters, is unquestionably the first in Europe; supported as it is by such names as Wilson, Gainsborough, Old Crome, Constable, Calcott, P. Nasmyth, Morland, Müller, Bonington, and, greatest of all, Turner. The works of Turner are now, however, so universally appreciated, and they have been criticised so exhaustively by Mr. Ruskin, that any attempt on our part to give an estimate of them would be supererogatory.

The very sudden rise of the British school — the almost simultaneous appearance of such men as Hogarth, Reynolds, Gainsborough, Barry, Wilson, and Romney—was not the least extraordinary of the great events which marked our national history in the latter half of the last century. And little less remarkable is the rapidity of the increase both of the supply and demand of works of art within comparatively the last few years. The paintings executed in the course of the century during which the British school has been established, have exhibited almost every kind of excellence; and the selection gathered with the other Art Treasures at Manchester in 1857, and again in the International Exhibition of 1862, would, we believe, lose little, if at all, by comparison with a similar collection of the productions of any Continental school during the same period. At the present time we see, on all hands, a happy promise of artistic activity—in public appreciation—in Government Schools of Design taking root all over the land—in the questions created by the introduction of photography—in the opposite principles involved in the practice of artists—and last, and perhaps not least, in the differences of critics and connoisseurs.

Chapter 9

Painting in Watercolours

We have seen that the use of, more particularly, earths and minerals of different colours, diluted with water alone, or water with which some ingredients not oleaginous has been combined, and applied for pictorial and ornamental purposes, is of the highest antiquity, and that painting with oils, or oleo-resinous vehicles, is a comparatively modern invention. The modes of water painting to which we allude are, of course, tempera, encaustic, and fresco. Watercolours have also been extensively used even in the execution of oil pictures, of which practice our own Turner affords a notable instance. But many, especially of the Flemish and Dutch oil painters, from the earliest period arrived at considerable technical excellence in the separate practice of watercolour painting. Adrian Ostade, and that universal genius Albert Dürer, have left us several examples in the shape of detached studies; and portfolios of Rembrandt's drawings are preserved in the British Museum. These, and even the distemper cartoons of Raphael and Mantegna, are, however, little more than simple washes of watercolour: the more recent processes by which effects are obtained nearly equalling the depth and power of oil painting, and which seem to promise to render watercolour painting the rival of oil in its age, as it was in its infancy, were then unknown.

The Paper

Watercolour painting surpasses oil in the purity and clearness of its tones, which arise from the transparency of its medium; it therefore excels in expressing the freshness, vivacity, and brilliancy of nature. But its most distinctive merit is seen in the realization of aerial effects and varied depths of distance. These peculiar excellences — the refreshing brightness and pervading sense of atmosphere — which can be obtained by a novice in watercolours almost as successfully as a Pynacker or a Claude could secure the same effects on canvas, result chiefly from the textural and absorbent properties of the paper employed to receive the Colours.

The surface of paper is *granulous;* that is to say, it presents so many little hollows and projections, which, while receiving general flat washes of colour, still maintain an alternation of light on the latter and half-light in the former. The minute cavities of the paper permit the eye, as it were, to penetrate the flat surface and follow the vanishing colour; and thus the eye receives illusive impressions of intervening air and distance; while the little prominences of the grain, receiving less colour (if a wash), and therefore retaining their reflective lustre, afford the truthful and beautiful luminousness which watercolour shares in common with fresco.

The facility of obtaining effects of aerial perspective has, however, tempted artists to render them too prominent in this medium by forcing them also in the colour. We find, for instance, the most distant objects, through various gradations of cold colour, too often represented with the brightest blue, and looking like so many holes in the picture. A tendency to rawness and crudeness, and the want of the mellowness of tone of oil, are indeed the commonest faults of painting in watercolours.

Paper is used from the greatest extremes of roughness to hot-pressed smoothness; the latter seldom, however, not having the recommendation of texture. The paper is also sometimes tinted, as in many of Turner's watercolour paintings. There is, in fact, paper of scarcely any surface or texture which this great artist did not employ. Nothing came amiss to him: and some of his drawings are executed upon pieces of crumpled brown paper which had probably enfolded a parcel. Card, or Bristol board, like hot-pressed paper, is seldom used, on account of its smoothness; but Cattermole has boldly covered with his opaque sketches some of the very coarsest millboard.[120]

Alterations, Corrections. There are other secondary advantages resulting from the grain of the paper. Rough surfaces, such as walls, gravel and sand, are imitated very felicitously by merely scraping the projecting granulations of the paper with a knife, rubbing them with sandpaper, or passing over them a wet cloth or sponge; by which operations different degrees of roughness are given with the removal of more or less colour from the projections, or by the driving it into their interstices. The hardness of the paper used will admit of these operations, and also of repeated dampings and complete immersions, without becoming what is called 'woolly.'

So that, if to these be added the greatest facility in erasing or effacing—even the power of cutting out a spoiled portion and inserting clean paper in its place; the use at will of transparent or body colours, either mixed or separately, or the one upon the other; together with all the styles of execution common to oil, such as hatching, stippling, scumbling, glazing, or spreading an opaque tint—it will be sufficiently evident, contrary to what is generally supposed to be the case, that the painter in watercolours can make alterations and modifications in his work with as much success as the painter in oil.

Sketches. The artist in the progress of his work is generally beset with unforeseen difficulties: for a thousand purely accidental circumstances occur in the course of the material realization of his idea. The colour, for example, dries irregularly, or collects in unsightly blots; or his brush is too playful, thoughtless, and disobedient, or too stiff, formal, and mathematically exact; his eye wanders, or sees either too much or too little, and his hand quivers with nervousness, or is cramped with rheumatism. These accidents the young artist, intent upon the exact imitation bit by bit of what he sees, believes to be unmitigated evils. Gradually, however, he becomes more certain of his ability of surmounting the obstacles thus presented, and with experience he can more readily anticipate the ultimate effect of the union of the various parts; his attention is therefore more at liberty to examine the nature of these unforeseen effects—when, to his great astonishment and delight, he finds the accidental blots and blurs may be easily 'worked in,' and often suggest beautiful little passages, which excite his imagination, and enable him with a little tact to snatch 'a grace beyond the reach of art,' at least of commonplace mechanical art. He will find, for a single instance, that if he wants a firm outline, he can obtain it by applying the colour in a very liquid state and waiting for the dark edge which it forms in drying; and he knows at the same time that colour thus laid suddenly, and confidently left to dry, preserves a much greater beauty and purity of tint than if dragged about and disturbed.

But nothing is found to contribute to variety of accidental effect more than the inequalities of the surface chosen for painting. The taking advantage of such effects permits the more rapid completion of a sketchy generalized resemblance of an object. This is the reason, also, why very rough paper is always chosen for sketches in watercolours. But the rough paper has another recommendation for this purpose; which is, that the inevitable imperfections of a sketch are hidden, and an appearance of general harmony and finish given by the recurrence at regular intervals of the granulations of the very coarsest paper. Besides this, watercolours are much better for sketches than oil, for another reason—namely, because sketches in oil, though kept in portfolios, undergo great discolouration in a short time, owing to the quantity of oil necessarily used to enable the artist to paint with sufficient freedom and rapidity; while watercolour sketches so protected will remain unchanged for an indefinite period.

Hanging. There are yet other considerations connected with the effects resulting from the texture of the paper which remain to be mentioned. The artist works, as already stated, with the light above and on one side—generally the left, in order to avoid the shadow from the brush falling in front of him on his work. Consequently, he looks at the paper in a lateral light, which brings out all the inequalities of its surface very forcibly. To illustrate the effect of this in the completed work, we will suppose the artist to make a sketch and a small highly-finished portrait of the same person; the former executed in flat washes, and the latter receiving a great quantity of minute stippling in the flesh—each touch possibly no larger than each little protuberance of the paper's grain. When both are ready for inspection, the artist's subject arrives, and looking at them on the easel, thinks one (the sketch), a mere daub, and the other equal to a highly-finished miniature. He then takes both in his hands, and turns to the artist, with the intention possibly of complimenting him, when the highly-finished portrait of himself looks, to his unpleasant surprise, nearly as coarse as the sketch: he turns back to replace them, when, as if by magic, the minute finishing he has so much admired is all again restored—the sketch remaining the same throughout. A similar effect occurs when persons make fresh arrangements in a room, and find a pet little drawing of this kind in its new place loses half its charm without any assignable reason.

Now these effects are all attributable to the grain of the paper. The highly-wrought picture is finished by the artist with the point of the brush, and every little summit of the granulation, from its prominence, the more readily catches and retains the comparatively dry colour employed in the stippling process: and not only this, but the painter involuntarily works on the projections. For, let the paper be magnified, and it will be found that each of these little hills, so to speak, receives the slanting ray on the acclivity next the source of light, and throws its shadow into the adjoining valley, so that the surface is a chequer-work of light and shade; and as every point of light attracts the eye, the artist insensibly and involuntarily, in finishing with the point of the brush, touches these slopes of light till they disappear and become blended with and as dark as the shadows they cast. But the necessary consequence, when the picture is reversed, and the light falls from the opposite side, is that not only the original coarseness of the paper is restored, but it is greatly aggravated by every slope upon which the colour basked in light, being now in turn enveloped in shadow, with, in addition, this shadow deepened by unilluminated paint. A sketch, on the contrary, upon which the colour is broadly floated, it will be readily understood, is not liable to much variation.

Of course finish, with no other object than that of obtaining mere smoothness, is very contemptible; but our motive in attempting to give the *rationale* of some watercolour paintings looking so different in different lights, is to draw the attention of the possessors of such works to the importance of hanging them as nearly as possible in the same position in reference to the light as that in which they were painted. Artists, knowing the importance of this, often inscribe in the corner of the work the professional directions—*jour à droite,* or *jour à gauche,* according as the light should be on the right or left. But when these are absent, the right position may be easily discovered in almost every case by observing from which side the light is gradated. It is also very desirable to observe this gradation of the light as a guide for the hanging of oil pictures.[121] A landscape, for instance, may have the sky very tenderly gradated from left to right (having been painted with the light on the left); but if this picture is hung with the light from the opposite side, the gradation of tone will be partly neutralized. And, further, the effect of the surface and texture of the oil paint demands attention to the rule. For, it will be observed, that where the artist has 'loaded' his colour in order to give brilliant 'catching' lights, when the illuminating rays impinge at a different angle, much of the spirit and feeling with which these have been touched will be lost; and, even if the surface has been clogged with varnish, either a shadow is projected instead, or the light altered in position, and the whole work rendered more coarse and rough.

Such contingencies as these—so prejudicial to the artist together with the still more injurious one, in a general exhibition, of the juxtaposition of unforeseen colour in neighbouring works (which the most careful collocation of pictures cannot prevent)—these and such like agencies have so powerful, though unsuspected, an effect upon the eye, and consequent misleading influence upon the judgment, that they should be frequently pointed out to the public, for few but artists themselves are sufficiently sensible of their existence.

Even miniatures, which, from the perfect smoothness of the ivory on which they are painted, might be supposed to be free from the variable effects at least of grain and texture, are yet found by miniature painters to be not beyond their influence. For, though the texture is so dense and the surface so perfectly smooth, yet in the substance of the ivory itself, especially those parts of the sheet not sawn out of the very heart of the tusk, there is a kind of wavy striated appearance, resulting from the alternation of layers or threads (somewhat resembling the grain of wood), of more or less transparency. And as in miniatures the soft tone of the ivory is seen through the more thinly painted passages—as in the face—one becomes, upon close examination, just sensible of an effect analogous to that of paper, though in a less degree. For a few additional remarks on the subject of 'Hanging,' see Appendix, note B.

PIGMENTS, BRUSHES, ETC

The Pigments. The same great distinction obtains in watercolours as in oil between the transparent and the opaque colours; and the former may be converted into the latter by the addition of white. Colours thus rendered opaque, together with those pigments in their own nature opaque, are (as already observed), from their greater solidity and substance, termed body colours. The permanent earthy and mineral colours were chiefly used in ancient works; and these, together with a few transparent colours, such as sepia, indigo, and Indian ink, satisfied the early watercolour artists of this country. As the art advanced, richer as well as more delicate, though less permanent, colours were quickly added; and as the demand increased, various improvements were made in the preparation of watercolour pigments by the artists' colourmen. Chemistry has supplied many entirely new colours, several of which are as fugitive as they are beautiful. It is, indeed, somewhat strange that in the wonderfully rapid advance of this science it has not discovered any means of rendering permanent such colours as the beautiful transparent vegetable yellows, the splendid red, carmine, and other tints obtained from the cochineal insect—colours which are almost indispensable in flower painting.

The necessity for the use of the colours from cochineal no longer exists, however, in such force since the introduction of the improved methods of preparing pigments from the colouring matter of the root of the madder plant. The colours extracted, called rubric or madder lakes, though not very vivid in abstract power of line, vary in tint from the most delicate rose to the deepest purple; and being more transparent and far more permanent than the old lakes, and working well both in water and oil, they are exceedingly valuable to the painter. These pigments, now so extensively used in dying and the industrial arts, we owe to the investigations of science. The artist is likewise indebted to the chemist for another pigment, pre-eminently serviceable as a watercolour. We allude to the white[122] prepared from zinc, called 'Chinese white.' This, though a metallic white, appears to be quite permanent, unlike all the whites prepared from lead, which when used with water are changeable even to blackness, sully other tints with which they may be brought in contact, and are far from innoxious to the person using them. This pigment, so eligible in other respects, has hitherto not been prepared with sufficient 'body' for use in oil. It has, however, been stated recently that a Mr. G. Lewis of Philadelphia has succeeded in giving the requisite opacity to this white oxide of zinc, by subjecting it to powerful pressure while grinding in oil.

Now, the use of white constituting, as we have seen, the great distinction in practice termed 'body-colour' painting, and nearly all that is characteristic in the watercolour art of our own time, in so far especially as it is imitative of oil painting, being attributable to the abundant use of white, it is evident that an eligible white pigment is extremely desirable. The leaden blackness which we often find in the place of the highest lights in old watercolour paintings proves that the whites then used cannot be relied upon. And although the terrene and barytic whites have enough body to allow of being applied in thickness and quantity sufficient to imitate the embossed effects of oil painting, yet the terrene whites, from their alkaline nature, are injurious to many colours in water, and barytic white does not work pleasantly—does not, from its clogging, pasty nature, deposit itself on the paper freely, following the lithesome play of the brush; and therefore does compete with the fascinating freedom of handling we admire so much in the oil pictures of, for example, Teniers and Wilkie. Barytic white—called 'constant white' by the colourmen—dries, moreover, many degrees lighter than when wet, so that the artist cannot easily calculate upon the ultimate pitch of his tones. Its extreme brilliancy, however, when used alone, sometimes recommends its use for the very highest lights.

But Chinese white is undoubtedly the nearest approach to the desiderated white watercolour—that colour which should be generally serviceable; which, while permanent itself, should not attack other colours when united with them; which should maintain the same tone when wet as it had when dry; which might be applied in opaque washings, and would cover and conceal a ground darker than itself; which should have so much strength and body as to afford, if required, actual relief to each touch, and yet be susceptible of extreme tenuity—a colour, in fine, which, like gold itself, should be precious from its own intrinsic beauty, and yet capable of receiving at the hands of the artist the greatest possible amount of extrinsic value, whether wrought and fashioned in dense masses, or scattered in airy waifs, or spread out in floating films.

Pigments, when employed with water, differ very much more than when united with oil in their several working qualities. Unfortunately the most permanent are the most unmanageable. The beautiful transparent but fugitive vegetable colours may be laid in even washes with the utmost facility; but the opaque earths and minerals, having greater specific gravity, will not float so readily; their particles remain where left by the brush, and yet are too coarse to penetrate the pores, so to speak, of the paper. The general rule, that a much purer compound hue may be produced by passing one tint of different chemical character over another than by applying them mixed together, holds good with more force in watercolour painting than in oil. In such operations, however, as the earthy and mineral colours will not bear friction, they must be applied last.[123]

Brushes. The smaller kinds of brushes are still sometimes termed 'pencils;' but the use of the word 'pencil' instead of 'brush,' as distinctive of and peculiar to watercolour painting, has become almost obsolete; and with reason, for to cover rapidly with floating colour the large surfaces of modern works in watercolour, requires brushes almost as large as those needed for painting ordinary pictures in oil; although, to avoid abrading the more delicate texture of paper, the brushes must not be made (at least for all ordinary practice) of anything so coarse as hog's bristles. The word 'pencil' still, however, retains its place in a semi-metaphorical sense, as generally allusive to the artist's work, whether he be painter or draughtsman, and in a still more figurative manner it is applied to anything delicately marked, as 'pencilled eyebrows.'

Brown sable is the hair generally used, being pliant, yet firm; but brushes made of red sable, and also of the squirrel—or 'camel hair,' as it is called—are useful for some purposes. Brushes of brown sable are made by the insertion of the hair into quills; hence the size of the brush is recognized by the various names of the birds which supply the quills employed—as eagle, swan (of various sizes), goose, duck, and crow. The eagle brush is very large and expensive, and seldom used. The duck and crow sables are employed for delicate markings, as in branches, foliage, and architectural details. Flat brushes, in German-silver ferules, are likewise employed; round brushes are also similarly enclosed, and they have the recommendation of not splitting like the quills.

LEGITIMACY OF PRACTICE

Few subjects in art have been more contested than that of legitimacy of practice in watercolour painting. We have already seen the distinction of 'body' colour, and for and against its use the contention has been principally raised. To show the diversity of opinion maintained, we may quote from two or three writers on the subject in question. Mr. Frank Howard, *Colour as a Means of Art,* says to this effect: 'It is to be regretted that, in some few, and those popular instances, the advantage of transparency arising from the legitimate use of watercolours should have been thrown away without obtaining any equivalent other than that of hiding or correcting blunders, and that attempts should have been made, by the use of opaque body colours and a similar method of working, to imitate the effect of oil painting. It is true, that opaque watercolours are supposed to have an advantage over oil colours in light and brilliant parts, and particularly in distances, in consequence of the tendency of the oil to come to the surface. On this account they are said to be used by Turner in distant parts, when he desires to attain great clearness and purity of colour. But used for watercolours, the only advantage of watercolours is abandoned without obtaining the equivalent of richness arising from texture in oil, and the purity of the one art is lost without obtaining the force of the other.' A somewhat similar view is taken by Mr. Burnet in the following remarks, from his *Practical Essays on the Fine Arts*: 'The freshness, the luminous property in fresco painting, is a charm which no watercolour drawing ought to be deprived of, and which no oil picture can contend with. The strongholds of oil painting lie in the deep-toned darks, and those juicy shadows where lighter half-tints are seen floating half-way down. The characteristic beauties of water-colour are in the pearly lights, and in those flat washes unattainable in oil colour without giving an inferior look to the whole work . . . The power, then, of retaining and giving back light is the peculiar property of watercolour, or rather of the paper, which ought, therefore, to be preserved at any sacrifice, as the artist has not the rich, pulpy, and unctuous glazings to give in compensation for its absence.' Then Mr. Burnet adds: 'And though the genius of Girtin and Turner did wonders in removing watercolour drawings from mere topographical achievements, it is only now that the capabilities of watercolour paintings are beginning to be perceived and spread over England. The drawings of Lewis, Cattermole, Harding, and [W.] Hunt, show what can be done in effect, texture, and colour; and we shall regret if the introduction of so perishable a material as body colour, or a meretricious perversion of talent, for the sake of attracting applause, destroys all remains of simplicity and truth.'[124]

Mr. Ruskin, on the contrary, says, in his *Elements of Drawing,* that he is inclined to think there should be no touch without white, and in several passages in his works speaks highly in praise of body colour. The earliest artists themselves, long after they had emerged from their sepia flat washes, generally, however, considered the use of opaque colour illegitimate. Turner was one of the first to break through this, as all other material restraints. 'To this master, in fact, we owe,' it is observed by Mr. Holmes, 'all the great improvements which have taken place of late years in watercolour drawing; for, in the course of his career, he introduced the use of warm tones into the shadows in the picture, and gradually discarding the use of the vegetable colours, he attained even a higher degree of brilliancy in his work, by reintroducing the use of those which are formed from mineral bases, and which we have seen in the instances of the pictorial representations on the most ancient monuments, still, after many ages, preserve their brilliancy unimpaired. Turner's works, however, are strictly examples of watercolour drawing; but since his time a style has arisen which appears to set aside the careful execution by which he and his contemporaries gained their effects, and to charge the drawing with heavy and unnecessary masses of material.' Contemporary artists, we may add, sometimes boldly sacrifice, as well as often virtually increase, the texture of the paper by scraping and other manipulations. In this, however, they resemble Turner; Mr. Ruskin thinks it even probable that in some of Turner's elaborately completed drawings, textures were prepared by various mechanical means over the general surface of the paper before the drawing of detail was begun.

From the foregoing we find that writers, having apparently claims to speak authoritatively, yet differ so much as to compel us to think for ourselves.

The question, then, appears to us simple enough. It is presumed that there can be no disputing the fact that a watercolour drawing is executed upon paper for some advantage exclusively possessed by the paper—else why not paint on some other material? Now, the peculiar and distinctive quality of the paper is, no doubt, the luminousness of its granulous texture. It should then be asked, What particular effects in nature will this distinctive quality afford better than can be furnished by other means? And when we know what these are, we contend, that to preserve them is the only limit we ought to place to legitimacy—these effects should never be altogether surrendered—they should always give a character to the finished work, whatever besides might be borrowed as auxiliary. Well, then, we have seen that the effects of light and atmosphere are those obtained with washes of colour more readily on paper than on any other surface. These washes need not, however, consist invariably of transparent or semi-transparent colours, for frequently an opaque wash will afford the happiest effect of light and air in the distance, through, be it especially observed, in a great measure, not being laid thick enough to obliterate the grain of the paper. We do not see the necessity, moreover, to restrict the use of body colour to these pearly washes. On the contrary, the effect of the granulation of the paper may be heightened, in some respects tenfold, *by stippling;* especially if the colour in nearly a dry state is merely touched on the prominences of the paper, and lodged as delicately as the bloom on a plum, and each little atom applied in a pure state, for the eye with its wonderful unconscious facility to blend into harmonious hues—as we see in the admirable works of Mr. W. Hunt.

Again, in foregrounds there are, of course, no breadths of aerial gradations; and therefore body colour maybe used with advantage on account of the greater vigour of handling and variety of marking it favours. It is also particularly eligible for rendering the minutiae of ornamental or other detail, from the crispness and sharpness which the artist can communicate to each touch. A remarkable example of this is afforded in the really marvellous watercolour works of Mr. John Lewis. Where, however, this definiteness of touch and body of paint is apt to give unnatural hardness and fixity, as it is if used in modelling the face, and where the artist does not aim at expressing or suggesting intervening atmosphere, but rather seeks to obtain the transparent glow of flesh, the use of body colour is 'illegitimate,' if we choose so to term it. But where we see the evident intention of rivalling the distinctive qualities of other technical appliances, merely for the purpose of exciting astonishment at the success of the rivalry, irrespective altogether of whether it be the best mode of imitating nature—where we see the artist wilfully resign all that is so peculiarly fresh and brilliant and lovely in watercolour, for the sake of obtaining the powerful impasto and intense glazing of oil painting—it is there the cry of illegitimacy may be fairly raised, because it is a manifest waste of means. The same objection may be made to those miniature painters who sacrifice the exquisite semi-transparent surface of the ivory; and to those oil painters who stain their canvases with pigments diluted to the neutral pallor of watercolours.

A watercolour painting may be worked with or without the glossy appearance inseparable from a varnished painting in oil; and the employment of gum for thus deepening and adding lustre, particularly to the shadows, is frequently considered illegitimate. We have given our reasons for believing in the legitimacy of the use of varnish in oil paintings. The same principle is here involved, but only so far as the glaze of gum may be used in passages where the grain of the paper is already with good reason sacrificed—its use is not necessary elsewhere.

PERMANENCY AND PRESERVATION

It is singular as well as painful to reflect that there is only too much reason to expect that in a few years by far the greater part of the beautiful watercolour paintings which gladden our eyes in the annual exhibitions will have become pale miserable ghosts of what they were; while certain simple efforts in watercolours as ancient as the pyramids preserve their freshness to this day; and wall paintings of two thousand, and some miniatures of not much less than one thousand years old, are still in excellent condition. With such permanency as this, oil paintings can hardly compare; for the oldest and most permanent are surely, though perhaps slowly, hastening to decay —losing in the first place transparency in the shadows, to end, however, with the obscuration of the whole picture.

Such being the excellent state of preservation of many ancient works, we naturally inquire how it happens that the works of our own time are so fugitive. One great cause of the fading of the early watercolour paintings of the present century (as also of miniatures) was, as already remarked, the reckless employment of vegetable colours. The manner in which missal paintings are protected no doubt in a great measure accounts for their preservation; and it was the observation of this which was probably one of the recommendations of the use of folding triptychs,[125] &c. (See Appendix, note D.) But those missal miniatures, it is found, are in the best condition which were almost entirely painted with colours of mineral or earthy extraction. Mr. Ruskin says, that 'any painter may get permanent colours from the respectable manufacturers if he chooses,' by which we presume can alone be meant—if the painter selects those of known permanency.

Some pigments, such, for instance, as indigo (a colour of very extensive use in modern watercolour paintings) and similar blues, appear to have their natural want of permanency greatly increased by the conversion of the vegetable mucilage with which they are prepared into an acid by the action of air. Many portions of Turner's paintings in which indigo has been used, either alone or mixed with yellow, to form a green, are turned to a rusty red; while in the midst of this unnatural hue, a part which has been accidentally covered is found to be pure blue or green. The importance of any change in a colour employed so universally as blue in skies, water, and mixed with yellow for the greens of foliage, will be immediately understood. But this same change of the mucilage into an acid will render even the permanent watercolours mechanically fugitive, that is to say, they return to their original powdered condition.

The greatest present cause of deterioration appears, however, to reside in the paper used. Mr. Ruskin, in one of his published lectures on the *Political Economy of Art, says,* in his usual graphic way, speaking of the common disregard whether either the colours or the paper will stand: 'In most instances neither will. By accident it may happen that the colours in a given drawing have been of good quality, and its paper uninjured by chemical processes. But you take not the least care to ensure these being so. I have myself seen the most destructive changes take place in watercolour drawings within twenty years after they were painted. And from all I can gather respecting the recklessness of modern paper manufacture, my belief is, that though you may still handle an Albert Dürer engraving, two hundred years old, fearlessly, not one-half of that time will have passed over your modern watercolours before most of them will be reduced to mere white or brown rags; and your descendants, twitching them contemptuously into fragments between finger and thumb, will mutter against you, half in scorn and half in anger, "Those wretched nineteenth century people! they kept vapouring and fuming about the world, doing what they called business, and they couldn't make a sheet of paper that wasn't rotten."' Mr. Ruskin adds, with much assumed *naïveté,* that he hopes to see a paternal government, one of the functions of which will be 'to supply its little boys with good paper.'

The chief cause of the deleterious preparation of paper is the use of chlorine as a bleaching agent, and which is never wholly washed out. We should, therefore, always be suspicious of very white paper. The old missals were executed on vellum, and consequently not exposed to this source of deterioration. The paste used for 'mounting' watercolour paintings often has alum in it, or has become acid with age; in either case it should carefully be avoided.

THE RISE OF MODERN WATERCOLOUR PAINTING

Painting in watercolours has received such unrivalled development in this country, is so extensively practised, and so generally patronised, that we naturally look upon it as a peculiarly national school of art. The art as now understood is almost of contemporary origin, and can hardly be said, therefore, to have as yet a history.

The honour of founding the English school of watercolour painting is generally claimed for Paul Sandby, who was born in Nottingham in 1732, and died 1809. He was certainly the reformer of mere topographical art, and not only studied much from nature, but probably, also, from the watercolour paintings of the Dutch masters, for he used considerable variety of method. He ordinarily, however, brought forward his drawings with Indian ink alone, afterwards staining them with a few tints of thin colour. The drawings of Paul Sandby deserve notice chiefly as 'showing the ocean of flat washes out of which modern watercolour art has risen, as bright as Aphrodite, with all her environing splendour of sea-foam, sea-colour, and sea-shell.' Such works as these of Sandby, being little better than studies of light and shade, we can readily understand how paintings in watercolours came to be called simply 'drawings,' a denomination they still retain.[126] In the early catalogues of the Royal Academy Exhibitions they are designated 'water-tinted drawings,' or 'water-washed drawings.' By degrees improvements were effected: a little blue was mixed with the ground-work tint, and the foregrounds were worked out in sepia; and upon this tints of colour were struck over the whole, commencing with a generalizing tint of some warm colour. An innovation was then made by John Cozens in substituting a mixture of indigo and Indian red as a neutral tint for the shading of his paintings, and with this sombre hue he produced works of great effect, and frequently of romantic grandeur.[127]

This principle was long retained of using a mixed colour, or *neutral tint,* for the shadows of every kind of subject and season, whether the picture was to represent a land or sea-piece, stone or brick buildings, evening or morning, sunshine or storm, summer or a winter snow-piece. The neutral tint was laid in first, and generally left untouched for distances, while every kind of object, from the clouds to the foreground, such as trees, water, cattle, sheep, and the bronzed faces of their attendant shepherds, was most impartially shaded with neutral tint. In general, the artists of those days followed the theories of the schools of oil painting in breaking down the warm lights with colours of the opposite quality, and represented shadows by cold tints only. For the finishing, these early practitioners trusted to the feeble lines of the lead-pencil, or the coarser markings of the reed pen.

Girtin, though a close student of Cozens, was, however, the great pioneer of modern practice, for he was the first to break through the trammels of the old school by painting objects at once with the tints which they appeared to possess in nature. With him Turner was closely associated; and in the works of this, the greatest master of the art, every stage of development may be distinctly traced up to a degree of perfection which can scarcely be surpassed, and we can hardly hope to see equalled. Turner is even greater in watercolours than in oil; but several other eminent oil painters have distinguished themselves also in watercolour painting. The following are some of the principal deceased masters of this branch of art, viz. Paul Sandby, Cozens, Girtin, Rowlandson (the caricaturist), Bewick, Stothard, Clennel, Chambers, Blake and Dadd (who both died insane), Robson, Barrett, Varley, Samuel Prout, Turner, Dewint, Copley Fielding, David Cox, and J. D. Harding.

Chapter 10

Stereochrome or Water-Glass Painting

We have endeavoured to show that fresco painting should, theoretically speaking, be a perfectly durable description of painting; it has (though more rarely than is commonly supposed) proved a permanent form of painting in Italy; yet the frescoes in the New Palace of Westminster, and a large proportion of those in Germany, afford conclusive evidence that the method has not in northern Europe withstood the effects of time and climate nearly so well as painting in oil would have done under the same circumstances. The irretrievable decay of nearly all the early frescoes at Westminster, in the Poets' or Upper Waiting Hall, and in the House of Lords, may be partly attributed to ignorance of the old methods of preparing the lime and colours. Another mischievous agency has probably been the improper preparation of the wall—the painting not having been cut off from possible absorption of moisture, which has so destructive an influence in northern climates. This last defect we would say *en passant* has been avoided in the more recently executed works; Mr. Herbert, R.A., Mr. E. M. Ward, R.A., and we believe other artists, having placed their couch of plaster upon a bed slightly detached from the actual wall, or upon slabs of slate. Returning to the causes of decay, we may add the probable circumstance —indeed the fact has been betrayed by the pictures themselves—that some of the works were not wholly executed in true fresco — the *buon fresco* already described — finishings in tempera having been added, which quickly blacken in an impure and are dissolved in a humid atmosphere. One of the most eminent of the painters engaged at Westminster has also expressed his belief to us that a particular pigment freely used in the early frescoes at the palace has had a most damaging influence. Terra-verte, the pigment alluded to, and the use of which is as tempting to the fresco painter as bituminous preparations are to the painter in oil, is said by our authority to form a pellicle which will not combine in that crystallization which, if it once unite the colours with the basis of fresco, must absolutely form one of the hardest and most durable substances in nature.

But after making all possible allowance for the failure of the earliest attempts at fresco painting in this country, there can, we think, be little reasonable doubt, after the researches and evidence of the many witnesses summoned before the various Royal Commissions on the fine arts, and after the lengthened experience of the artists themselves, that everything relating to the proper management of the material is now understood. And yet, not only are some of the early frescoes already complete wrecks, but even in the best preserved, the best situated, and the most recently finished, there are some traces and symptoms of incipient decay. What is, then, the conclusion which seems, however, reluctantly forced upon us? Can we do other than infer, despite every presumption to the contrary, that fresco is not adapted for a damp climate, as it is not likely to remain unchanged for the centuries that mural paintings, from their very situation, are intended to endure? The absence of ancient frescoes and the early substitution of oil painting for tempera in the north of Europe, with the importance attached to the drying properties of the new vehicle, point to the same conclusion. And it is further borne out by the fact that where the colours have been applied as thinly as possible, as in Mr. Herbert's scene from 'King Lear,' 'Lear disinherits Cordelia,' which is the best preserved early fresco at Westminster, though peculiarly exposed from bad drainage—there the surface remains least affected by mould and fungus. For our part, however, we do not permit the evidence, strong as it is, to shake our belief in the theoretical inference that water can never affect a fresco in the least if once the colours and lime of the plaster are combined in the crystallization of which we have spoken. There are frescoes in the open air in Italy, and we also know that Mr. Herbert has thrown quantities of water over his fresco of Lear; yet it is quite clear, whatever may be the real cause of the decay, that our best artists have been unable to execute their works in such a way as to ensure their resisting the attacks of a humid atmosphere, perhaps more insidious in London and on the banks of the Thames than elsewhere.

Mr. Maclise, R.A., among other mural painters, long since felt the necessity therefore for a more permanent medium. Accordingly this artist proceeded in the autumn of 1859 to Germany, to inform himself of the merits of stereochrome or water-glass painting, which had been adopted by Kaulbach in his great works in the Berlin New Museum, by Kuhlmann at Lille, and many other German artists. Mr. Maclise returned fully satisfied of the greater suitability of this method; he has wrought in it with perfect success in his vast picture in the Royal Gallery, Westminster, the 'Interview of Wellington and Blucher after Waterloo,' and the artist is now painting the companion picture on the opposite wall of 'The Death of Nelson' by the same method. We must pause for a moment to remark that these great pictures will certainly mark an era in the history of British art. Each forty-seven feet long, and each containing or to contain upwards of fifty life-size figures, their merit will be considered fully commensurate with their size. From the finished picture, and from the progress already made with its *vis-a-vis* at the date of our going to press, we may unhesitatingly predict that these great works will rank as the noblest examples of monumental painting commemorative of national military and naval achievement hitherto executed in England, and fully equal to anything of their kind in Europe.

Returning to the method by which Mr. Maclise executed his great Waterloo picture, we may mention that Mr. E. M. Ward is already a convert to the new process, and Mr. Herbert intends to adopt it as a final fixing agent.[128] Mr. Ward has employed it successfully in a portion of his last picture in the Commons' Corridor, the 'Escape of Charles II;' and he is now using it alone for the next painting, the 'Landing of Charles II.' But we must hasten to describe the process itself.

Stereochrome, or water-glass, is then, chemically speaking, a tetra-silicate of potash, a compound of silica, otherwise called silicic acid, and potash. It was the discovery, or the invention, as we might more properly term it, a process of reasoning having led up to it, of the late Dr. Johann Fuchs, of Munich. The inventor shared the common fate of having his invention slighted and misunderstood. It was confounded with a bi-silicate, and even the 'liquor silicum,' which is a mono-silicate. Now, however, it is acknowledged that there are few other bodies capable of being put to so many various applications. It is said to have been successfully applied in Germany to the preservation from decay of the stones of buildings exposed to the open air. Experiments upon the durability of water-glass have been made in exposed situations in Germany, and have proved perfectly successful. At Berlin a crucial experiment was made by suspending a stereochrome painting for twelve months in the open air under the principal chimney of the New Museum, during which time it was exposed to sunshine, mist, snow and rain, but nevertheless retained its full brilliancy of colour. The late Prince Consort was one of the very first to bring this invention before the English public, he having translated and allowed to be published in the *Journal of the Society of Arts* the pamphlet which Fuchs wrote shortly before his death, and left as a kind of legacy.

The water-glass method of painting is extremely simple. A surface of stone, slate, or cement is prepared in a manner to receive colours which are levigated with water. The colours are applied with no other vehicle or medium than pure distilled water; the brushes being the same as those used for similar paintings in oil. It is, in fact, thus far the purest and simplest form of tempera or watercolour painting. When the painting of the subject is finished, the picture is fixed on the wall or surface by means of the liquefied glass (or tetra-silicate of potash in a state of solution), which gives the name to the process. This is simply syringed on, and left to dry. The numerous minute holes of the syringe allow the water-glass to be ejected onto the picture in an almost impalpable form, half vapour, half mist, and in any quantities, little or much. The object is, of course, simply to fix the painting, not to continue depositing the water-glass until it shall perform the function of a varnish; because this would give the surface the glossiness which is one of the disadvantages of large oil paintings, and the absence of which is justly prized in fresco. In a short time after the water-glass has been carefully and in moderation syringed on, the carbonic acid of the air, and the earths in the surface, throw down the silica, or flint; the alkali partly combines or effloresces out, when it is easily washed off, the picture remaining adherent and only removable by mechanical disintegration.

The advantages of water-glass over fresco are manifold. Besides its grand recommendation of apparently perfect durability, it allows the use of all those pigments which would suffer from the action of lime. The range of the pigments which may be employed appears, indeed, to be quite indefinitely extended. It admits, unlike true fresco, of any rate of execution, and also of any number of alterations, corrections, and retouchings. We understand, for example, that Mr. Maclise has washed out whole figures and groups during the execution of his Waterloo picture. There is consequently less necessity for the preliminary coloured sketch, which are almost indispensable in fresco; though a 'study' of a large composition is always extremely desirable, by whatever method the work may have to be executed.

It will, in short, be perceived that the greatest difficulties and disadvantages in fresco, namely, the necessity of painting the picture piecemeal, of executing only that piece for which the plaster was freshly prepared for the day's work, the inevitable, and in an elaborate subject the very numerous, joinings this involves, and the impossibility of retouching without cutting out a portion of plaster entirely, are thus altogether removed or obviated.

The advantages afforded by water-glass of permitting the artist to work at any time, and as unhurriedly as he pleases, can hardly be too much insisted upon. We have said that the glory of real fresco is that it compels a primary attention to the essentials of art. But practically we find that its severe limitations are very frequently betrayed in exaggerated breadth, emptiness, slightness, and incompleteness, and very rarely made the best of by simple purity of outlines and tones, and a noble indication of expression. We naturally applaud when difficulties are vanquished; and when the conditions of an art are perfectly understood, any attempt to evade them should meet with the strongest condemnation. Yet every limitation in the vehicle of art is *per se* an evil, not a good. The artist should never be a slave to his mere material. The more time you give a poet and the richer his vocabulary, the riper and the more choice will be the fruit of his genius. In the same way, the more time you give a painter and the more varied the means of expression you place within his reach, the more comprehensive and complete will be the reflection of his heart and brain and soul on wall or canvas. It is something almost pathetic to see an artist with a lofty conception of his subject and extreme conscientiousness struggling in the fetters of fresco. There is really a touching instance of this now at Westminster. Mr. Herbert—who is devoted to his art with the whole energy of a most enthusiastic nature—is known to have knocked out portions of his illustration of King Lear four and five times before he would allow himself to be satisfied with the harmony and permanency of those passages of his work. And beneath the flooring of the great picture of 'Moses bringing down the Tables of the Law,' which Mr. Herbert is on the point of finishing, there are buried the *débris* of two years' continuous toil. From the commencement of the cartoons in 1856, till the anticipated completion of this picture, the artist is known to have been engaged upon it, with some very trifling interruptions, no less than seven years—the time Michael Angelo was occupied on 'The Last Judgment,' and Titian, as is supposed, on the 'Peter Martyr.' We may venture to say—and it is hardly more than might be expected—that Mr. Herbert's picture is an assured triumph in the most elevated walk of art fully as exceptional in this country and in modern Europe as are in their kind the neighbouring achievements of Mr. Maclise.

In the belief that our artists are now in possession of a simple, comparatively easy, and durable method of wall painting, we hope to see that application of art which is of the highest national and educational importance receive a new development. Why should not the walls, not only of our churches, palaces, and museums, but of our universities, schools, and railway stations, and also—if not before — all those of our courts of justice, hospitals, prisons, and workhouses — be covered with appropriate and noble paintings, historical, religious, or moral?

If the reader will turn the section on fresco painting in England, he will see that not only in the metropolis, but in various and remote parts of Great Britain, a demand for mural paintings has sprung into existence. This is in a measure a natural consequence of truer knowledge and taste in architecture; but on all sides, also, we see indications of a recognition of the educational as well as the decorative value of art. And now that the public has begun to evince a large and liberal appreciation of the noblest functions of painting, the government will, not improbably, be induced to extend the patronage hitherto confined to Westminster. It is true that occupation will still be furnished for years to come to some of the artists now engaged at the New Palace, but other signal opportunities for state encouragement of mural painting will occur at no distant periods. First, we shall have the noble pile of new government offices; and perhaps a still finer and more appropriate occasion will arrive when all our courts of law are united in one great palace of justice—a project which can hardly be much longer delayed. It is surely incumbent on the government to be well informed of the growing demand for mural painting for churches and the mansions of private patrons. But especially does it befit artists to prepare themselves to meet creditably the severe requirements of this class of work. We are satisfied that ability would be forthcoming, but organization would be much needed in the event of numerous cyclical or epical subjects being proposed for execution, similar to those undertaken in the Italian schools during three centuries, and in those of modern Germany. In a series of paintings, however vast, if closely related in meaning or intention, there should be unity of conception, and the ideas of one great designer should give consistency and keeping to the whole. To do this the artist must either devote a great part of a lifetime to one series of works (as we have discovered at Westminster), and then perhaps leave them unfinished, or he must at times gather round him a body of trained pupils. This latter system, though unknown in this country, has much to recommend it, and is we know approved by some of our best mural painters. To be carried out effectually, however, it should be attempted only, of course, by eminent artists. It would be of the greatest importance, too, that these painters should be perfectly independent, quite free to follow their own judgment in all things, and not subject to interference from any quarter; otherwise the scheme would certainly fail. Two of our most thoroughly competent masters—Messrs. Herbert and Maclise—are, we believe, not unwilling to undertake the formation of schools of monumental painters, arduous as the task would be at first. An experiment of more importance to the future of British art could not be devised; and we cannot close our labours with a sincerer wish than that the attempt may be made, and, when made, crowned with success.

Appendix

Note A. On Photography and Coloured Photographic Portraits

The extensive patronage given by the public to coloured photography, is sufficiently proved by the number of establishments for its supply in all our thoroughfares. In the occupation thus afforded, a number of artists are necessarily engaged, indeed the great body of ordinary miniature painters have been gradually absorbed. As far as mere pecuniary remuneration is concerned, we believe the artists themselves have no reason to complain at this change of employment; but we cannot help regretting a consequence which has already begun to ensue, namely, that the *bona fide* art of miniature painting—that pleasing art in which our countrymen have always distinguished themselves—will be comparatively neglected. The practice of colouring photographs, it will be readily understood, almost precludes real artistic advancement in any direction. Whatever merit the colourist may display must have been gained in other employment. The peculiar hue of the photograph vitiates the eye for correctly appreciating colour without the accustomed groundwork; and power of drawing is necessarily lost from its never being called into requisition. Thus the photographic colourist, after a time, when left to his own resources, must find how insidiously injurious and delusive is the influence of his employment upon his character and progress as an independent artist.

The value of photography when kept perfectly distinct, as an auxiliary to the artist, is, however, unquestionably great, though only beginning to be duly and correctly appreciated. Our younger artists have naturally been the first to submit to its teaching and suggestions, and although by it they also occasionally allow themselves to be misled, their works indicate already some few important results from its study. Even in historical painting, stricter regard to detail does not always attract the attention from higher qualities according to the old-established opinion; but, on the contrary, frequently helps the realization of the subject and incident. In landscape painting, however, its influence has hitherto been most conspicuous. It is only quite recently that an effort has been made to unite perfect topographical accuracy with the leading spirit of a scene, and thus give the representation of remarkable or sacred localities historical, or, so to speak, documentary value, as well as artistic importance. Photography has, in fact, incited artists to make renewed efforts to solve that most difficult of all art-problems —the harmonious union of breadth and finish.

In portrait painting, also, photography is of service, though it should be scrupulously kept separate and subordinate. It is impossible that the photograph can ever supersede the work of art, for the simple reason that the unthinking camera cannot usurp the artist's highest prerogative—that of choosing the best of the subtle and ever-varying traits of expression. But though, in regard to expression, photography is far more likely to lead astray than to direct, it can furnish the painter with trustworthy data for the *logic* of his drawing and proportions, and supply him with memoranda of accessories which will leave him free to concentrate his attention upon more essential facts. In all—and there is much—that in art is comparatively speaking mere mechanical copying, its assistance is invaluable, and the more it borrows of the painter's principles, the more abundant interest will it repay him. 'Photography,' as Sir David Brewster has well said, 'in place of being a rival, as was once imagined, is an auxiliary to art, giving it new powers and new fields of operation, and receiving from it in return the most valuable aid.'

We have alluded to the principal defect of photographic portraiture—the inability to choose the most characteristic and agreeable expression; and this becomes painfully evident from the impossibility most people feel of commanding a natural expression when *posed* in the photographer's chair, and in momentary consciousness of being caught alive in that mysterious camera. And, even in the drawing—that stronghold of photography—though the artist cannot approach its mathematical accuracy, still, if he has secured the general resemblance, he, with his agile pencil, sets our imaginations more pleasantly at work, and we follow his lines with a pleasure the other cannot afford; and although we detect them here a little within, and there a little beyond the exact truth, still the eye, with wonderful and unconscious facility, supplies the happy medial line, and at the same time receives an impression of notion, vivacity, and life which nothing else affords.[129] This power in the eye no doubt explains why the most imperfect of pictures—a mere slight sketch—will sometimes convey a more striking impression to the mind than even the most perfect photograph. 'Untouched' photographic portraits are, nevertheless, invaluable to relative or friend; because they supply a plan, chart, or map of the face almost as correct as honest; and upon this groundwork of fact memory may supply what a stranger would not suspect could exist. We have just said advisedly '*almost* correct,' because the different focal distances of objects and the convexity of the lenses prevent absolute truth of forms.

We need scarcely allude to other defects equally inseparable from photography. Where we see the art comparatively successful in portraiture, it must assuredly be admitted that the photographer is entitled to great praise; for certainly no object presents him with so many difficulties as the few square inches of the human face—most especially if that face is young and beautiful. For example: from the blue rays which enter into the composition of light possessing so much photographic power in the 'negative' the deep blue eye comes out in the positive colourless as skimmed milk, and for the same reason the delicate bloom of youthful epidermis, and the atmospheric tints which soften the lines of age, are absent. The yellow rays, on the contrary, are greatly intensified, so that 'freckles' appear to be cruel traces of small-pox; hair looks dyed if golden or red; and worse, exactly in proportion as it is more carefully combed and greased. But this latter defect arises from the great activity of all shining lights, which make their size in the photograph much beyond their extent in nature. And to this, likewise, is due the exaggeration of the spectrum, or point of reflected light in the eye, which frequently gives a vacant stare; while the blanched lifelessness of the lips results from their greater smoothness of texture and nearer approach to a shining or polished surface. Seeing, then, with all its merit and marvel, that the photograph before the application of colour has certain inevitable defects, we have next to consider the advantages, if any, of the colouring process.

In the first place, it must be premised, and we think it will be readily conceded, that at least the broad characteristics of the photograph have to be preserved. But, further than this, we may venture to assert that, whether desirable or not, many likewise of the peculiarities of the photograph cannot be obliterated—or evaded; except indeed by the most unconscionable and altogether unjustifiable application of opaque colour. The coloured photograph, therefore, cannot legitimately possess the distinguishing qualities of a work of art; it cannot exhibit largely the *mind,* the poetical suggestiveness conveyed by artistic selection and adaptation of form and expression, nor many of the more delicate beauties of colour. The coloured photograph can, for example, possess scarcely any of the charming transparency in the flesh which we so much admire in the miniature on ivory. This arises from the opaque ground and necessity of using body colour, in order, by its opacity to 'kill'—using the painter's phrase, or *bury,* to suggest another metaphorical expression—the unpleasant hue of the photograph. Transparent colours, if used in quantity sufficient to effect this interment, would insensibly lead to what Mr. Ruskin would call 'saddened colour and sorrowful heaviness of tone;' and it is found that on the prepared paper a 'forcible' effect involves less labour and is more showy and generally taking than a quieter, though richer effect, albeit possessing the additional merit of preserving more faithfully the original photograph.

As for the so-called photographic miniatures on ivory, the disadvantageous effect upon the colour produced by the photograph showing through must in the very nature of things be visible, if indeed the photograph be used at all. But in no instance that we have seen is the soft, true, delicate milkiness of the ivory preserved, if the photographic image has actually been fixed on its surface or sunk into its texture; for the solution (or whatever it may be or is called) which renders the ivory photographically sensitive, converts it at the same time into something resembling horn, and totally ineligible for the artist's operations. If, again, the ivory is reduced sufficiently thin for the purpose, and is only used as a medium to transmit the photographic representation, the former objection of course recurs. But, though we have not seen one successful coloured photograph 'on' ivory, we have seen passed off as such a mere coloured copy on ivory traced or taken from a photograph. We do not wish to make invidious remarks, but the public cannot be expected to detect misrepresentations which require a knowledge of many minute petty technicalities to expose.

Nevertheless, we freely admit that it is far more desirable to have a good photograph than a bad picture; but we have had, and still have, in view a work of real art-value in our comparison. There is, then, in addition, this further *primâ facie* objection to a coloured photograph, that it is a nondescript production—neither picture nor photograph—having neither the higher beauty of art nor the approximate truth of science; and therefore, as a matter of individual taste, many persons infinitely prefer, to its generally dauby meretriciousness, the photograph *pur et simple.*

But this consideration, it may be said, is somewhat beside the real question. A few coloured photographs we have seen are, in point of fact, undoubtedly effective, pleasing, and passably truthful: but in this case the art element preponderates, and an artist of very considerable ability must have been employed to render them so attractive. Whether the chemical nature of the photograph as a substratum will have any effect in hastening the fugitiveness of the colouring or its inevitable gradually-increasing discordance, we are not prepared to say; and until we are assured of the permanence of the photograph itself, it does not much signify.

But, in regard to the statement involved in what we have said above, 'that the approximate truth of the photograph is sacrificed in the colouring process,' we can confidently assert that the moment a photograph is touched with colour, it at once loses its fine scale of light and shade; and, however careful the artist may be, he will insensibly efface some of the exactitude of the forms and detail. Generally, in fact, the artist works upon a very faint *positive* 'impression' (to use the term borrowed from the printer's and engraver's art), and entirely covers it with body colour, or a still more opaque oil paint, with the express intention of concealing the tone of the photograph, using as a guide another and darker 'positive.' Here, then, it becomes apparent (if we are to admit the compromise at all) how necessary it is that only competent and experienced artists should be employed in order that the product of the camera should not be altogether falsified, but, on the contrary, receive all the compensating advantages it may derive for the loss of much of its own proper merit, by being passed through the nobler alembic of the artist's brain. This is recognised in some respectable photographic establishments; but, as ability of any kind commands its price in the market, so, for the better description of coloured photographs, a high price is necessarily demanded—a price, indeed, little short of that which was formerly paid for an average miniature—say from five to twenty guineas for a head, and thirty, forty, or fifty for a full-length. From this very circumstance, however, there is much temptation to practise deception, which the public should be warned against. We strongly suspect that many photographers who ask a low price for the additional colouring, employ a far superior artist to colour their 'show pictures' than they would engage for their actual commissions. Photographs are, however, simply 'tinted;' and this rapid process need not greatly enhance the price.

Note B. The Distribution, Hanging, Framing, and Care of Pictures

When apartments are devoted entirely to the exhibition of pictures, two or three large works may be placed, as in the picture gallery of the Vatican, in one small room: but in private houses, and for domestic decoration, they should always have relation to the dimensions of the chamber in which they are placed. As large pictures then apparently diminish the size of a small apartment, smaller easel and cabinet pictures have been with good taste preferred for our contracted English interiors. In the spacious entrance halls and corridors of country mansions, large hunting and sporting subjects and whole-length portraits of ancestors, are, however, appropriately placed. In dining-rooms, also, from the more massive and simple character of the furniture, a few life-size portraits, together with, of course, subjects of a cheerful and festive character, are admissible. In all cases the juxtaposition of oil pictures, watercolour paintings, and engravings, should be avoided; as they greatly injure each other's effect. For the drawing-room, subjects of a refined and elegant character would naturally be chosen; and watercolour drawings would form a fitting decoration for a *boudoir,* or an inner drawing-room; while framed prints might be reserved for sleeping apartments.

We see no reason, however, why the possessor of pictures, who has a separate apartment for his books, and a conservatory for his flowers, should not also have a gallery with a suitable light for the proper display of his pictures.

At all events, due attention should be paid to the important facts already mentioned relating to the *hanging* of pictures. The paper of the wall against which pictures are suspended should have no strongly-defined pattern, and be of one uniform colour (red inclining to crimson, or tea-green, are the best colours); and if borders are introduced they should not contain flowers. Bright carpets and all gaudy colours are likewise injurious. Pictures, indeed, should, if possible, be painted for their situation.

As a general rule, the centre of the picture should not be much above the level of the eye. In an exhibition, the pictures in this most favourable situation are said to be on the 'line.' If the work be a landscape or a portrait with a background, the horizontal line will require to be so placed. The artist, be it remembered, when painting his picture fixes this line (at least theoretically) on a level with his eye—in fact, the two things, the horizontal line and the level of the eye, are identical—and he paints accordingly. If the spectator, therefore, does not regard the picture from the same relative position, much of the work will be foreshortened, and the general effect consequently falsified. Paintings on ceilings are, of course, not subject to these conditions, though they often show a very arbitrary use of the horizontal line. Hanging pictures low has the additional recommendation of increasing the apparent height of an apartment. In viewing pictures, the proper *focal distance,* which is determined by their size and the character of the execution, should also be strictly observed.

The extension and repetition of form so conducive to harmony is taken advantage of in the boundary line; thus the head of a child, or a group, consisting of an assemblage of curved lines, reaches the eye more agreeably through a circular frame; so likewise with the repetitions of form in the square or oblong aperture. Frames should harmonize in style with the other ornaments of the apartment, particularly the mouldings and cornices. Frames which project much appear to contract a room. Massive frames convey a painful impression of suspended weight; but this is partly obviated by 'open work' patterns. In apartments with lateral light, the pictures should never slant as if toppling over. Pictures should not be suspended from one nail; the diagonal lines formed by the cord have a very discordant effect. Two nails and two vertical cords, or, what is far more safe, pieces of wire cordage, should be used. There is an admirable contrivance for concealing the attachment of pictures, and allowing them to be slung forward into the room so as to receive the full light.

For watercolour paintings it is especially important that the frames should not be heavy or too profusely ornamented. A massive frame will almost destroy the effect of delicate work in watercolours. Burnishing small points of the frame is, however, from the greater vivacity of watercolours, less objectionable than when the frame is intended to enclose an oil picture. The glass of the frame, should not touch the face of the painting. The 'mount,' or margin intervening between the watercolour painting and its frame, is almost invariably white; though it might not unfrequently with great advantage be tinted, especially if the painting is merely a vignette. For all delicate work light in tone, a paper mount is preferable; and for such, a simple gold bead frame with a gold edge to the mount next the picture is very suitable. But more powerfully and intensely-coloured water paintings, especially if warm in tone, might often be rendered far more effective and harmonious by substituting a gold mount. In all cases, however, we recommend to allow the artist to select or advise the choice of frame for his own work; or to let him know if it is desired that the frame for his picture should match others, in order that he may paint with a view to the influence of the frame. Where large collections are to be framed, useful suggestions will be found at the end of Mr. Ruskin's notes to the Turner Gallery, and examples may be seen in that gentleman's arrangement of the Turner collection.

Pictures require light and air; the habit, therefore, of covering up pictures in town houses during the many months that families are away is very injurious. Washing pictures should be undertaken on a warm, dry day, and nothing but clean cold water should he used. The surface should be wetted with a sponge or soft leather, but the water should never be allowed to float, and all moisture should be carefully removed by gentle friction with an old silk handkerchief. The *backs* of pictures should be frequently cleaned, and it is desirable to protect them with sheets of tin-foil or oil-skin. The relining of pictures is often an excellent precaution for their preservation. Some remarks on the use and abuse of varnishing have already been offered. The operation of transferring pictures from panel to canvas is too delicate and tedious to be undertaken except for valuable works. The 'Raising of Lazarus,' by Sebastiano del Piombo, in the National Gallery, has been transferred from panel to canvas.

'Pictures, like people, are not only subject to the inevitable decay of age, but to a variety of diseases, caused by heat, cold, damp and foul air. Many (and they, too, are among the most delicate and beautiful) have, like Leonardo's "Last Supper," and a large proportion of the works of Watteau, of Reynolds, and of Turner, unsound constitutions given to them by the authors of their existence, and are thus subject to premature and rapid destruction. These liabilities, and the many accidents to which they are exposed, have made picture restorers as important a class in art as physicians and surgeons in life; and, as might naturally be expected, there are many unskilful among them, and many ignorant quacks.'—Leslie's *Handbook*. Picture doctors are, however, a necessary evil, and to choose men of well-known respectability is the only advice we can offer the public, when it is necessary to entrust paintings to their tender mercies. But 'restorations' and 'repaintings' should be avoided as much as possible. The oil in old pictures has undergone all its changes; not so the oil in the new tints, which are made to match the old; but, as the changes must take place, after a time the restorations and repairings must necessarily cease to match, and become apparent from their discordance.

Note C. Scene Painting: Dioramas, Panoramas, etc

Scene Painting is an extensive and peculiar area of art, with its own laws and practical and scientific rules. The scene painter should be well able to decide on the effect of those colours he employs by day, when they shall be subjected to a strong artificial light; and it is of the highest importance that he should be well versed in linear and aerial perspective. He uses chiefly watercolours, on account of their operating promptly, and presenting no glossy surface. One of the difficulties which the scenic art cannot overcome is, that the perspective is frequently violated by the actor moving about at the very back of the stage; when all those objects placed there, which, whilst the performers kept in front (where everything is suited to his actual size) appeared in due proportion, lose their verisimilitude, and appear insignificant, and disproportioned. The man becomes as tall as a rock or tree, and the imagination of the spectator has not power sufficient to preserve the illusion of the scene. This can only be obviated by the actor remaining as little as he can at the back of the stage.

In the early days of the English stage, painted scenes were not displayed before the audience. Inigo Jones was the first who introduced appropriate decorations of the kind in England. But the great reformer of the stage in this particular was John Rich, who spared no expense in the decoration of Covent Garden, while it was under his management, in the early part of the last century.

The application of scene painting known as a panorama was first introduced by Robert Barker, the builder and original proprietor towards the close of the last century of the rooms in Leicester Square, and who was succeeded by that excellent artist, the late Mr. Burford. In a panorama the spectator is, as it were, placed on a central eminence, commanding a view on all sides. The pictorial representation surrounds him as would the natural scenery; the painting being executed on the inside of the hollow cylinder which forms the wall of the exhibition building. The picture is lighted from a skylight. But the effectiveness of the lighting is greatly increased by covering the space immediately above the platform on which the spectator stands, and thus concealing the source of the light which falls on the painted surface. A picture placed in light and viewed through a medium of shadow is known to acquire more than ordinary optical illusiveness. A difficulty in the execution of a panoramic painting is the application of the rules of perspective where the point of sight is indeterminate and would in nature move with the spectator. This difficulty should be met, as far as possible, by making all the visual rays meet in the centre of the circle. A painting of this kind requires an appropriate building; and two have been erected in London — that known so long as Burford's Panorama, but now finally closed, and the Colosseum in the Regent's Park. The Germans name a similar exhibition 'Rundbild' or Cyclorama, which more accurately indicates its nature. The two great pictures of London and Paris at the Colosseum, Regent's Park have been exhibited many years. Of these the view of London from the top of St. Paul's was the first, and has always been most attractive. The sketches were made and the painting was commenced some forty years since, by the late Mr. Horner, and after his death the work was taken up and completed by Mr. E.T. Parris, the artist who repainted in monochrome the pictures of Sir James Thornhill in the dome of St. Paul's.

The word Panorama has been also made to apply to a series of panoramic views painted on a flat surface, and made to pass before the eyes of the spectator. In this case the conditions are reversed—the spectator becomes the fixed object, and the picture the moving one. The most beautiful example of a 'moving panorama,' as it is called, is that which was painted for Mr. Macready by his friend Mr. Stanfield, in illustration of the chorus of 'King Henry the Fifth,' the last of the Shakespearian plays so magnificently put upon the stage by that distinguished manager and actor.

The Diorama is a still more illusive and beautiful application of science and skill to the purposes of art than the Panorama. Those who remember visiting the building in the Regent's Park, where dioramic pictures were exhibited several years ago, will bear witness to their pre-eminence over the 'dissolving views' and other optical illusions which have since attracted the public. While the Panorama was the invention of an English artist, the Diorama was conceived and perfected by two Frenchmen, MM. Daguerre and

Bouton. Although in some respects more limited in the power of representing nature, it produces a far greater degree of optical illusion. The means of lighting the picture are more complicated, the light and shade being chiefly managed by the admission and exclusion of actual daylight on the surface of the painting; certain parts of the work being transparent, the light can also be admitted from behind and through the canvas, thereby producing great brilliancy—an artifice which causes an appearance of solidity and reality in the parts exposed to the action of the ordinary daylight on the surface. A combination is secured of transparent, semi-transparent, and opaque colouring, which is still further assisted by the power of varying both the effects and the degree of light and shade on the surface of the picture. Thus the accidental effects of nature, sunshine, and storm, and moonlight, and even motion, as the fall of an avalanche, or the tumbling waters of a cataract, can be represented with an appearance of truth that renders the diorama the most perfect scenic representation of nature in existence. In the power of representing architecture, and especially interiors, it is unrivalled; a powerful relief may be obtained without exaggeration; and colour need not be sacrificed for the sake of effect. As a panorama requires a building specially suited for its display, so the diorama cannot be exhibited in its perfection except in a building expressly suited to its necessities, both as regards the display of the picture and the position of the spectator. There is no longer any such building in London; and, since the death of Bouton, there has been no exhibition which could be properly called a diorama. We are indebted for a portion of the preceding facts relating to panoramas and dioramas to an article in the excellent recently-established periodical, *The Reader*.

Note D. On Triptychs, Retables, Antependia, etc

The art of the Middle Ages had a specific use. Artists did not paint, as now, on speculation. The uses to which the tabular or wooden pictures were applied, suggested certain forms and modifications. Altar-pieces were originally portable; which explains the practice of enclosing pictures in cases with doors, called diptychs, triptychs, or polyptychs, accordingly as they consisted of two, three, or many portions. A reference to the origin of these terms may be not uninteresting.

The diptychs are of very early date. They were among the Romans formed of two little tablets, of wood or ivory, folding one over the other like a book, and the interior presented a surface of wax prepared for writing. These tablets, or *pugillares,* as they were called, sometimes served, when sealed, for conveying secret messages; but they were soon employed for a more interesting purpose. From the time of the emperors, it was the custom for the consuls and superior magistrates, on their elevation, to make presents of ivory diptychs carved externally, with sculptures in bas-relief. On one leaf was carved the portrait and titles of the new consul, and on the other a mythological subject, or the games of the circus with which he had amused the people at the period of his elevation. These interesting diptychs are known by the name of *consulares.* At a later period, when the Roman empire had adopted the Christian religion, the consuls sent diptychs to the principal bishops also; and these, receiving them as a testimony of goodwill and respect to the Church, placed the diptychs upon the altars, that the magistrates who gave them might be recommended to the prayers of the congregation at the celebration of mass. Such is the origin of ecclesiastical diptychs. The subjects of the carvings which enriched the exterior of these diptychs being taken from the New Testament, they appeared, after the fall of the Empire, very suitable for decorating the covers of books of prayers—to which use we owe the preservation of a great number.

The following difference existed between the Christian diptychs of this period and the Consular diptychs—viz., that the principal representation of the former was inside instead of outside the covers. This difference, no doubt, arose from the desirability of folding up and concealing the contents of these portable diptychs in time of persecution. Afterwards they were again exhibited on the altar open. 'When the persecution had ceased, the use of these pictures [or sculptures] was universal, and continued in succeeding centuries. The crusader, the traveller, the poorest pilgrim, enclosed in diptychs and triptychs of wood and ivory the holy images he carried with him [as do the Russians to this day]; and before which he daily prostrated himself, to offer his prayer to God. Some were also made of large dimensions, and placed over a *'prie-dieu'* or devotional chair in private rooms.'—*Labarte.*

In the oldest triptychs the portions were *united* by hinges, and it was only at a comparatively late period that the chief portions of the altar-piece were separated by pilasters, and bore heavy cornices. An example of the simple folding-doors or wings on each side of a gabled picture may be seen in the painting by Duccio da Siena, in the National Gallery. The outside of the doors had, almost universally, subjects painted on them in black or brown and white *(chiaroscuro),* probably from a traditional imitation of the sculptured back of the original diptych.

The form of the triptych when opened suggested what is called the 'retable,' 'retablement,' which is flat and does not admit of being closed. As altar-pieces became more decorative, certain supplementary or complementary pictures were painted on the *predella.* The 'predella' or *gradus* was the wooden base (on the top and back of the altar) on which the altar-piece rested, and to which it was attached. On this panelling were depicted in miniature different events in the life, or other circumstances connected with the saint or divine personage represented above on the altarpiece proper. When—as it frequently was—the altar-piece was presented to the church, the heraldic arms of the 'donor' were often added at the extremities of the predella, in addition to his portrait, generally introduced into one of the compartments above. As the decorative capabilities of these works became recognised, they were variously ornamented, and their frames assumed architectural importance—the architectonic enrichments following the taste of the place and period. The original Roman diptychs were generally rectangular, but sometimes the upper edges are raised and ornamented somewhat like the tympanum of a building. The Byzantine diptychs have often circular tops. Later Italian and German works of this class commonly finish in more or less pure forms of Gothic: the early decorated style occurring most frequently. The architectural importance of an altar-piece may be seen (and would be still more advantageously if all the portions were united) in the very extensive retable by Andrea Orcagna in the

National Gallery. A picture by Jacopo di Casentino, in the same collection, is a still more elaborately constructed though less extensive altar-piece. It has gables and medallions or roundels, a predella and side projections, or buttresses, which are adorned with panels in different tiers, containing small full-length figures, which arrangement serves to account for the immense number of similar small paintings of secondary merit dispersed in various places and assignable to this period. The great altar-piece of the Van Eycks at Ghent is a polyptych (that is, of more than three leaves). It originally consisted of two tiers of leaves, seven above and five below. Of the seven, three, were fixed, and the portions closing upon them were divided on each side into two subjects. Of the five, one large centre subject was fixed, and two leaves (one on each side) closed upon it.

The older method of *artistic arrangement* in pictures of this description was to place the principal subject in the centre, and single figures of saints on the doors. The figures of saints and evangelists were, however, soon brought into the centre picture, which generally represented the enthroned Madonna[130] or Christ holding a globe (termed a 'Majesty'). The saints were also greatly increased in number, and groups belonging to different periods were introduced to share in this presumed heavenly adoration. Hence, the origin of the *Sacra Conversazione.*

We have glanced at the practice of presenting pictures as offerings to a particular church. These were frequently simple panels. Such panels were inserted in the sides of shrines and reliquaries, as they were also in coffers, furniture, and domestic utensils. The numerous side chapels of churches were of course dedicated to various saints, hence these votive pictures frequently contained a confused jumble of incredibly ludicrous, and, not unfrequently, even indecent representations of various events in the life of the patron saint, painted often with Chinese disregard of relative proportion. At other times the commemorative tablet recorded some local legend or fact.

There was yet another, and in some respects a more important class of panel picture—viz., the altar 'frontals' or 'antependia.' These altar-facings were movable, and, according to the usage of the Church of Rome, four or five of them were provided for each altar, in order that they should harmonize in subject with the nature of the sacred office to be performed. These frontals being, from their position, very conspicuous, the highest order of ability was engaged for them; and from extant continental examples, no decoration appears to have been too costly, and no material too rich to lavish on their embellishment. To prove this, we need only refer to the precious 'palliotto' at Venice, the golden casing of St. Ambrogio at Milan, and the silver, gold, and enamelled antependia of the altars of San Giovanni Batista at Florence, and San Giacomo at Pistoia. One beautiful specimen of a 'precious frontal' is placed under glass in the south ambulatory or processional path next the choir in Westminster Abbey; though, situated as it is among the tombs, it may be mistaken for part of a monument. It is an extensive work, measuring about eleven feet in length and three in height. The paintings, on a gold mosaic ground, are extremely well and carefully designed, and are attributed to the close of the thirteenth or commencement of the fourteenth century.

Messrs. Digby Wyatt and Waring remark[131] that the striking difference between this beautiful production as a work of art, when compared with the commoner decorative painting practised at this period in England and Germany, leads to the inference that in the Middle Ages for the finest decorative work we were under great obligations to Italian artists. In this frontal the processes are exactly similar to those of the early Florentines and, curiously enough, 'in the Close Rolls of the 44th of Henry III (1260), is to be found a mandate from the king commanding the sheriff of Surrey to cause that "immediately the pictures and *frontal* of the altar of the great chapel at Guildford be made as we have instructed *William of Florence our painter.*"' From this mandate these gentlemen infer that William the Monk, mentioned in the records of the decorations at Westminster, is the same artist, and that this frontal was probably executed by him. It is, however, satisfactorily proved in Gage Rokewode's *Account of the Painted Chamber* (p. 25), that William the Monk of Westminster was a distinct person from William of Florence; and more than this, that while the latter was only paid sixpence a day, William of Westminster was receiving two shillings.

Although beyond the scope and intention of this book to have carried out, we would take the opportunity of a new edition to record our coincidence with an opinion expressed in a very kindly estimate of our labours in the *Saturday Review* of April 2, 1859. The writer of the critique alluded to, observes that the history of early English art would reward a diligent inquirer for all the pains he might bestow on the investigation. 'The more documents are searched, and the more our ancient buildings are examined, the more clearly it will appear that a native school of art flourished in this country, whose works, moreover, were probably in no way inferior to any other specimens of painting on this side the Alps. Why does not some one collect the scattered notices of English pictorial art—the story of Benedict Biscop, the legend of St. Dunstan, the fragments of English embroidery and illumination, the mural paintings still preserved in many churches, the Painted Chamber, St. Stephen's Chapel, and the Liber Eliensis? Here is a mine which needs working. Nor need the search be confined to painting.' In sculpture, we may add, the great cycle of religious subjects in the West Front of Wells Cathedral, which Flaxman, the late Professor Cockerell, and the best authorities consider the work of English artists, though executed at a period dating somewhat before the revival of the art in Italy under Donatello, would form a great *point d'appui.* But the whole history of British art has yet to be written.

Note E. The Glory, Nimbus, Aureola, etc

The golden 'glory' is the representation of a kind of halo, supposed to emanate from the bead or body of divine persons. When it surrounds the head it is a *nimbus,* when it envelopes the body it is an *aureola.* The 'glory' also applies to the union of both. The symbols, emblems, and legends, employed in early Christian art, form a curious and extensive study (Hagiology and Christian Iconography), upon which the late Mr. Pugin, M. Didron, Mrs. Jameson, and others, have written very learnedly. The various forms and attributes of the Glory is a most important branch of this interesting subject. In classical times it was a great honour to have a portrait painted on a circular golden shield, and suspended in temples and other public places. The distinction was conferred upon heroes and those who had served their country; Greek inscriptions decreeing these honours are still in existence. In course of time, from the head being painted on a circular gold shield, the shield was attached to the head alone in full-length representations. This is the origin of the *nimbus* which frequently appears in Pagan pictures, especially those discovered at Herculaneum and Pompeii. Little discs, attached like flat hats to the heads of their statues, were also employed by the sculptors as a mark of distinction and sanctity, although in earlier times sculptors had employed the same kind of plates over their statues simply to protect them from rain or the excrement of birds in the open air. Some painters, from seeing the effect of these plates on the statues, imitated them in actual perspective in their pictures, while others (the earlier ones probably) kept them flat and perfectly round, as in the works of Giotto and Cimabue. The nimbus being of Pagan origin there was, however, at first some opposition to its introduction into Christian art. But after the eleventh century, it was invariably employed to distinguish sacred personages, as the Saviour, the Virgin Mary, angels, apostles, saints and martyrs. Nimbi are sometimes of various colours in stained glass windows.

'They are of various forms; the most frequent is that of a circular halo, within which are various enrichments, distinctive of the persons represented. In that of Christ it contains a cross more or less enriched; in subjects representing events before the Resurrection, the cross is of a simpler form than in his glorified state. The nimbus most appropriate to the Virgin Mary consists of a circlet of small stars; angels wore a circle of small rays, surrounded by another circle of quatrefoils, or roses, interspersed with pearls, &c. Those for saints and martyrs were similarly adorned; but in the fifteenth century it was customary to inscribe the name of the particular saint, and especially those of the apostles, round the circumference. A nimbus of rays diverging in a triangular direction, which occurs but seldom before the fourteenth century, is attached to representations of the Eternal Father; and his symbol, the hand in the act of benediction, was generally encompassed by a nimbus. When the nimbus is depicted of a square form, it indicates that the person was living when delineated, and is affixed as a mark of honour and respect. From the twelfth to the fifteenth century the nimbus appears as a broad golden band behind the head, composed of concentric circles, frequently enriched with precious stones.' —*Fairholt.* After this it was defined merely with a line or thread of gold, sometimes quite round, sometimes as a small disc in fattened perspective. As an attribute of *power,* it was often attached to the heads of evil spirits and Satan himself. The use of the *aureola,* or enlarged nimbus, which surrounds the whole body, is much more limited than that of the nimbus, being confined to the persons of the Almighty, Jesus, and the Virgin Mary. Sometimes, however, it is seen enveloping the souls of saints and of Lazarus. The aureole varies in form. That in which our Saviour is represented, and which was a very early symbol of our Lord, is called 'vesica piscis,' from the elliptical form resembling a fish. Then there is the 'divine oval' and the 'mystical almond.' When the person is seated, the aureola is circular: sometimes it takes the form of a quatrefoil, each lobe encompassing the head, the feet, or the arms; and it is frequently intersected by a rainbow, upon which is seated Jesus or the Virgin Mary.

Note F. Painting in Embroidery

In embroidery, the ladies of antiquity and mediaeval times found (if we maybe permitted to say so) a more artistic, if a less useful, employment than that furnished their fair descendants in the 'knitting, netting, and crochet,' or even the *potichomanie* of the present day. Embroidery must indeed have been one of the very earliest forms in which art developed itself. Embroidery was commonly practised in Egypt, and Sir J. G. Wilkinson says, 'that the Hebrews, on leaving the country, took advantage of the knowledge they had there acquired to make 'a rich hanging for the door of the tent, of blue, and purple, and scarlet, and fine twined linen, wrought with needlework.' 'Needlework' and 'embroidery' is mentioned in various parts of Holy Writ. From Homer we learn that it was the employment of Andromache, Penelope, and Helen.

In the first centuries of the Christian era, and especially in the Greek Church (as it is to this day), the Christ, the Virgin and saints were embroidered upon the pontifical ornaments, upon the tissues that decorated the altars, and the 'veils' or curtains of the churches. In the fifth century the art of weaving silk stuffs of the most brilliant colours, and enriching them with subjects executed in gold and silver thread, was carried to great perfection. The embroidery upon the priestly vestments was particularly sumptuous and elaborate: the whole history of Christ was embroidered on the toga of a Christian senator. The Anglo-Saxon ladies were especially skilful in this art; they showed their great devotion to the Church by supplying the richest ornaments to its ministers, and their productions were renowned over the Continent under the title of *Opus Anglicanum.* The Norman ladies showed equal talent; and we owe the tapestry preserved in the library at Bayeux—one of the most interesting historic monuments—to the skill and patience of Queen Matilda, the wife of William the Conqueror, who, like another Helen, embroidered the incidents of his victory in England for the use of the cathedral at Bayeux.

Arras in France, all through the middle ages and down to the sixteenth century, was famous for its tapestry. The name of the town was given in England and Italy (Italicé as *Arazzi)* to the pictorial hangings that adorned the palaces of kings and nobles. Raphael's Cartoons, Dow in Hampton Court Palace, were, as already observed, designed for the tapestry-workers of Arras.

The tapestries themselves are now preserved in the Vatican, and are called Arazzi della scuola vecchia (of the old school) to distinguish them from a second series of Arazzi della scuola nuova (of the new school), which are supposed, from the great inferiority of their drawing and style, to have been executed from cartoons made by Flemish masters from small sketches by Raphael.

Note G. Study at the Royal Academy, etc

In the Royal Academy the study from 'the Life,' that is to say, drawing and painting from the 'figure 'or 'living model,' is conducted by gaslight during the winter. The model is *posed,* or 'set,' as it is otherwise expressed, in some particular attitude, and either nude, for the study of anatomy, or clothed, for the study of drapery. Etty's studies from the life, now so much prized, were for the most part rapidly executed by gaslight. Before the pupil is admitted to this Life School, he has to go through a course of chalk drawing, commencing with three probationary drawings—the first an outline from the skeleton; the second, the 'anatomical figure' in outline—generally Houdin's *ecorché* (a figure by the French sculptor displaying the muscles without their integumentary investment); and the third, a shaded drawing from a classical statue. The course of drawing from the 'antique' is then entered upon, in which six finished chalk drawings are made from several of the beet remains of ancient sculpture. Drawings and paintings in these schools are always somewhat less than half the size of life, and are called 'Academy figures,' though the term is generally limited to studies from the nude. For the study of anatomy the pupils have also the privilege of drawing from dissections at King's College.

In addition to these facilities there are—a Painting School, conducted exclusively by daylight, in which pictures of established reputation are copied—a Library of valuable books on art and prints; and on Thursdays and Fridays the students are allowed to copy from pictures in the National Gallery (Old Masters), Trafalgar Square, and on Mondays, Tuesdays, and Saturdays from pictures in the National Gallery (British School) at South Kensington. Students of architecture and sculpture have similar advantages. Visitors are appointed from the ranks of the Royal Academicians to the different schools; so that the diplomatic honour of membership is not without its duties, and these, especially in the case of the portrait-painting R.A.'s, are, it may be conceived, sometimes onerous.

The course of instruction in academies generally, though it may teach to avoid defects, cannot supply native genius; yet this necessary limitation has alone, it would seem, sometimes led to a bad sense being attached to the epithet 'Academic.' The model is of course *posed* in a conventional attitude to display muscular action, form, light and shade, or colour, to the best advantage, and as many even of the easiest attitudes are painful to preserve quite immovable, the artist sometimes unconsciously imitates the constrained appearance weariness soon induces; and so it happens that when a painter introduces a figure that is wanting in repose or in its parts inharmonious, or else, apparently merely to parade his knowledge or his taste, and either a figure inappropriate altogether, or bearing an evident disregard of higher qualities, such, for instance, as expression—in all these cases, it is at once called 'Academic,' or an 'Academy Figure.'

Note H. Crayon, or Pastel Painting

Painting in coloured crayons is of German origin; but has been carried to the highest perfection in France, where Greuze, Nattier, Girodet, and other eminent painters, practised the art. The facility and rapidity with which a picture may be executed with the dry crayons are very great, and render them very useful for studies of effect, particularly in landscape; but crayon paintings have a certain meretriciousness which has prevented their extensive adoption for finished works among English artists.

Coloured crayons, or pastels, are made by the mixture of colour with a colourless base. A mucilage is used to bring the colour and its base to the consistence of a soft paste (whence the name *pastel),* when it is formed into small round lengths, or 'sticks,' which, when dry, are ready for use. 'The material upon which the painting is executed is commonly a paper manufactured for this purpose, in such a manner that the texture becomes loosened, and forms a woolly surface, which at once assists the blending of the tints, and receives and retains the crayon powder.'[132] For finer work vellum is used, to the surface of which a 'nap' has been communicated by friction. The tints are rubbed in, and blended for the most part with the finger, although 'stumps' (Fr. *estompes),* and the point of the crayon or pieces of its length are also used. There is no satisfactory method of 'fixing' pastel paintings, and the chief objection to them is want of permanency—friction, damp, and sunlight being particularly injurious.

Note I. What Is Pre-Raphaelitism?

Pre-Raphaelitism, according to the explanation of it given by its champion, Mr. Ruskin, is intended to combat the tendency of modern art to the pursuit of beauty at the expense of manliness and truth; and the servile imitation of the Post-Raphaelite painters, to the neglect of the exact imitation of

Nature, thus resting in an imperfect reproduction of electric merit, which must result in conventional mannerism, and hinder, if not prevent, the artistic discovery and reproduction of new truth from the inexhaustible fountain of Nature herself. To escape from this tendency, 'the Pre-Raphaelite Brethren,' as they styled themselves, propose to follow the track of art from its infancy; in the words of Lord Lindsay, the student must 'ascend to the fountain-head; he must study Duccio and Giotto, that he may paint like Taddeo di Bertolo and Masaccio;—Taddeo di Bertolo and Masaccio, that he may paint like Perugino and Luca Signorelli;—and Perugino and Luca Signorelli, that he may paint like Raphael and Michael Angelo.' Mr. Ruskin repudiates the idea of the Pre-Raphaelite artists imitating any pictures; he avers that 'they merely oppose themselves to the modern system of teaching, and paint Nature as it is around them, with the help of modern science, and with the earnestness of the men of the thirteenth and fourteenth centuries.' He has, however, more recently gone to a much greater extreme: for instance, he insists that mediaeval art was *religious,* and all modern art is *profane;* that mediaeval art *confessed* Christ, while modern art *denies* Christ.

Against this schism in art it is objected that its very title is likely to mislead; for, judging from their works, we may well say, with Mr. Ruskin himself, that 'these Pre-Raphaelite pictures are just as superior to the early Italian in skill of manipulation, power of drawing, and knowledge of effect, as inferior to them in grace of design; and that, in a word, there is not a shadow of resemblance between the two styles.' And even if there are errors in the modern system of teaching, they do not prove it to be wrong by availing themselves of it only so far as it gives mere skill in exact technical imitation, and rejecting its higher principles, while professing to substitute a style in which these technical merits do not exist, but whose qualities of grace, purity, beauty, and expression they confessedly miss. Let us have, if possible, closer study of Nature, and more conscientious imitation of her; but why should the artist, more than the poet, resign his noble prerogative of educating his mind and eye to the appreciation for purposes of selection of all that she offers of tender or lovely, expressive or beautiful? Why should he not do what even Nature herself refuses to do, unite, for harmony or contrast, many diverse beauties together, provided he cull the flowers from Nature herself, and they be not artificial? Again, these painters profess to imitate Nature, and eschew the plagiarism of modern art; yet some of them imitate the productions of a period when almost the only excellence was expression, which they do not reproduce, while they borrow much that is merely grotesque. Not that the ancient painters intended it to be so; but it was the nearest approach to the imitation of Nature which their imperfect scientific and technical resources permitted them to make. The truth appears to be, that there is some analogy between the progress of act and science,—every step has been the vantage-ground for further progress,—both are infinite, and no one mind can master every branch of either; still, by following the natural inclination, a proper use of the knowledge of what has already been done, and the conscientious study of Nature, there will ever be room for originality.

The religious spirit of early art being the product of totally different tendencies from those of modern society, we can no more recall it than we can return to the manners and customs and entire mode of thinking of that age. As Mr. Leslie happily says: 'The spirit of Chaucer is not to be caught by adopting his phraseology, or by printing in black-letter; so neither shall we catch the spirit of any school or master by adopting that from it which is merely temporary.'

We have, however, in various parts of this volume, acknowledged the service rendered to art by Pre-Raphaelitism in the way of protest against the conventionality into which the English school had fallen—against a system of mere picture manufacture, and against the substitution of flippant execution for honest labour, and the intelligent reverential rendering of Nature.

Notes

1 An Italian word, compounded of 'chiaro' and 'oscuro,' signifying literally *light-dark*.

2 A *medium* or 'vehicle,' as it is otherwise called, is the fluid in which the colour is held in suspension while transmitted or conveyed to the picture.

3 It may be mentioned that the words cloth, linen, and canvas are used indiscriminately, and simply in contradistinction to wood, stone, &c.

4 From the Italian *cartone,* stout paper or pasteboard

5 Cennino Cennini wrote a valuable and interesting *Treatise on Painting* (1437), which describes the practice of tempera, secco, fresco, &c., in Italy before the introduction of the improved oil painting. This treatise *(Trattato della Pittura)* has been translated, together with the excellent notes of the former editor Tambroni, by Mrs. Merrifield. Cennini was the pupil of Agnolo Gaddi, who derived the method he taught through Taddeo Gaddi from Giotto.

6 The word 'ancient' is now commonly applied to the 'old' masters and their works, in order to coincide with ordinary usage in the apposition of the words 'ancient' and 'modern.' The only objection to the substitution of the word ' ancient' for ' old' in this case is, that it may sometimes occasion ambiguity as to whether ancient be meant for classical.

7 *Tints* differ from each other in being simply lighter or darker, but *hues* differ in colour. Therefore, we may have many tints of one colour, and various hues of one particular degree of intensity in relation to black and white. In ordinary usage, however, by 'tints' we frequently mean colours generally, and the word is often substituted for 'hues.'

8 Many of the greatest sculptors, painters, and architects of the best period in Italy, either issued from the goldsmith's workshop or successfully practised the goldsmith's art. We need only mention, in addition to Ghirlandajo, Brunelleschi, Lucca della Robbia, Ghiberti, Paolo Ucello, Antonio del Pollajuolo, Andrea del Verocchio, and Cellini.

9 Mordant, the adhesive matter used by gilders to secure the gold leaf; also a substance used in dyeing or calico printing to fix or *bite in* the colours—hence the name mordant, from *mordeo* to bite.

10 Tempera pictures of the fourteenth and beginning of the fifteenth century frequently exhibit an inequality of surface, some portions having thick edges and being considerably more raised than others. This generally results, as we shall see more particularly later, from the partial oil painting used for those

portions, and the viscidity of the oil; but it may also have been occasioned, in some instances, by the different consistence of the tempera media employed for various colours.

11 *Tone* is either general or particular: it may mean simply the degree of light or shade in some specific part; or it may refer to the generic character and complexion, so to speak, of the whole picture. We may say indifferently of an engraving or a picture that it wants more tone—meaning, in the first, simply harmony of shading; but in the latter we may also mean that it wants more general accordance with one individual hue, warm or cold, just as all the notes in a pianoforte are tuned to one particular key-note.

12 Cabinet pictures are so named because they are so small in size as to be readily contained in a cabinet.

13 Glazing is effected by spreading thin tints of various transparent colours. This term is explained more fully in the article on Oil Painting.

14 'Colours' and ' pigments' are commonly confounded; but pigments, or, as they are popularly termed, 'paints,' are those substances possessing colouring power in so eminent a degree that they are used on account of that property. Pigments are, so to speak, material colours. 'Colours' have a generic signification, including the phenomena of colour, whether considered in the abstract or the concrete.

15 To Pliny alone, among the ancient writers, are we indebted for a connected and critical history of the fine arts. This is contained in the 34th, 35th, and 36th books of his *Natural History*. Pausanias relates numerous facts and particulars respecting the fine arts and the ancient artists, in his account of the statues, pictures, and temples of Greece, but he does not furnish historically connected notices.

16 The cestrum was a pointed graver; but it must have been formed like the stylus, flat at one end and sharp at the other; since designs in wax executed with the point could only have resembled the *sgraffiti* (of the Italians) on ivory; and there can be no doubt that the early wax pictures were much more finished. — Eastlake, *Materials, &c., p. 149.*

17 Haydon says that it was then rubbed with wax candles, and finally with white napkins, till the polish was exquisite. His principal authority for this was probably the passage in Vitruvius, 1. vii. c.9. But here the wax candles, *cum candelis linteisque puris,* are only mentioned as a cerate, or nearly colourless varnish for polishing walls.

18 The ancients, though ignorant of the modern mode of distillation, were acquainted not only with naphtha, but with a method of obtaining the essential oil of turpentine.

19 'The child and the uninstructed in art alike seem to consider it of the greatest importance to omit nothing which they are able to see. Continuity of form

appears to them a point of first necessity. A boundary line studiously even and unbroken [the chief characteristic of Egyptian painting] of an object so situated as to afford the fullest view, is deemed the best and most natural expression of it. This impression is but conformable to the first notions entertained concerning the appearance of objects, such notions being entirely referable to the most familiar and habitual associations.' Fielding on the *Philosophy of Painting.*

20 For further popular information on the various kinds of writing, as the *hieratic,* or sacerdotal manner; the *demotic,* or *enchorial;* the popular, or epistolary, see Mr. Samuel Birch's *Introduction to the Study of the Egyptian Hieroglyphs.*

21 *Foreshortening* is the apparent diminution of the length of an object in proportion as the direction of its length is brought to coincide with the direction of the visual rays. Hitherto, in the history of art, we have had no foreshortening, but only the profile view of objects, placed, as it were, flat on the wall. Foreshortening was therefore a bold invention. Correct foreshortening is one of the greatest difficulties in art, and almost peculiar to painting, for the sculptor does not require a knowledge of its principles, excepting in bas-relief. Michael Angelo was perhaps the greatest master of foreshortening.

22 Aesthetics is a term derived from the Greek, denoting *feeling, s*entiment, imagination. The term, like some others used in art, was originally adopted by the Germans, but is now regularly incorporated into our own vocabulary of art. By it is generally understood the 'science of the beautiful'.

23 Wornum's Epochs, &c., p. 51

24 Pliny mentions a picture by this painter at Thebes of the sack of a town, which so impressed Alexander the Great when he saw it, after the storming of Thebes, that he took it for himself, and ordered it to be sent to Pella. The chief incident of this picture is one that has been closely imitated by Poussin, in his 'Plague of Ashdod,' in the National Gallery. A wounded mother was lying with her infant near her at the point of death, and the expression of her face was remarkable for the intense agony she felt lest the child should suck blood instead of milk from her breast.

Aristides received apparently very high prices for his works, and after his death they rose to an enormous value. Mnason, tyrant of Elatea, paid him for a Persian battle a sum not much short of 4,000 £. sterling. About two centuries later, or about 146 B.C., Attalus III, King of Pergamon, gave six times this amount for a single picture by Aristides. This same king bought from the plunder of Greece by Mummius another picture by this master for nearly 6,000*l.*; but this price appeared so extravagant to the uninitiated Roman soldier, that, suspecting the picture possessed some hidden value, he withheld it from Attalus, and sent it to Rome, where it was dedicated in the Temple of Ceres.

25 Other well-known savings are attributed to Apelles. It is said to have been a rule with him never to spend a day without in some way or other exercising his pencil: hence his maxim—*nulla dies sine linea*. Again, it was the custom with Greek painters to expose their pictures when finished to the public view, in the front or in the porches of their houses; and Apelles having in this way 'exhibited' a picture, a cobbler found fault with the sandal of one of the figures of Apelles, a criticism to which the painter carefully attended; but the cobbler perceiving the fault corrected on the following day, was bold enough to venture to criticise the leg also; when Apelles came out and indignantly said, in the words of Pliny, *Ne supra crepidam sutor judicaret,* which have supplied the English proverb—'let the cobbler stick to his last.'

26 *Still-life* is the exact imitation of immobile objects, such as fruit, flowers, eatables, and dead animals. *Genre* is a French word applied to those subjects for which there is no other name, and which are, therefore, classed as of a certain 'genre' or kind. The subjects of *genre* painting need not be low, as in Dutch pictures, but they must be comparatively familiar or domestic. A genre picture, though it may not admit of being otherwise classified, yet may partake of something of the qualities of all. The want of patronage for the stricter historical style in England has led to a compromise—the historical *genre,* of which some of Mr. E. M. Ward's pictures are illustrations.

27 Pictor *[painter],* the cognomen of a Roman painter, usually known by the entire name Fabius Pictor.

28 This description of decoration discovered at Pompeii and elsewhere constitutes the principal remains of ancient painting. The Arabians borrowed this style of ornament, and thus it acquired its name; but they were obliged to suppress the forms of men and animals, the representation of them being forbidden by Mahomet; and in the place of fanciful convolutions, they substituted exact geometrical forms. The most wonderful monument of Moorish arabesque is, we need scarcely say, the Alhambra. The old Roman style was, however, revived by Raphael, from the admiration excited in him by the discovery, in his time, of the paintings of this description in the Baths of Titus. But in the famous Loggie of the Vatican, he not only improved upon the beauty of his model, but, by introducing the element of allegory, he gave poetical meaning, and therefore far greater interest to the composition. In France, in the time of Louis XIV, the love of splendour and gaudy display was particularly manifest in the arabesques, the ornaments being loaded till meaning and propriety were entirely sacrificed and the eye insufferably wearied. Arabesques of great excellence have been painted by several modern German fresco-painters, particularly by Kaulbach and Neureuther, the former at Berlin, the latter at Munich—in the Glyptothek, or sculpture gallery.

29 The artists who practised at Constantinople were Greeks, and they preserved traditionally, if not the ancient art, the ancient name of the city where they painted: hence the 'Byzantine' style.

30 For several reasons there is not the least doubt this was done with designed. See Appendix, note E.

31 *Le Pitture Antiche delle Grotte di Roma, e del Sepulchro de' Nasoni.*

32 'The Catacombs of Rome, most of them lying at a short distance from the city gates, were originally, and probably from the time of the Republic, *puzzolana* pits. They were also early made use of as places of sepulture for the lowest classes of the people, and for slaves. For these and other reasons, being avoided and decried, they were chosen by the persecuted Christians as places of resort and concealment, and more especially also as places of burial for their martyred brethren; Christ having condemned the heathenish custom of burning the dead, which, independent of this, had already much declined since the establishment of the Empire, several excavations of this kind, which had been abandoned for generations, and probably forgotten, were secretly enlarged by the Christians into extensive and intricate labyrinths, composed of narrow intersecting passages, along the sides of which sepulchral recesses were disposed. Many of these passages terminate in small, architecturally-shaped, vaulted spaces, where, in periods of persecution, divine service, and especially the festivals of the martyrs, were held. In the sixteenth and seventeenth centuries, when a new impulse was given to the Catholic church, these resting-places of the martyrs were again opened and eagerly examined, when the sides and roofs were found to be covered with a great variety of paintings. Since then, these have, unfortunately, been almost obliterated by the admission of the air and by the smoke of torches, while such engravings as were taken from them at the time give us no adequate conception of their style.' —Kugler's *Handbook of Painting, vol. i. p. 13.*

33 The resemblance is, of course, purely imaginary; for not the least reliance can be placed on the numerous legends respecting the actual bodily appearance of our Saviour, although the painter of this portrait probably followed a traditional type, for it differs materially from the Grecian ideal. A letter, describing the person of Christ, was pretended to have been written to the Roman Senate by Lentulus; but it appears for the first time only in the writings of Anselm, Archbishop of Canterbury in the eleventh century. The letter referred to runs thus: 'A man of stately figure, dignified in appearance, with a countenance inspiring veneration, and which those who look upon it may love as well as fear. His hair, rather dark and glossy, falls down in curls below his shoulders, and is parted in the middle after the manner of the Nazarenes; the forehead is smooth and remarkably serene; the face without line or spot, and agreeably ruddy; the nose and mouth are faultless; the beard thick and reddish, of the colour of the hair, not long, but divided; the eyes bright, and of a varied colour.' Two traditions respecting the 'holy true image' are deserving notice for their connection with works of Christian art. The first is related by Evagrius, a writer of the sixth century, and is as follows: 'Abgarus, King of Edessa, in Mesopotamia, who was confined by sickness, which his physicians could not relieve, having heard of the miracles performed by Christ in Judea,

sent a messenger to him to invite him to come to Edessa, to cure him of his complaint. This messenger was a painter named Ananias, and the king ordered him that, if he could not persuade Christ to come to him, he was at least to bring his portrait. Ananias delivered his letter, but, on account of the crowd, retired to an eminence close by, and there attempted to make a drawing of his face. This he found impossible to do owing to Christ's repeated movements, or, as a later authority says, the refulgence (brilliance) of his countenance. Christ himself, however, accomplished his purpose; for, having called for water to wash his face with, he wiped it with a napkin, which be gave, with an answer for the king, to Ananias, who found a likeness miraculously imprinted on it.' Abgarus, as he anticipated, was cured by this portrait, and it became an object of universal veneration at Edessa, until it was removed to Constantinople by Nicephorus Phocas, in A.D. 964. It was subsequently carried to Rome, and is claimed to be identical with the painted head of the Saviour preserved in the church of S. Silvestro in Capite; although another account states that it was taken to Genoa and deposited in the church of S. Bartolomeo; and although this and various other images of Christ, still held sacred in the Roman church, have been repeatedly declared spurious in councils of the same church. The other tradition is, that a woman presented a handkerchief to Christ to wipe the perspiration from his face as he passed to Calvary, and that upon this handkerchief the Redeemer left his likeness. This woman was canonized by Leo X, under the name of Sta. Veronica, and the handkerchief is said to be preserved among the four 'great' relics of St. Peter's! A representation of this kind — the head of the Saviour on a cloth, and called a 'sudarium'—is common in the works of early painters.

34 *Original Treatises on the Arts of Painting,* 2 vols.

35 'The use of this word in a new and technical sense, as applied to works of art, becoming general in our own, as it is already in other languages, a definition may be offered. The word may often be rendered *intention,* but it has a fuller meaning. In its ordinary application it means the principle of action, attitude, and composition in a single figure or group; thus it has been observed, that in some antique gems which are defective in execution, the motives are frequently fine. Such qualities in this case may have been the result of the artists' feeling; but in servile copies, like those of the Byzantine artists, the *motives* could only belong to the original inventor. In its more extended signification the term comprehends inventions generally as distinguished from execution. Another very different and less general sense in which this expression is also used, must not be confounded with the foregoing; thus a *motive* is sometimes understood in the sense of a *suggestion.* It is said, for example, that Poussin found the *motives* of his landscape compositions at Tivoli. In this case we haves *suggestion* improved and carried out; in the copies of the Byzantine artists we have *intentions* not their own, blindly transmitted.'—Sir C. Eastlake: note to Kugler's *Handbook,* vol. i. p. 18. In the last case the difference of the sense is perhaps more apparent than real—the

'suggestiveness' is only an accident; *intention* has also something restricted and not essential in its signification; hence, in fact, the advantage in using the word *motive* in the new sense.

36 It is scarcely necessary to relate the old legend that Giotto was originally a shepherd boy, and one day he was discovered drawing a sheep upon a slab of stone by Cimabue, who, astonished at the boy's talent, asked him to go and live with him, and become his pupil; an invitation which, with his parents' consent, he accepted with delight, and followed the great painter to Florence.

37 The Italian diminutive *ino* is often employed in this way for scholars, even should they greatly surpass their masters.

38 It was conjectured by Vertue and Walpole that Cavallini was the architect of the crosses erected to Queen Eleanor and of the shrine of Edward the Confessor in Westminster Abbey. The Petrus Romanus Civis mentioned in the inscription on the tomb may possibly have been Cavallini; but the date (1279 or 1280) would make him only twenty years old, according to Vasari. Vasari is, however, so frequently incorrect in dates, that no reliance can be placed upon his statements.

39 Or *beatified brother:* the beatification of a holy person was an honour solemnly conferred by the Roman church, and only inferior to canonization.

40 Kugler's *Handbook, &c.*, vol. i. p. 165

41 The works in *Pietre Dure* and *Pietre Commesse,* so extensively carried on in Tuscany (and hence called Florentine mosaics), differ from the preceding mosaics in the materials, execution, and subjects chosen. Both are employed for merely ornamental or decorative purposes, and represent fruit, birds, flowers, &c. The *pietre dure* work gives the objects imitated in relief in coloured stones, and is generally used as a decoration for coffers or the panels of cabinets. The *pietre commesse of* the finer sort consists of precious stones inlaid, and is employed for caskets; cabinets, &c. The stones are cut into thin veneer, and the various pieces are sawn into shape by means of a fine wire stretched by a bow, aided by emery powder, and afterwards fitted at the lapidary's wheel. The materials are exclusively natural stones, as agates, jaspers, lapis lazuli, &c., the colours of which serve the purpose of delineating various ornamental natural objects. The walls of the chapel of the Medici attached to S. Lorenzo at Florence are lavishly decorated with this costly material.

42 This description of work we have found in modern times to lead immediately to engraving, and something of the kind—some means of multiplying impressions—seems to have been not unknown to antiquity, judging from the much-commented on passage in Pliny, xxxv. 2. Marcus Varro, says Pliny, made *(aliquo modo)* and inserted in his writings the portraits of seven hundred distinguished men, and dispersed them to all parts of the world; and this he did for the gratification of strangers. The process, whatever it was—and

Pliny's allusion is so concise, that any explanation of the means can be merely conjectural—must have been transient and imperfect, or some traces of the art would have been preserved, or some mention of it made.

43 Frequently also the Saviour holds a book (the New Testament), on which are inscribed the words, 'Ego sum lux mundi'—I am the light of the world.

44 As believed to be intended by Ezekiel, vii. 1-10, viz., a man (St. Matthew), a lion (St. Mark), a bull (St. Luke), and an eagle (St. John). Various other symbols are of frequent occurrence, such as stags approaching a vessel, which stand for the souls of the faithful thirsting after the living waters. These souls, while here below, appear in the shape of doves; after the resurrection, and in a glorified state, in that of the phoenix—also an emblem of eternity. In this form they are often perched in the branches of a palm, symbolical of the tree of life. Subsequently the disembodied spirit was represented as a newborn infant, and we often see it thus borne to heaven in a napkin by angels.

45 Published under the title of *Manuel d'Iconographie Chrétienne.*

46 It is a remarkable fact that the Byzantine style of art, even in these times, is congenial to the feelings of certain Western races, who, with small knowledge and great devotion, find in these strange and dismal pictures fitting incentives for their zeal. A genuine Byzantine Madonna picture, or one executed in the same style, with dark face and stiff gold garments, will everywhere most readily obtain the repute of a miraculous picture—an honour seldom bestowed on the most finished work of art. In those parts of Italy where the Byzantine dominion lasted the longest, the cultivation of the stiff Byzantine type, for popular devotion, was maintained in juxtaposition with that of the most perfectly developed form of painting. In Venice, as late as the last century, painters of 'sacred pictures' still existed; and in Naples, to this day, a lemonade-seller will permit none other than a Byzantine Madonna, with olive-green complexion and veiled head, to be painted up in his booth. We here stand upon ground to which Titian and Ribera, with all their influence, have not yet penetrated.'—*Handbook of Painting*: The Italian Schools, vol. i. p. 91.

47 *Art Treasures in Great Britain*: The MSS. of the British Museum.

48 Mrs. Merrifield's *Ancient Practice,* &c., p. xxix.

49 So named—*dai Libri,* literally 'of the books'—from his employment. His father, Francesco dai Libri, was also a celebrated though inferior illuminator.

50 *Monuments d'Art, &c.*

51 *Northern Tour,* p. 603.

52 It is foreign artists, however, particularly those of Munich, who have chiefly distinguished themselves in this branch of art. The late Mr. Bone was one of the best English enamel painters of our time.

53 Where, for example, can two large portraits be produced of greater historical interest than those two small highly finished miniatures by Holbein in the Meyrick collection—the portrait of Henry VIII, sent to Anne of Cleves, and the returned one of Anne.

54 The reader will find the subject of coloured photography treated in note A of the Appendix.

55 Translated in the *Illustrated Handbook of the Arts of the Middle Ages.*

56 For instance, the pieces in the Bibliothèque Impériale at Paris, the one in the Museum at Poitiers, and the vase found in Essex.

57 The claim of the Limousin artists to this invention has, however, been disputed. In the Loan Collection, South Kensington Museum, there was exhibited in 1862 a drinking-cup, which put back the art some fifty years before the earliest date previously known, and moreover seemed to rob Limoges of the honour of the invention, for the cup was certainly Flemish or German.

58 The dawn of the revival of painting, we have seen, commenced with the thirteenth century; but the period known as the *Renaissance* (or new birth) dates particularly from the fifteenth century, when the study of the remains of ancient sculpture infused a new life into art.

59 Alluding to those in the well-known Debruge-Labarte collection, for which M. Labarte wrote his admirable descriptive catalogue, and of which he was co-inheritor.

60 *Grisaille,* or *camaïeu*—painting in grey; resulting in a chiaroscuro or monochrome picture.

61 *Accessories* are those objects in a picture, auxiliary, 'accessorial,' or complementary to the general effect, but not being the principal subject or figure.

62 Labarte. *Illustrated Handbook, &c.*, pp. 74 and 76.

63 The word 'plaster' is here used in a general sense; it is not to be understood that plaster or gypsum is mixed with the lime. Plaster, strictly speaking, is the Italian gesso of which we have already spoken, and in old books on art, plaster casts are commonly called 'gessos.' The word stucco is sometimes used indifferently for plaster, for the exterior coating of a house, and for compositions used in making ornaments. A wall may, of course, be composed of any materials, if it is to be painted on when dry in distemper with colours simply diluted with water and size.

64 Mr. Field, the author of *Chromatics* and other quite valuable works, says, in reference to the last restriction: 'This need not, however, be a universal rule for painting in fresco, since other cementing materials, as strong or stronger than lime, may be employed, which do not have the action of lime upon colours, such as calcined gypsum, of which plaster of Paris is a species; which, being neutral sulphates of lime, exceedingly unchangeable, have little or no

chemical action upon colours, and would admit even Prussian blue, vegetal lakes, and the most tender colours to be employed thereon, so as greatly to extend the sphere of colouring in fresco, adapted to its various designs; which also calls the attention of the painter in crayons, scagliola, and distemper.

'So far, too, as regards durability and strength of the ground, the compo and cements, now so generally employed in architectural modellings, stucco and plaster would afford a new and advantageous ground for painting in fresco; and as it resists damp and moisture, it is well adapted, with colours properly chosen, to situations in which paintings executed in other modes of the art, or even in ordinary fresco, would not long endure.' We are very doubtful, however, whether any material would be found to endure where the plaster of lime and sand fails. Moreover, the word fresco is here applied to various kinds of painting which have not the fine properties of fresco, and which, therefore, we shall find it necessary to distinguish from the true fresco employed by the greatest masters.

65 Michael Angelo is reported to have said: 'To paint in oil is an art fit only for women, and easy and lazy persons like Fra Sebastiano'—il colorire ad olio era arte da donna, e da persone agiate ed infingarde, come Fra Bastiano. We need not, however, infer that the first clause of this sentence (which is all that is generally quoted) was Michael Angelo's absolutely unqualified opinion. The remark was perhaps coloured by the great master's angry feeling against Sebastiano del Piombo, who had earned his reputation by oil painting, and had tried against the wish of Michael Angelo to persuade Paul III to have the 'Last Judgment' painted in oil.

66 We have already explained that these joinings are unavoidable: 'These divisions in the patchwork (for such it may be called), of which all works of the kind must consist, are among the tests of fresco painting properly so called. Whenever the extent of a surface of plaster without a joining is such that it would be impossible to complete the work contained in it in a day, it may be concluded, even without other indications, though such are seldom wanting, that the mode of execution was not what is called "Buon fresco." Walls decorated by the earlier Italian masters exhibit no joinings in the plaster having any reference to the decorations upon them. The paintings must, consequently, have been added when the entire surface was dry; and must either have been executed in tempera, or if with lime, by means of a process called "secco."—Eastl.ake's *Materials, &c*

67 *Second Report of the Commissioners on the Fine Arts.*

68 It is to be observed that this is the customary contracted form used by the Italians, and they do not, like ourselves, in a given date, include the current but unexpired century.

69 The life of Fra Lippi was a romance. When a child he was made a member of the Order of Carmelites; but disliking monastic restraint, he left the convent

in his seventeenth year. Amusing himself one day in an excursion at sea with some friends, they were suddenly attacked by pirates, and carried as slaves to Barbary. During eighteen months Filippo bore his chains, when one day he drew a likeness in charcoal of his master on the wall, which was so striking, that the Moor rewarded him with his freedom; and, after he had painted several pictures, gave him rich presents and sent him home. When forty-six years of age, while painting in the convent of Sta. Margherita, at Prato, he won the affections of Lucrezia Buti, a young Florentine lady, who was being educated there. She afterwards bore him the son who became a much more distinguished painter than the father. Fra Filippo died suddenly, eleven years after the abduction of Lucrezia (not without suspicion of having been poisoned by this lady's relatives), and just before the Pope's dispensation for his marriage with her, obtained by the interest of his patrons, the Medici.

70 Mantegna was one of the first great Italian painters who practised the art of engraving, and engraved their own designs. It is generally represented that the art of engraving was discovered in 1452 by Masso Finiguerra, a gold and niello worker of Florence. Designs were engraved on metal plates, and in order to render them more visible, niello (*Ital.* for black), a black composition of lead and silver, was rubbed into the incisures. In order to see the effect of the design, Finiguerra is said to have been in the habit of taking sulphur casts from his niellos, and printing with them on damp paper; and either this habit or some accident led him ultimately to print with the niello itself. Sir C. Eastlake, however, says (*Materials,* &c., p. 92*)*, that various passages in a Venetian MS., preserved in the British Museum, prove that the art of etching was understood and practised long before it occurred to the monks, or to Masso Finiguerra, to take impressions from plates. There are wood engravings of certainly an earlier date.

71 A copy of the 'Last Supper' was made by Marco d'Oggione, a friend and scholar of Leonardo, with the sanction of the great Lombard. This picture was purchased on the Continent by Sir Thomas Lawrence for the Royal Academy, for 600*l.*, and is now preserved in the rooms in Trafalgar Square, This copy was exhibited in 1858, at the British Institution, and from some judicious notes on the exhibition, by Mr. Scharf, we extract the following upon the disposition of the figures on one side only of the table in the 'Last Supper.' 'The arrangement of the table and the position of the figures as we see them here, was not the original device of Leonardo. In this he merely followed the traditional composition accepted by all Italian painters since the revival of art among them. A picture of the Last Supper was always considered the most appropriate decoration for the refectory of a convent, which was generally a large square room, with long tables placed round three sides of it. Between the tables and the walls the monks sat at their meals, whilst the serving brethren occupied the centre of the apartment. For their convenience no seats were placed along the outer sides of the table. The prior and superiors of the convent sat at a long raised table, as in our college halls, at the upper end of

the room, and the picture of the Last Supper was usually placed on the blank wall facing them, whereby the painter contrived by his work to complete the arrangement of the tables on the fourth side of the room. In this manner the apostles being confined to one side of the table becomes intelligible.'

72 Leonardo died in 1519, and according to Vasari, in the arms of the king, who had come to visit the beloved artist in his last illness. The following will, however, show that this story is without foundation: Leonardo died at Cloux, near Amboise, May 2, 1519. According to the Journal of Francis I, preserved in the Imperial Library at Paris, the Court was on that day at St. Germain-en-Laye. Francesco Melzi, in a letter written to Leonardo's relations immediately after his death, makes no mention of so noteworthy an incident. Lastly, Lornasso, who communicated so much respecting the life of the great artist, distinctly says, that the king first learned the death of Leonardo from Melzi.

73 All that is known of this gigantic genius has been embodied in the work by Mr. Harford, *The Life of Michael Angelo Buonarotti; with Translations of many of his Poems and Letters*. This biography also contains a memoir of Raphael, and a notice of the curious episode in the history of art at this time, occasioned by the fanaticism of Savonarola. This famous monk, it is well known, deprecated all naked, or indeed any, female representation, and obtained such influence over his followers as to procure the public burning in Florence of a number of valuable works of art; Fra Bartolommeo, Lorenzo di Credi, and other artists actually contributing their own pictures to the blazing pile. Mr. Harford's work includes also an interesting memoir of Vittoria Colonna. The change in the feelings of Michael Angelo, as he advanced to old age, and the gradual ascendency obtained by religion over philosophy, is traced, on his own authority, to his friendship with Vittoria Colonna, Marchesa di Pescara, who lived at Rome for a year after the commencement of their acquaintance (1537), and resided several years at Viterbo afterwards. During that time Michael Angelo made several drawings for his illustrious friend, and they exchanged letters. 'Some have imagined, perhaps from misunderstanding Condivi, that Michael Angelo was smitten with a hopeless passion for Vittoria Colonna. Mr. Harford calmly examines the facts of the case, and appeals to the testimony of his poems addressed to her—five in number—and to sundry unpublished letters in the possession of the Cavaliere Buonarotti, at Florence, to prove that it was a religious friendship. The discussion of this question is carried on with judicious calmness, and is marked by candour and good sense; and ought, we think, to satisfy every one that, although Michael Angelo was not insensible to the beauty of Vittoria, it was her religious elevation of sentiment, her condescending courtesy, and the nobleness of her character which attracted his admiration; and that when Condivi spoke of him as "enamoured of her divine spirit, and beloved by her in return with much affection," he spoke of "Such love as spirits feel, In worlds whose course is equable and pure."', *Edinburgh Review* (No. 216).

74 The Sibyls, according to mediaeval legends, stand next in dignity to the

Prophets of the Old Testament. These reputed prophetesses are represented to have foretold the coming of the Saviour to the ancient Pagan nations, as the Prophets predicted his advent to the Jews. Ten Sibyls are enumerated as having been alluded to by Greek, Roman, and Jewish writers, and by most of the Christian fathers. They take their names, for the most part, from the particular place or country to which they belonged. Sir Charles Eastlake says, in a note to Kugler's *Handbook:* 'The authority of the Sibylline writings with the Pagans soon suggested the pious fraud of interpolating them; the direct allusions to the Messiah which they contain are supposed to have been inserted in the second century. But, notwithstanding the occasional expression of some suspicion as to their authenticity, these spurious predictions continued to be held in veneration, not only during the Middle Ages, but even to a comparatively modern date; and the Sibyls were represented in connection with Scripture subjects before and after Michael Angelo's time by various painters. The circumstance of their appearing in works of art, as equal in rank with the Prophets, may have arisen from the manner in which St. Augustine *(De Cicit. Dei,* xviii. 47*)* speaks of the Erythræan Sibyl's testimony immediately before he adverts to that of the Prophets of the Old Testament.'

75 The 'Last Judgment' has been allowed to become so much obscured by dirt and smoke, that (speaking from our own experience) it is almost, impossible to 'make out' any portion. There is a copy by M. Sigalon, the size, we believe, of the original, in the Palais des Beaux Arts, at Paris.

76 By far the best life of Raphael is the German work of Passavant—*Rafael von Urbino u. sein Vater Giovanni Santi*—lately published in French.

77 This beautiful ceiling is excellently imitated in the Italian Court of the Crystal Palace at Sydenham.

78 Richardson's *Theory of Painting, &c.*

79 'He [Raphael] has departed from historical truth in the pillars that are at the Beautiful Gate of the Temple. The imagery is by no means agreeable to the superstition of the Jews at that time and all along after the captivity. Nor were those kinds of pillars known even in antique architecture, I believe, in any nation; but they are so nobly invented by Raphael, and so prodigiously magnificent, that it would have been a pity if he had not indulged himself in this piece of licentiousness.'—*Richardson.* These spiral decorative pillars are, however, altogether assigned to Giovanni da Udine.

80 The 'Fornarina' (i.e., the Baker) is a name which, as applied to the obscure person to whom Raphael was attached, even to his death, does not, according to Kugler, occur before the middle of the last century. There is much uncertainty respecting several of the so-called portraits of this female. The most undoubtedly authentic is the picture in the Barberini Palace, in Rome. The forms of the figure (which is uncovered to the waist) are fine, and even beautiful; but the features are not entirely free from an expression of common life.

A portrait, said to be of the same person, in the tribune of the Uffizj, is of the purest beauty, but does not resemble this. Dr. Kugler believes it to be by Raphael, but the colouring is quite Venetian; and in a note he gives an hypothesis of Missirini, that it is by Sebastiano del Piombo, after Michael Angelo, and that the subject is Vittoria Colonna. The German critic says further: 'A draped female portrait, of Raphael's later time, which appears to represent the same individual, though at a younger period, is of higher beauty and most enchanting grace and true Roman character. This figure may possibly have served as Raphael's model for the Sistine Madonna.'

81 The Dominican monk, St. Peter Martyr, was an active agent of the Inquisition in the thirteenth century; in consequence of which, he made himself many enemies, by one of whom he was at length assassinated at the entrance of a wood, on the road from Milan to Como. He was accompanied by another brother of his order, who fled and escaped. This assassination is the incident of Titian's great picture.

82 Tibaldi, called by the Carracci Michael Angelo Riformato, the Reformed Michael Angelo, was a Bolognese artist; but his finest works are his frescoes in the Escurial at Madrid.

83 Nicole dell' Abbate was an excellent painter, but few of his works remain.

84 Albani is said to have been led into this particular choice of subject through the numerous family he had by his second wife Doralice Fioravante, who belonged to a noble Florentine family. By this lady, who is said to have been beautiful, Albani had twelve children, all remarkable for their loveliness; and his wife and children were the models for the numerous Venuses, Nymphs, and Cupids which are the principal productions of his pencil in later life. Fiammingo is said also to have studied the children of Albani for his celebrated ivory carvings.

85 We may perhaps venture to remind our readers that Mr. Thackeray is an artist, and, we believe, studied art with a view to make it his profession, before he devoted himself more particularly to painting in words.

86 See *Rembrandt and his Works,* by J. Burnet.

87 Much of the study at the Royal Academy is conducted by gaslight. For further particulars see note G in Appendix.

88 'Cast shadows' are always to be distinguished from other shadows incidental to an object. In this instance the side of the brush itself turned from the light would of course have its shadow, and another shadow would be 'cast,' or projected on to the first object with which it came in contact. Cast shadows are always darkest, because least susceptible of modification by reflections. An eclipse is a vast 'cast shadow.'

89 The hog-hair brushes may recall an anecdote which is so well known as to scarcely require repetition. However, we venture to give it. Giotto, on one

occasion, while taking a walk with some friends, met a herd of swine, one of whom ran against Giotto and upset him. The good-humoured painter immediately sprang up, and exclaimed, 'Well done! I have made many a florin out of your bristles, and yet have never offered you a single bowl of soup.'

90 'Drapery' is the generic term for every kind of textile fabric susceptible of folds; it also includes fringes, tassels, &c. The 'cast,' or adjustment of draperies, is made the object of a special course of study in some foreign schools, especially by German painters for their works in fresco, as well as by sculptors generally. The salient parts of the body and limbs should always be seen through the drapery, though it is unnecessary to carry the principle so far as the ancient sculptors, who wetted the drapery to cause it to adhere more closely to the figure. In the works of the higher schools generally, and for a particular example in Raphael's Cartoons, thick stuffs are chosen, because they have few folds, and are therefore broader and grander in character. The specific quality of the fabric is indicated by the size of the folds; the smaller having a tendency to become angular, and the larger to form 'eyes,' as the abrupt terminations of the longitudinal division of folds are named. The texture is also indicated by the quality of surface, whether rough or smooth, dull or brilliant. Thus satins (witness the 'Satin Gown,' by Terburg) resemble polished bodies in the reception of glossy lights in the midst of dark half-tints; but distinct shadows are seen, though modified by strong reflections. The folds are generally conical, with sharp breaks of a crescent shape and sudden terminations, in consequence of the stiffness arising from its polish. The folds of silk are more angular, and the 'sheen' of its lights less brilliant. In furs the light glistens just within the edges; and velvets have a similar peculiarity, viz. that, in retreating parts of the folds, where other stuffs would have half-shadows, they display vivacity and light. The characteristics of cloth are very simple. It is desirable to preserve an angular disposition of the folds; for if they be too curved, it conveys the impression of the drapery being full of something—as a sack of flour. Albert Dürer used to study his drapery from models made with wet paper, which he copied in all its stiffness and angularity. Zurbaran made great use of the lay figure; and his draperies, especially the white, give evidence of careful study. It is only less difficult to give lightness to 'flying drapery' in painting than in sculpture. In the 'Bacchus and Ariadne' of Titian, in the National Gallery, the scarf escaping, ruffled by the wind, from the figure of the god, is a fine instance of motion being suggested even in a comparatively heavy material. Haydon, in his *Autobiography,* gives an amusing account of the number of times he had to paint out some flying drapery in his picture of Dentatus — because it seemed always to want a prop. Wardour Street is at present a great depôt for draperies, armour, and other artistic 'properties.'

91 In the successive application of the coats of colour to a picture, the oil in each superimposed coat is apt to 'dry' into that previously laid (especially if the latter is not perfectly dry), and then the colour applied last loses some of its

force. Previous to fresh applications, therefore, the artist generally spreads a thin couch of oil or varnish over the colours already laid, in order to make them 'bear out,' and to ensure the uniting of the subsequent with the previous painting. This operation is termed 'oiling out,' and such thin glazes of vehicle are sometimes called 'preparations.' The 'sinking in' of the vehicle should be distinguished from that of the pigment: in the former the surface becomes dead, in the latter it becomes shining, from the supernatant oil.

92 The plural of the Italian noun *dilettante,* a lover or admirer (of any art, &c.). 'Amateur' and 'connoisseur' (from the French) import, the first a lover of, the second a person skilled in the knowledge of, art.

93 The softer kinds of varnish are especially liable, when exposed to damp, to produce this appearance on the surface of pictures; so called from resembling the 'bloom' on fruit: it is otherwise termed 'chilling.'

94 *Keeping* is the proper subserviency of tone and colour in every part of a picture, so that the general effect is harmonious to the eye. When this is unattended to, a harshness is produced, which gives improper isolation to individual parts, and the picture is said to be *out of keeping.*

95 The term 'balsam' was formerly, and is still frequently, applied to liquid resins generally. The modern French chemists, however, restrict the word 'baume' to those resins, whether liquid or solid, which contain benzoic acid.— Eastlake's *Materials, &c.*

96 The word *amber is* derived from the Arabic *ambar,* which was probably applied originally to ambergris. The attractive power of amber after friction was evidently known to the ancients from the names employed to designate it. The attractive power after friction is not, however, a test of amber alone, for it is known to be a property common to resins generally, to sealing-wax, and other substances. The analogy between copal and amber evidently indicates a similar origin. Their consistency, their colour, their nature, and the fact that they both enclose organic remains, prove the resemblance; and concur in showing that amber, like copal, and many modern resins and gains, has flowed from the trunk and branches of a vegetable. The great quantity thrown up by the Baltic sea is probably owing to the existence of a considerable bed—the site of the forest which produced it.

97 Richardson says, speaking of the St. Cecilia of Raphael, that the surface of the picture opposite the flame of the candles on the altar was 'perfectly fried.'

98 'Piers Plowman (whose *Vision is* supposed to have been written in 1350), in describing the dress of a lady richly clad, says, that her robe was of "scarlet in grain," that is, scarlet dyed with grana, the best and most durable red dye. The import of the words "in grain" was afterwards changed, and the term was applied generally to all colours with which cloths are dyed which were considered to be permanent; in this sense it is still used.'—Mrs. Merrifield's *Ancient Practice, &c.*

99 It was only in the sixteenth century that the word, in the form of *vernice,* was applied to liquid compositions.

100 One curious circumstance connected with the English polychromy of the thirteenth century is the partiality exhibited in all the royal records of the period to use green as a preponderating colour, and as a ground for other decorations. The recommendation of the white lead and verdigris (vert-de-Grèce) used, was that they were both 'dryers;' and, therefore, even when mixed with oil—as they probably often were—the oil paint would quickly dry.

101 *Priming* is the house-painters' term for the first or primary coat or coats of paint, or the preparatory oil ground for the finishing coat.

102 *The Early Flemish Painters,* p. 42.

103 That is to say, the oils which had been converted into a varnish by the 'other mixtures of his'—that this is Vasari's meaning is apparent from many considerations, which, as they are indicated in various places, it is unnecessary to state in detail here.

104 White copperas is known to have been used by early Flemish painters.

105 The exact arrangement of the entire altar-piece is described in note D of the Appendix.

106 An ancient copy of the 'Adoration of the Mystic Lamb,' formerly in the Aders collection, was exhibited in the Art Treasures Exhibition at Manchester, 1857.

107 The fame of Albert Dürer rests, however, principally upon his engravings; in which we do not know whether to admire most the surprising richness of invention, or the wonderful delicacy of execution. It is a disputed point whether Albert ever engraved on the wood himself; but his woodcut designs are, though far coarser in execution, like his copper-plate engraving, full of fantastic invention. The following are the most remarkable woodcuts and engravings of this manly and prolific genius; and they are enumerated in the order of their production. The woodcuts illustrating the Revelation of St. John; the engraving of the coat of arms with Death's head; the engraving of Adam and Eve; sketches of the sufferings of Christ; an excellent woodcut of a Penitent, and another of Death seizing an armed warrior; two great series of woodcuts known as the *Greater and Lesser Passion of Christ;* and another well-known series of the *Life of the Virgin;* the grand woodcut composition of the Trinity; the very celebrated engraving of *The Knight, Death, and the Devil* which has been considered 'the most important work which the fantastic spirit of German art has ever produced;' the allegorical engraving of *Melancholy;* an engraving of St. Jerome in his study; the large woodcut, the triumphal Arch of the Emperor Maximilian; the series of woodcuts which form the triumphal car of the Emperor Maximilian; and, lastly, the remarkable engraved portraits of some of his distinguished contemporaries, including Melancthon and Erasmus.

108 Altdorfer, as an engraver, is one of the best of the so-called German 'little masters,' from the smallness of their prints and cuts; the French call him *le petit Albert* [Dürer].

109 Some of the engravings of Lucas Van Leyden—as, for instance his Eulenspiegel (a notorious clown)—are among the very greatest rarities of print collectors: there are not more than half-a-dozen impressions extant of the print we have named.

110 The words *Connubialis amor de Mulcibre fecit Apellem* are written on his monument, erected at Antwerp one hundred years after his death.

111 Although the honour of introducing oil painting into Italy is ascribed, probably with justice, to Antonello, yet not only were specimens of the Flemish method imported before the return of Antonello from Flanders, but pictures were actually painted in Italy by some Flemish artists; among which were Roger of Bruges (Roger Van der Weyden), and Justus Van Ghent. The latter resided for several years at Urbino, and painted works in oil there; but as the native artists, such as Giovanni Santi (the father of Raphael), continued to paint in tempera, the inference is that the Flemish painter contrived, like other of his countrymen, to keep the secret of his process.

112 The marketable value of Rembrandt's etchings has of late years risen amazingly. The 'Christ Healing the Sick,' called 'The years Guilder Print,' as having once fetched that price, about 10*l*., then considered enormous, would now command, if a good impression, perhaps as many guineas as guilders. The presence or absence of scarcely perceptible appearances in the impressions indicating the exact state of the plate, will cause the most startling differences in the value. Of the portrait of 'Rembrandt with a sword,' hence called 'The Sabre Print,' only four impressions are known, and for one of these Mr. Holford is said to have paid 400 guineas.

113 The creator, as Dr. Waagen says, of 'conversation-painting;' and, as Sir Edmund Head calls him, the painter of 'genteel comedy.'

114 Of this artist the following, among other amusing anecdotes, is related: In 1658 Cano received a commission to carve a statuette of St. Anthony of Padua for an *Oidor* or judge of Granada. When finished, the judge came to see it, expressed himself pleased, and inquired the price. The answer was one hundred doubloons. This excited astonishment in the patron: he therefore ventured to inquire how many days the artist had spent upon it. To this Cano replied, five-and-twenty days. 'But,' said the calculating Oidor, 'that comes to four doubloons a day.'—'Your lordship reckons wrong,' answered Cano, 'for I have spent fifty years in learning how to execute it in twenty-five days.' —'That is all very well,' replied the other; 'but I have spent my patrimony and my youth in studying at the university, and in a higher profession, and now here I am *Oidor* in Granada, and if I get a doubloon a day it is as much as I do.' The artist scarcely stayed to hear him out. 'A higher profession, indeed!'

he exclaimed. 'why, the king can make judges out of clods of the earth, but it is reserved for God alone to make Alonzo Cano.' Upon saying which, he took up the figure and dashed it to pieces on the floor. The judge, in the utmost alarm for his own safety, rushed away from a man who could thus demolish a saint. The offence was indeed a capital one, but appears never to have reached the ears of the Inquisition.

115 Better known through his poem, *De Arte Graphicâ,* which has had the honour of translation by Dryden. Dufresnoy is also the subject of an epistle by Pope, and the text for some valuable notes by Reynolds.

116 This enormous picture is larger by three feet than the 'Marriage at Cana' by Paul Veronese.

117 It would appear, however, from the anecdote told by Walpole, that this was not always the character of his works. Holbein was sent by Cromwell, the king's minister, to take a miniature portrait of lady Anne of Cleves; and, says Walpole, in his *Anecdotes of Painting,* 'by practising the common flattery of his profession, was the immediate cause of the destruction of that great subject [Cromwell], and of the disgrace that fell on the princess herself. He drew so favourable a likeness that Henry was content to wed her; but when he found her so inferior to the miniature, the storm which really should have been directed to the painter, burst on the minister, and Cromwell lost his head because Anne was a *Flanders mare,* not a Venus, as Holbein had represented her.' This interesting miniature, together with that of Henry sent to Anne, was in the Manchester Art Treasures Exhibition of 1857. We think that one glance at the portrait of Anne would exculpate Holbein from the charge made by Walpole. The miniature has certainly a delicacy of finish commensurate with its extremely minute size, but it has also that striking individuality and palpable honesty which, although unknown to the portrait painting of the time of Walpole, and rarely tolerated in our own, distinguishes all the genuine works of Holbein, and indeed is so remarkable, that one might in every case asseverate the faithfulness of the likeness. The face of Anne is in point of fact almost as far removed from the 'Venus' of Walpole as it is from what the king's coarse brutal comparison would suggest. The miniature does not give the figure, but the expression of the features, and the known character of the king afford apparently to us sufficient clue to the catastrophe. Meekness, inclining almost to shallowness, or a temperament unsusceptible of lively and sympathetic emotion, however capable of constancy and devotion, would be little appreciated by the exacting imperious Henry. A shrewd observer might actually gain considerable insight into an interesting historical episode from this miniature of Anne.

118 Jonathan Richardson was one of the best critics and writers on art whom we have had in the English language. The perusal of his *Theory of Painting* awakened the ambition of Reynolds when a boy to become a painter.

119 The union of the daughter of Sir James Thornhill with Hogarth (then in his

thirty-second or thirty-third year) was without the consent of her parents: and Sir James, the rich, prosperous, and highly-honoured artist, was, very excusably, not easily reconciled to the match, considering the youth of his daughter, then barely eighteen, and the slender finances of her husband, who was as yet , 'all unknown to fame.' The marriage seems, however, to have been a great stimulus to Hogarth's genius, for immediately after it he began his celebrated series of the' Harlot's Progress.' Mrs. Hogarth now contrived, at her mother Lady Thornhill's suggestion, to have some of Hogarth's pictures introduced into Sir James's dining-room as a surprise. This being accordingly done, when Sir James learnt they were the productions of his son-in-law, he merely said, 'the man who can produce such representations as these can maintain a wife without a portion.' He soon afterwards, however, became both reconciled and generous to the runaway couple. The young lady Hogarth had married, though bred in comfort and affluence, made the poor painter a truly excellent wife. In the International Exhibition (1862) there was one portrait, and in the Manchester Exhibition of Art Treasures (1857) there were three portraits by Hogarth of this estimable woman. The first of these last represented her young and pretty, as she may have been soon after the marriage; the second, in matronly middle-life — both indicated a sensible, kindly, amiable nature; in the third (with the features somewhat idealized), she appeared as 'Sigismunda' holding the urn with her husband's heart. This last portrait illustrates a curious passage in the artist's history. A 'Sigismunda,' believed to be by Correggio, but now attributed to Furini (a far inferior painter), had been sold at Sir Luke Schaub's sale for 400*l*. This price, fetched by a poor specimen of an 'old master,' so excited Hogarth's indignation (who was wretchedly paid for his best works, and had just received only 160*l* for his series of six pictures of 'Marriage à la Mode,' now in the National Gallery), that he is said to have resolved to paint in competition this picture for which his wife served as model. Be this as it may, Hogarth — who after all did not over-estimate his high-art qualifications so much as Walpole and Reynolds have given the cue for supposing — would not sell his picture for a smaller sum than the 400*l*., and charged his wife not to part with it for less than 500*l* after his death — an injunction which she obeyed during twenty years of widowhood, the declining circumstances of the latter part of which were relieved by a small pension from the Royal Academy.

120 The paper most generally used is of what is called 'Imperial' size (30 in. by 21 in.) under which name the best and greatest varieties of texture and thickness can be obtained. For large drawings, cartoons, and engineering plans, colossal cartridge paper, as it is termed (manufactured by Fourdrinier's ingenious process), may be purchased 4 ft. 6 in. wide, and more than long enough to reach doubled from the top to the bottom of the Monument. Graduated tinted papers are also sold of various groundwork preparatory lines, for daylight, moonlight, and other effects, and from which the 'lights' of the painting are scraped out. Papers of Whatman's manufacture are esteemed for possessing sufficient hardness to resist moderate friction. That

the paper should be properly sized is of great importance. If sized too strongly, colour will not float or work well upon it, but will look hard and streaky. If sized too little, the colour will be absorbed into the fabric, and appear poor and dead.

121 Mr. Ruskin, however, in the Appendix to his eloquent *Notes on the Turner Gallery*, says: 'Even interiors, in which lateral light is represented as entering a room, and none as falling from the ceiling, are yet best seen by light from above; for a lateral light, contrary to the supposed direction of that in the picture, will greatly neutralize its effect, and a *lateral light in the same direction will exaggerate it.'* To the last observation we must certainly venture to dissent; for an artist would naturally, and in the case of watercolour paintings almost (as we have seen) necessarily, paint in a light coming from the same direction as that in the representation, and could not, if he would, paint for the picture to look better in any other light.

122 As may have been observed, we have for greater convenience occasionally used the terms colour and pigment as convertible. However, 'the term colour is equivocal when attributed to the neutrals white, black, and grey; yet the artist is bound to regard them as colours, and in philosophic strictness they are such latently, compounded and compensated, for a thing cannot but be that of which it is composed, and the neutrals are composed of and comprehend all colours.'—Field.

123 The pigments are prepared for use in three forms: viz., as dry *cake* colours, as *moist* colours in earthenware pans, and in the compartments of tin boxes, and in a still softer state enclosed in metal collapsible *tubes.* The first is the earliest of the modern modes of preparation; but cake colours were long subject to many objections, such as drying and crumbling with age or in warm climates: with more careful grinding, however, and other improvements in their manufacture, they are now less liable to crack; and from being hard and gritty, they have become comparatively smooth and yield a firmer body of tint. A numerous class of artists consider them to have advantages over the moist colours, as regards purity of tone and perfection of wash, and to be therefore especially suitable for miniature and flower painting. When the colours are required for use, the supply is obtained by dipping the cakes in water and rubbing them on china palettes, or, when a larger quantity is wanted, in the troughs of china tiles, in plates or saucers. The *moist* colours are now very extensively employed for ordinary watercolour painting. For sketching from nature, from the readiness and facility with which an inexhaustible supply of powerful colour may be obtained, they supersede all others. They are especially convenient and advantageous for the learner. The colour is obtained by gentle friction with the point of the brush charged with water directly on the pigment itself. The colours prepared in tubes are still more moist, and necessarily so for moderate compression to be sufficient to eject them from their collapsible receptacles. These metal tubes are precisely of the same description as those which contain oil colours, and the water pig-

ments in them are of, as nearly as may be, the same consistence as those in oil. Watercolours so prepared are only needed for large works, and when a very considerable body and breadth of colour is required to be laid on in a short time. When used, the top of the tube is unscrewed, and the pigment pressed out till it forms a little hillock, as large as needed, on the palette: the whole is, in fact, simply borrowed from the practice of oil painting.

124 There appears to be an inconsistency, or a *non sequitur,* here, seeing that at the date when these Essays were published (1848), three out of the four artists last named employed almost exclusively body colours. Mr. Burnet probably intended to allude to the earliest practice of those artists, when we believe they all worked in washed tints, and used opaque colours sparingly.

125 In Italy curtains are often drawn over pictures to protect them from the sun.

126 The term 'drawing' is however so little adapted to express the elaborate processes of the present system of watercolour painting that we have throughout this section ventured generally to substitute the words 'painting' and 'picture.'

127 Cozens was a grandson of Peter the Great. His father was the son of the young Drury Lane actress with whom the Czar lived while working at Deptford. The works of Cozens were passionately admired by Constable.

128 Mr. Herbert's very remarkable picture, to which we have referred, is executed by a method peculiar to the artist. It is in some respects analogous to 'fresco secco,' but Mr. Herbert has covered his plaster with a coating of flour of zinc, which prevents any subsequent action of the lime in the plaster upon the colours, and secures a brilliancy greater than *buon fresco* itself. Over the picture when finished the water-glass is to be syringed.

129 This phenomenon—for it is no less—is no doubt due, like the marvels of the stereoscope, to the beautiful ordering of our binocular vision; although the effect is totally dissimilar, for in the stereoscope all is preternatural stillness. Apropos of the stereoscope, there is, we may remark, a growing tendency to exaggerate the effect of relief in stereoscopic pictures, for the purpose palpably of exciting vulgar wonder: we have seen an arm and a leg apparently project forwards several yards. This is, of course, the effect of placing the two cameras much farther apart than the distance which separates our two eyes; thus altogether falsifying nature. In some books on practical photography, there are directions for placing the cameras at so many feet or yards apart for distant objects!

130 See the picture attributed to Cimabue in the National Gallery, which is very similar to the Cimabue in Santa Maria Novella at Florence.

131 *The Mediæval Court* in *the Crystal Palace,* p. 34.

132 *The Art of Painting in Coloured Crayons.* By H. Murray.

Index

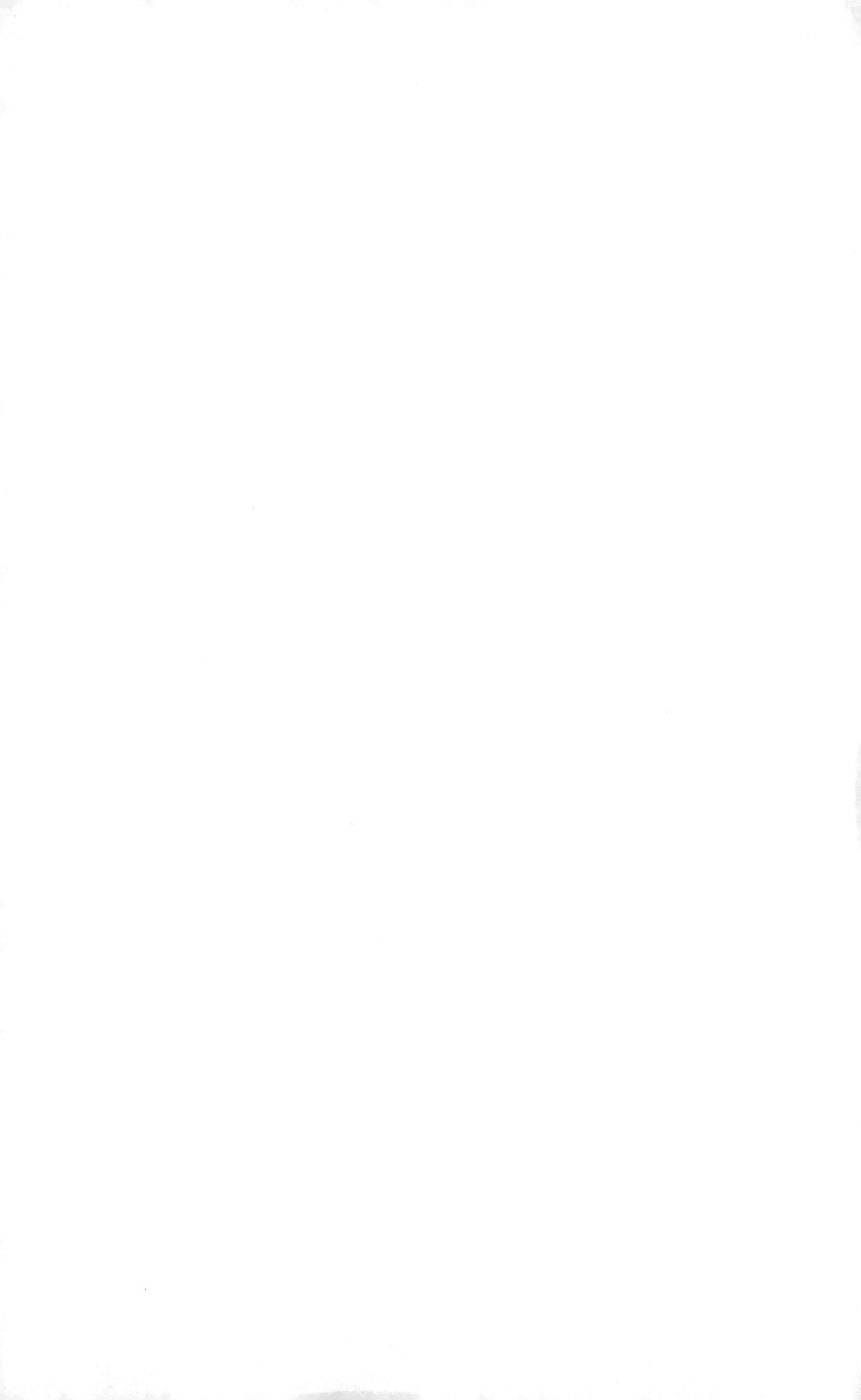